Peasants and Tobacco in the Dominican Republic, 1870–1930

Peasants and Tobacco

in the

Dominican Republic,

1870–1930

Michiel Baud

THE UNIVERSITY OF TENNESSEE PRESS

Knoxville

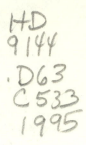

Every effort has been made to locate the original source of figure 1, but the
author has been unsuccessful in this effort. Any information regarding the source
of this photograph should be directed to the author in care of the University of
Tennessee Press.

The paper in this book meets the minimum requirements of the
American National Standard for Permanence of Paper for Printed
Library Materials. ∞ The binding materials have been chosen
for strength and durability.

Library of Congress Cataloging-in-Publication Data

Baud, Michiel, 1952–
     Peasants and tobacco in the Dominican Republic, 1870–1930 /
    Michiel Baud. — 1st ed.
       p.   cm.
    Includes bibliographical references and index.
    ISBN 0-87049-891-6 (cloth: alk. paper)
     1. Tobacco industry—Dominican Republic—Cibao Valley—History.
2. Tobacco farmers—Dominican Republic—Cibao Valley—History.
3. Peasantry—Dominican Republic—Cibao Valley—History. I. Title.
HD9144.D63C533 1995
338.1'7371'0972935—dc20
                                     94-18760
                                        CIP

Contents

Illustrations

FIGURES

MAPS

TABLES

Acknowledgments

An important analogy between academic research and peasant agriculture is that, although both peasant producers and academics often work in isolation, their success and survival depend on the help and support of others. This book is an obvious proof of this statement. Although the process of writing has been an individual undertaking, its completion owes much to the help of many people in the Dominican Republic and Holland.

Let me start by expressing my gratitude to all the people working in libraries and archives who provide essential support for a historian. Especially the people of the library of the Center for Latin American Research and Documentation (CEDLA) in Amsterdam and the Archivo General de la Nación in Santo Domingo have been very sympathetic and helpful. In the Dominican Republic, many people, inside and outside the academic world, helped me to understand Dominican society and supported my research, each in her or his own way. I will always be grateful for the way Jaime Domínguez supported me in my first stumbling steps into Dominican history. In a later stage, Antonio Lluberes, Roberto Cassá, Rafael Emilio Yunén, and Raymundo González explained to me many of the mysteries of Dominican history. It is impossible to exaggerate the importance of their friendship for my understanding of Dominican society. The same is true for my friendships with Estela Rodríguez, Sonia Vásquez, Rosajilda Velez, and, of course, Laura Faxas. Rosemary Vargas and Jan Lundius have been my loyal supporters from the beginning. I also received support from Carlos Dore, Norís Eusebio, Fernando Ferrán, Frank Moya Pons, Walter Cordero, and José Del Castillo. In Santiago, Minerva López helped me to understand Cibao society. I am most grateful for the support and friendship of Iturbides Zaldívar from the Instituto del Tabaco. Theo van Velzen helped me comprehend the intricacies of the tobacco trade.

Acknowledgments

My research in Villa González depended on the cooperation of many people whom I cannot mention here but to whom I am very grateful. Above all, I thank the family of María and Modesto, who accepted me as a researcher, treated me as a son, and trusted me as a friend. What more could one desire? I feel sad that Alcedito Mirabal was not given the time to see the completion of this study, to which he contributed so much.

In Holland, many people have lived with me through my research. Some I have lost along the way; others have seen only the final stage. Frank van Vree has been an unwavering friend through all these years. My colleagues at Erasmus University helped me through the last stage of writing this book.

The book has benefited from the advice of several people. Peter Boomgaard, Willem van Schendel, Gert Oostindie, and Alex van Stipriaan read parts of the first draft and gave useful suggestions. Richard Price and Sidney Mintz were very supportive when this work finally reached the publication stage. Most important were Harry Hoetink and Peter Geschiere. Both left an invaluable imprint on this book. They shared their knowledge with me in a way that I hope to emulate with my own students. I am deeply grateful for their support.

Finally, I must thank my family. Without them I might not have finished this project. I am most grateful to my parents, who, for better or for worse, enabled me to start and finish this project. To them I dedicate this book.

PART I

Introduction

1

About This Book:
Social and Historiographical Context

This book is about the history of tobacco agriculture in a relatively small region of the Caribbean: the northern valley of the Dominican Republic, generally known as the Cibao. This work attempts, first of all, to arrive at an understanding of the history of the men and women for whom tobacco cultivation was the basis of their existence as small-scale agricultural producers. Second, the book analyzes the place of the tobacco sector in the national and international economies and the consequences of the increasing presence of the national state in rural society. Here I shall try to answer the questions of why so many peasant families in the Cibao felt attracted to the cultivation of tobacco and how they managed to maintain a degree of autonomy in the social and economic organization of their lives.

Tobacco cultivation in the Cibao began in the early colonial period, when small-scale agriculture developed around the Santiago–La Vega axis, in the so-called Vega Real. Part of this agricultural production was consumed within the region, but some of it was sold to the ships that frequented the northern coast. Tobacco quickly became a favorite cash crop of the northern population. In the sixteenth and seventeenth centuries, when tobacco production developed in the shadow of Spanish mercantile control (and often in opposition to it), its cultivation became the realm of the creolized Spanish population.[1] Impoverished whites and colored groups—*gente común* as they were called in the seventeenth century—gradually integrated tobacco into their subsistence agriculture and began its commercialization.[2] They cultivated tobacco for their personal use and sold a part of it to cover the expenditures they inevitably had to make. In an economy where the circulation of money was very limited, an easy-to-handle cash crop such as tobacco allowed the poor agrarian population to fulfill its religious and civic obligations and to

3

acquire basic necessities. In the seventeenth century, various religious officials exported to Spain the tobacco that they had received as tithe or prebend.[3]

Tobacco production made the provinces of Santiago and La Vega symbols of prosperity and economic development in the nineteenth century. They were "much more hardworking than the southern provinces," wrote the Spaniard Mariano Torrente in 1851, adding that the region exported almost four million kilos of tobacco.[4] A few years later, a local newspaper wrote, "The people of the Cibao . . . are the most important group in Dominican society because of their regional wealth, their industrious activity, their material progress, and their progressive ideas."[5] The export of tobacco generated substantial profits for the regional mercantile class. It was the foundation of the proverbial prosperity of the Cibao region in the last decades of the nineteenth century and at the beginning of the twentieth. Many changes occurred in this period, and much capital was invested in other sectors, but tobacco continued to be the focal point of the region's agriculture. As late as 1924, it was said that tobacco was the region's only source of wealth (*única riqueza*), and the regional tobacco expert Luis Carballo in 1934 called the crop "life or death" (*vida o muerte*) for the regional capital Santiago.[6] This resilience of the peasant production of tobacco is, in and of itself, interesting enough. It is even more remarkable in light of the dramatic transformation of Dominican society between 1870 and 1930.

SMALLHOLDERS, TOBACCO, AND THE TRANSFORMATION OF DOMINICAN SOCIETY, 1870–1930

The establishment of large capitalist sugar-cane plantations in the southern part of the Dominican Republic in the 1870s meant a decisive break with the past. Dominican politicians and observers were enchanted with the economic vigor of the sugar plantations and with their image of progress. "The production of sugar will be the salvation of the country," wrote the *Gaceta de Santo Domingo* jubilantly in 1877.[7] However, the world sugar crisis of 1884 demonstrated the danger of a model of economic growth which depended on one agricultural product. Many enterprises went bankrupt, resulting in a drastic concentration of sugar capital that led, in the first decades of the twentieth century, to monopoly control by a limited number of large, mainly U.S.-owned, companies. Many sugar entrepreneurs favored political intervention in Dominican politics by the United States because they hoped that this would open the way for Dominican sugar to attain preferential access to the U.S. market.[8] The U.S. government indeed assumed formal control over the country's finances in 1907 and occupied the country militarily from 1916 to 1924. The U.S. occupation led to consolidation of the process of capitalist expansion in the country and tied the Dominican economy firmly to the U.S. market.[9] The sugar industry's "enclave" character was reinforced by the predominance of immigrant labor in the 1920s. When Dominican workers, protesting low wages and bad working conditions, turned their back on the sugar plantations in the 1880s and 1890s, the work force of the plantations came to consist almost exclusively of British West Indian and Haitian immigrant labor.[10]

These developments changed the face of the Dominican economy. New means of transportation and communication facilitated agricultural production and commercial relations. Steamships now regularly called at Dominican ports, and telegraph lines connected the country with the important commercial centers of the world. Gradually, an industrial sector came into existence which was geared toward national consumption. Some industrial production of matches, ice, soap, and liquor (rum) existed in the last decades of the nineteenth century. The first decades of the twentieth century saw the emergence of factories producing shoes, hats, chocolate, and tobacco products.[11]

These changes also affected the Cibao. The regional economy became firmly linked to the world market, giving rise to a strongly dominant class of merchants and landowners. Still, the cultivation of tobacco remained almost exclusively the domain of a multitude of smallholding families who produced increasing quantities of this crop. The basic characteristics of this smallholder economy differed little from those of other peasant societies. First, the cultivation of tobacco in the Cibao was a household activity. Labor was provided by the members of the family, and productive activities were basically geared toward their subsistence.[12] Second, the cultivation of a cash crop such as tobacco linked the peasant families to the market, but did not mean the immediate destruction of their economic autonomy.[13] As long as access to land was guaranteed and the subsistence agriculture of the household was not restricted, peasant producers maintained control over the social and economic organization of peasant society. Even when they had to yield part of their produce to the holders of political and economic power (a group hereafter often designated as "the elite"), they managed to retain elements of autonomy in the daily practice of agricultural production.[14]

The interesting feature of this development is that the regional export economy depended on the continuing production of peasant households. While it is often suggested that the strengthening of the export sector in Latin America has automatically implied large-scale agriculture, the history of the Cibao demonstrates that this is not necessarily the case. In this sense, the Cibao tobacco sector may be linked to the small-scale export production of tobacco in Brazil and northern Colombia (and to a lesser extent Cuba) and of coffee in Costa Rica and Colombia (Antioquia). These cases show that small-scale peasant agriculture very well could lead to increasing production for the (export) market. We should therefore ask ourselves when and under what conditions such small-scale export-oriented agriculture is viable.

It is often suggested that the specific nature of tobacco and coffee as crops must be considered the principal explanation for the continuing existence of small-scale agriculture. This idea is especially appealing in the case of tobacco. The continuous care required by the tobacco plant has attracted the attention of virtually every observer of tobacco agriculture. The Cuban writer Fernando Ortiz based his famous comparison of tobacco and sugar cane on this aspect of the tobacco cultivation: "The special requirements of tobacco cultivation have made it necessary for tobacco to be grown in small plots, like vegetable gardens, and not on great acreage like the cane fields of the sugar plantations . . . Each *vega* is a unit in itself, where the complete agricultural cycle of tobacco begins and ends."[15]

This is too simple a picture, however. Ortiz does not take into account that in many regions—Brazil and the Dominican Republic among the most outstanding—tobacco was a favored cash crop, because it could be cultivated without too much labor investment. In other parts of the world— the most conspicuous example being Sumatra in the Dutch East Indies— tobacco *was* cultivated on plantations.[16] Moreover, Ortiz was talking only about dark tobacco. In the twentieth century, the cultivation of flue-cured light tobacco has turned into a highly sophisticated, large-scale, capital-consuming activity.

The case of coffee is no less complex. While it is a crop that does not require much attention and therefore often has been cultivated by smallholders, large-scale plantation production also occurred in many parts of Latin America. Brazil is an obvious example of large-scale coffee production. Unlike tobacco, the coffee tree requires three or four years to start producing. The cultivator therefore needs some production or income in the intervening years. The quality of both crops is dependent upon the way they are processed. Many small-scale producers did the processing themselves, but there has been a general tendency to transfer that responsibility to the mercantile class in the case of coffee. Especially in the Colombian and Costa Rican coffee sectors, this has led to an increasing dependency on the part of the cultivators.[17]

6

It is necessary, then, to look beyond the characteristics of the specific export crops cultivated by smallholders. An important condition for the viability of small-scale agriculture appears to have been access to land. Continuing access to agricultural land was linked to population density. Thus small-scale agriculture often shifted along with the frontier, where few people lived and land was abundant.

Another factor was the social and economic basis of the regional and national power groups. Small-scale agriculture was more likely to persist when it was in, or at least not contrary to, the interest of local elites and the state. It cannot be a coincidence that, in regions where small-scale export agriculture predominates, merchants and sometimes industrialists form the most powerful block within the elite. Of course, here we are confronted with a problem of causal relation, but it seems evident that small-scale agriculture for the market often coincided with the existence of an elite which did not have the financial and technical means or the wish to take charge of agricultural production itself.

Finally, it is important to take account of the market in which smallholders sold their products. In the case of tobacco and coffee, the world market played the most important role. World market demand and prices determined the profits to be made in the cultivation of a certain crop. Small-scale agriculture often seems to expand with low world market prices. Catherine LeGrand suggests that the position of small-scale agriculture improves in periods of economic recession.[18] Low world market prices for an export crop may increase the comparative advantage of peasant producers. In this context, it is also interesting to know the extent of the internal market. Most export crops were also consumed locally. These local markets could be quite substantial, thereby diminishing the weight of the world market.

DOMINICAN HISTORIOGRAPHY AND THE TOBACCO SECTOR

As in other regions in the world where peasant agriculture formed the basis for an expanding export-oriented economy, in the Dominican Republic the tobacco sector has always elicited contradictory opinions. With the rapid expansion of capitalist relations of production in the period 1870–1930, many people came to consider peasant production an obsolete remnant of the past, which needed to be adapted to modern times. They were convinced that large-scale production was the only road to economic development of the country. They believed that the state had to subdue the peasant population and force it to modernize its agricultural production.

7

Other observers saw the decentralized tobacco sector as the foundation of a harmonious and democratic social and economic development. This sector was often favorably compared to the large-scale sugar cultivation in the southern part of the island. Opposing the idea that peasant production was a sign of backwardness, a romantic idealization of the tobacco sector in the Cibao took place in this period. As early as 1881, the influential intellectual Pedro F. Bonó lauded the democratic character of the tobacco cultivation, by which every family was able to procure its own livelihood.[19] In 1893, Rafael Abreu Licairac wrote an eloquent defense of Cibao rural society in *El Eco de la Opinión,* a journal which had always favored the interests of the sugar industry:

> The excellent organization of labor which prevails in that region . . . fits the fine theory of the distribution of the productive forces. We can say that in this fertile countryside everyone is producer on a greater or lesser scale. Every family possesses its well-cultivated piece of land, which proportionally accrues to the general production. . . . There, the life of the peasantry is really rural life with all its attractions and advantages; remunerative work and relative wealth prevail, accompanied by contentment, satisfaction, and welfare, which are their consequences.

Explicitly emphasizing the contrast with the southern sugar sector, he went on: "The egotistical form of the monopoly is negative and counterproductive. We prefer thousands of small producers . . . over a limited number of large producers who feel themselves king, because of this feudal sentiment which is created by the excessive concentration of wealth."[20] Other people also pointed to the tobacco sector as an alternative model of economic development. Peasant society was seen as the place where traditional norms and honorable values were (still) respected. It was also believed that peasant production, in which every family possessed its own means of subsistence, would lead to a more democratic and egalitarian society.

These opposing visions have also influenced Dominican historiography. In many historical works the tobacco sector is shrouded in a veil of romanticism. For the authors of these works, the cultivation of tobacco brought out the best qualities of the Dominican people. The tobacco producers were hardworking, honest, and thrifty, and they formed the backbone of Dominican identity. During the Trujillo dictatorship, these ideas were used to forge the image of a robust, white class of cultivators that constituted the core of Dominican national identity, much as the *jíbaro* in Puerto Rico or the *guajiro* in Cuba did.[21]

Prevalent in the Marxist-influenced historiography of the 1960s and 1970s was the idea that peasant production was doomed to disappear. This vision was informed by a strong anti-imperialist rhetoric, stressing the dominance of U.S. capital in the Dominican economy. Historians influenced by this current of thought directed their attention to the U.S.-owned sugar plantations and their pernicious influence on the country's social and economic development; they largely ignored the existence of peasant production in the countryside.[22] When the peasantry was mentioned, these historians tended to stress the inadequacy of peasant production and the exploitation of the rural population which they saw as the inevitable outcome of that production.[23]

Only recently, research on the Cibao peasant sector has superseded these preconceived ideas about the sector's virtues or imminent demise. A number of studies have analyzed the insertion of the Dominican Republic into the world economy. The work of Patrick Bryan and David Bray demonstrates the varying and sometimes contradictory effects of the world economy on the Dominican peasantry.[24] Far from always destroying the viability of peasant production, links with the world economy sometimes even stimulated small-scale production. The new approach to the peasantry as a historical factor is also clear in the studies done by Kenneth Sharpe or Pedro San Miguel, which take peasant production as an autonomous field of research, worth studying in its own right.[25] For tobacco cultivation, there is, of course, the book by Fernando Ferrán, an invaluable starting point for any scholar studying the tobacco-producing peasantry in the Cibao.[26]

In this book I want to combine the advantages of these two last approaches. My research shows that it is just as dangerous to neglect the logic of peasant production as it is to neglect the place of the peasant producers in society as a whole. To account for the viability of small-scale export agriculture, it is necessary to look into both the internal dynamics of the peasant economy and its social and economic context. Apart from the theoretical third chapter, all chapters deal with the Cibao in the period 1870–1930. The book is divided into four parts. Following the introductory section, the second part focuses on peasant society. It attempts to determine the logic of peasant tobacco production and analyzes the commercial system that linked the peasant producers to the market. The next part centers upon the efforts of the tobacco exporters and the Dominican state to obtain control over peasant society. In the concluding part, the situation of the Cibao peasantry will be compared with that of other peasantries in the world.

HISTORICAL SOURCES

Some people may regret the paucity of statistical material in this book. I agree to the need for more detailed statistics, but I believe that we must use data from archival sources with great care. The figures for Dominican history up to the 1920s (except perhaps those of the Dominican Customs Receivership[27]) are very unreliable. Statistical evidence is absent, and information by contemporaries is almost always impressionistic and descriptive. A look at the widely diverging tobacco export figures (see table 2 in appendix 1) may be enough to convince readers of this. As late as 1927, agricultural experts bemoaned the absolute absence of reliable data about the tobacco sector in the Cibao.[28] When possible, I have used the available statistical data, but I remain very skeptical about their reliability.

The principal sources for this book are documents in the various archives of the Dominican Republic. For more information about their contents and their exact location, the reader is referred to the Essay on Sources. Written documents have not been the only source of information, however. This study is also based on two fieldwork periods of two months each in the Villa González region, one of the areas most famous for production of dark tobacco. The results of my first visit were published as a short case study in 1984.[29] Later I went back to seek additional information about the daily practice of peasant production and to increase my understanding of the historical vision of members of the peasant population itself. Although it was not possible to obtain oral information about the entire period covered in this book, fieldwork enabled me to supplement my data with valuable insights.[30] The stories of elderly people about the history they themselves have lived through provide a wealth of new information about Dominican history, making it possible better to understand historical change on the micro level of the peasant community. Such stories give social and economic history a "human face." In addition, they form a useful counterweight to the written sources and enable the historian to unravel the latter's implicit biases. It is important to remember Sabean's dictum that written sources for studying peasant culture "implicate in one way or another those people who to some extent exercised domination over the peasant."[31] Apart from new data, oral history provides a completely different perspective on historical change. This perspective is essential if we want to understand the history of peasant production. It must be remembered that many ideas presented in this book would not have been formulated without the stories told by the tobacco producers themselves.

2

Tobacco and the Cibao, 1870–1930: The Regional Economy

> Thousands of individuals and families have rested their hopes on tobacco cultivation. When the harvest is abundant and good prices are paid, the cultivators and merchants all are content; with the income of the tobacco harvest, everyone takes care of his most pressing needs and buys the goods that he may require during the rest of the year. Others pay off debts they have incurred in previous years because of exceptional circumstances and buy pieces of land which they need.
>
> —Amado Franco Bidó, 1924

As a region, the Cibao lived off income generated by the production of tobacco in the nineteenth century. Dominican tobacco found easy acceptance in the world market; its quality was widely eulogized. Dominican tobacco often was used as a wrapper for Cuban cigars. A French diplomat who investigated the Dominican tobacco sector in 1849 wrote: "The tobacco leaf of Santo Domingo has a better taste and looks more pleasant than other kinds, and offers a perfect elasticity and good strength."[1] Tobacco linked the northern part of the Dominican Republic to the world market, and in so doing, it shaped regional society. The amount of currency circulating in the region was a direct function of the volume of the tobacco harvest and the prices on the world market.[2] The Santiago-based newspaper, *El Eco del Pueblo,* wrote in March 1886: "It can be said that the tobacco season here is the blessed golden age in which, as the legend tells, everything was contentment and happiness."[3] This statement was exaggerated, but it stressed the regional importance of the tobacco trade in the nineteenth century.

The tobacco sector was an important source of seasonal wage labor. Tobacco had to be selected, processed, and packed before it could be transported. Part of the tobacco was manufactured and consumed within the

11

country, in the form of *andullos* (pressed tobacco), cigars, and cigarettes. Added to these economic functions were activities linked to tobacco cultivation, such as manufacturing *serones* (bags) and thread, domestication and care of pack animals, and transportation.[4] Although peasant production formed the majority of Dominican tobacco production, some larger landowners and richer peasants also cultivated the crop for the market, often making use of seasonal wage labor.

The tobacco sector gave the Cibao a specific pattern of social and economic development. In order to understand the development of productive forces in the region, we must therefore analyze the regional importance of tobacco as an agricultural commodity and see how its fate changed with the vicissitudes of the world market. This chapter, then, focuses on the tobacco economy in a period when the economy of the Cibao as a whole underwent important changes. We shall see how tobacco production influenced the region's economic and financial development, its labor market, and its infrastructure, and also how the tobacco sector itself changed in response to changing world market conditions.

REGIONAL GEOGRAPHY

The Cibao is a fertile valley which lies between two mountain ranges, the Cordillera Central and the Cordillera Septentrional in the northern part of the Dominican Republic (see map 1). The long valley begins as a very wide, humid lowland area in the southeastern corner, leading via a narrow stretch of dry, low land toward the northwestern port, Monte Cristi. The fluvial system of the Cibao Valley is divided into two subsystems. West of Santiago, the Yaque del Norte is the principal river. It receives all the water from the slopes of the western Cibao and discharges into the ocean near Monte Cristi. The Yuna del Norte has the same function in the eastern part of the region. This region is far less mountainous, and the Yuna has always been a calm and navigable river.

The Cordillera Central forms the southern frontier of the Cibao. It contains the highest peak of the Caribbean, the Pico Duarte (3,087 meters). The Cordillera reaches its highest points in the western part of the national territory and gradually slopes down toward Bonao. The arable highland plains are called *la sierra* in contemporary speech. It must be noted that until the nineteenth century the name *Cibao* was used to indicate these mountainous regions. Only in the course of the nineteenth century was the name adopted for the valley. The Cordillera Septentrional, which separates the Cibao Valley

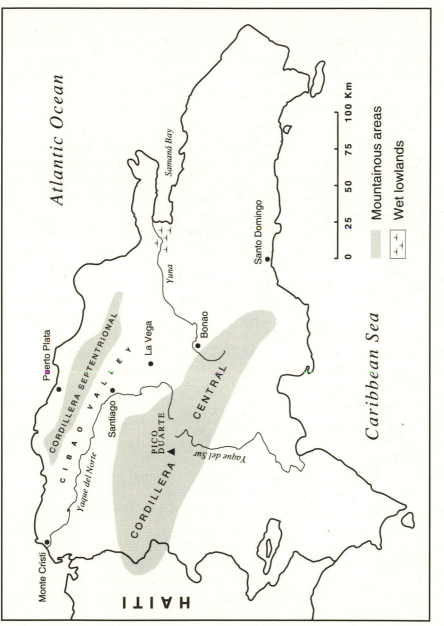

Map 1. Major mountains and rivers in the Dominican Republic. Map by Willem A. Baud.

from the northern coast, contains lower mountains reaching a maximum altitude of only 1,250 meters. Nevertheless, it has always been a formidable obstacle to transportation between the valley and the principal port of the region, Puerto Plata.

The climate of the Cibao Valley is very favorable to human settlement. In the summer, temperatures oscillate between 25 and 35 degrees centigrade. Here the air always retains some of its freshness, in contrast to the normally hot and humid southern part of the Dominican Republic. In the winter, temperatures may drop to 18 degrees. Rain may fall at any time of the year, but the periods of July to September and December to January are considered the "wet" seasons. However, rainfall is not uniform in the region. Averages diminish following the line from Samaná Bay to Monte Cristi. The lowlands around Sánchez are very humid. In the nineteenth century they contained extensive marshlands, due to excessive rainfall and subsoils which prevented the water from draining. Along the *Linea Noroeste*, as the lowland toward the Monte Cristi region is called, humidity sharply decreases, resulting in a dry, hot environment less salubrious to plants and animals.

Thus, in the Cibao Valley we may distinguish three ecological zones: the humid and marshy lowlands toward Samaná Bay; the relatively densely populated, fertile agricultural region around the axis Santiago–La Vega, often called the *Vega Real*; and the drier, less fertile region toward Monte Cristi. Compared with other Caribbean islands, the population density of the Cibao—and of the Dominican Republic in general—has been relatively low. Most of the valley was covered with forest. Only in the agricultural center of the valley had the landscape already been "tamed" and brought under cultivation. Here the forest had given way to villages and agriculture. This was the only region in the country where, in the late nineteenth century, the continuous competition between cattle holding and agriculture already had been decided in favor of the latter.

In the Dominican Republic as a whole, which measured almost fifty thousand square kilometers, the population increased from 207,000 in 1863 to almost 900,000 in 1920.[5] In 1875, the Cibao Valley had a population of 90,000. The province of La Vega was the most densely populated of the country, with La Vega being the second largest town after Santo Domingo.[6] In the last decades of the nineteenth century, the population of the region began to grow. In 1908, it had increased to approximately 250,000, and in 1920 it reached 350,000.[7] In the process, La Vega lost its position to Santiago. The latter city became the center of the tobacco trade and the largest town of the Cibao. The city grew steadily, from 5,500 inhabitants in 1874 to 17,000 in 1920.[8]

14

Smaller towns formed the center of the regional economy. They were small urban conglomerates that blended almost imperceptibly into the countryside. The writings of the traveler Samuel Hazard, published in 1873, give a good impression of their appearance. In the center of town, houses and stores were made of stone and sometimes had two stories, there was usually a church, and streets were paved. Here most merchants had their offices and storehouses, generating much commercial activity. Toward the periphery, the majority of houses were made of wood and roofed with palm leaves, and streets were unpaved.[9] The rural character of the Cibao towns remained clearly visible, despite their gradual expansion, until far into the twentieth century.

TOBACCO AND THE REGION'S FINANCES

Commercial dealings in the nineteenth century implied little more than an exchange of tobacco for cash. At the beginning of the harvest, German importers sent money to the region through Dominican exporters. This money enabled the latter to buy and export the tobacco. In the twentieth century, the monetary system became more sophisticated, as banks took over part of the creditor role from the European importers. The mechanism remained basically the same, however: the money entering the region depended on the prospects for the tobacco harvest.[10]

The Dominican economy suffered from a structural scarcity of money in this period. Many kinds of different currencies were used within the country—U.S. dollars, Peruvian *soles*, Mexican pesos, gold, and silver—but there was never enough. Commercial dealings were greatly hampered by the unreliability of the money. Many people made it their business to diminish the silver content of coins, producing what was called *moneda gastada* (worn-out money).[11] As a result of this situation, the Dominican economy functioned on the basis of paper IOUs, *vales*, which often were used as money. This practice pervaded the entire society. The government paid its daily expenses with money borrowed from the mercantile class, which formed *juntas* or *compañías de crédito* (credit associations), often in exchange for part of the customs duties. The *papelitas* (little papers) on which these contracts were written were used as money in the large merchants' commercial dealings. Government employees usually were paid with *hojas de sueldo* (salary sheets).[12] The same was true of workers in most of the larger agricultural enterprises.[13] This system was highly susceptible to inflation.

As a consequence of this situation, the region directly experienced the ups and downs of the world market. When prices were good, the region prospered. In strictly economic terms, prosperity often resulted in strong inflation. The expanding money input tended to increase regional consumption. A large portion of the goods consumed was imported from overseas and could not be replenished rapidly; the result was an inflationary pressure on prices. Low prices usually led to a financial crisis. When events on the world market depressed prices, money ceased to flow into the region. The scarcity of money paralyzed commercial activities. When the Franco-Prussian War of 1870 interrupted the export trade to Germany, the governor of Santiago, J. V. Núñez, wrote: "The inhabitants of this region have been, and still are, very sad, because of the lack of circulating currency. This situation has affected all social classes, even more so because, as a consequence of the European War, we cannot sell our tobacco, the principal or even the only product which has always flooded the region with gold and silver."[14] Civil warfare and climatological disaster also led to depression and hunger. Numerous sieges disrupted the economic activity of Santiago.[15] Sometimes the Cibao economy approached a standstill. During a long drought two years later, the region reportedly experienced "the greatest monetary scarcity ever, because the lack of tobacco and consequent inability to pay transportation costs, have limited the importation of money."[16]

A major crisis occurred in 1879, when the German government more than doubled its import duties on tobacco, from 40 to 85 German marks per hundred kilos.[17] The increased customs duties favored German tobacco, and the demand for Dominican tobacco was sharply reduced. The price of Dominican tobacco on the German market dropped some 30 percent.[18] This decline led to a sharp decrease in the region's capital stock and inaugurated a strong deflationary trend. In 1881 it was reported that real estate prices "from the year 1875 until the present day have decreased to some 50 percent of their [prior] value, eloquently demonstrating the miserable conditions that afflict us."[19] The demand for tobacco slumped, and many mercantile firms had to close their doors. In the three years after 1879, Santiago lost some twenty-five commercial establishments.[20] The tobacco crisis lasted throughout the 1880s. In 1886, "the principal houses of this city hardly [had] money to take care of the purchasing of the tobacco."[21]

The position of Dominican tobacco in the world market improved again in the first decades of the twentieth century. As we shall see in chapter 7, this was the result of increasing European demand and the establishment of a national tobacco manufacturing industry. These developments produced a steady increase in tobacco production in the first decades of the twentieth century. Appendix 1 shows that annual tobacco production in the Dominican Republic in the 1870s oscillated around 100,000 bales (*bultos*, each containing fifty or sixty kilos), or five million kilos.[22] Steady growth began in the first decade of the twentieth century, and tobacco production reached a peak of 22 million kilos in 1925. Thus an upward trend is obvious in this period—tobacco production more than quadrupled in sixty years.

However, we should be aware that these clean production figures are deceiving. Production showed extreme variations from one year to the next. Sometimes the cause of this variation was civil warfare. Especially in the late nineteenth century, political instability disrupted agricultural activity and caused repeated loss of crops.[23] However, the most important source of variation was tobacco agriculture itself. The low level of agricultural technology and the absence of irrigation made tobacco cultivation strongly weather-dependent. It was noted in 1883 that "tobacco is still being cultivated with the means presented to us by the natural environment. As a consequence of the lack of irrigation, the mere absence of rain in the months of sowing and resowing leads to great quantitative and qualitative variations in the harvest."[24] The fact that tobacco is an annual crop, together with such considerations, made for widely varying production figures. In 1889, the harvest amounted to hardly more than 50,000 *bultos*, while it had been at 127,000 the previous year. A similar sudden decrease occurred in 1894, when exports to Germany were 75,000 *bultos*, compared to more than 150,000 in each of the two previous years.[25]

We can distinguish roughly three periods in the market position of tobacco. In the late nineteenth century, especially after the tobacco crisis of 1879, little attention was paid to tobacco production. Merchants bought the tobacco as a bulk product for a low price and were little interested in its quality. Peasant producers reacted by using less labor-intensive methods and by sacrificing quality to quantity. In the first twenty years of the twentieth century, the tobacco market became more profitable, and merchants and public officials tried to increase production. Prices paid to the cultivators remained low, however. In the third period, which began in 1918, the booming world market after World War I (the so-called "Dance of the Millions") sent prices to unprecedented heights (see appendix 1). Foreign importers established themselves in the region, joining efforts by the cigarette factory "La Habanera" to improve tobacco quality. With improved technology, the variability of tobacco crops tended to diminish, but considerable variation still occurred from year to year in the 1920s.[26] In this period, a group of clearly market-oriented cultivators emerged, alongside a growing group of poor cultivators. The continuing dependence of regional commerce on the tobacco trade became clear in the late 1920s, when the agricultural expert of the government, Luis Carballo, wrote: "The buying of tobacco by exporters has all but ceased. This, and the fact that this crop is the only one which sustains our commerce at present, has caused a noticeable decrease in commercial activities."[27]

Thus the fate of the Cibao elite was closely linked to profits from the tobacco trade. During crises, regional entrepreneurs looked for alternative agricultural and commercial activities, but such a strategy became a real possibility only in the twentieth century. Despite these problems, only a few individuals ventured to criticize the tobacco monoculture.[28] The profits to be made in the tobacco sector were too attractive. The interests of the commercial elite were sufficient to guarantee that tobacco exports would continue. During periods of high prices, optimism and self-confidence reigned in the entrepreneurial ranks. A prolonged upward trend of the tobacco market led to an expansion of the commercial sector in the Santiago region.[29] The optimism was demonstrated by construction of buildings and investment in new technology. It also spawned new commercial activities and strengthened the political and economic position of the mercantile class.[30] During such periods, politicians, public employees, and journalists again saw confirmed their belief that tobacco was the undisputed mainstay of the Cibao.

LARGE-SCALE TOBACCO PRODUCTION

Although tobacco was a smallholder crop, even in the 1850s some tobacco was already being produced by a group of rich, market-oriented cultivators. These tobacco growers, often members of the local elite, were scattered throughout the Cibao. They cultivated tobacco in order to make a profit and sometimes maintained direct contact with the European importers. In later years, these tobacco cultivators became proverbial figures. *El Orden* wrote in 1874: "Fifteen or twenty years ago the cultivation of tobacco was done with much more dedication. The cultivators took care of [the plant] scrupulously from the moment it was sown and followed the agrarian rules strictly. . . . In all aspects they obeyed the rules which they learned from their fathers."[31] The letters of the French planter Dubocq, written in the late 1850s, give an impression of a sharply calculating agricultural entrepreneur, who possessed very precise information about the situation of the market.[32] Notary records of the same period contain elaborate written contracts as far back as the 1840s between cultivators and merchants. They indicate that some producers committed themselves to sell fixed amounts of tobacco in exchange for credit with local merchants.[33] These cultivators were thoroughly market-oriented producers who experimented with seeds and techniques and used wage labor for some of the menial tasks. The quality of their tobacco was often very good, giving Dominican tobacco its good name on the international tobacco markets. General Sosa, for instance, was widely known in the nineteenth century for the high quality of his tobacco.[34]

Some members of the elite continued to grow tobacco themselves after the 1870s. Well-known entrepreneurs like José Joaquín Díaz and the brothers Espaillat had larger farms and employed wage labor to care for their crops. A few attempts were even made to foster large-scale tobacco plantations in the Cibao. The Cuban-Dominican revolutionary Máximo Gómez ran a plantation called "La Reforma" in the Monte Cristi region during the years 1889–96.[35] In 1889, a Dutch company started a large-scale tobacco plantation in the heart of the Cibao, some ten miles north of Santiago. The Dutch engineer W. C. van der Veen, who had worked in the Dutch East Indian colonies, was the director of this plantation, "La Carmelia." During the three years of its existence (1889–92), the enterprise employed more than one hundred men, who cleared some sixty hectares and planted them with tobacco.[36] This enterprise seemed so promising that the governor wrote in 1889: "The farm *Carmelia* is the major source of wage labor in this province and constitutes one of its most cheerful hopes."[37] These hopes were quickly dashed, however. The Dutch pulled out of the country in 1892, leaving the British consul-general to report: "The tobacco estate formed with Dutch capital . . . has been abandoned, experience having taught the planters who were interested in them that the cost of raising tobacco from Sumatra seed on Dominican soil is too high to allow remunerative speculation."[38] Also in 1889, Baron von Farensbach planned to establish a number of state farms, or *fincas modelos*, which were to function as an example for the peasantry. This project never got off the ground. Above all, the baron was interested in tax exemptions and stopped his activities when the Dominican government did not comply with his demands.[39]

After the tobacco crisis in 1879, many members of the more market-oriented peasantry in the La Vega region switched to cocoa, which promised high profits. Some regional merchants, under the leadership of Casimiro de Moya and Gregorio Rivas, had started to stimulate the cultivation of cocoa in the eastern Cibao in the 1880s.[40] They made this part of the Cibao the center of the new sector; San Francisco de Macorís was its principal commercial city. Cocoa cultivation required a greater investment, however, especially because the trees started to produce only after three or four years.

A writer stated in 1908: "There is no doubt that cocoa is the most profitable crop for the cultivator, but only the relatively well-to-do are able to dedicate themselves to this crop"; tobacco "is the best crop for the poor cultivator."[41] For forty years, cocoa production showed steadily increasing export figures. However, the cocoa sector lost its impetus in the beginning of the twentieth century. Competition on the world market from West African producers and the increasing incidence of diseases of the cocoa trees severely affected the sector in the 1920s and brought its prosperity to a close.[42] By then cocoa had replaced tobacco in the eastern Cibao, and the cultivation of tobacco had been pushed gradually westward. The history of peasant production of tobacco thus became a spatial phenomenon, too, slowly extending first as an expanding circle around the axis Santiago—La Vega, and later moving westward toward Monte Cristi and into the Sierra.

The tobacco sector rebounded in the early decades of the twentieth century. This resurgence reflected better world market prices, as well as the emergence of a regional tobacco industry. New technology was introduced in the region that made possible mass production of cigarettes. This innovation, and an upward trend in the Dominican economy overall, caused a proliferation of tobacco factories in the country. E. Deschamps mentions the existence of 112 tobacco-processing enterprises in 1907.[43] Many of these belonged to small entrepreneurs, but a few were modern industrial enterprises employing steam energy. Such factories were José Tolentino's "La Anacaona," E. León's "La Aurora," and "La Matilde," the property of Simón Mencia Sucs., all three in Santiago. Each employed more than fifty people in 1900, sometimes making use of a "putting out" system.[44]

The most important of these new factories without doubt was "La Habanera," established in 1901 by the German entrepreneur Richard Söllner. With the most modern machines of the period, tended by German technicians, this establishment became Santiago's largest factory, employing hundreds of workers. "La Habanera," renamed "Compañía Anónima Tabacalera" (CAT) in 1914, was the undisputed king of the tobacco industry in the Cibao. Until the company opens its archives for historians, however, we can say very little about its historical development and its social and economic influence on the city of Santiago and on the Cibao in general. The vertical integration of the agricultural and industrial parts of the production process is the most likely explanation of its success.[45] In the shadow of Söllner's successful enterprise, more traditional cigar factories flourished. "La Matilde" and "La Aurora" also became large-scale, modern factories.

Alongside the tobacco sector, some other agricultural enterprises came into existence in the central Cibao. J. Armando Bermúdez established a sugar-cane plantation in Banegas in 1918. About one thousand tareas were planted with cane, and the hacienda produced "sufficient to satisfy the local consumption of Santiago."[46] The enterprise, under the name "Central Bolívar," continued its production during the 1920s and supplied a newly founded distillery in Santiago owned by the same entrepreneur.[47] In 1929, the enterprise was joined by a U.S. company, the "Compañía Agrícola Dominicana," which bought large tracts of land to produce starch from cassava. The company started producing in Quinigua in 1931 and used a large number of wage laborers.[48] Similar enterprises came into existence in other parts of the Cibao countryside. They often took advantage of irrigation systems constructed in this period. Large-scale agriculture provided new wage-labor opportunities for members of the surrounding peasant society, and wage labor gradually became an integral element of peasant existence.

In the first decades of the twentieth century, then, many changes occurred in Cibao society. In this process of change, a new social structure came into existence. First of all, the composition of the elite underwent a transformation. While the traditional cattle holders virtually disappeared, the class of agrarian entrepreneurs swelled rapidly, becoming an important pillar of the regional elite.[49] Native and immigrant entrepreneurs bought land and started large-scale capitalist agricultural undertakings. They often lived in the countryside but maintained close contact with members of the urban elite. The large exporters were the most influential members of urban society. Their import-export trade was central to the welfare of the region. Industrial entrepreneurs constituted a new elite group. They, with the merchants, became the strongest pressure group in twentieth-century politics.

Rural towns such as Santiago, La Vega, and Moca expanded and gave rise to a nascent middle class. It was a diffuse and diverse group, consisting of employees of commercial and industrial firms, public servants, and medium-scale commercial entrepreneurs. In the countryside, the intermediate class consisted of local strongmen, petty traders, and more prosperous peasant producers. These men mediated between the peasantry and the urban commercial elite. They were often intermediary traders, *corredores*, who secured the tobacco from the producers and sold it to urban merchants.[50]

New urban wage-labor opportunities and demographic growth drew a growing migration toward the cities. Gradually, a class of people came into existence who were dependent on wage labor. This development led to an embryonic labor movement in Santiago in the 1920s. The workers in the tobacco industry organized themselves in "La Hermandad Cigarrera." Their struggle for recognition of their union and their demands for improvement in labor conditions caused two serious labor conflicts in 1919 and 1924.[51] Other people earned a living in the informal sector, as ambulant saleswomen, artisans, shoeshine boys, prostitutes, or beggars. This group became so numerous that in the 1920s municipal councils took measures to suppress it.[52] The urban poor originated in the rural population and often remained in close contact with their families in the countryside.

The remaining group in this new social structure was, of course, the peasantry, the subject of the rest of this book. The peasant population was the most numerous social group in the country until well into the twentieth century. Its existence often was taken for granted, but its agricultural labor was of crucial importance to the tobacco economy.

THE REGIONAL LABOR MARKET

> Daily, teams of mules (*recuas*) enter the city loaded with the aromatic leaf. The storehouses are being filled, and the large halls of the storehouses are busy and animated by the presence of the women who select, store, and classify the tobacco. The female workers arrive in the early morning to take their places and sweeten the monotonous atmosphere of the trade with their happy songs. Similarly, the men who classify the tobacco and the sweaty, content porters shout the *to le lá* which, rhythmical and melodious, incites them to the work which they do happily because they know it guarantees them their daily bread.
>
> —"Tabaco: Ya hierve la colmena," *La Información,* Santiago, May 22, 1917

The many activities connected with the cultivation and export of tobacco gave many employment and provided the income necessary for a growing group of semiproletarianized families. Tobacco export itself was the most important source of seasonal wage labor. Many tasks had to be performed before the tobacco could be exported. Some of these were done by the peasantry, but the exporters, as their trade became professionalized, began to do much of the processing and preparation of export tobacco themselves.[53] Even in the late nineteenth century, some of the tobacco was dried, fermented, and classified in the exporters' storehouses.

The main workforce in the storehouses always consisted of women, most of them from the countryside. As Deputy Andrew put it in 1889: "Hundreds,

Figure 1. Front porch of storehouse of a tobacco exporting company, beginning of twentieth century. Photograph from Dominik Photo.

even thousands of women make their living with hard work, but at least they can buy food and clothes, thanks to the preparation which the tobacco undergoes before it is put in *serones* or packed."[54] In this way, many women found temporary jobs. The work had a seasonal character and was not very demanding physically, but it is unclear whether these factors alone account for the predominance of women in this labor force. To be sure, the brunt of the work took place during the harvest season, when most men were busy with agricultural activities. Another incentive for the employer to use female labor was the women's willingness to work for low wages.

At the turn of the century, an average exporter employed some thirty women during the harvest season.[55] When, in the 1920s, more foreign companies settled in the region and tobacco processing was expanded and modernized, the number of women working in this sector increased. It was reported that, in the 1920s, two thousand women and four hundred to five hundred men were engaged in the preparation of tobacco during the harvest season.[56] At the height of the harvest season, it was estimated that, in Santiago, some one thousand laborers were employed in the storehouses. A workforce of fifty workers, with an average of three women to every man, was not exceptional. Men earned from eighty centavos to one peso a day, classifying and storing tobacco. Women earned twenty centavos for preparing fifty kilos of tobacco. They could make forty to sixty centavos a day, but even the most experienced women often did not manage to finish more than two quintales.[57] Because of the availability of cheap female labor, many firms opened storehouses in rural areas.

Other forms of wage labor existed on the larger tobacco farms. The cultivation of tobacco was predominantly carried out by the peasantry, but, as we have seen, there were a number of larger-scale cultivators. The failure of the Dutch plantations put an end to attempts to foster large-scale tobacco plantations in the Cibao, but regular wage labor continued on the tobacco farms of the more prosperous cultivators. In this way, wage labor was introduced in the countryside. In the twentieth century, agricultural wage labor became a normal practice in the rural economy and an accepted part of peasant livelihood.

The cultivation and export of tobacco generated collateral types of work as well. The *serones*, in which the tobacco traditionally was exported, were made of palm leaves by women in rural villages, especially in the mountains. In the nineteenth century, places like Janico, Sabaneta, Mao, and San José de las Matas derived part of their prosperity from the "industria del tejido de guano," which produced thousands of *serones* needed every year in the tobacco export. As Bonó put it, "Entire communities are engaged in making them, and thousands of men, women, and children make a living by collecting and weaving the fibers."[58] Deputy Andrew even characterized this production as their "only industry, only livelihood" ("única industria, único elemento de vida").[59] It was estimated in 1885 that this industry produced ninety thousand *serones*, each of which sold for fifteen centavos in the place of production and thirty-five centavos in Santiago.[60] This sector continued to be a necessary element of the tobacco economy in the first decades of the twentieth century. Only in the late 1920s, when exporters started to export their tobacco in *pacas* of textile or jute, which were more acceptable internationally, did *serón* manufacturing decline.[61]

Transportation too was linked to the tobacco trade. Traditionally, tobacco was carried to coastal towns by so-called *recuas*, herds of about twenty mules, each mule being able to carry two *serones* of sixty kilos. In the historiography, the *recueros* as a group are romantically depicted as honest and reliable.[62] This image probably derives from the adventurous and risky character of this form of transportation. There is no doubt that mutual trust and personal relations played an important part in this activity. Nevertheless, complaints about the *recueros* also were heard. They were a volatile and evasive group, and it was often difficult to reclaim lost possessions. Sometimes *recueros* accepted a mission under a false name and disappeared.[63] Others tampered with the loads and replaced tobacco with leaves or stones.[64] In any case, the *recueros* belong to the romantic age of the tobacco sector in the Cibao. After the construction of the two Cibao railroads in the last decades of the nineteenth century, animal transport declined rapidly, and the professional *recueros* disappeared. As a collateral activity of the tobacco-producing peasantry, tobacco transport retained its importance until the 1920s. Then, the expansion of truck transport put an end to it.

Manufacture of tobacco products was an important source of nonagricultural wage labor. In the cities, many specialized cigar-producing enterprises existed. It is not entirely clear when this small-scale cigar industry emerged, but in 1867, urban *tabaquerías* existed in Santo Domingo.[65] The cigar industry expanded rapidly in the final decades of the nineteenth century.[66] As Bonó wrote in 1881, "The production of cigars . . . gives work to countless inhabitants of rural and urban communities, who count on it to secure the future of themselves and their families." However, he stressed that these were modest enterprises working with simple technology.[67]

As we have seen, the tobacco industry changed dramatically with the establishment of some large factories in the beginning of the twentieth century.

The consumption of cigarettes rapidly increased, within years surpassing the consumption of cigars. New technology which made mass production of cigarettes possible was introduced into the region. The proliferation of tobacco factories in the country expanded the demand for labor.

A large, capitalist enterprise, the Compañía Anónima Tabacalera, came to symbolize the deepening division between the few large-scale firms and the much more numerous small-scale, informally organized, economically weak tobacco manufacturing sweatshops. The latter manufactured hand-made cigars in primitive circumstances, often using unpaid family labor exclusively.[68] Most of these were very weak financially, and, under adverse circumstances, many temporarily went out of business. Their existence was increasingly threatened by the central government, which tried to increase its income by raising duties on cigars and cigarettes. In 1911, the *Ley de Estampillas* was passed, which burdened every thousand cigars with a tax of two and a half pesos. According to Deputy Amado Franco Bidó, the law's effect on the Cibao was "sad and painful" ("de manera triste y dolorosa"). Bidó stated that "the people who engaged in the production of cigars have completely stopped their activities, while others have reduced the salaries of laborers."[69] In the 1920s, the government made a new attempt to gain control over the informal sector of cigar producers. It raised taxes on cigars from two and a half to ten pesos per thousand and declared illegal all unlicensed manufacture and sale of cigars. This state intervention, which was intensified during the Trujillo regime, inhibited small-scale tobacco manufacture. According to the same Amado Franco Bidó, countless small factories ("infinidad de fábricas") closed their doors in 1924, and state regulation severely restricted the operations of others, causing a tragic loss of employment for thousands of cigar makers. Bidó accused the government of deliberately "putting an end to the factories."[70]

Although there was some politically motivated exaggeration in these accusations, in subsequent years the authorities indeed waged a barely concealed war against what came to be called the *cigarrerías clandestinas*.[71] This campaign reflected the increasing strength of the Dominican state and the ambition of many politicians to increase state control over civil society. Although many people acknowledged that this policy threatened the livelihood of a great number of poor families, small-scale tobacco manufacturing was actively discouraged. However, the informal sector never was completely destroyed. Even today, small-scale illegal manufacturing of cigars continues in towns and in the countryside.[72]

The Infrastructure of an Export Economy

No problem was lamented so much in Cibao society as the region's deficient road system. Regional dependence on the export of agricultural commodities made the improvement of regional infrastructure an absolute necessity. This need was felt most urgently by the commercial elite. Its businesses depended on cheap and efficient transport to the world market.

The merchants certainly had reason to complain; transportation of goods over the fifty-mile stretch from Santiago to Puerto Plata was a hazardous and expensive undertaking. Foreign travelers such as Sir Robert Schomburgk and Samuel Hazard could hardly find words to describe their travel adventures. Schomburgk wrote in 1851 that "the enormous prices for freight to the only shipping port surpass the value of the article and counteract the full development of this trade."[73] In the 1870s, transport from Santiago to Puerto Plata still was more expensive than the trip from Puerto Plata to Germany. In addition, transportation by *recuas* was slow and often goods were damaged en route. The roads were very dangerous. It was estimated that, between 1870 and 1884, more than 1,500 animals perished, causing a loss of 75,000 pesos for animals alone.[74]

The commercial elite of the Cibao initiated many plans to improve regional infrastructure, but most fell through because of a chronic shortage of capital. As it turned out, railroad construction supplied the desired outlets to the sea.[75] These railroads caused a decisive change in the economic geography of the Cibao. Construction of the Sánchez-Santiago railroad, a joint venture of the Dominican state and a British–North American company, started in 1881. The state's contribution to the project was a share of the import-export duties of Samaná. The enterprise encountered many problems owing to marshy land in the eastern Cibao, internal conflicts, and financial difficulties. The railroad reached La Vega in 1887, but almost twenty years and a lot of public money were required to complete the stretch to Santiago. By that time, the Santiago elite had become so indignant and impatient that it had embraced another project to connect Santiago and Puerto Plata by rail.

The *Ferrocarril Central Dominicano* (FCD), as this new railroad was called, was financed by a Dutch loan and supervised technically by Belgian engineers. Construction began in 1890, but the mountains proved a formidable barrier to which the technology of the time was not equal. The line was inaugurated in 1897, but it never functioned completely satisfactorily. Derailments occurred frequently, and many investments had to be made later.[76]

Construction of the Sánchez–Santiago and the Puerto Plata–Santiago railroads required the labor of a number of men unprecedented in the region. The latter railroad, which traversed part of the valley of the Central Cibao, was built exclusively with Dominican labor. In the first years of its construction (1890–95), it employed an average of 500 men, a number that increased to 1,500 and even 1,800 in the last stage of its construction in 1897. The agrarian population of the Cibao could not supply this labor, and men were brought in from all parts of the country.

The two railroads facilitated regular transport of increasing quantities of tobacco to the harbors and brought down the cost of transportation. When the Sánchez–Santiago railroad started to function in 1887, the line became the principal means of transportation for tobacco from the La Vega region. For a number of years, Sánchez seemed to be replacing Puerto Plata as the principal export harbor,[77] but with the completion of the FCD, Puerto Plata recaptured its primary position in the tobacco trade. Transportation of tobacco was the most important source of income for the FCD. In 1910, some 60 percent of the freight on the FCD consisted of tobacco.[78]

Construction of the Ferrocarril Central also stimulated agriculture in the Cibao Valley west of Santiago. The railroad traversed some fifteen miles of the valley before cutting northward into the mountains. As we shall see in chapter 6, well-to-do businessmen started to buy land on both sides of the railroad, fostering agricultural enterprises. The emergence of the town of Las Lagunas (later called Villa González), some ten miles from Santiago, and the growth of Navarrete resulted directly from the construction of the railroad.[79] Altamira, in the mountains, prospered similarly, developing into a commercial center.[80]

The FCD was quite profitable until the assassination of President Cáceres in 1911. In the revolutionary unrest which followed, tobacco production, along with the profits of the railroad company, decreased.

Many practical problems also continued to hamper the operation of the railroads. The two lines had different gauges, preventing them from connecting to form a regional railroad system. The steep gradients in the Cordillera Septentrional and the marshes and inundations in the eastern Cibao caused frequent accidents and extra expenditures. Both were one-track roads, and, in case of an accident, all traffic came to a halt. The vagaries of a railroad trip became proverbial in local folklore.

In addition to these technical problems, the railroads became a target of political strife. Control of the railroads meant access both to the region's principal means of transportation and to public customs revenue. Especially the

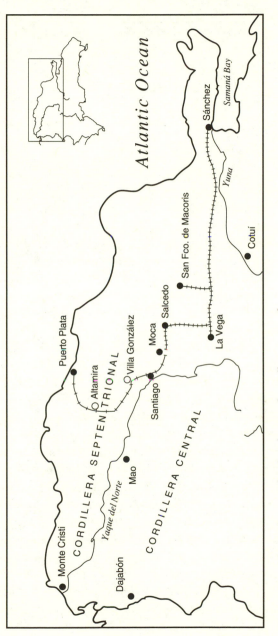

Map 2. The Cibao: Places and railroads. Map by Willem A. Baud.

Table 1
Dominican Tobacco Prices and Costs of Transportation (in Dominican
pesos per quintal)

	1849	1872	1887	1912
Price Paid to Peasant	14-20	9	4	3.50
Internal Transport Costs	1.50	2.25	3.75	2.35
International Transport Costs	2.50	2.25	?	1.75

Sources: For 1849: Victor Place, "Memoria sobre el cultivo, la cosecha y la venta de los tabacos" (1849); rpt. in Jacqueline Boin and José Serulle Ramia, *El proceso de desarrollo del capitalismo en la República Dominicana (1844–1930)* (Santo Domingo: Editorial Gramil, 1979), 1:196. For 1872: *El Porvenir* 1, no. 25 (6 July 1872). For 1887: *El Mensajero* 7, no. 13 (28 Aug. 1887). For 1912: Patrick E. Bryan, "The Transformation of the Dominican Economy" (Ph.D. diss., Univ. of London, 1978), 139.

FCD repeatedly became the subject of political intrigues in the first decades of the twentieth century; in consequence, its operations often were suspended.[81]

These problems kept regional transportation costs high. The commercial elite complained constantly about the excessive cost of railroad transport, particularly in view of the poor service and the "deplorable condition" of the rolling stock.[82] At various times, the state ordered price reductions to assist the mercantile class, but such measures could not stem the tide. There was a bitter complaint in 1923 that "Santiago cannot develop its immense agricultural wealth, because of the barbarous rates of the Central Railroad."[83] That same year, the FCD encountered financial problems owing to competition from road transportation; it was reported that "the absence of loads has created a difficult situation for the FCD and caused a partial standstill in the trade of Puerto Plata."[84] The railroad company reduced its tariffs in an attempt to recapture the tobacco freight, but by 1927 some 40 percent of the import-export trade already had been transferred to Santo Domingo.[85] When the road system was improved during the U.S. occupation of the country, and especially with the construction of the Santiago–Santo Domingo highway, the tobacco merchants did not waste much time in taking advantage of the new opportunities offered by this connection. In the 1920s, much of the Cibao's tobacco was shipped through Santo Domingo, definitively reducing the importance of Puerto Plata and Sánchez, but also threatening the regional preponderance of Santiago. Competition from cheaper and more efficient road transport dealt the deathblow to the Cibao railroads, and they stopped functioning in the 1950s.

The railroads, then, played a complex and contradictory role in the historical development of the Cibao's tobacco economy. There can be no doubt that the needs of the agricultural export economy provoked their construction. The region's commercial elite fully supported these initiatives and cherished high hopes for their positive impact on agricultural development. And, despite the problems during construction, the railroads initially lived up to these expectations, becoming the main arteries of the regional economy. The expansion of cocoa cultivation and the growth of tobacco export in the first decades of the twentieth century can be considered direct consequences of railroad construction. On the other hand, the regional elite was only marginally involved in the railroad enterprises. The latter were financed by foreign capital, and regional merchants never succeeded in obtaining a decisive voice in their management. This may have accounted for the ultimate failure of the enterprises. Tensions always existed between the regional elite and the railway companies, the latter being accused of incompetence, excessive prices, and corruption.[86] As soon as cheaper means of transportation became available, the Cibao merchants, without the slightest compassion, abandoned the railroads and left them to wither away.

In the period 1870–1930, a new kind of society came into the existence in the Cibao Valley. Demographic growth, expansion of the agricultural frontier, and construction of new means of transportation changed the social and economic geography of the region. While cocoa transformed the economy of the eastern Cibao, tobacco cultivation formed the basis for a regional export economy in the central Cibao. Many people in the rural and urban areas depended on the tobacco sector for their livelihoods, and a plethora of economic activities resulted from the cultivation, preparation, and export of tobacco.

It is remarkable that tobacco continued to be the principal cash crop amid all these changes in the central Cibao. Even more, it is notable that smallholding peasant producers continued to produce the majority of the crop. The particular characteristic of Cibao society was that capitalist relations of production expanded without undoing small-scale production of tobacco. The growth of the export economy took place by integrating—not by destroying—peasant production. The integration certainly was facilitated by the failure of experiments with large-scale tobacco production, but it also reflected the structure of tobacco production. Specific historical conditions in the Cibao gave the peasant producers such an autonomous position that they were not easily subdued. It is to the analysis of these peasant producers that we now turn.

31

PART II

Peasants and Tobacco

3

Peasants and Historians: A Theoretical Survey

From the point of view of the national economy of countries, agriculture can be divided into two different periods. In the first, which we may call *domestic*, land produces only for consumption. The other is the period of *industrial* agriculture, which especially produces in order to sell. We find ourselves in a time of transition from domestic to industrial agriculture.

—S. E. Valverde, Minister of Justice and Public Instruction,
Santo Domingo, 1897

CARIBBEAN PEASANTRIES

The existence of Caribbean peasantries has long been ignored by social scientists and historians. Their attention generally has been devoted to the plantations, which were singled out as the most characteristic social and economic institution of the Caribbean. This was true for research on slave plantations in the seventeenth and eighteenth century, as well as the modern agro-industrial complexes.[1] Research into Caribbean peasantries is of more recent origin. One could say that attention to the (continuing) existence of peasant societies in the Caribbean began with the ambitious research project in Puerto Rico in the 1950s, directed by Julien Steward. The results were published in an important study, *The People of Puerto Rico*. This book left no doubt that manifold forms of agricultural production existed on that island. Alongside plantation agriculture, there existed an important small-scale agricultural sector composed of family farms.[2]

One of the collaborators on this project, Sidney Mintz, later extended its results to the history of the Caribbean in general. In a number of groundbreaking articles, he identified the existence of small-scale agricultural producers in the Caribbean, which he called "reconstituted peasantries."[3] His work broke radically with the idea that plantations had been the only decisive force in Caribbean history. He showed that slaves created niches of peasant production alongside the plantations. Some peasantries were created within the plantation economy. This was what T. Lepkowski and C. F. S. Cardoso later baptized the "peasant-breach" in plantation society.[4] Others were created outside the reach of the plantations by ex-slaves and *maroons* who had fled the plantations. Caribbean peasantries thus were created *within* the capitalist world economy, but that did not mean that they were created *by* it. Mintz argued that the birth of Caribbean peasantries must be considered as an act of resistance to a colonial order based on slavery and plantation production. Caribbean peasantries, in his eyes, represented "a *mode of response* to the plantation system and its connotations, and a *mode of resistance* to imposed styles of life."[5] After emancipation, these peasantries continued to exist and became an important social sector in the modern Caribbean.[6]

Mintz's ideas did not go uncontested. Some historians argued that he exaggerated the unique character of the Caribbean peasantry. Peasantries were equally oppressed all over the world, and they considered it useless and even politically dangerous to distinguish a separate "Caribbean" kind of peasant. Such arguments often were based on a schematic application of Marxist concepts, but the general idea certainly was not held exclusively by Marxist scholars.[7] Others argued that Mintz ignored differences in the patterns of development characteristic of the Caribbean islands, paying too little attention to the variations in plantation economies.[8] These critics alleged that Mintz's ideas were based on the history of those Caribbean islands where plantation slavery had been predominant and that it was not possible to speak of reconstituted peasantries everywhere in the Caribbean. In the Spanish Caribbean, especially in Puerto Rico and the Dominican Republic, an independent peasantry came into existence in the seventeenth century which did not have any relation with plantation agriculture. It consisted of the creolized rural population of Spanish and African descent, which established itself in the rural interior of the Spanish islands. This peasantry did not form itself in opposition to a dominant plantation economy, but, on the contrary, originated in the political and economic vacuum left by the impotent Spanish colonial administration. Where slaves and ex-slaves on most Caribbean islands were forced to establish themselves in the extremely restricted space not occupied by the plantations, the "creole" peasantry in the Spanish Caribbean colonies in the seventeenth and eighteenth centuries took advantage of the absence of political control and the abundance of uncultivated land.

Still, Mintz's work remains an essential starting point for any scholar investigating Caribbean peasantries. Recently, the Puerto Rican historian Angel Quintero Rivera recast Mintz's ideas to make them applicable to the case of Puerto Rico. Reformulating the element of resistance, so important in Mintz's analysis, Quintero argues that the rural interior of the island functioned as a countereconomy. The smallholder economy of the interior existed in opposition to the central town, which was the seat of an authoritarian colonial state.[9] In his recent history of peasant production in Dominica, Michel-Rolph Trouillot tries to combine Mintz's ideas and Marxist concepts. He calls for a historical analysis of peasant production which relates the relations of production, on the level of peasant production, to the influence of the capitalist world system. Repeating a statement made by Mintz a decade earlier, he suggests that the history of Caribbean peasantries may offer new perspectives in the more general "peasant debate."[10] Thus Trouillot closes the circle. After "discovering" a Caribbean peasantry in the 1950s, stressing its uniqueness in the 1960s and 1970s, and denying that uniqueness in the 1970s and 1980s, scholars now tend to integrate the analysis of Caribbean peasantries into the wider peasant debate without ignoring the specific historical circumstances of the peasantries' origins.[11]

The fact that Caribbean peasantries came into existence only a few centuries ago provides a strong argument for a dynamic approach to the history of peasant production. It is impossible to speak of destruction or disintegration of a natural economy in the Caribbean case, such as is often assumed in the analysis of peasant societies. Quite the contrary: "Caribbean peasantries are made up of populations whose very physical presence in the territories they now occupy came as a consequence of world capitalist development."[12] It does not suffice merely to analyze their existence, it is necessary to focus on the creation and *re-creation* of peasant production in history. At the same time, the history of Caribbean peasantries provokes questions as to the content of resistance and autonomy often implicit in peasant production. The Caribbean experience seems to indicate that small-scale agriculture was not just a fate inflicted upon hapless peasant producers. The social and economic organization of peasant production represented an option, sometimes even a conscious choice on the part of the peasants. Decisions, taken as individual producers and as a group, were based upon consideration of social behavior and moral codes operating within peasant society, *and* of changes in the outside world. Peasant production often took place in reaction to an expanding world economy, just as, for instance, plantation agriculture did. Historical research must try to explain this uneven and dynamic development of peasant production in the Caribbean.

Before I address myself to the particular situation of the Cibao peasantry, it is necessary to examine briefly some of the relevant issues in the peasant debate. No attempt will be made to summarize the entire debate.[13] Rather, I shall concentrate on three basic problems, which are of particular importance to the history of peasant production in the Cibao: (1) the logic of peasant production, (2) the influence of the market on peasant agriculture, and (3) the relation between peasant producers and political powerholders and the state.

THE LOGIC OF PEASANT PRODUCTION

The household is the axis of peasant production. It is simultaneously the unit of production and the unit of consumption. The peasant household furnishes the nonwage labor (sometimes temporarily supplemented by unpaid help from outsiders) and at the same time consumes the majority of the agrarian production. This fact limits the size of the peasant farm. As a general rule, we may consider the limits of a peasant farm to be a function of the available (family) labor. Tobacco often has been considered a crop perfect for peasant production, because it fits so well the requirements of family labor. Other crops, such as sugar cane, are almost impossible for peasant producers to grow profitably.[14]

If we assume that no outside labor is employed, we see that the expansion of cultivated land beyond a certain limit automatically leads to decreasing marginal productivity or less intensive agriculture. When the land is too small to feed all members of the household, some of them will be pushed out, and the family will become smaller.[15] Only a change in methods of cultivation or technological knowledge may break this vicious circle. It therefore is not surprising that peasants in many parts of the world have responded eagerly to labor-saving improvements—even where economists perceive underemployment—but have been much more reluctant to accept quality-improving but labor-intensive innovations.

The centrality of the household renders discussion of the adequate size of landholdings virtually irrelevant. The extent to which a piece of land can sustain a household depends upon the needs of its members, the fertility of the land, and the crop being cultivated. Sometimes a very small patch of land is sufficient to feed and keep busy all members of a household. This is the case in the cultivation of paddy-rice and, more or less, of tobacco. On the other hand, in the colonization areas of the Amazon, where the topsoil is extremely thin, properties of forty hectares are considered very small and are barely sufficient to feed a family. Many observers therefore assume that

38

peasant holdings, as agricultural enterprises, are incapable of achieving a sustained accumulation of capital. There is a tautological element in these observations. Peasant producers are seen as essentially incapable of accumulation. When they accumulate anyway, they are no longer considered peasants.

Many theories also depict the peasantry as an immobile class of agricultural producers who are stuck to their land and possess an extremely local world view.[16] Such theories tend to ignore or disguise the fact that individual members of peasant society often are extremely mobile and spend an important part of their lives in migratory and off-farm activities. Migration was an integral part of the life cycle of male members of the Cibao peasantry, just as it was for male peasants in other parts of the world.[17] The role of migration became even more evident when agricultural resources became scarcer and the viability of peasant production was undermined. For many rural households, labor migration then became a means to survive as agricultural producers.[18] Family ties and the redistribution of consumption goods often extended far beyond the physical boundaries of the household.[19]

The character of rural society is not determined only by its economic organization, however. The hierarchy and the redistribution of goods among peasant households is regulated by rules (more or less strictly enforced) about loyalty, moral conduct, and responsibility. James Scott speaks therefore of a "moral economy."[20] Peasants could endure a great deal of injustice and hard labor, but they considered the physical survival of their families a moral responsibility of all members of the community, rich and poor.[21] More recently, Goran Hyden coined the term "economy of affection"—one characterized, in his view, by "the affective ties based on common descent, common residence, etc."[22] These ideas may caution us against an excess of economism. However, they are also dangerous in the sense that they may engender a simplistic and rather ahistorical vision of the organization of peasant production.[23] Hyden's ideas tend to confirm the image of peasant producers as an undifferentiated mass of poor producers with shared interests. It is important not to overlook the conflicts and competition also implicit in peasant production.[24] Within households, there is always a potential tension between solidarity and competition. This tension is most easily seen in the repeated quarrels about inheritance of land and goods, that have been the subject of several studies.[25] Considerable differences in power may exist within peasant society: between men and women, parents and children, family and nonfamily. The distribution of goods within the household often was unequal. "Patriarchal" peasant households were characterized by a systematic pattern of age- and gender-based inequalities in access to resources, to income, and to household decision-making power, with the male head of the household as the ultimate authority.[26] Not unjustly, Kasfir asks how many members of peasant society may have felt themselves *entrapped* by Hyden's economy of affection.[27] Historians may ask: How, then, were the positions of dominant members of the household legitimated? And in what ways were their positions affected by changing social and economic circumstances?[28]

Finally, it is important to remember that most peasant studies (like this one) have a definitely local character and are presented as monographical studies. This means that groups with widely diverging economic and cultural characteristics have been presented as "peasantries." We can agree with Roseberry when he states that "the concept of 'peasant' encompasses and obscures a wide variety of social, economic, and cultural forms."[29] It may be argued that the use of the denomination "peasantry" often obscures more than it illuminates.[30] Yet, so long as we do not possess other concepts which allow us to connect our empirical research to theoretical discussions, we had better stick to what we have. A more positive argument exists, too. Trouillot writes: "If the word *peasant* as such may be devoid of analytical validity, it reflects nevertheless a range of commonalities."[31] Academics may not agree completely on the meaning and significance of peasant production, but the concept of "peasantry" still provokes pertinent questions about the variety of developmental processes in different parts of the world, and about the continuing existence of modes of production that are not (completely) dominated by capitalist relations of production. The concept of "peasant" points at the various and uneven development of capitalist relations of production and warns us against simple linear models which see a uniform capitalism as the inevitable result of historical change. The task is to distinguish the different forms peasant production may take and the variations in its subordination to capitalism.[32] Doing so may give us an instrument for dealing with the crucial problems of social and economic transitions in agrarian societies.

PEASANTS IN RELATION TO THE MARKET

Peasant producers have an ambiguous relation to the market. Production for the market normally complements their cultivation of food crops. Satisfying the needs of the household is their principal aim, but this goal does not prevent them from participating in a marketplace governed by the rules of accumulation. This situation provokes various questions.

Many observers have expressed the opinion that peasant producers are structurally antagonistic to the market. In their eyes, the subsistence-oriented logic of peasant production stands in opposition to market mechanisms.[33] Marxist and modernization theorists alike consider peasant production as an obstacle to the development of productive forces. In their opinion, "archaic" forms of production such as peasant production had to be superseded before development could occur.[34] As we have seen, there are two important problems with this vision. First, it is strongly informed by a linear way of thinking in which every society has to undergo the same stages of development. Second, it presupposes a static peasant sector which is unable or unwilling to react adequately to market forces. The general, underlying idea is that noncapitalist societies cannot change of their own accord and will do so only under the influence of external forces.

Recent research has underscored the idea that the market behavior of the peasantry is more complicated than these simple notions suggest. The reactions of peasant producers to the increasing presence of the market can take various forms. There can be no doubt that expanding world capitalism often had unfavorable consequences for peasant economies. Traditional economies often were forcefully opened up by imperial taxation and forced commercialization. Local societies sometimes reacted by fencing themselves off and making themselves invisible to the intruders. However, it would be an error to suggest that peasant reactions to the market were necessarily negative. Where they could, peasant producers did not hesitate to take advantage of new opportunities offered by infrastructural developments and the market.[35] Wage labor and production for the market often generated extra income which enhanced the economic autonomy of the producers. On other occasions, such producers used integration into the market economy as a means to escape the demands of local landholders.[36] Terence Ranger therefore rejects the idea that peasant producers *per se* would be opposed to the market. He observes about the African situation: "I do not believe that the protests of African peasants were always against the penetration of capitalist relations or that they necessarily bore the pathos of the structurally determined losers. In some circumstances at least, the protest of African peasants could take the form of an unequivocally class struggle *within* the context of capitalist relations rather than against their penetration. Indeed, in some circumstances there were peasant victories to be won even in colonial Africa."[37]

The difficult economic position of the peasant producers and their subordinate social and political position may make it difficult to believe in "peasant victories," but the active part played by peasantries in shaping market production is worth stressing. Analyzing the historical role of the peasantry in Zimbabwe, Ranger therefore argues for a reorientation of peasant studies. Instead of analyzing peasant production as a residual category—surviving as a historical freak and bound to disappear under the onslaught of colonialism and capitalism—we should see peasant production as an *option,* as a result of what he calls *self-peasantization.* The creation of a peasantry in Zimbabwe is, in his eyes, not a historical accident, but the result of "the deliberate and painful adoption of a number of strategies" by the rural population: "The resistance to the planned colonial economy was made possible by the determined self-peasantization of most of the African population."[38] Similar remarks could be made about peasant producers in Latin America.

It is thus useless to define peasant production as "pre-capitalist." It may be true that the viability of peasant production tends to decrease in the long run, but up to the present time, that fact has not made it disappear. The economic logic of the peasant household is influenced by extant market opportunities, as well as by reciprocity, redistribution, and labor pooling. Peasant production is characterized by a combination of subsistence and commodity production. It is not the dominance of one of these over the other that must inform our research, but the historical logic of their changing combination.[39]

I would argue—and not only for the Caribbean—that we can only account for the enduring existence of systems of peasant production if we accept the fact that, within capitalism, a constant creation and reproduction of peasantries takes place. These processes of "peasantization" must not be considered the result of a "capitalist masterplan," but as the result of the adaptation and change of peasant society. Diana Wong writes: "The concept of "peasantization" . . . is designed in part as a polemical corrective to those who see peasants as being necessarily transformed into proletarians as a consequence of their incorporation into the capitalist world-economy. . . . By "peasantization" is *not* meant a return to a closed peasant economy; on the contrary, it is conceived here as the development of a form of production which arises in the course of its increasing incorporation into the factor markets of the national and the international economy."[40] This perspective on peasant production—as an optional reaction to the market, rather than a fate—may point the way to new questions and conceptualizations. It abolishes the simple contradiction between peasants and the market, and it may lead us away from the vision of the peasant producer as a hapless victim of capitalism, without turning him into a "rational" entrepreneur tailored to a universal Western design.[41]

These problems have been at the core of the so-called "modes of production" debate. This debate has above all concentrated on the question of the "articulation" of capitalist and noncapitalist modes of production. In what ways did the state and capitalist entrepreneurs try to get a foothold in systems of peasant production? And how did peasant producers manipulate their own and other people's institutions to protect themselves against, or to take advantage of, outside influences?[42] These questions defy simple answers or generalizations. The advantage of formulating, and of trying to answer, them is that they bring us back to the focus of social change, the organization of production: to "the specific, historically occurring set of social relations through which labor is deployed to wrest energy from nature by means of tools, skills, organization, and knowledge."[43] What have been the motives and the underlying reasons for peasant producers to engage in specific commodity relations? Why did they use certain technology, and why did they cultivate specific crops? Which segments of peasant society were responsible for the perpetuation of peasant production? And, finally, how and why do peasant households continue to produce for the market, when it is clear to outsiders that they receive too little for their product?[44]

PEASANTS AND POWERHOLDERS

The "modernization" envisaged by most Latin American governments in the late nineteenth and twentieth centuries meant, more than anything else, the introduction of large-scale agricultural production. Private enterprises had to be given free rein to occupy uncultivated lands and to increase production with the use of modern technology. Politicians influenced by technocratic positivism set themselves the task of transforming traditional society. Because most Latin American governments were unable to direct this process themselves, they generally relied on private capital to modernize their societies. A similar situation could be seen in the European colonies in Africa and Asia. The state limited itself to creating the conditions necessary for the expansion of private capital. It lowered tax barriers, granted concessions, and facilitated production for the world market by improving the infrastructure.

A crucial point in this expansion of capitalist production was the supply of labor. Plantations could only produce profitably when they could rely on a stable labor force. In most countries with rapidly expanding capitalist sectors, a struggle for the labor of the peasant population was the immediate result.[45] Mintz writes of the Caribbean that "so-called peasants, and other groups in their respective societies, were in active contention, during the greater part of the Caribbean history, for finite resources, the most important of which being the labor power of those selfsame 'peasants'."[46] When the agrarian population was reluctant to sell its labor, entrepreneurs looked to the state to solve this problem. It was considered the duty of the state to take measures to break open the structures of agrarian organization. In many countries, successive governments therefore enforced laws aimed at the creation of labor. In Puerto Rico, the notorious *libreta* was created in 1847. In Guatemala, the Amerindian population in 1877 lost a major portion of its common lands and was forced to work on the coffee plantations. In almost all Latin American countries, people suspected of "vagrancy" could be arrested without trial and put to work on the plantations.[47]

Until recently, this state intervention in rural society was considered a more or less unambiguous and uniform process. Classical Marxists saw the state as the representative of the dominant classes, and the followers of the *dependencia* school showed how imperialism and state intervention irreversibly swept away precapitalist structures of production. Nowadays, the picture is considerably less coherent. Two factors fractured this simple picture of imperialist exploitation and destruction. On the one hand, the interests of the elite were shown to be far from coherent, and state intervention therefore could not be nearly as unequivocal or influential as previously had been supposed. On the other hand, local structures of social organization and production proved to be more resistant and adaptive than had been predicted in the apocalyptic visions of the *dependencia* school.[48] The Latin American elite was a very fluid group during the heroic period of capitalist expansion, and elite groups held widely divergent ideas concerning the road by which their society should travel toward modernization. Regional interest groups disputed each other for control of the state apparatus. Native landowners competed with foreign-owned plantations over the control of labor. Traditional elite groups lamented the loss of old values and resisted innovations. Barely concealed animosities often existed between those elite groups who controlled the state apparatus and the rural elites.[49] The creation of large-scale enterprises often collided with the development of a prosperous rural sector of native producers. While the administrative elite favored the former, provincial elites tried to preserve and slowly adapt rural society, so as not to endanger their own dominant positions. The recently established Latin American states were too weak and loosely organized to harmonize the contending interests. The result generally was a contradictory state policy, engendering uneven and divergent results.[50] On the local level, elite-peasant relations were very complicated.[51] Landowners who felt themselves on the defensive favored preservation of the existing order. They often found their interests threatened by the state. Consequently, they pursued their interests just as often by taking advantage of state measures, as by ignoring or actively opposing them.[52]

It is interesting that rural elites in this way sometimes ended up defending peasant production. Peasant production belonged to the "old order" from which the rural elite derived its social position. In the countryside a mutual loyalty often existed, symbolized in a vertical patron-client relation.[53] These relations, in which peasants showed loyalty to regional powerholders in exchange for protection, could be very hard on the peasantry, even amounting to outright exploitation. They could also be mere common-law agreements in which rights and duties of both parties were clearly regulated. It may be important for the study of Caribbean "creole" peasantries, which were not racially separated from the elite, that this "contractual" reciprocity seems to have prevailed in the case of populations that were more or less homogeneous ethnically.[54]

The protective attitude of rural elites toward the peasant population was not only the result of conservatism, however. Peasant society could provide cheap periodic labor. This was an important asset for rural entrepreneurs who lacked liquid capital. Capitalist merchants therefore often supported existing peasant economies.[55] Their enterprises depended upon the continuing availability of cheap agricultural commodities supplied by peasant producers. Thus, the protective attitude toward the peasantry depended both on the social and economic interests of the elite and on the elite's linkages to the world market. It cannot be explained simply by referring to tradition. We must ask why this "tradition" was maintained, or even reinforced, under changing circumstances. The elite attitude toward the peasantry cannot be caught in a simple dichotomy, exploitation vs. protection. Both elements were present in the relations between elite groups and the peasantry, and it is necessary to explain why one of the two prevailed in specific circumstances.

When outsiders tried to obtain a hold on peasant society and to interfere with its social and agricultural organization, their attempts often failed. The evasiveness of peasant society has become proverbial. It infuriated modernizing politicians and entrepreneurs and underlay the myriad negative stereotypes of the cunning peasant or "lazy native."[56] Peasants defended that part of their way of life which they considered essential for their material and immaterial continuation. This statement applies to social relations and productive techniques, as much as to cultural institutions such as witchcraft, rituals of birth and death, and popular religion.[57] The results may be different in each peasant society. What makes these societies comparable is their efforts to create niches that outsiders cannot penetrate.

Peasant producers rarely resorted to violence or open resistance. Their reactions mainly consisted in what Michael Adas has called "avoidance protest" and James Scott "everyday forms of peasant resistance."[58] Many regulations or government decrees failed in the face of peasant producers' purposeful but elusive obstinacy, "like a snail drawed back in their shell."[59] Analyzing the position of the African peasantry, Goran Hyden concludes that what makes the peasant family invulnerable to outside influence is the continuing capacity to produce enough food for its own subsistence. Subsistence agriculture provides peasant families with an "exit-option"; it allows them to withdraw from the market economy. Emphasizing the numerous examples of passive peasant resistance, he observes: "The dilemma in which most African countries find themselves can best be summarized in the statement that the peasants, who are the majority of the producers, do not need the state, but the state needs the peasants."[60] Although it may be argued that Hyden exaggerates the potential for resistance of the African peasantry and underestimates the inroads of the state and the market economy,[61] his emphasis on the relative autonomy of the peasant producers has relevance for peasantries in other parts of the world. Peasant producers undergo many forms of exploitation and political subordination, but often they are able to maintain a degree of autonomy. They have multiple opportunities to evade state control and to limit the effects of subordination, especially when their access to land is more or less guaranteed.

The position of peasant producers, then, was strongly affected by their place in society as a whole. The relationships among peasant producers, rural elites, and the state were fraught with ambiguity. If a state was weak, there might be room for negotiation, and often the peasantry could maintain a degree of autonomy. Peasant producers could take advantage of these opportunities as long as their organization of production allowed them to play an active role in adapting, manipulating, and creating changes in the structure of agrarian society. On the other hand, the peasantry lacked political power and depended on the support of powerful social groups. The positions of rural elite groups were crucial in this respect. In their efforts to take advantage of an expanding market economy, members of a rural elite often encouraged peasant production and many times ended up defending it.

THE DYNAMICS OF CONTENTION

All history is specific, and most historical studies tend to stress the exceptional or even the unique. In part, this book, too, will do this. The history of tobacco production in the Cibao, and the people who were responsible for it, are important and interesting in their own right. Here we are discussing not abstract concepts like class formation and the like, but groups and individuals who are consciously and unconsciously acting in history. We should not forget Scott's dictum: "For the victims as well as the beneficiaries of the large abstractions we choose to call capitalism, imperialism, or the green revolution, the experience itself arrives in quite personal, concrete, localized, mediated form."[62] But it cannot be left at that. Historical facts are not just there, lying dormant until someone comes to compile them and put them in order. The sources must be analyzed and interpreted. Sometimes, as in the case of oral history, they are even purposefully "created" by the historian. A study that aims at understanding historical processes on a regional and local level cannot ignore more general discussions of this topic. Writing a book like this implies a number of assumptions that are informed by the ongoing academic discussion and by the specific questions and fields that are of interest to the historian.

What assumptions, then, emerge from our selective look at the peasant debate? First of all, to understand the logic of peasant production, it is necessary to take peasant society as point of departure. Clearly, I do not posit a simple dichotomy between a capitalist (world) economy and a noncapitalist peasant sector. It is necessary to understand how peasant society changed over time as a result of its changing context. Only by analyzing the relation between the changing organization of the household and the wider changes taking place socially and economically may we hope to understand the history of peasant production.

Secondly, it is important to understand the relation between peasant producers and the market. The Cibao tobacco growers had a long tradition of participation in the market without becoming irreversibly dependent on it. The tobacco sector in the Cibao can be understood only if this characteristic element is analyzed and explained. Another issue is the differences among peasant producers themselves, which resulted from their participation in the market. The differential advantages that individual producers could draw from this confrontation seem to have heightened social differences within the peasant community. This differentiation challenges the assumption that peasant populations are socially homogeneous. It is important to see how the increased differentiation has changed the nature of peasant society.

A third cluster of questions refers to the class position of the peasantry, and especially its subordination to the state and to rural elite groups. The state tried to increase its hold over the peasantry, but many times these efforts were not coherent or successful. Regional elite groups lived close to the peasantry and often functioned as buffers against an encroaching state.

When regional elites ended by defending peasant producers, it is necessary to explain the origins of this (temporary) convergence of interests. How did members of the elite perceive the peasantry? And how did the peasant producers try to take advantage of the existence of regional elites to protect themselves against undesirable interventions from outsiders?

The crucial historical problem, then, refers to the interaction of different logics of economic and social behavior. Scott may be right when he suggests that capitalism is after all the dynamic, "revolutionary" force breaking up old patterns of social and economic organization.[63] However, it is the struggle over the extent and direction of these changes that explains regional variations. Social and economic transformations are not the monopoly of one group, but the result of confrontations (which, to be sure, can be quite harmonious at times) among different social groups. If we want to account for the history of social and economic transformation, we must focus on this struggle.

The consequence of the foregoing is that this book does not restrict itself to the history of one social group. Rather it focuses on the interaction— the cooperation and the confrontation—among different individuals and groups. This focus may enable us to understand the social and economic position of the Cibao peasantry and to ascertain the degree of autonomy it possessed in different eras. Our hypothesis is that, even though the Cibao peasants were vulnerable to many kinds of pressure and manipulation, they succeeded in defending part of their social and economic organization. This struggle for autonomy, however, was not always unambiguous, especially because the shared cultural background and the occasional support of the local elite made it impossible always to distinguish peasants and elite groups. It is therefore important to understand the links connecting peasants and the local elite. Such links are not only social and economic, but also cultural and ideological in nature. The ultimate question is this: how did the tobacco-producing peasantry, which from all obvious viewpoints would seem to be a politically weak class, manage to maintain itself during sixty years of intense and sometimes dramatic changes in the Dominican Republic? This is not a simple question about continuity or absence of change. On the contrary, it leads us directly to the historical analysis of an adaptive peasant society. If we want to explain the continuing peasant production of tobacco in the Cibao, we must look for the causes of its continual regeneration—that is, we must look to the capacity for change and adaptation on the part of the men and women cultivating tobacco.

4

The Tobacco-Producing Peasantry in the Cibao: The Logic of Small-Scale Agriculture

Every time it rains, you sow tobacco to scratch out a livelihood ["para salvar la vida"].

—Félix Mercado, cultivator in Villa González, during
a session of the Tribunal de Tierras, 1960

The character of the Dominican people demands a certain independence in actions and work . . . No one likes to give up the independence of action to which he is accustomed.

—*El Eco de la Opinión*, 1885

The history of the Cibao tobacco sector was the result of a complex relation between changes in the organization of peasant society and changes in the regional economy. On the one hand, both the regional economy and the mercantile elite depended on the continuing production of tobacco. On the other hand, the expansion of capitalist relations of production in the Cibao caused a gradual and sometimes contradictory transformation of rural society, which might undermine the viability of peasant production. What we have to assess is the susceptibility of the tobacco-producing peasantry to market forces. It is important to analyze the adaptive strategies of the peasantry and its changing position in capitalist society. We do not have to agree with "dualist" visions such as Scott's "moral economy" or Hyden's "economy of affection" to concede the specific character of peasant societies.[1] The combination of subsistence agriculture and production for the market gave the peasant producers margins of autonomy which were usually unavailable to exclusively market-oriented producers.

The question, then, is not *if* subsistence agriculture was an important aspect of peasant production, but *how* its place changed within the peasant

49

economy. We must also explain why tobacco was the favorite cash crop of the peasantry and in what ways this crop was instrumental in creating and maintaining an independent peasant sphere. How was agricultural production organized, and who controlled access to the means of production, especially land? What was the relation between the cultivation of food and of cash crops? What differences existed within peasant society, and how did these differences affect the market position of the various groups? Answering these questions can yield information about the historical development of peasant societies and may ultimately lead us to an understanding of the resilience of peasant production within capitalist society. In the Cibao such questions are especially interesting because of the specific aspects of peasant production. Given the abundance of land and the absence of extra-economic coercion, why did the peasantry produce for the market at all?

This chapter tries to answer some of these questions. The relation between tobacco production and subsistence-oriented activities is a central issue in this analysis. Exploring it leads us to a discussion of the characteristics of tobacco as a cash crop, the pattern of landholding in the Cibao, and the subsistence strategies of peasant households. Although this chapter focuses on the internal organization of peasant production, we must not forget that peasant society was part of a wider society. The historical development of the Cibao peasantry and its confrontation with external influences originating outside its control will be treated in chapters to come. It is impossible to understand the system of tobacco cultivation without understanding the internal logic of the Cibao peasant economy, but it is just as dangerous to analyze the history of the peasantry without referring to its changing position within larger social and economic structures.

Tobacco Production in Nineteenth-Century Cibao

Rural society in the Cibao at the end of the nineteenth century was basically a frontier society. Land was abundant in the Cibao, and the agricultural frontier pushed relentlessly forward. Rural villages hardly existed in the region, and clusters of two or three houses were dispersed throughout the forest-covered countryside. Peasant families lived in small huts, *bohíos*, at the center of a courtyard inhabited by pigs and chickens. Each dwelling housed a nuclear family which was considered a separate unit, but relatives, especially of the older generation, normally lived close by and often shared the courtyard. Close to the houses, small patches of land were cleared which were cultivated with plantains (*plátanos*), cassava (*yuca*), corn (*maíz*), and sweet potatoes (*batatas*), sometimes planted in the shadow of coffee, cocoa, or mango trees. At the appropriate season, some plots would radiate the bright green color of young tobacco plants.

When the population increased and tobacco agriculture expanded, the landscape gradually became domesticated. The forests in the northwestern Cibao, the eastern swamp region, and the mountain ranges gradually were transformed into agricultural land. From the center around the Santiago–La Vega axis, the frontier expanded in periodic waves into the uncultivated frontier areas, which until then had been used exclusively for cattle (see map 3). Bonó described this process in 1881, pointing out its two dimensions: the expulsion of the seminomadic cattle economy toward the regional periphery, and the incorporation of some of the cattle holders into a more market-oriented agricultural economy: "In this way, the old cattle holders who hold fast to their pastoral customs . . . have sold, and continue to sell, their lands to agrarian cultivators from Moca and Santiago and withdraw to more distant areas which are still deserted and therefore allow them to continue their pastoral life. Others who are perhaps better informed and see these immigrants as their more progressive brothers, worth imitating, follow their example and start working their land."[2] A last, important development occurred in the late 1920s, when an irrigation system was constructed in the region west of Santiago. Access to water made it possible to push the agricultural frontier far into the western part of the Cibao, which formerly had been too arid to cultivate.[3]

This "conquest" of the agricultural frontier is an important feature of Cibao history.[4] At the same time, the Cibao had a centuries-old tradition of producing and exporting agricultural commodities. Tobacco production had established stable commercial networks that linked the Cibao to the coastal towns—the most important of which undoubtedly was Puerto Plata—and the world market. The combination of frontier agriculture with a commercial system geared to export of agricultural commodities determined Cibao history.

Reflecting this dual nature of Cibao society, the tobacco-growing peasantry in the second half of the nineteenth century consisted of two main groups. A more or less stable sector of peasant production occupied the central Cibao, around the La Vega–Santiago axis. Population density was quite high in this area, and the land was clearly demarcated. Growing tobacco was an important means of survival here, one that tied peasant families firmly to the market.[5] The contemporary romantic image of the hard-working, respectable rural population was modeled on this group. On the fringes of this stable agricultural sector lived a second group of cultivators who exemplified

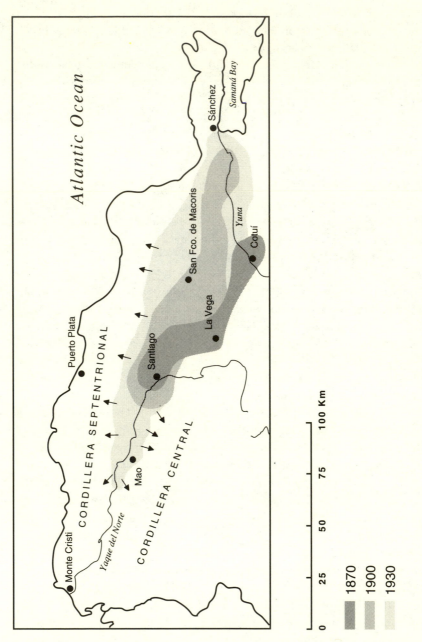

Map 3. Expansion of the agricultural frontier in the Cibao, 1870–1930. Map by Willem A. Baud.

the frontier character of Cibao society. These peasants grew tobacco using a slash-and-burn system, gradually in this way penetrating into the forest. They often lived in isolation in the woods, combining pastoral activities such as hunting and cattle holding with agriculture. They consisted partly of the heirs of the early-nineteenth-century seminomadic Cibao economy, and partly of cultivators who had been pushed out of the agricultural center and had sought land on the frontier. The organization of peasant agriculture depended on the two productive cycles of food crop and tobacco cultivation. Traditionally, these were not—as is the case today—strictly separated. The cultivation of food crops demanded permanent attention. Plantains and cassava could produce fruits all year and were the favored staple crops of the rural population. Tobacco usually was sown during the rainy period in the last two months of the year, but peasant producers might sow tobacco during any time of the year which promised prolonged rains. The productive cycles of tobacco and food crops thus coexisted.

Figure 2. View giving an impression of the region. In front is a tobacco field; in back are the foothills of the Cordillera Septentrional. On the right is a *rancho,* in which tobacco is hung to dry. Photograph by Michiel Baud.

TOBACCO AS A PEASANT CROP

Tobacco is an annual crop that sprouts, grows, and flowers within a period ranging from 60 to 150 days, depending on the climate. The plant can reach a height of 1.5 to 2 meters. Its leaves can reach a length of 1 meter, but they are usually smaller. At the end of its growing period, it bears flowers with a pink or sometimes yellow color. One plant can produce up to 40,000 seeds.[6] The crop belongs to the family *Solanaceae* and originates, as far as we know, in the New World.[7] When the Europeans arrived in the Caribbean, different types of tobacco plants existed, of which only *Nicotiana rustica* and *Nicotiana tabacum* were consumed by the indigenous population. It was this latter type which the Spaniards started to cultivate and which eventually became the commercial crop referred to as "tobacco."[8] In time, through spontaneous hybridization or purposeful selection, many varieties of *Nicotiana tabacum* have come into existence.[9]

Tobacco grows easily and spontaneously and does not require any special attention. It matures rapidly. Although the plant is potentially a woody, shrublike perennial, it is normally grown as an annual. Within a mere two months after sowing, the tobacco leaves can be picked and hung to dry. This makes it a highly seasonal crop whose cultivation leaves ample time for growing food crops. The short agricultural cycle also tends to diminish the risks involved in tobacco cultivation. Finally, the plant can sustain relatively long periods of drought and therefore can be cultivated in semiarid zones such as the western Cibao.

Tobacco is a cash crop, meant to produce a large, aromatic leaf. As such, it requires careful attention and much processing. This has made tobacco one of the most labor-intensive cash crops of the modern world. However, Dominican producers cultivated local types of black tobacco and aimed at a voluminous harvest rather than high-quality tobacco. This fact set the Dominican tobacco grower apart from his Cuban (and perhaps also his Puerto Rican) colleagues. Where these latter were meticulous agriculturists who used sophisticated techniques and tuned their agriculture closely to the market, Dominican producers usually cultivated the crop with minimum labor. For them, tobacco was part of a subsistence economy geared to the perpetuation of the household. The crop, as an addendum to the more important food crop agriculture, took second place within the peasant economy. One could say that the Cuban producers had domesticated the tobacco plant, while in the Dominican context it was an untamed cash crop. The peasant producers favored the cultivation of tobacco because of its ready market and its capacity to mature without too much attention.[10]

The dark tobacco grown by the Cibao peasantry consisted of two types: *criollo* and *olor*. The origins and exact botanical characteristics of both kinds are subject to debate (see appendix 2). The two held different market positions.[11] *Olor* tobacco produced a more aromatic leaf and was used in the production of cigarettes. *Criollo* tobacco was dark and had a less identifiable taste. It could easily be mixed with other types of tobacco and was mostly (although not exclusively) used in cigar production. In the twentieth century, *olor* tobacco was bought and processed by the national cigarette industry, while most of the *criollo* tobacco was exported.

For the tobacco growers, other differences were important. *Criollo* plants tended to produce a larger quantity of tobacco, but *olor* prices were usually higher. Cultivators affirm that the *criollo* tobacco plant was stronger. It could stand long periods of drought and, even when sown very late, always produced something. High-quality *olor* tobacco demanded considerable labor. Thus, the type of tobacco a grower preferred depended on his calculations. As long as subsistence agriculture was the essential activity of a peasant household, it usually grew *criollo* tobacco. More market-oriented tobacco growers tended to switch to *olor* tobacco and try to obtain better prices by dedicating more time to its cultivation. This was not a static opposition. According to the vagaries of the market and tobacco prices, structural changes occurred which affected producers in diverse ways.

Figure 3. Rural dwelling. Note tobacco growing almost to the front door. Photograph by Michiel Baud.

Before varied chemical processes were invented to manipulate the taste of tobacco, it was the soil more than anything else which gave a specific taste to a certain type of tobacco. Perhaps for this reason tobacco was generally designated by the name of the place where it was cultivated. Before the discovery of artificial fertilizers late in the nineteenth century, manure (animal or human) was used in European agriculture, but it was generally recognized that organic fertilizer gave a bad smell to tobacco. Production areas with abundant virgin lands which did not need fertilizing therefore were favored for tobacco cultivation. It is no coincidence that the heyday of many new production areas was in the nineteenth century when there was ample virgin land to be cultivated and that many of these regions experienced severe problems in the twentieth century, when artificial fertilizers obliterated their relative advantage. At that point, the archaic production techniques often used in agriculture on virgin lands became evident.[12]

In the Dominican Republic, tobacco was grown on recently cleared land. Until well into the twentieth century, agriculture in the Cibao would start with slash-and-burn clearing of a patch of virgin land—the *tala y tumba*, in local jargon. Trees were cut down and underbrush burned. The felled trees were used to make fences, necessary to protect the crops from roaming animals. Such a fence had to be, in the words of Abad, "a real Chinese wall, solid and impenetrable."[13] When the land had been cleared, stumps dug out, and stones removed, the soil was turned with a machete. Small plot size and imperfect clearing, which always left debris in the field, precluded the use of a plow. The plow was introduced in the region late in the nineteenth century but found general acceptance only in the 1940s.[14]

The peasants usually preferred a plot of some ten to twenty tareas (sixteen tareas make one hectare), which they called a *conuco*. However, the size of the cultivated land could vary with its fertility, with the size and composition of the household, and with the ambition of the peasant.[15] According to the governor of La Vega in 1872, forty tareas was the maximum which could be cultivated by one family.[16] After two or three years, a new patch of land was opened up and sown with tobacco. The previously cultivated land was left fallow—*botado,* as it was called—and thereafter was considered inferior for tobacco cultivation. The use of virgin lands resulted in high yields and a dark, heavy type of tobacco.[17]

Clearing the *conuco* was a labor-intensive way of preparing land. However, the trees which were cut down to clear a *conuco* fulfilled many functions in the peasant household. Apart from being essential for protecting the crop, they provided wood to build houses and firewood for cooking. Furthermore, land clearing was done in the dead season, between August and November, when there was little agricultural work to do. Weed control was hardly necessary on recently cleared land. Thus much labor was avoided in the busy period when the tobacco was in the field. Discussing agricultural practices in Africa, Fresco writes: "In the forest, weed infestation, rather than just yield decline, seems an important reason why farmers abandon fields at the end of the cropping cycle."[18] In addition, it may be assumed that male peasants liked the rough and rewarding work of clearing a *conuco*. It affirmed their manhood and showed the world that they were responsible men who took care of their families.[19] I never heard a cultivator complain about the work involved in clearing land.

Tobacco and food crops usually were cultivated on the same land. When the tobacco was sown, it was the normal procedure to intercrop it with staples such as corn, cassava, and beans. This intercropping was strongly criticized by agrarian advisors and tobacco merchants,[20] but it was an essential element of the subsistence economy and continued until the 1960s. In the present day, it can still be seen in the more remote tobacco areas. Some peasants cleared two plots, each of about six tareas. One of these was dedicated to tobacco and was always called *conuco*. The other contained the food crops: corn, cassava, sweet potato, sometimes coffee, and, of course, the rural staple, plantains (*plátanos*). These plots were sometimes called *platanales*.[21] Women and children had an important role in the provision of food, and a distinct preference therefore existed for cultivating food crops close to the house. In the course of the twentieth century, as these food plots became smaller and more clearly separated from commercial agriculture, they were sometimes designated by the term *hortaliza*.

The animals which posed such a threat to field crops were an integral element of the peasant economy. Chickens, pigs, and goats could be seen everywhere roaming around the peasant *bohíos*. They functioned as both savings account and insurance in the peasant economy, enabling the family to survive in periods of sickness or drought. As a seventy-five-year-old peasant from Moca commented, "In former times you could buy a lot of things for one peso. You could buy a pig, for instance. And when you had fattened it up, you could get land for it or clothing and much more."[22]

THE CULTIVATION OF TOBACCO

In the nineteenth century, the sowing of tobacco consisted of broadcasting tobacco seeds in the cleared *conuco*. The land was fertile, and when rainfall did not fail, the tobacco would grow without any further human intervention. When necessary, a second round of sowing (the *resiembra*) was done after a few weeks. Rainfall was of crucial importance at this stage. Cultivators waited for the winter rains before sowing, and, since these were irregular, the planting season could vary widely. Usually tobacco was sown in November and December, but in years when it did not rain, planting could take place in March and even April. It was only in the twentieth century, when the growers started to use seedbeds, that tobacco was sown in September and the harvest took place in December.

The weather during the first weeks after sowing determined the fate of the crop. Heavy rainfall could have disastrous effects on the young tobacco plants while they were still small and their roots were weak. The young crop was similarly threatened by periods of drought.[23] However, tobacco growers built some security into their agricultural system and rarely lost the entire crop. First of all, a recently cleared *conuco*—often surrounded by forest— had an extraordinary capacity to retain moisture. Secondly, sowing tobacco required hardly any labor and could be repeated endlessly. These "resiembras" guaranteed the cultivators at least some tobacco production. It is true that bad harvests frequently occurred, due to prolonged drought, hail, or torrential rains, but peasants affirm that tobacco always "produces" something ("tabaco siempre da algo)."[24] Most tobacco growers say that this is why they prefer tobacco over other cash crops.

The use of virgin lands for tobacco cultivation precluded any problems in connection with fertilizing. Although in 1865, an agronomist—probably Cuban—already was recommending the use of *guano* "as a first-class fertilizer for the cultivation of tobacco,"[25] fertilizing was virtually unknown in Dominican tobacco cultivation until late in the twentieth century. In 1948, two officials of the U.S. Department of Agriculture observed that "fertilizers are not in general use in the Dominican Republic."[26] Some people argued that intercropping with food crops such as sweet potato, pumpkin, or watermelon helped the soil recover after the tobacco harvest.[27] However, one factor probably was responsible for the slow introduction of fertilizer and the continuation of slash-and-burn agriculture. Dominican tobacco was sold to German importers who were interested, above all, in cheap, dark tobacco which could easily be mixed with tobacco from other parts of the world. The virgin Dominican soil, cleared by burning the underbrush, was highly suited for the production of such a tobacco. The fertility of the land made for a strong plant with large leaves, while the burning, which took most of the organic material out of the topsoil, produced a tobacco that had little aroma and therefore blended easily with other varieties.[28]

The most labor-intensive stage of tobacco cultivation was the harvest. It began when the plant reached maturity and the lowest leaves, the "sandleaves" (*barresuelos*) turned yellow. The best picking technique was to begin with the lower leaves, wait for the next leaves to mature, and so on, until the plant was without leaves. This method sometimes was used by the peasants, but often all the leaves were picked at once.[29]

When the leaves were picked, they had to be hung to dry immediately or the leaf would lose its texture, start to rot in the piles, and—very important in a practical sense—lose its strength. Then it could hardly be manipulated. In principle, men picked the tobacco, while women attached the leaves to long strings made of palm leaves (*sartas*) and hung them in drying sheds (*ranchos*).[30] This distribution of work was very flexible, and I have often seen women picking tobacco and men making sartas.

Family labor alone often was insufficient to cope with the work of the harvest, and the harvest therefore saw the organization of communal labor gangs (*juntas gratuitas* or *juntas de vecinos*; sometimes the word *convite* was also used). We do not know when the peasant producers started to use this institution of reciprocal labor exchange, but it already existed at the beginning of the nineteenth century.[31] It seems to have been a logical response to the periodic need for extra labor in the money-scarce peasant economy.[32] It did not reflect some indiscriminate "peasant solidarity" but was part of a survival strategy in which individual peasant households chose to link their fates. Apart from the economic convenience, such a system of cooperation reaffirmed and consolidated networks of friendship and social obligation.

The tobacco grower would advise his family, friends, and neighbors that on a certain day he wanted to pick his tobacco: "This day is mine" ("Este día es mío"), as old peasants recall the accepted formula. In the twentieth century, Monday was set apart for *junta* activities in the Villa González region, but it is not clear whether this was a general custom. On the prearranged day, men and women assembled at the specified *conuco*. In general, only people living within walking distance were invited. If a person could not come, someone would be sent as a replacement. In the twentieth century, these substitutes sometimes were paid. Men picked the tobacco, women tied the leaves to the *sartas*, and the *junta* finished the harvest within a few days. There is no doubt that *juntas*, although implying hard work, were merry occasions at which rural songs (*décimas*) were sung, the latest news was exchanged, and matches were made. Many old people vividly remember the happiness of these busy days, when one worked with family and friends and celebrated the completion of the harvest with a communal meal accompanied by bottles of rum.[33] The tobacco owner's only obligation was to provide food and drink for his workforce. He and his family would in their turn help their neighbors. The same system was applied when a *rancho* had to be built. The system accomplished labor-intensive tasks without resorting to wage labor.[34]

It took about twenty-five days for the tobacco to dry in the *ranchos*. When the leaves had a uniformly reddish-brown color, they were ready to be taken down, and the fermentation process could start.[35] Sometimes some fermentation was induced in the *ranchos* by hanging the *sartas* close to each other, but this practice disappeared in the nineteenth century. The *sartas* were laid down on the floor in a huge pile (*troja* or *troje*).[36] In the *troja*, the actual fermentation took place. The packed leaves were heated, and a chemical process transformed the living, organic leaf into a dead, manageable commodity. The productive cycle ended with tobacco being packed in *serones* and transported via mule to the city.

While the fermentation required no capital, a certain expertise was needed to avoid damaging the tobacco. It was the most delicate stage of the production process. Many observers claimed that defective fermentation was the principal reason for the low prices of the Dominican tobacco. When the fermentation process was not completed properly, the tobacco continued to ferment during its ocean passage and reached the European importers in bad condition—*quemado* (burned), as it was called.[37]

Land and the Peasant Economy

The autonomy of the tobacco-growing peasants in the Cibao depended on their access to land. As long as the peasant producers were able to find new pieces of land without monetary compensation to the landowner or the state, they could perpetuate their subsistence agriculture. "Open" land resources were an essential pillar of the Cibao peasant economy. Later we shall see how rural entrepreneurs and state officials tried to curb this access to land, but, before the 1930s, they succeeded only partially in "capturing" the peasantry in this way.

Juridically, free access to land in the country was closely tied to the so-called *terrenos comuneros,* pieces of land held collectively by a number of proprietors who all possessed shares (*pesos* or *acciones*) in the landholding. The origins of the *comunero* system must be sought in the colonial period and, more particularly, in the economic neglect of the island by the Spanish colonial government. The Spanish Crown had given large land grants to the first colonists. In the long period of economic depression which began in the sixteenth century, these *hatos,* as they were generally called, came to be owned collectively by the heirs of the original landowners.[38] Since an abundance of land existed in the colonial period and the land was used principally for extensive cattle grazing, no need existed for an exact subdivision of the hatos.[39] It is not clear whether this process of collective ownership came to a temporary halt during the Bourbon reforms at the end of the eighteenth century, but it developed further during the eventful years after the Haitian Revolution. The scarcity of money and administrative insecurity stimulated expansion of communal landholding patterns.[40] In the nineteenth century, these patterns had developed into a complicated system of landholding, which could perpetuate itself only because of low population density and an underdeveloped economy. In practice, every co-owner of a communal property had the right to use the resources of the property. He could take water and wood, cultivate the land, and pasture his cattle, so long as there was no infringement on the rights of other owners. The *comunero* system practically guaranteed Dominican cultivators access to land. This right received legislative backing in the final quarter of the nineteenth century, when the government decreed that merely cultivating export crops conveyed property rights over land.[41] It is probable that Knight referred to this situation in 1928, when he stressed that *use* and not *property* was basic to the Dominican land system.[42]

In the Cibao, the situation was more complex. The region had a long agricultural tradition, and the central part of the region, where large-scale cattle operations were absent, possessed a clear pattern of land ownership. It therefore is not immediately clear what the importance of the *comunero* system was in the Cibao in the second half of the nineteenth century. Bonó's statement in 1857 that the comunero system was the principal system of landholding in the Dominican Republic "except the surveyed land of the Cibao," is somewhat ambiguous.[43] What he probably meant was that, while *terrenos comuneros* existed in the Cibao, a relatively large proportion of the land had been demarcated and was owned privately. He referred to the central region of the valley around the axis La Vega–Moca, where most land was demarcated. Tulio Cestero described the Moca region in 1901 as "the most agricultural province of the Republic," adding that "in its territory, which is the smallest [in the country], not a piece of land is unused."[44] San Miguel rightly suggests that the laws on the division of *comunero* lands enacted in the first two decades of the twentieth century were largely superfluous in the central Cibao, since market forces already had accomplished the task undertaken by these laws. He writes: "In Santiago, many of the common lands had been subdivided among shareholders before the enactment of the aforementioned laws. . . . The laws on the partition of common lands acknowledged a process that had begun years before."[45] It is important to remember, however, that land was still very cheap. This was true even in La Vega, the oldest agricultural region of the Cibao. An old man in La Torre (La Vega) recalls that in his youth "it was possible to buy a farm or a considerable amount of land for one calf."[46] And outside this relatively small agricultural center, the cheap land was even more abundant until the 1930s.

Small-scale cultivators were not very interested in the legal aspects of land tenure. They did not care whether the land they cultivated was public, private, or *comunero* land; what mattered to them was access to land. Especially important for the cultivators was the right to make use of natural resources that were not situated directly on their property. This right allowed the peasant family to fetch water in one spot, get firewood in another, and have their cattle roam around freely. Above all, however, the right was crucial for slash-and-burn agriculture. It may well be that legal co-ownership had become rare in the twentieth century, but, for many peasant producers, it had become normal to refer to unoccupied, freely available land as "comunero" land.[47] Interviews in the Villa González region tend to confirm this interpretation. Elderly peasants in the Cibao nowadays remember hardly anything about the land laws issued during their lifetimes, but unrestricted access to land—in strong contrast to the situation today—is a recurring theme in their stories. They often talk about "comunero" lands, vaguely waving their arms to indicate land which, in days long past, was unclaimed and free to take. It may well be that in the Cibao the *comunero* system lost its significance long ago. In that case, contemporary use of the term "comunero" among elderly peasants might be the result of land legislation at the beginning of this century, which reintroduced the term into the local vernacular.[48]

Land gradually became less abundant in the twentieth century. Demographic growth generated increasing pressure on available land resources. In addition, members of the elite started to invest their money in landed property and became owners of relatively large tracts of land. In addition, new legislation curbed communal landholding. However, the peasantry did not immediately lose its access to land. Only in the "old" agricultural region between La Vega and Moca was land more or less divided in the 1920s, re-

moving the last possibilities of free access to land. In the "newer," more recently settled areas, landowners often lacked the funds to put their properties to profitable use. Many landowners were glad when they could take advantage of the presence of peasant families who would clear their land. The
latter could freely settle on their land, under the sole condition that, after
two or three years, they would leave their *conuco* sown with guinea grass. In
this way peasant agriculture paved the way for commercial cattle raising,
which became an important activity for many of the new landowners.[49]

The open land frontier in the northwestern valley and especially up onto
the mountain slopes surrounding the valley continued to provide the peasantry with a safety valve. When their independence was threatened or peasant agriculture became impossible, the peasants moved into the mountains
and continued their peasant agriculture there. In his interesting study of an
agricultural community in the northern mountains, David Bray stresses the
peasant character of the colonization of the mountainous regions. He notes
that the settlement of the northern mountains was not undertaken by landless laborers, but "of already established farmers who were seeking to expand their holdings and achieve a greater land base for their family's labor."[50]

The principal explanation of the peasant producers' continuing access
to land, of course, was the Dominican Republic's low population density in
the period under study. As we shall see, however, the slow development of
productive forces and, above all, the weakness of the elite and its internal
contradictions were just as important. In the absence of a strong entrepreneurial class which might have established large-scale plantations or at least
monopolized access to land, and a politically strong elite which might have
forced the rural population into subjection and coercive labor, the Cibao
peasantry was able to maintain its independence.[51]

The Subsistence Economy of the Peasant Household

The cultivation of tobacco was only one, and often not even the most important, of the elements of the peasantry's subsistence economy. Indeed,
one of the amazing things about the tobacco sector was the contrast between its production and its commercialization. In the latter, all aspects of a
monoculture were apparent. The regional press depicted the Cibao as a region completely dependent on tobacco monoculture. The government was
equally inclined to focus on tobacco and ignore the importance of subsistence agriculture. These institutions were aware of subsistence agriculture's
importance, to be sure, but, in this era of "progress," with its one-sided bias

63

toward export agriculture, food crops were considered uninteresting. Not for nothing were (and still are) such crops as corn, beans, plantains, and cassava called "lesser fruits" (*frutos menores*)!

The cultivation of food crops was essential for the peasant economy, however. For peasant families, these crops were as important as the tobacco crop. They guaranteed a family's continued existence and decreased its dependence on an unpredictable market. Food cultivation explained the alternating participation in and withdrawal from the market, so characteristic of the history of peasant production. Peasant households used the income provided by tobacco to buy consumer goods. Sometimes that income allowed them to obtain credit, but most families were not dependent on the sale of tobacco. With reason we may doubt that tobacco cultivation was the center around which the peasant agricultural cycle revolved.

The fortunes of the peasant producers depended not so much on the market as on the success or failure of their food crop agriculture. It may be significant that older peasants hardly recall years of extremely low tobacco prices, while they remember very accurately the years in which food shortages occurred. When adverse weather conditions destroyed the food crops, despair could grip the rural population. At such times, families had to consume their animals and their small savings. These were also occasions for religious processions—usually dedicated to San Isidro, the patron saint of the cultivators—through the fields to beg for rain.[52] At the worst of times, peasant families had to move away to places where they could wait for rain.[53] Traditionally, the mountains were the place of refuge in these circumstances. The men, with or without their families, moved up and hastily cleared a conuco. It was reported in 1935 that, in times of distress, "the peasants flee to the mountains where after a period of suffering they are able to establish another *conuco* which provides them with their daily food."[54]

When the rural inhabitants were in danger of starving, some migrated toward the cities. In 1924, *La Información* reported that "the sharp crisis caused by the prolonged drought in the surrounding countryside has resulted in a rural exodus toward the city [of Santiago]." City people started to become alarmed about "this immigration of destitute people (*infelices*) who do not possess the means to survive in the struggle for daily bread in the city" and asked the authorities to solve the problem.[55] Many people in Villa González still remember the year 1944, the "Año del Centenario," when an extremely long drought drove people into the mountains, where they survived on cassava bread. Although these were exceptional years, periods of food scarcity became increasingly frequent in the countryside in the twentieth century. It is unclear whether this was the result of the new emphasis on export agriculture or whether increasing dominance by the market caused a withdrawal of foodstuffs to the cities.

The peasants themselves processed certain tobacco products—rural cigars and *andullos*. Cultivators often kept their best tobacco for themselves and rolled their own cigars, which they smoked and sometimes sold at retail. *Andullos* were made by compressing densely-packed tobacco leaves in a long, stretched cloth. By gradually increasing the pressure during several months, the processors squeezed all moisture out of the tobacco leaves. The result was a solid substance, which was smoked in a traditional pipe, the *cachimbo*. The production of the *andullos* complemented agricultural work.[56] However, some specialization took place in the second half of the nineteenth century. Small entrepreneurs in mountainous rural towns such as Jarabacoa and Janico started to import tobacco from other places and fostered a prosperous business. Many people were engaged almost exclusively in this sector. Bonó, perhaps exaggerating somewhat, states that a fifth of all the tobacco exported was in the form of *andullo*.[57] Popular lore has it that many people became rich from this *andullo* production.

Tobacco growers also made cigars and *andullos* for their own consumption. Nowadays, this is often done to generate extra income, but peasant cultivators take special pride in smoking their best tobacco themselves. When market prices went down, many extended this activity. They kept a larger part of their tobacco and increased the amount of tobacco they processed themselves. This possibility of processing tobacco within the household economy bolstered the independent market position of the peasant. In 1909 Amiama Gómez wrote in the *Revista de Agricultura*: "When the merciless or greedy merchant does not want to pay a just price for first-class tobacco, the cultivator makes good cigars [*buenas brevas*] in his homestead, or excellent *andullos* in his tobacco sheds: but he does not *burn* it, he does not sell it under its just value."[58]

Many peasants also complemented agriculture with transport activities. Members of the rural communities domesticated mules and transported tobacco. Some of them could be considered "professionals" (like one of the principal characters in Juan Bosch's novel *La Mañosa*), but many cultivators traveled with a few animals, as a profitable and attractive sideline to their agriculture. An observer in Santiago stated in 1889, "A multitude of cultivators—and we refer to the poorest—possess three or four pack animals, which transport loads to Puerto Plata or La Vega and in this way, for better or worse, manage to support their families."[59]

65

Thus agriculture was embedded in an intricate mosaic of activities. Peasant production implied a good deal of collateral work. Some of it, such as the construction of ranchos and the making of sartas, was linked to tobacco agriculture. Other activities simply formed part of rural existence. Many people had their own herbal medicines, sewed their clothes, and made their own furniture.

The Organization of the Peasant Household

We know little about the internal organization of peasant households in the nineteenth or even the twentieth centuries, but the few sources that we have suggest that peasant society consisted of nuclear families under patriarchal control. When a man reached adulthood, he chose a woman, built a house, and cleared land, as a means of taking care of his wife and children. The tobacco harvest played an important role in the timing of marriage. A young man would start timidly to court a local girl. When his prospects were good, he built a small house with the help of his father and family and cleared a piece of land. Tobacco was sown and harvested after a few months. Selling his tobacco gave the man his first private money and enabled him to marry. Amado Franco Bidó wrote in 1924, "In the middle of the harvest, abundant or not, marriages are frequent, because when our rural people receive money, they feel only one primeval and immediate desire, the formation of a household."[60] Because of the surplus of women (partly the result of prolonged civil warfare in the nineteenth century), many men had more than one wife at one time. A favorable harvest might enable a man to give a mistress a small house and some possessions.

Agriculture was essentially a family affair. The male head of the family was in charge of its organization, but all family members were actively involved in agricultural labor. Schooling hardly existed until deep into the twentieth century; as soon as children could walk, they were put to work at daily chores. They carried water from the river or well to the house, swabbed the floor, fed the chickens. When older, they had to help in agricultural tasks. The boys helped to clear the forest, took care of the *conuco*, and accompanied their father on errands. The girls helped their mother in her domestic work, washing clothes, cooking, and cleaning the house. Agriculture was also predominantly a household activity. All family members performed agricultural tasks as needed.

Access to sufficient hands to take care of the agricultural chores was an essential precondition of peasant agriculture. Larger families—more family labor—meant more land cultivated and could mean greater prosperity. Control over labor became more important with the increasing dominance of the market and in the twentieth century this control began to play a more important role in the organization of rural families. The economic fortunes of the family depended on the control that the male head of the family exercised over the labor of his family members. His ability to deploy that labor determined his possibilities for accumulation.[61] According to Bray, control over labor was an important principle of peasant agriculture in the Cibao in this period, leading to increased differentiation among the peasantry: "Men strove to accumulate wives and children when their material resources permitted it."[62] Multiple households then became instruments in a process of accumulation and differentiation. Not surprisingly, richer cultivators tended to have large numbers of children. My village sample in Villa González shows that most men had children with more than one woman. Several men had more than twenty living children.[63]

The need to control family labor reinforced patriarchal tendencies that already existed in rural culture.[64] Children were kept under close control until an advanced age. Many elderly men recount how they could only change their shorts for long pants when they were eighteen; even then, the father watched his son's behavior.[65] Grasmuck and Pessar suggest that such tactics postponed the moment when the sons' labor had to be shared with another household.[66] The "honor" of daughters was guarded even more jealously. Courting could be a tedious affair when done according to parental rules. Prospective candidates (male and female) were severely scrutinized, and a young man was expected to visit the house of his beloved many times before her parents would approve the engagement. Many elderly people recall that young people had to wait a long time before they could become involved with the opposite sex or establish a separate household. The paradoxical result was that many young couples fled (often making it appear that the girl had been abducted) and by sleeping together formed a consensual union that could not be dissolved by the parents.[67]

A wife had to take a subservient role. It was the man's duty to generate income to feed and cloth his family and to guarantee the safety of his wife and children. As long as he complied with these obligations, he could do what he liked. Even when he had relations with other women—often hardly concealed—or went off drinking and stayed away from home without any explanation, his wife was not to complain. She had to cook food, raise the children, and wash his clothes. In addition, she did her share of the agricultural work. It is not improbable that her responsibility for the *hortaliza* and the cultivation of food crops in general constituted a kind of subsistence guarantee in case her husband left her. There was one important condition in the matrimonial "contracts" in peasant society. When a husband failed to take care of his family as custom dictated he should, the wife had the fullest right to go her own way and secure the survival of herself and her children as she saw fit.

Women had very few opportunities for a life outside marriage. They could return to their parents, but in that case they just exchanged one type of patriarchal control for another. Female-headed households, such as existed in other parts of the Caribbean, were uncommon in the Cibao. Public opinion and women themselves looked down upon this alternative, not least of all because peasant society had no ideological place for women in such an unprotected position. The only liaisons approaching such a construction were the households existing separately in a polygamous situation. Here the woman lived alone with her children, but the man was expected to guarantee their subsistence.

With the increasing dominance of the market and new wage-labor opportunities, women gained some economic independence. As in other peasant societies, women often possessed a quite independent and responsible position in Dominican rural society, a fact that tended to be obscured by the dominant patriarchal ideology. In the nineteenth century, women already were working in the storehouses of the tobacco merchants. In the twentieth century, a regional market for food crops also came into being, providing women with extra income. Peasant women became very active in this food market, generating extra income for the family. The *marchante* became a well-known feature of rural society. Rafael Espaillat wrote in 1935, "In many rural regions, it is the woman who goes to town to sell the superfluous agricultural production, and when she has sold everything, she turns into a petty trader, buying cheap products in the countryside to sell in town."[68] In rare cases, a woman ran a farm on her own. This was usually the case after the sudden death of her husband and was seen as a transitory situation. In later times, when wage labor was more common, women sometimes ran a farm with hired labor.

Migration and Changing Peasant Existence

It would be a serious mistake to analyze the peasantry exclusively from a village perspective.[69] The picture of stagnation and immobility painted by written sources hardly fit the facts. Certainly agriculture was not the only activity peasants engaged in, and frontier agriculture *ipso facto* implied some degree of mobility on the part of the peasant household. The fact that tobacco was an annual crop with an agricultural cycle of only a few months made for great flexibility. Migration was a normal part of the male life cycle from the nineteenth century on. The origin of this peasant mobility must have been the political instability of the nineteenth century. Civil warfare was endemic in the Dominican Republic before 1930. Soldiers were recruited from the ranks of the peasants, and military campaigns took them to all parts of the country. Such campaigns accustomed the peasant population to traveling throughout the country. Military service could also facilitate upward social mobility. Hoetink has stressed the opportunities that existed to ascend the politico-military ladder during military campaigns and revolutions. Important late-nineteenth-century political leaders such as Heureaux and Luperón, who came from marginal social groups, took advantage of such opportunities. This phenomenon also existed on a lower level, and many local and regional leaders owed their positions to a military career.[70] On the other hand, young men sometimes tried to evade conscription by migrating. The governor of Azua complained in 1870 that some two hundred men had deserted the army and were living in the Cibao.[71]

The experience of migration created adaptations in peasant society in which the remaining family labor absorbed burdens created by male absence.[72] When, in the last decades of the nineteenth century, sudden opportunities for wage labor lured the men away from their agricultural plots, these networks insured the continuation of the household economy. During the early years of the sugar industry, many men migrated to the sugar plantations during the harvest (*zafra*). The construction of the two railroads in the Cibao in the final decades of the nineteenth century also provided opportunities for wage labor. The majority of the 1,500 men who worked building the Ferrocarril Central in the 1890s were peasants.

The consequences of this migration for peasant society were highly ambiguous. Wages were a welcome supplement to income from peasant agriculture, allowing rural inhabitants to buy desirable consumer goods and pay unexpected costs associated with sickness or accidents. Florencia Mallon has shown how wage labor in the Andes supplemented and supported the subsistence economy but in the long run increased differentiation within the peasant economy and undermined the peasant household.[73] This same process took place in the Cibao, though more gradually and with less dramatic consequences. Wage opportunities were too few and too irregular, and wages too low, to have had conclusive effects on the peasant economy.

Peasant laborers also tried to restrict their wage labor to the "dead season" between May and November, when the few agricultural tasks could easily be left to the women and children. Before the 1920s, most peasants refused to engage in wage labor when their presence was necessary at the *conuco*. Thus they still saw agriculture as their primary responsibility. This attitude, which made them highly unreliable as a workforce, was a constant source of frustration for employers.[74] The U.S. consul in Puerto Plata wrote, "The habits of the working class are not very steady, especially in the country, as when they have worked hard and accumulated a few dollars, they are apt to want a rest."[75] The fact that the Dominican worker had few needs was often mentioned as the principal reason for the Dominican economy's underdevelopment.[76] This was another way of saying that Dominican workers were not fully proletarianized. Their solid base in peasant agriculture enabled them to evade the discipline of the workplace.

Although the men might not have objected to travel, migration gradually became more of a necessity than they would have liked to admit. Migration certainly became an accepted and often necessary part of peasant existence in the first decades of the twentieth century. It diminished consumption within the family and provided financial means to invest in agriculture. We have already seen how drought could push the peasant population into the mountains.

Most travel by the men took place during early adulthood. Many peasant men had worked and lived in several places before their twenty-fifth birthdays. Present-day oral history confirms this pattern. When asked about the places where they have resided, most interviewees name at least four or five places, some near their birthplaces and others far away, in distant regions of the country. One old man had lived in Monte Cristi, Puerto Plata, Santiago, Sabana de la Mar, Higuey, and Santo Domingo.[77] He may have been an exception, but most male peasants had worked in distant places during parts of their lives. Listening to aged men tell about their lives and the activities they have engaged in, one is struck by the variety of work they have done and their remarkable love of travel.[78]

Peasant men give two reasons for their travels: adventure and work. These are often inextricably intertwined. Most say that, as young men, "they wanted to see something of the world." Migration also was a means of escaping patriarchal control and acquiring independent income.[79] Most men did this traveling while still unmarried, but marital status seemed not to make much difference in whether a man traveled or not. A young man without a family may not have needed an excuse to leave, but even if he had family responsibilities, work was a legitimate reason for going. It was generally believed that men were freedom-loving and volatile. As long as they fulfilled their responsibility to sustain their families, parents and wives more or less grudgingly consented to their absences.[80] Migratory wage labor shifted part of the responsibility for agricultural production to the female and younger members of the family. These members of the household formed the center of gravity of the peasant economy, to which the men returned after their various social and economic activities.

In the twentieth century, migration and wage labor became increasingly necessary within the peasantry. Wage labor became an essential source of income for many poor peasant families, as access to land became more difficult and peasant production no longer could sustain the family. Peasants provided labor for the increasing number of capitalist enterprises, and some joined the urban proletariat. Migration also could be an instrument of upward mobility. Rich peasants sent their sons and daughters to the cities to be educated and to secure a better or different life. It may be that many of them failed, but some succeeded in ascending socially.[81]

For the peasant producers who remained behind, subsistence agriculture remained the basis of their existence and independence, and few wanted to lose the security it provided. Thus subsistence agriculture and the freedom to travel became the two fundamental supports of the peasant population's autonomy.

In this chapter I have tried to give a picture of the Cibao peasantry and its changing place in Dominican society in the period 1870–1930. If questions and inconsistencies remain, they stem in part from the lack of source material, and in part from the problems involved in analyzing a peasant population over a long period of time. There is something inherently misleading in the static and tautological concept of "the peasantry." We tend to talk all too easily about the peasantry as if no changes occurred in its composition. But who were these peasants in 1870, 1900, or 1930, whom we are wont to presume equivalent? Many different groups of cultivators existed. "Traditional" peasant producers, who were hardly interested in the market and persisted in their frontier agriculture, managed to maintain their independence. Others tried to hold onto their subsistence base while becoming more dependent on the cultivation of tobacco as a cash crop. Simultaneously, the number of market-oriented peasant producers, who tried to take advantage of new opportunities offered by the market economy, increased. In general, it can be said that tobacco as a cash crop linked the peasants to the market but did not require that they be dominated by the market's rules. Although they very well could use the income provided by tobacco, they could fall back upon the food crops they cultivated. Only when food production failed did the structure of the peasant economy collapse. Many producers supplemented their agricultural income with periodic wage labor. As the twentieth century advanced, some households lost their subsistence base and became dependent on wage labor. Others succeeded in accumulating some capital. They bought land, went into trading, or sent their children to town to be educated.

Hyden's concept of an "uncaptured" peasantry has been severely criticized,[82] but it nevertheless may help us better understand Cibao peasant society. When older peasants in the Cibao talk about the past, they recall an idyllic age when poverty and jealousy were absent. Behind this apparently romantic nostalgia, we can detect two basic tenets of peasant society as it existed until the 1930s. First, there was a period in which people enjoyed extensive freedom and autonomy. Second, the elders lament the disappearance of a society in which social and economic relations were not yet exclusively determined by the market and in which "everyone helped each other." They remember, in fact, the period in which the Cibao peasantry was not yet the "slave" of the market and the peasant economy was not completely monetized.

The position of the Cibao peasantry was determined by four specific elements. First, there was an abundance of land, allowing the peasantry access to land at no cost. This availability enabled peasant producers to maintain an agricultural system which safeguarded the production of food crops. The resulting subsistence base constituted the second element of peasant autonomy. A third, more ambiguous element was the mobility of the peasant producers. They were able to move freely and look for supplementary income in other regions of the country. However, migratory wage labor in the long run played an important role in the penetration of the market economy into the Cibao countryside. It gradually diminished the importance of subsistence agriculture and stimulated differentiation within the rural community.

A final pillar of the peasant economy was tobacco itself. The crop was well suited to smallholder production. It produced a yearly cash income and left ample time for other activities, agricultural and nonagricultural. Tobacco was well suited to smallholding agriculture because it required careful attention and left enough time for the cultivation of food crops. Another factor was that the Cibao peasants were accustomed to tobacco growing. The cultivators felt sure of tobacco and were not prepared to abandon this crop in spite of occasional crises. It was their favorite cash crop, and they knew they could always sell it. The tobacco expert Luis Carballo wrote in 1931, "They have inherited their knowledge of tobacco from their ancestors and know that it has a secure market . . . ; and they do not feel the need to experiment with other crops which may lead them to even greater failure."[83] Peasants often say, chuckling, that the cultivation of tobacco is a vice (*vicio*), impossible to abandon.

5

Peasants and the Market:
Organization of the Rural Tobacco Trade

When the cultivator has his tobacco half-grown [*a medio crecer*] and lacks the means necessary to support himself and his family, the intermediary presents himself with money in hand and proposes to buy the tobacco for a very low price. Under pressure to meet his most immediate needs, the cultivator is obliged to accept these conditions, and sells.

—Temístocles Herrera Borr, 1926

One of the topics debated most hotly in peasant studies is the relation between peasant producers' market participation and their fundamental orientation to subsistence agriculture. We can distinguish roughly two positions in this debate. Modernist observers have stressed the positive consequences of the peasantry's participation in the market. In fact, these theorists consider the market a prerequisite for improving the material position of the peasantry and for economic development in general. The modernist vision is shaped by a neoclassical belief in the free market—a market in which all participants have equal chances and conditions are regulated by the free interplay of market forces.[1]

Squarely opposed to this position is a more critical approach, strongly influenced by Marxist thinking. Here the market is viewed as one of the principal arenas where surplus is extracted from peasant producers. Far from being a freely accessible, impartial place of economic exchange, the market is, in this opinion, completely controlled by the dominant classes and utterly disadvantageous to the small producers. The fact is stressed that participation in the market often is far from voluntary and in some cases even results from "forced commercialization."[2]

Both these camps tend to see market influence as an outside force to which the peasantry is forced to submit. They envision the inevitable and

73

unilinear disappearance of peasant production as a result of the development of productive forces.[3] As I have suggested earlier, the market position of peasant producers is somewhat more complicated than these theories suggest. The market may destroy systems of peasant production, but it may also support them. It may be that many peasant producers have objected to the conditions under which they were allowed to participate in the market, but this is not to say that their subsistence orientation *prohibited* this participation. Reviewing the ideas of Goran Hyden, René Lemarchand recently has pointed out that many examples exist of peasant producers who have reacted very effectively to market opportunities. He writes: "The important issue is not whether African peasants are inherently receptive or averse to capitalist economies, but the terms on which they are incorporated into such economies."[4]

For the Caribbean, Mintz has shown that peasant producers created their own market systems which linked them to the world market. This permitted them to take advantage of the market as an instrument for accumulation and upward mobility without abandoning their subsistence orientation.[5] These ideas converge with Terence Ranger's concept of peasantization, mentioned in chapter 3. Peasant production for the market must be considered an option which is determined by the needs of the household and the conditions of that market. Aversion to the market may exist within peasant society, but it cannot be considered its innate characteristic. It should be explained rather than taken as a point of departure. Such a viewpoint qualifies theories which suggest that the peasantry's insertion into the market economy is a unilinear and uniform process. As long ago as 1955, Eric Wolf warned that it is dangerous to suppose that "the line of development of particular peasant communities always leads from lesser involvement in the market to more involvement."[6] His emphasis on the inconstancy of market involvement of peasant producers has not lost its value. As long as the subsistence base of the peasantry was guaranteed and no extra-economic force was applied, peasant producers were, to a certain extent, free to enter or leave the market economy. The subsistence strategy of the peasant family thus implied a constantly changing relation to the market economy.

This is not to say that peasant production can be analyzed without taking into account the peasantry's political subordination. An analysis of the market position of the peasantry leads automatically to a discussion of its political position. Peasant producers do not trade in a free market of the type assumed by neoclassical economists. Their freedom of decision is severely curtailed by their subordinate position and their dependence on local strongmen. Abstract market forces expressed themselves in very concrete

74

forms on the level of the peasant community. The tobacco trade implied direct, person-to-person negotiations with the local traders who bought their tobacco. Peasants depended on the mercantile class for credit and political protection. When local landowners bought the tobacco, the peasants also depended on them for access to land. Moreover, traders often held key political positions in local society, which they used to improve their market position within the community. Rural society in the Cibao gave a clear example of the web of dependency relations woven around peasant producers.[7] These highly personalized relationships could offer peasant producers certain advantages and insure a degree of protection. At the same time, they created gross inequalities in bargaining power.[8]

An analysis of the market position of tobacco-producing peasants in the Cibao must address various problems. First, it is necessary to see how the relation between subsistence and market agriculture changed in the period under study. In this respect, the most difficult problem is to determine the importance of the market in the peasant economy. Second, we must analyze the organization of rural trade. What differences existed within the class of peasant producers, and what were these producers' relations with the mercantile class? It will be clear from the foregoing that in answering these questions we cannot limit ourselves to economic relations. The market position of the peasant producers was a function of complex relationships with local traders, relationships that were economic as well as noneconomic. We therefore conclude this chapter by considering briefly the social and political positions of the rural traders.

THE RURAL TOBACCO TRADE

In its simplest form, the tobacco trade consisted of the exchange of tobacco leaves for money. Bonó gives the earliest detailed description of the tobacco trade at the level of the cultivator, and of how credit functioned in the commercialization of the crop:

> [A young peasant] clears a piece of land, sows the tobacco, and offers to sell it to the shopkeeper, if the latter will give him what he and his family need. The shopkeeper does not have the means to do so . . . , but he recognizes good business and runs to the foreign merchant, whom he asks for an advance. The merchant, who already knows that the peasant has sown the tobacco and that it will only take four months for the tobacco to be dried and packed, gives the money to the shopkeeper with interest. The shopkeeper passes it on with more interest to the peasant, who now is able to look after himself and his family.[9]

This description, written in 1881, is a useful starting point for an analysis of the tobacco trade in the Cibao.[10] The access to money—or rather, to credit—was the principal incentive for the cultivation of tobacco. Capital was very scarce in the nineteenth-century rural economy. Although incorporation into the world economy made shortages of capital less acute in the twentieth century, access to credit remained one of the most valued advantages of the cultivation of tobacco. Peasant households received consumer goods in exchange for (part of) their coming tobacco crop. The crop was the basis for the majority of commercial transactions.

Intermediary traders lived in the countryside themselves and were often engaged in other commercial activities, such as running a small rural shop (*pulpería*). This location facilitated their performing dual roles as creditor and purchaser of tobacco. In rural discourse, the *comín* was considered to be the person who traded at the lowest level of rural society. He normally limited his commercial activities to his own community, whereas the *corredor* traveled through a larger region.[11] M. C. Grullón described the activities of these traders in 1918: "They only engage in this profession during the tobacco harvest. They go from field to field, where this crop is cultivated. They take an option on the tobacco by way of cash advances bearing a more than onerous interest; this process regularly causes the ruin of the peasant. They give him ten pesos in order to receive fifteen as soon as the tobacco is harvested and dried. Others buy the tobacco in advance for two to five pesos per quintal. Both these methods aim at doubling the capital within a year, and many succeed in doing it within six months."[12] The cultivators dried and fermented their tobacco in their *ranchos* and then sold it: "When the leaves have been taken out of the *ranchos*, the cultivators collect them in small heaps in which the leaves can dry without fermenting. Then they normally await the visit of the buyer."[13] After the tobacco was sold, the peasants normally packed the tobacco in *serones* and carried it to the storehouse of the purchaser.[14] In the twentieth century, merchants sometimes took care of the packing themselves. They paid laborers to prepare and pack the tobacco in the *rancho* of the cultivator.

Bonó described the stereotypical transaction. The shopkeeper or a fellow cultivator advanced money to the peasant producer when the tobacco was still in the field, under the explicit condition that he would receive the tobacco after the harvest. This tobacco was "promised" (*comprometido*).[15] Such advances hardly ever were delivered in real cash and normally took the form of consumer goods. Tobacco sold *before* the harvest garnered lower prices than the market price ultimately would be. It was observed in 1907

Figure 4. Rural church. In front is a man riding a mule, carrying two (empty) *serones*. This was the traditional way to transport tobacco. Photograph by Michiel Baud.

that "the majority of the cultivators in the Cibao find themselves continually obliged to sell part of their crops before the harvest. When they hand over the tobacco, they receive only half the going price."[16] The same article estimated that one-fifth of the entire production of the Cibao was sold in this way. This situation did not change in later years.

Why did so many peasant producers sell their tobacco in such an unprofitable way? Why did they not wait a few months longer and receive a fair price for their tobacco? The most important reason must have been that, although subsistence agriculture formed the foundation of the peasant economy, it could not supply all the family's needs. The peasant household as an economic unit was quite vulnerable to adverse circumstances. Usually there was sufficient food, but cash money for necessary expenses was lacking. For the peasantry, local traders were the only source of credit, and the low tobacco prices must be considered as reflecting an "implicit" interest. The profit of the intermediaries was in the overpriced consumer goods they sold to the cultivator and the low prices they paid for tobacco. There are no indications that they charged interest for the advances they gave.[17] Significantly, cultivators remember landlords and traders as the ones who "gave" money (*daban pesos*).

We may understand some of the advantages of this system for the cultivator when we consider the high rates of interest paid on borrowed money in the first decades of the twentieth century. It was reported that interest rates from 25 to 100 percent for short-term loans were quite normal in 1907.[18] In later periods, these seem to have remained normal rates. When we consider that present-day interest rates can reach 100 percent for a three-month credit, there is no reason to doubt the 1928 estimate that cultivators usually paid 50 percent interest for a short-term loan.[19] Analyzing notarial records of the region, San Miguel suggests that rates of interest could be even higher for small-scale cultivators.[20]

The relation between producers and traders, then, was highly ambiguous. Their short-term interests often coincided. Without the local traders, the producer could not dispose of his product. The traders were dependent on the peasants' continuing tobacco production. On the other hand, many conflicts existed. The cultivators were subject to various forms of unequal exchange, and, although they tried to counter its negative consequences, they often suffered under the commercial monopoly of the local traders.

TOBACCO AND SOCIAL DIFFERENTIATION

The peasantry reacted in various ways to the vagaries of the market and the changing tobacco prices. After the tobacco crisis of the 1870s, when prices fell dramatically, cultivators withdrew labor from tobacco cultivation. More peasants grew tobacco, but, instead of focusing on quality, they tried to obtain as much weight as possible: "Thus, knowing that there is demand for quantity, not quality, they gain much time in this way and act as the best speculator."[21] Growers began to add weight to the tobacco by adding stones or water, in an effort to counteract the low prices.[22] The process reversed in the 1920s, when prices started to rise and demand increased. Many producers started to dedicate more time to tobacco cultivation. In this period, social and economic differences among tobacco producers widened, and these differences were reflected in patterns of tobacco marketing.

These differences were seen most clearly in the ways tobacco was transported to market and, above all, in its classification. The different forms in which the tobacco was sold suggest the relative importance of tobacco as a cash crop in the household economy. Peasant producers in the nineteenth century always sold their tobacco without any classification whatsoever. Most small-scale cultivators continued to sell their tobacco in this way in the twentieth century. They usually cultivated *criollo* tobacco and received a bulk price for it. These transactions were normally called *uno y otro* or *al barrer.* One tobacco expert, Máximo Grullón, strongly criticized this "erroneous and fatal custom of selling 'uno con otro'."[23] Many people believed that the cultivators would receive more money for the tobacco if it were classified. Others alleged that the system prevented producers from trying to improve quality. However, peasants themselves state that the difference in income used to be too small to compensate them for the extra labor involved in selecting the tobacco.

The economic activities of market-oriented cultivators followed the tendencies of the market. When possible, they tried to take advantage of the opportunities of the tobacco market. They selected their tobacco according to size and quality and sold it in different classes. In the nineteenth century, three classes were usually distinguished: *primera, segunda,* and *tercera.* Sometimes subdivisions of *superior* and *inferior* were made in each category.[24] In the twentieth century, three classes were normally distinguished. *Olor* tobacco was divided in two classes: *primera* and *segunda. Criollo* tobacco was added as a separate class. Sometimes the distinctions became more sophisticated. *Criollo* tobacco always remained a separate class, but *olor* tobacco was sold in four classes: FF, F, A, and *picadura.*[25] These classes reflected differences in quality. "Picadura," sometimes taken together with "A," was the lowest-quality tobacco and consisted of small and damaged leaves. The FF, "doble F," were the largest and most beautiful leaves. Sometimes the tobacco was sold in strings of rudely classified tobacco leaves. This form was called *enmanillado* and was supposed to guarantee a better quality of tobacco. On rare occasions, tobacco was sold in *tongas* or *manos* (bundles of leaves tied together at their shafts).[26] Only high-quality tobacco or extremely large leaves, which fetched higher prices, were sold in this form.

It was in the manipulation of these classifications that profit could be made. The quality, uniformity, and selection of the tobacco determined its price. It is generally accepted that the market price of tobacco depended, above all, on its skillful classification. Therefore it is not surprising that social differentiation within the producing class expressed itself clearly in the marketing of tobacco. Some cultivators succeeded in taking advantage of the market and gradually increased their material welfare. They bought land, built a house, and sometimes even became traders. It is difficult to trace the exact origins of such successful peasant entrepreneurs. They seem often to have used their subsistence agriculture to strengthen their position on the market. Their orientation to the market expressed itself in a sharp, calculating attitude, combined with extreme thrift, especially in the initial period:

R. T. is one of the successful cultivators of the Villa González region. Wage labor provided him with some money in the 1920s, which he used to buy land. He started to cultivate tobacco in 1928, already having considerable knowledge of the market. Over time he acquired 30 tareas of land. His ability to select tobacco and his sharp eye for the market enabled him to obtain high prices. He was a very successful cultivator and the first man in the neighborhood to build a stone house and to buy a television. Out of necessity or conviction, he always remained in the peasant milieu, where he acquired a reputation for having expert knowledge of the tobacco market. He ended up establishing and presiding over one of the first peasant associations of the country.[27]

For the majority of the peasant producers, however, the market was a mixed blessing. On the one hand, selling tobacco enabled them to acquire certain consumer goods that they could not produce themselves. On the other hand, it rendered them vulnerable to outside pressure and facilitated outside intrusion into the peasant economy. Peasant producers grew tobacco in order to satisfy their immediate monetary needs, but the cultivation of tobacco sometimes competed with their subsistence agriculture. We have already noted that the collective memory of the peasant population attaches more importance to the fate of food production than to the irregular fluctuations of the tobacco market. This may serve as circumstantial evidence for the continuing importance of the subsistence orientation in twentieth-century peasant agriculture, but it must not blind us to various forms of market orientation on the part of the tobacco growers, or to their changing market behavior. We have seen that it would be a fallacy to assume that the Cibao peasantry possessed an essential aversion to the market. Centuries of market production demonstrate the contrary. The transformation of rural society was not a matter of *introducing* market principles but rather of changing the relation between subsistence-oriented and market-oriented behaviors of the peasant producers.

The scarce historical evidence we have suggests that this changing emphasis has been a rather uneven and erratic process. The small tobacco growers had a notoriously weak position in the market and received very low prices for their product. Because of these low prices, their subsistence agriculture remained of crucial importance. Paradoxically, this allowed them to maintain a degree of independence. In this way their weak market position functioned to maintain the resilience of peasant production, while sustaining a subordinate position.

It is interesting to note that some elderly peasants express a profound distrust of the market, which is absent in the younger generation. These older ones still hold onto the combination of tobacco and food crop cultivation, trying to retain the independent market position it used to guarantee them in former days. Some explicitly state that they see their food production as the principal weapon against untrustworthy traders and an unreliable market. Today's tobacco cultivators, they say, because of their exclusive focus on tobacco, have turned into errand-boys of merchants, agronomists, or landowners. They criticize the contemporary monocultural, technocratic approach to tobacco growing. Their attitude thus expresses both a rejection of the market-oriented attitude prevalent today and a proud remembrance of their past independence of the market.

The tobacco trade, as described by Bonó, has survived until the present time, but the peasant class itself has changed. Individual peasant households held onto their subsistence agriculture, but they were prepared to increase their participation in the market when prospects were good. They were not averse to wage labor, as long as it did not endanger their subsistence agriculture. Some smallholders, for various reasons—practical intelligence, access to some capital, better education, family or political relations—were able to obtain a stronger, more independent market position. We know very little about the exact causes of these differences. Continuing access to land was very important, as we have seen, but it is difficult to ascertain who succeeded in reaching that goal and who did not.

Successful peasant producers often gave up agriculture and invested their savings in other activities. Some migrated away and turned their backs on the countryside. Others became petty money lenders and sometimes

Figure 5. Old peasants telling their story to the author. Photograph by Michiel Baud.

started to buy up tobacco in their neighborhoods. Rural intermediaries often started out as cultivators, and income from agricultural production provided their first capital. It was observed in 1929 that the small-scale rural traders "have almost always been cultivators."[28] These were not necessarily peasants with superior starting positions. Shanin has emphasized that chance played an important role in differentiation within the peasantry. Relatively insignificant events could lead to a complete change in the socioeconomic position of the peasant household.[29] Some families reached material well-being through hard work and an austere lifestyle, but others never made any progress despite such characteristics. Along with chance, personal qualities of the producers played an important role. Families saw their small savings dwindle when a member became sick, but just as many families suffered because of drinking or gambling habits. We must not forget these individual lives when we try to trace the general tendencies of the tobacco market.

Peasants and Traders

Small-time traders (*corredores*) worked with borrowed capital and were pressed to return the money as soon as possible. They were therefore always in a hurry to secure the tobacco that was owed to them. The cultivators often were forced to hand over the tobacco before it was properly dried. In 1893, Rafael Abreu Licairac suggested two principal causes for the decline of the tobacco sector in the Cibao. First, of course, was the "characteristic, dull apathy" (*genial rutinaria apatía*) of the cultivators. Second was "the objectionable impatience of the speculator and the exporter, who oblige the cultivator to deliver the product of his work before it possesses the conditions necessary for sale in the market. They do so because they want to recover their loans rapidly and they erroneously believe that in this way they will obtain higher profits."[30] *La Información* wrote in the 1920s that the peasants "in the beginning of each harvest find themselves surrounded by these commercial mosquitoes, who are greedy for wealth and almost always extremely avaricious in dealings with the laboring peasant."[31] Contracts in the twentieth century sometimes stipulated that the tobacco had to be delivered before a certain date.[32] When the harvest promised to be small, this behavior became even worse. In 1917 it was reported that "various cultivators complain that the so-called *comines* take their still-green tobacco out of the *ranchos* as compensation for their debts. The traders believe that the harvest will not be sufficient to pay back all their creditors."[33] The pressure to deliver the tobacco as soon as possible is also evident in another practice.

When the tobacco picking was coming to an end and many smallholding families were desperately short of money, most shopkeepers and money-lenders refused to give any more credit. Ferrán calls this period the stage of *tiroteo* ("juggling").[34] Some of the tobacco was already hanging in the *ranchos* and, from this moment on, money could be obtained only by offering tobacco in exchange. Today it is normal for a peasant family to pay for its daily necessities during the harvest period with small amounts of tobacco. One can sometimes see people entering a small rural shop with a handful of dried tobacco leaves.

Critics of these aspects of the tobacco trade claimed that measures to improve the quality of the Dominican tobacco could not succeed as long as this type of commercial transaction continued: "It is clear that the peasant's need to sell, and the claims of the merchant on the tobacco crop (for which he has advanced money and which he wants to ship), do not leave time to the one to harvest at the opportune moment, and to the other to let the tobacco dry for the necessary time."[35]

Sometimes the intermediaries took advantage of the scarcity of cash to increase their commercial profits. When money was not available or when they could convince the cultivator that it was not available, they did not pay for the tobacco, but gave the cultivator an open credit in their store for the

Figure 6. Peasant with a bundle of *sartas* made of palm leaves; they are used to hang tobacco in the *ranchos*. Photograph by Michiel Baud.

Figure 7. Picking tobacco, starting from the bottom and moving upward. Photograph by Michiel Baud.

amount of money they owed. This practice amounted to a forced truck system. In 1909 in was reported that "the (usurious) merchant does not pay the cultivators with current money, so that the latter are obliged to spend the income of their harvest during the dead season to pay ridiculous prices [*precios de ganga*] in gold money for imported articles."[36] It is not clear how widespread this practice was, but its existence shows again that the intermediaries derived their crucial position mainly from their dual function as supplier of consumer goods and buyer of tobacco. The scarcity of money in rural society also worked to their advantage.

THE ECONOMICS OF SMALL-SCALE TRADE

Local traders had an important position in the rural economy, but often they were squeezed between the cultivators and the urban merchants. It must be remembered that, although the intermediaries wielded great economic power in rural society, they did not belong to the elite. They were as far removed from the wealthy urban merchants as were the peasants. The urban merchants tolerated the intermediaries as long as they had no other way to obtain the tobacco, but they were keenly contemptuous of these men coming from the country (*campo*), with their rude manners and lack of sophistication. They accused the *corredores* of shifting all the commercial risks to other parties. On many occasions it was asserted that the "poor" and "defenseless" peasant had to be protected against the intermediaries' abuses and manipulations of the market. In the 1880s, the *corredor* and the *comin* already were being publicly condemned as parasites, living on the backs of the peasantry. This kind of criticism never stopped.[37] Urban merchants also complained about the fact that the intermediaries often did not pay their commercial taxes (*patentes*), thereby distorting free commercial competition.[38] Many observers, then, saw the intermediaries as the cause of commercial losses. F. A. Vicini observed in 1929, "The sums of money which the exporters advance to the *comines* normally are lost in much greater proportion than would occur in a well-disciplined trade."[39]

There was a grain of truth in this observation, but above all an overdose of hypocrisy. The elite conveniently preferred to ignore its own role in the commercial process and to blame the petty rural traders. As chapter 7 makes clear, the market was dominated by a small number of prominent companies. Many observers worried about the lack of free competition. Urban merchants tried in many ways to manipulate the market and did not hesitate to decrease prices with little tricks. They systematically undervalued the tobacco brought to them by cultivators or intermediaries.[40] When this was not sufficient, they resorted to outright fraud. In the closing decades of the nineteenth century, merchants were repeatedly accused of using false scales. They appeared to offer prices higher than before but deceived the seller with their scales.[41] They also bought tobacco from the coastal regions in the North, which was cheaper because of its reputedly worse condition, and mixed it with tobacco from other provinces.[42]

Everyone knew that the merchants complained about the inferior quality of the tobacco, to justify the low prices they offered. An observer noted in 1920, "At this moment—and this happens every year—incredible tales about the tobacco price make the rounds. Merchants who have an interest in the trade declare that the tobacco 'will be worthless'."[43] Sometimes rumors were circulated that the harvest was going to be extremely large. When prices went down as a result of this incorrect information, the merchants tried to buy as much tobacco as possible.

Although the merchants were unable to control the commercial process completely, they tried to increase their influence on tobacco buying. The urban firms were competing for the tobacco, but this did not stop them from making informal agreements and manipulating the market. Their social affiliations, class interests, and shared ideology bound them together. They belonged to the same social group, and competition was mitigated by mutual agreements and informal cooperation. In the twentieth century, denunciations of price manipulations and secret agreements became a regular feature of the tobacco trade. Price agreements became the normal practice in the 1920s. In June 1924, for instance, *La Información* reported that the low prices of tobacco were not the result of "the situation of the international market, but of the manipulation of local speculators." It continued: "From the beginning of the harvest there have been agreements and bargains between two or three buyers in order to bring about low prices for this year's tobacco."[44] The next year, accusations were made in Moca that "the mercantile houses are demoralizing the trade. They pretend that they have no interest in the tobacco in the hope of buying it later at a lower price."[45] These agreements normally had a temporary character. Sooner or later, the common front was broken. All the firms had contractual obligations to supply tobacco to their European customers and there was always the threat that the competitors would cheat and suddenly start buying the tobacco for a slightly higher price. Usually prices would increase after weeks or months of tense waiting. One of the merchants would break ranks, and the others would follow rapidly. Sometimes the *corredores* were the first to start buying tobacco for higher prices, speculating on prices rising later on.[46] After the urban merchants increased their control over the intermediaries in the 1920s and turned them practically into paid employees, this became more difficult.[47]

The intermediaries could do very little against this manipulation of the market. They borrowed their working capital from the urban merchants, who had to be repaid after a few months. The only asset they had were their good contacts in rural society, but these created their own obligations. Traders sometimes felt a moral obligation to give advances to cultivators from whom they knew it would be difficult to recover their money. Often they had to accept tobacco of inferior quality. A former *corredor* recounts: "In 1928, the Tabacalera loaned me some fifty pesos to buy tobacco, and they gave one peso commission in order to eat and pay for the pack animal. Sometimes they gave me two pesos commission, or three or four. I had to make my profit in the countryside. It was not fixed. There were days that I was losing money because the Tabacalera refused to accept tobacco of inferior quality. I had to take this tobacco back to my house. There, I classified it to sell it afterward to the storehouses for a lower price."[48] The commercial activities of the small-scale rural traders were often quite hazardous; and, more than once, they were unable to repay their money lender. Intermediaries sometimes borrowed money from many different sources, in this way obtaining a certain degree of autonomy vis-à-vis the urban merchants. The result was that they often could not repay all their creditors.[49] They did all they could to end up on the good side of the line. They squeezed down the prices they paid to the producers and tried to take advantage of their own crucial position in the commercialization of tobacco. They often used the same tricks as the peasantry, hiding badly cured tobacco or stones in the middle of the *serones* and resorting to other devices to fool the merchants.

For their part, the cultivators tried to use the security of their subsistence agriculture to obtain a stronger market position. With the security of an ample harvest of food crops, family members could engage in commercial activities or do extra wage labor. In this way, a peasant family could maintain a fairly autonomous position, which enabled it to wait for optimal market conditions for the tobacco. Cultivators sometimes refused to sell their tobacco because prices were too low. For instance, it was reported in 1891 that tobacco growers withheld their best tobacco "because they do not want to *burn* [*quemar*] it, as they normally say."[50] The independent market position of the tobacco growers in the nineteenth century enabled them to take such an attitude. When prices remained unsatisfactory, they also increased their production of cigars and *andullos*, which they could keep without risk of putrefaction and which could easily be sold.[51] They often retained the best tobacco for their *andullos*.[52]

In the twentieth century, many cultivators lost this "exit-option."[53] They were bound to the local traders and had become dependent on the market. This made part of the peasantry intensify efforts to take advantage of market forces. Many producers tried to counteract low prices by augmenting the weight of their tobacco. The peasants' entire process of cultivating and preparing the tobacco—beginning with their preference for virgin lands, which gave a high yield, and ending with the picking of worthless leaves, against all the admonitions of agricultural experts—was geared toward this objective.[54] When they packed the tobacco, they artificially added more weight. A way of saving labor and adding weight at the same time was to put green, undried leaves in the *serones*, a practice which in the long run could produce putrefaction. As a rule they moistened the tobacco before it was weighed.[55]

Many cultivators preferred to sell their crop in bits and pieces, keeping the best quality tobacco as long as possible. When *La Información* lamented the low tobacco price in 1918, "hardly favorable and even ruinous for the peasantry," it observed with delight that the peasants did not want to sell their tobacco for this price: "They say with the wisdom of the hick [*yico*]— The tobacco does not putrefy, and we have sweet potatoes and plantain for the rest of the year."[56] It was observed in 1929 that "the peasant prefers to sell his tobacco little by little. He keeps the best part to himself and speculates to receive higher prices later on."[57]

Some growers tried to get around the intermediary traders and sold their tobacco in town, where they normally could obtain higher prices. This practice was as old as the cultivation of tobacco but must have received an impetus when the two railroads were completed and the export trade moved into the Cibao and became more accessible to the cultivators. Cultivators in Jarabacoa started to bring their tobacco to La Vega themselves in 1907 in hopes of obtaining better prices.[58] Some years later it was reported that tobacco purchasers traversed the countryside around Mao, searching in vain for tobacco, "because the exploited peasantry has decided to sell its tobacco in the provincial capital."[59] Some of the peasants took the tobacco to the urban storehouses themselves and there bargained for higher prices.

This behavior reflected an improved understanding of the market and greater assertiveness on the part of the peasantry. And when prices diminished to an unprecedented low in the post-1929 crisis, peasants demonstrated that they had not lost their combativeness. Confronted with the extremely low prices in town, they took their tobacco home again, and some actually burned it. As was reported: "The low price has brought so much dejection among the cultivators that there already have been cases of peasants burning their tobacco. Others return to their houses with their tobacco."[60]

THE SOCIAL POSITION OF THE TRADERS

It would be inaccurate to view the market situation of the local traders as merely a matter of economics. Their commercial dominance was reinforced by the social and political structures of rural society. The Dominican Republic came into existence in the nineteenth century as a predominantly agricultural country with a weak and ineffectual central government. As a result, local strongmen wielded great political power. Rural politics had strong patriarchal and personalistic overtones and rested upon a complex edifice of informal leadership. Local traders occupied a central position in this rural political system. Apart from playing a central role in the rural tobacco market, many traders occupied a central position in other spheres of rural society as well. They often owned the local shops and bars (*ventorillos*). As *corredores*, they dominated the local market and furnished the rural population with consumer goods. Their relations with urban merchants gave them access to credit and commercial information. In addition, they often were in charge of the few recreational activities available in rural areas. They had the money to organize cockfights and rural dances (*fandangos*).

Some of the intermediaries started acquiring land, especially in the years when the tobacco trade appeared unprofitable. San Miguel gives a number of examples of creditors' acquiring land through purchase or in compensation for defaulted loans.[61] In the Villa González region, many traders bought land in the late 1920s and 1930s, becoming powerful landholders.[62] Some *corredores* gradually expanded their activities even into the realm of processing. In the late 1920s, Don Felipe A. Vicini, in a concise overview of the commercial situation in the tobacco sector, mentioned a new group that he called "country packers" (*empacadores campesinos*): "They have a small depot and buy tobacco, paying only a small sum in cash and paying the remainder two or three months later at the price then in force." Vicini was at pains to stress the speculative nature of these operations, but his description suggests that the *empacadores* were a new and more professional group of intermediaries. They unpacked and reclassified the tobacco that they bought from the cultivator, and then sold it. As Vicini notices, they often managed to sell directly to the "foreign houses" (*casas extranjeras*).[63]

The local power of these intermediaries, who originated in rural society, extended into the political sphere. Although often poor and illiterate, they could become key figures in the social and economic organization of rural society. In the peasant universe, they were the nearest nuclei of power. The limits of their authority often were unclear, and therefore they were even more menacing. The inspector of public education (*inspector de instrucción pública*) of Santiago, Augusto Ortega, observed in 1922, "The rural inhabitant obeys the chief not so much out of deserved respect as out of fear of the latter's continual abuses and arbitrariness, which have never been punished but, on the contrary have been rewarded."[64] These local strongmen were often invested with political power and became local representatives of the state. Many local traders were appointed *alcalde pedáneo, jefe comunal,* or *inspector de agricultura.* When the National Congress was discussing the problem of alcohol consumption in the countryside in 1906, it was observed that it would be very difficult to prohibit or restrict the activities of the rural liquor stores, because "almost all of these establishments have one or two bottles of rum in the back room and under the bed. Moreover, the people who are normally involved in this business are the *alcaldes pedáneos*, who also operate the cockfights, own the taverns, and organize rural parties (*fandangos*), etc."[65] This observation suggests the feeble financial base of many of the rural traders, but it also stresses that their position rested above all on the combination of functions they performed. After having stated that many *jefes comunales* in the countryside feel themselves "masters of life and property," an observer wrote in 1914:

> In the countryside, there are the so-called "Inspectors of Agriculture," poorly designated because of all the things they do, they are least interested in this. The inspectors have such a powerful position that they recruit and bring the people together when they are needed for military service. They also take care of the community when there are elections, and everybody will vote as they indicate. The inspectors expel individuals from the region; the inspectors destroy property which is not to their liking and execute civilians. The inspectors do justice, survey land, and authorize contracts.[66]

This may have been a slightly exaggerated picture, and many frustrated rural officials would have been surprised to read this account of their supposed power, but it gives an impression of the prerogatives that could be usurped by local strongmen with the right political connections. Any analysis of rural society has to take into account their potentially dominant position.[67]

As may be clear from these observations, many people were critical of the power of these local strongmen. Their existence often was mentioned as an important obstacle to improving Cibao agriculture. Urban merchants and state officials saw them as usurers who stood in the way of "normal" commercial exchange between cultivator and merchant. They were described as a "terrible plague" abusing the peasantry; "because they are educated in the art of lying, our present-day *corredores,* who are the same as yesterday's *jefezuelos,* always find means by which they can exploit the credulity of our rural population."[68] People who tried to improve the quality of Dominican tobacco stated that this could be done only when the power of the intermediary class was broken. They complained that it was impossible to strengthen the market position of the peasant producers as long as the intermediaries maintained their crucial position. These ideas show, among other things, the strong resentment felt by the urban exporters at their failure to control, let alone replace, the intermediary sector. Many predicted the superfluity and the extinction of the intermediaries as the tobacco trade developed, but this did not occur. On the contrary, there proved to be a continuing need for these middlemen, which actually increased with the consolidation of the tobacco sector in the twentieth century.

The concentration of commercial, social, and political power in the hands of local powerholders insured the "underdog" position of the Cibao peasantry. Because the *corredor* was so close to the peasant household, it was very difficult to escape his influence. The cultivator always owed him money. When a cultivator wanted a drink or decided to try his luck in the cockfights, he had to go to this same *corredor*.[69] The combination of social and economic functions was the *corredor's* most formidable weapon in the struggle for commercial benefits. He allowed the peasants to fill their material and immaterial needs in return for their loyalty and their tobacco.

The relation between peasant producer and intermediary could not be described exclusively in terms of exploitation, however. We must not neglect the specific logic of the peasant economy, in which security and survival were central objectives, and in which capital accumulation or the freedom of the capitalist market were only of secondary importance. The personal relationship with a local strongman in the Cibao had two sides. Along with the arbitrariness, it offered protection and security. Bonó's description shows how important the intermediary's credit was to the peasant family. It provided a buffer in an economic system that was continuously threatened by warfare, climatological disaster, or commercial depression. This protection—ambiguous as it might be—was an important condition for the perpetuation of the peasant economy. In addition, the peasants who cultivated tobacco as a part of their subsistence economy needed someone who could take care of the marketing. Many of the small-scale producers were aware that the prices they received for their tobacco were low, but most were primarily interested in prolonging a trade that enabled them to exchange tobacco for commodities. For many cultivators, the endless debt must have become an accepted and even, sometimes, a desirable part of their social existence. It functioned more or less as a guarantee of a continuing supply of consumer goods.[70]

Both parties attached importance to the personal character of debt-credit relationships. Loyalty and personal trust were essential features of the financial transactions. Credit was not a financial matter only, but also involved social and political loyalty. The advances received by the peasant had to be seen "as a proof of personal trust [*confianza*]."[71] Confianza was often the only asset the peasants had, and still have, to give in exchange for credit. This trust normally was established through family ties or personal (often *compadrazgo*) relations. These sometimes could lead to true patron-client relations, but normally they were less stable and enduring than peasant-elite relations.[72]

This emphasis on personal relations does not mean that negotiations and conflicts were absent in day-to-day relations between cultivator and creditor; we have seen the opposite. The moral boundaries of such behavior were fairly clear, however. While a cultivator might try to cheat the creditor with his tobacco, he would not easily repudiate a debt. The creditor might squeeze down the tobacco price as much as possible, but he would hesitate to deny additional credit when a family was in immediate trouble because of sickness or death.

Although a good deal of pragmatism thus existed within these relations, written and oral evidence confirms that the social sanction against failure to comply with one's obligations always was strong.[73] Peasants who did not sell their tobacco to the person who had given them advances were called "marked" (*cruzados*). For them, it was very difficult to obtain credit from other buyers the following year. This aspect of the commercialization of tobacco appears to have been internalized in the peasant culture over the years. Even cultivators who admit that, under certain circumstances, they had been forced to default on their obligations at some point of their lives, are emphatic in their condemnation of other cultivators who did the same. The meeting of credit obligations seemed to have become a matter of honor (one could also say of necessity) in agricultural society, deeply ingrained in the peasants' social psychology.

The tobacco market in the Cibao was predicated on the fact that tobacco was cultivated by a multitude of peasant families. This diffusion gave rise to an extensive system of intermediaries who could connect the producers with the world market. It also gave the tobacco market a specific logic, which explains why peasant producers continued to sell tobacco when prices did not seem to compensate them for their efforts.[74] Income from tobacco was not essential for the survival of most of the tobacco-growing peasant families. Even in the twentieth century, when access to land in the Cibao countryside was increasingly restricted, the majority of peasant families maintained a subsistence orientation and were only marginally involved in the market economy. This had nothing to do with an aversion to the market; the tobacco cultivators had a long tradition of market participation. Neoclassical economists may be right in claiming that few people feel inclined to reject the market economy, provided that they are allowed to enter it on their own terms and are not subject to forms of economic or extra-economic coercion. The problem, of course, is that such an ideal "free" market almost never exists. The Cibao situation suggests that peasant producers did not oppose the market or, for that matter, capitalism. Rather, they struggled for an acceptable place in that market. The degree of involvement in the market was an option that varied according to the period and the class position of the cultivator.

In the tobacco trade, two distinct systems of economic practice thus came together. The producers used tobacco to bolster their subsistence economy, while the *corredores* saw the tobacco market as an instrument for making a profit. Tobacco cultivation guaranteed that intermediaries would provide the cultivator with consumer goods all year. The fact that the traders lived close to the peasant producers and helped them in their daily subsistence created strong personal bonds. These bonds served to perpetuate this unequal relationship but did not lead to the definitive subjection of the peasantry, as happened in nineteenth-century Puerto Rico.

On the other hand, these paternalistic relations could not hide the potential for antagonism between producer and purchaser. In the twentieth century, competition between the two parties increased. This resulted, on the one hand, from the emergence of a group of more market-oriented cultivators, who tried to manipulate the market in their favor. Some of the more market-oriented cultivators improved their position and established what Lehmann has called "capitalist family farms."[75] On the other hand, rural traders in the twentieth century adopted an increasingly businesslike attitude. They were pressed by the urban merchants to adapt their commercial practices to the demands of the world market. This resulted in a gradual replacement of personal relations by the rules of the market. The political functions performed by the local traders strengthened their social and economic positions vis-à-vis the peasantry.

The intermediaries played an ambiguous role in the transformation of the regional economy. They were dependent upon the continuation of peasant tobacco production. Representing rural society to the outside world, they therefore sometimes defended the system of peasant production. On the other hand, they were the persons who translated state policy into daily reality. In their function as local strongmen or agricultural inspectors, they sometimes acted as agricultural modernizers; just as often, however, their control of rural society amounted to outright repression. They were instrumental in the subjection of the peasantry and the accumulation of commercial profits. Economically they formed the indispensable bridge between the tobacco producers and the market. We may view these local entrepreneurs as "brokers." They originated in peasant society itself and as such were able to mediate between the two spheres Wolf has labeled "nation" and "community."[76] As a result of their crucial position, they were able to wield considerable power on the local level of society. At the same time, lack of "background" and "civilization" blocked their social ascent into the urban elite. Indeed, they were subjected to constant criticism by the urban merchants, who resented the independence of this volatile group of intermediaries. They were described as exploiters and usurers. Such criticism certainly was not unique to the Dominican Republic,[77] but this is not to say that it was always justified. The intermediaries played an important role in rural commerce and made possible the rapid growth of the regional export economy.[78] The results of the peasantry's participation in the rural trade were not without irony. The peasant cultivators entered the market in the first place in order to safeguard the subsistence of their family. However, in pursuing this objective, they could not prevent the gradual transformation of the rural economy.

6

The Transformation of Rural Society:
Peasants and Landowners
in the Villa González Region

In those times we were all equal. There were no rich or poor people.
Nor was there so much pride [*orgullo*] as there is today.

—Cristino Enrique, cultivator, age 88, 1985

In former days, the rich gave a piece of land to anyone and, using the
same land, you paid them back.

—Juan Isidro Rodríguez, cultivator, age 76, 1985

Even though it is clear that tobacco was produced for the market by small-
scale peasant producers during the period 1870–1930, many questions remain
concerning the dynamics of peasant society in the Cibao. A coherent history of
the peasantry can be obtained only by analyzing its relation to other groups and
its place within the society as a whole. We must ask ourselves how the social
position of the peasantry changed in this key period of transition in the regional
economy. Perhaps even more importantly, which factors were essential in di-
recting the processes of change in peasant society? What footholds did outside
forces such as the state or the rural elite have in order to change peasant society, and to what extent did the organization of peasant society allow the peasantry to maintain an autonomous space for social and economic action?

To answer these questions we must account for the specific characteristics of Cibao rural society. First, there was the social and cultural organization of peasant society. Contrary to a common presupposition about peasant
societies,[1] rural society in the Cibao was not organized around a village or
some sort of rural community. Peasant families worked together if necessary—they formed a peasant "society" when confronted with outsiders—but
they possessed few institutionalized links with other families. Administrative

divisions had little practical value, and village populations were not spatially concentrated. In assessing changes within peasant society, we must therefore take individual households as our main reference point.

Second, we must look more closely at the emergence of a class of large landowners in the region and its influence on peasant society. These landowners were closely linked to the urban elite of Santiago. They tried to take advantage of peasant society to run their farms and increase their production for the market. This effort often created patron-client relationships which linked the peasant producers to the regional elite. Social scientists have argued that vertical relationships, although sometimes offering peasant producers security, are essentially exploitative and in the long run destroy peasant autonomy.[2] It may be more correct to argue that patron-client relations, like market relations, involved different social and economic logics confronting one another. Such confrontations could have widely divergent results. The benefits usually accrued to the elite, but during certain stages of social and economic development, they could also buttress the viability of peasant production and support peasant autonomy. On the other hand, landowners, by making use of personal relations, often were rendered incapable of exploiting their possessions in a completely businesslike fashion. The vertical relations between different social classes thus shaped the process of transformation in rural society and had important consequences for the social and economic position of the peasant producers.

These themes require analysis on the micro-level of rural society. Many changes may escape our attention if we take large regions as our units of investigation. This is particularly the case with historical studies, for which source material is usually inadequate. We shall focus, therefore, on a small region ten miles northwest of Santiago, around the present-day Villa González. Until recently this region was the center of tobacco cultivation, but its agriculture developed relatively recently, around the turn of the century.[3] Thus it provides us with an unusual possibility to study the genesis of an agricultural export sector based upon peasant production and to analyze some aspects of the historical development of class relations.[4]

THE CREATION OF AN AGRICULTURAL REGION: VILLA GONZÁLEZ IN THE TWENTIETH CENTURY

In 1873, the traveler Hazard could still describe the Villa González region as "uninteresting and unsettled," meaning that it did not have large-scale agriculture.[5] In this period, the major part of the region was covered with forests.

The population of the region was sparse and, apart from smallholder agriculture, cattle raising was the principal activity. The legal status of the land was unclear. Most of the land was in the public domain, and, although some land was privately owned, its value was insignificant.

All this changed in the final decade of the nineteenth century, when the Ferrocarril Central was constructed between Santiago and Puerto Plata. The decision to build the railroad was taken in 1890, and the next year construction of the tracks began. The directors of the company decided to follow the trajectory of the existing "main road" (*camino real*). This added some twenty-five miles to the railroad but reduced the technical problems of the enterprise. As a consequence of this decision, the line crossed some ten miles of the valley northwest of Santiago before turning northward into the mountains. Although it would take seven years to finish the railroad, the consequences of the project were felt immediately. Land alongside the (projected) railroad became more attractive for agriculture.[6] Las Lagunas was to be the first stopping place for the trains leaving Santiago for Puerto Plata. The railway station became the center of an urban settlement situated on flat valley land between the southern slopes of the Cordillera Septentrional and the wide riverbed of the Yaque del Norte. When the place became a proper village with a station building and a church, it was renamed Villa González, after one of its most distinguished inhabitants, Manuel de Jesús González.[7]

Because of the new prospects occasioned by the railroad and the growing population in the agricultural heartland of the Cibao, east of Santiago, agricultural entrepreneurs started buying land in the region around the railroad. They took advantage of the low land prices and acquired large amounts of land. These were mainly entrepreneurs from other parts of the Cibao and some recently arrived foreigners. The French-Cuban Manuel Boitel came from Otra Banda and started buying land in the early 1890s, becoming one of the founders of Villa González.[8] Another entrepreneur of French descent, Melitón Fondeur, bought more than a thousand tareas in 1894.[9] In subsequent years, the family Fondeur acquired more than 125 hectares in the Villa González region. These were large amounts of land in a region where the largest properties were no larger than ten or twenty hectares and the majority were much smaller.[10] Other families who acquired land in this period were Carbonell, Mera, Peña, and Fermín, to name only the best known. They were people with some capital who bought land from existing landowners or from the government. Some local landowners, such as José Vidal Pichardo, Carlos Díaz, and Francisco Bétancourt maintained themselves initially, but they were outdone by the newcomers and sold out in the early decades of the twentieth century.[11]

The land generally was not surveyed, and most properties in the region were sold as *cordeles*, long stretches of land of which only one side was fully demarcated. In the region of Villa González, *cordeles* were usually staked out between three more or less parallel lines: the river Yaque, the railroad, and the mountain ridge. Properties extended on both sides of the camino real. The properties were measured only at the roadside, and the price was based on the width of the cordel, called "the mouth" (*la boca*).[12] The far side of such a *cordel* was undefined; no one really cared about the more rugged land of the mountain slopes. As a consequence of these original contracts, nowadays most of these lands are possessed by members of these early families.[13]

The new landowners started out by combining agriculture and cattle raising. They cultivated only a small part of their land and held cattle on the rest. It was reported in 1895 that, in the region, "all the rural land is indiscriminately dedicated to cattle ranching and agriculture, on the understanding that the latter takes place behind fences and the former anywhere, under guarantee of the good faith of the rural dwellers and the signs placed by the respective owners."[14] Labor was scarce, and agriculture was much more labor-intensive than cattle raising. Peasant society consisted of families who combined food crop agriculture and tobacco farming. The population density of rural areas was low, and smallholders were dispersed throughout the countryside. Rainfall in the Villa González region was not as abundant as in the La Vega region, but it generally was sufficient to avoid loss of the entire crop. The climate especially favored tobacco, which did not need much water.

When prices for agricultural products increased in the early decades of the twentieth century, large landowners became more interested in agriculture. Agricultural production expanded, but the scarcity of labor remained a problem for commercial agriculture. Many newcomers combined landownership with commercial activities, especially in retail trade and tobacco export. By about 1900, men like Manuel de Jesús González, Rafael Fondeur, and Jorge Carbonell already had established extensive commercial networks in the region.[15] In the proximity of the railway station, they constructed storehouses. This made Villa González an important regional center of the tobacco trade. In 1908, a wooden church, built by the local community, was consecrated with extensive festivities.[16] The region was commonly described as bustling and full of commercial activity.[17] The storehouses which were constructed alongside the railroad became the center of feverish activity. During the tobacco harvest, hundreds of men and women worked day and night, unpacking, selecting, and cleaning tobacco. The entrepreneurs supervised the work themselves and were frequently seen in the

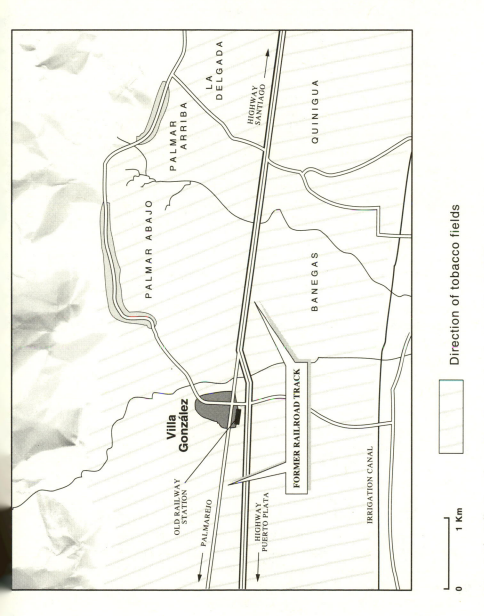

Direction of tobacco fields

Map 4. The Villa González region. Present-day situation. Map by Willem A. Baud.

Villa
González

OLD RAILWAY
STATION

PALMAREJO

HIGHWAY
PUERTO PLATA

FORMER RAILROAD TRACK

IRRIGATION CANAL

PALMAR ABAJO

PALMAR
ARRIBA

LA
DELGADA

HIGHWAY
SANTIAGO

BANEGAS

QUINIGUA

0   1 Km

storehouses, occasionally checking the tobacco and keeping an eye on the tobacco buying. Gradually, technological innovations were introduced. Until the 1920s, illumination was provided by gas lamps. When one of the merchants bought a generator, night work during the tobacco harvest was done by electric light.[18] Most commercial offices had their private telephone lines to Santiago installed in this same period. In 1928, the Vásquez government gave the village a windmill, which was supposed to regulate the water supply.[19]

The smallholders appear to have reacted to these changes in two ways. One group tried to jump on the bandwagon of progress. Producers who belonged to this group secured titles to the land they worked and sometimes even to additional land. Prices were very low in the early period, and several small-scale cultivators seem to have been able to accumulate enough money to buy land.[20] Other small-scale cultivators were content merely to preserve their access to land without acquiring land titles. The fact that the land market became livelier and land changed hands more frequently did not affect their slash-and-burn agriculture, geared as it was toward the fulfillment of their subsistence needs.

It was a unique feature of capitalist development in this region that most landowners did not try to expel the smallholding peasantry from the agricultural land. In fact—contrary, for instance, to what happened in the case of the *agregados* in the nineteenth-century Puerto Rican coffee sector[21]—the landowners actively stimulated peasant agriculture on their lands. The fact was that the local landowners lacked sufficient capital and labor to bring their land under cultivation. Especially the absence of a reliable labor force prevented rapid expansion of large-scale commercial agriculture. Local entrepreneurs could not recruit peasant labor by extraeconomic coercion and lacked the funds to attract laborers with high wages. They found a temporary solution by integrating peasant production into the exploitation of their property. Unable to clear and cultivate their lands themselves, they allowed peasant families to squat there. The relation between the landowning elite and the peasant producers thus cannot be considered a simple process of *enclosure*. Rather we see simultaneous development and integration of two systems of agricultural organization. Nascent capitalist agriculture took advantage of the presence of peasant producers in various ways. First of all, through their slash-and-burn agriculture, the peasant producers helped to clear the land. Second, peasant family members provided a stable, if restricted, source of wage labor. Finally, the peasants produced the tobacco which became the mainstay of commercial activity in the region.

It was only in the course of the 1920s that increasing state intervention and the modernization of the export trade brought fundamental changes in the situation of the small-scale cultivators. Especially the law of 1920, which made the registration of land obligatory, increased the gap between the elite and the peasant population. Registration was a costly affair, and many poor landowners could do nothing other than hand over part of their land to pay the cost of surveying their property.[22] In this way they lost the surplus of land which had been an important element of their agricultural organization. At the same time, the cost of land registration induced larger landowners to increase the returns on their properties. They intensified their agricultural activities and started to occupy more land. As a consequence, from the late 1920s onward, the peasants had to pay for access to land.

Peasant Existence and Social Mobility

During the period 1900–1930 (and thereafter, for that matter), the population of the Dominican countryside was growing. This resulted, above all, in the growth of the poorest segments of rural society. The village sample in Villa González gives a number of examples of people who ended up much poorer than their parents, due to bad luck, commercial misfortune, or personal weakness (often linked to problems of alcohol consumption). Many people had to sell the land they possessed as a result of sickness or debt.[23] Population growth and downward social mobility thus went hand in hand. However, upward social mobility also occurred, and within one family widely divergent social trajectories could be seen. As research on other parts of the world has also shown, peasant children born together could reach extremely dissimilar levels of material and social status.[24]

Access to land was the crux of peasant production. Customary law gave every heir an equitable share of an inheritance, and fragmentation of land was the greatest threat to the viability and well-being of a peasant family. Rural impoverishment was, above all, linked to the restricted access to land. In the older agricultural areas, around Moca and La Vega, the frontier was already closed in the first decades of this century. Only a few people held onto their land; others made a living through wage labor or sharecropping. A majority of the rural population emigrated to other rural areas or to the cities.

In the long run, possessing land proved of vital importance. Peasants who managed to hold onto their land were able to continue agriculture without too much infringement on their independence.

101

M. M. is a proud eighty-year-old man, living on land his parents left him.
His clothes are old and torn. His house is made of wood taken from his
parents' house (which was a house *de lima* [with a roof in the form of a
ship's keel], a style not in use anymore). He has no household goods but
the most basic furniture. Despite his age, he is busy all day doing odd jobs
around the house and taking care of his animals. He cultivates his land
with tobacco and food crops, in the "old way." His only concession to modernity has been planting the tobacco in rows. He refuses to give up inter-
calating his tobacco with food crops. His mother was the village teacher,
but he himself has remained illiterate like his father. His brothers and sisters live in Santo Domingo and New York, and he is the only one who has
stayed behind. The fifty tareas around his house are his property, and half
of them are cultivated by someone else, *a media* (M. M. receives half the
crop). He is not poor in the strict sense of the word, but he rejects modern
ways of living. While many old men like him complain bitterly about the
unjust course of history which has left them penniless, he likes to dwell on
the past, when people still held "sane" ideas and were not spoiled by
greed and pride [*orgullo*]. He is aware of the fact that other members of
his family are better off materially—he is proud that one of them has become a doctor—but he does not feel inferior. He knows that the way he
lives is the result of a deliberate choice that he sees no reason to regret.

This case shows, among other things, the importance of continuing access to
land. When peasant producers could hold onto their land, they were able to
resist market pressure. A similar example is provided by an old man in the
region who lives on a property of some one hundred tareas that he inherited
from his parents. He cultivates only a very small portion of his property, but
until now he has resisted all offers to sell it.[25]

Keeping landed property intact was also a mechanism of rural accumulation. Some members of peasant society managed to improve their economic positions because they were able to avoid fragmentation of their parents' properties. These peasants often had few brothers and sisters with
whom they had to share the inherited land. Some families continued to manage the inherited land collectively, as a *sucesión*.[26] Others avoided fragmentation of the land by allowing one heir to buy out the others. This last strategy played an important role in the increasing differentiation in rural society.
In the words of Luis Crouch, "[I]t is the ability of rising rural capitalists to
keep property intact by buying out their brothers that prevents properties
from being fractionated, and thus contributes to social differentiation."[27]

Upward mobility within peasant society usually occurred as a result of
nonagricultural activities. Few, if any, persons succeeded in accumulating money

solely on the basis of agriculture.[28] Peasant producers who managed to accumulate some capital often were active in mercantile pursuits. Trading was the principal means by which a process of continued accumulation began. Many richer cultivators established small rural shops, *colmados* or *pulperías,* in which the basic consumer goods of rural society were sold. This often led to giving small credits to poor relatives and neighbors. In exchange, these cultivators received the debtors' tobacco, which they sold at a profit to larger merchants. In this way the cultivator became a petty intermediary and sometimes a local strongman.

> The case of C. D. is illustrative. He was a member of an influential regional family, but everyone—he himself and other cultivators—confirms that he started out as a simple cultivator of tobacco on someone else's land. As a young man, he distinguished himself by his wits, and many people remember stories about his mischief (*maldad*) and cunning. After a few years, he started to buy small amounts of tobacco. He was so successful that he became a professional trader in 1925. In the 1930s, he possessed a storehouse in Villa González and had become one of the largest buyers of the region. He continued to be interested in agriculture and even developed his own kind of tobacco. When he invested part of his profits in land, he also became a large landowner, cultivating most of his land on a sharecropping basis. Many families in the region were dependent on him, working in his storehouse or farming his lands. He completely controlled the finances of the families who worked his land. People nowadays call him the greatest *explotador* of the region, but this judgment is often mixed with a sense of admiration for his ruthlessness and success.

This is an exceptional case, but it is exemplary of a recurring process—one that usually occurred on a smaller scale—by which successful cultivators consolidated and improved their economic positions by moving into petty trading.

Wage labor also could be a means of accumulation and differentiation. Some of the more successful cultivators had relatively well-paid and secure jobs during their lives. One of the leaders of a regional association of tobacco growers had been administrator of the Bermúdez sugar company in Quinigua. He earned some sixty pesos monthly, while tobacco prices stayed around five pesos per quintal. Others worked as *capataz* ("foremen") on the larger estates (*fincas*). To get such a job, it was necessary to have good relations with the employer. Such relations offered many economic opportunities closed to other cultivators and often paved the way for a process of accumulation.

Differences within peasant society were reflected in the market positions of individual producers. The more prosperous peasant producers were in a position to wait for the favorable prices typical at the end of the commercial season, and so they managed to get more money for their tobacco.

The poorer cultivators were unable or unwilling to wait and had to be content with the relatively low early prices. A vicious circle thus was created. Many peasant producers confirm that in the old days their lives were not bad; however, due to their unfavorable market positions and the scarcity of money, they had found it almost impossible to improve their economic positions. Different market strategies resulted in social differentiation. Most cultivators of tobacco received credit in anticipation of the tobacco harvest. It was the degree of this dependence that determined the differences within peasant society.

The peasant population came to be divided roughly into two groups. A minority succeeded in acquiring land and establishing themselves as commercial farmers. These market-oriented producers often became local powerholders, engaged in small-scale trading, and held political positions. The mass of the tobacco-growing peasant population continued its slash-and-burn agriculture squatting on others' lands, while new opportunities for occasional wage labor provided some supplementary income.

> The family history of Carmen and Antonio clearly exemplifies a life of peasantization and poverty. As a young man, Antonio had worked as a carpenter, living here and there. His father possessed only a small patch of land (*solar*) on which he had built a small house. When Antonio married Carmen, they had no financial or material possessions. They were allowed to build a small house in the yard of an uncle, but they did not like being dependent on his good will. Moreover, Antonio considered himself an "agricultor" and, as he says himself, longed to work the land. In their thirties, the couple started to work the land of landowners in the region, *a media*. They worked during some twenty years for several landowners in different places. With their four children, they lived on the land, screening off a small secluded space in the *ranchos* where the tobacco would be hung to dry after it was harvested. They survived with the food crops they cultivated and the income from their tobacco. In the dead season, they did odd jobs. Antonio worked as a carpenter, sometimes being away several weeks at a time, and Carmen sold snacks during rural holidays. They were barely able to feed their children in this period. Everyone agreed that they were hardworking, "decent" people, however, and therefore they received support in their most difficult moments. Eventually they built a small house in the yard of Carmen's mother. While Antonio continued to work as a sharecropper (*medianero*), Carmen contributed to the family income by ironing clothes for some well-to-do families. The change in the family fortunes came when Antonio, as a result of his connections (*amistades*) and the right political affiliation, received a piece of land in a program of land reform. This guaranteed the household access to land. The family no longer had to part with half of its agricultural production and now possessed a more or less secure subsistence base.[29]

Figure 8. Women attaching tobacco to the *sartas*. Note that this picture shows an almost empty *rancho*. Photograph by Michiel Baud.

Figure 9. The stack of filled *sartas* is growing higher. Photograph by Michiel Baud.

Figure 10. Detail of women working in the *rancho*. Photograph by Michiel Baud.

Figure 11. Work in the *ranchos* continues a tradition of conviviality during the tobacco harvest. Note that the *rancho* now is almost filled with drying tobacco. Photograph by Michiel Baud.

Social differentiation between and within families intensified the potentially disintegrating forces already extant in peasant society. Peasant production could be based on loyalty and mutual help, but never had it been immune to internal dissension or feuds.[30] A family member was first and foremost responsible for the survival of his own household. In moments of great distress, the household took undisputed priority over the wider network. As Wolf points out, "There must be a limit to the degree to which one's own resources can become committed to those of the neighbor, lest one be dragged down by his potential failure."[31] This priority limited solidarity within peasant society—between family members, to be sure, but especially between those who were not kin. Although an ideology of reciprocity prevailed, solidarity was often restricted by social and economic differences within peasant society.

Such conflicts above all concerned access to social and economic resources. Here interests were at stake, which directly affected the agricultural production and the survival of individual households. Rural inhabitants do not talk easily about their conflicts with other members of the peasant community, but broken promises, usurpation of land, and theft of crops figure abundantly in their stories about the past.[32] Conflicts also arose easily within

107

peasant families. Their ostensible cause usually was some transgression of moral codes or social hierarchies, but the underlying motives were often economic.

This kind of conflict could explode during wakes (*velorios*), when family, friends, and neighbors came together to commemorate a deceased person. These events used to last nine days, during which the relatives mourned and expressed their sorrow, crying and loudly wailing. Sometimes "professional" women were invited, who took care of these outward signs of grief. Food and drinks were offered by the organizing family and close friends. During the nights, those present prayed, sang religious songs, and told stories. These were social gatherings with important implications for the family network. Participation in a *velorio* was an indication of the position of an individual within the family. Hidden tensions among family members often surfaced during a *velorio*. Although the *velorio* was intended principally to mourn the deceased and to affirm mutual solidarity, the long duration of the ritual and the pent-up emotions, reinforced by the consumption of alcohol, might provoke open demonstrations of hostility.

Outward solidarity was based on a set of informal but generally respected obligations and behavioral norms. When more successful or richer members of the family felt themselves released from these obligations and did not comply dutifully with their obligations, conflict could evolve. This did not necessarily result in overt quarrels, but the behavior of all individual family members was under constant scrutiny.[33] During *velorios*, family members were forced to share the same surroundings and old wounds might be reopened. This might occur particularly when disagreements arose concerning the inheritance of the deceased.[34]

Such conflicts point to the continuous social change within peasant society. Social and economic hierarchies were fluid systems designed to regulate society, and conflict usually led to a partial restructuring of social relations. Economic change strained peasant society and called existing social codes into question. Potential conflicts exploded when one participant no longer saw any reason to avoid them. More research is needed to investigate whether the intensity of conflicts indeed increased in the first decades of the twentieth century, but many older people confirm that peasant society was gradually torn apart by jealousy and pride (*orgullo*). What they probably mean is that social and economic differences within peasant society became more significant during their lifetimes, and that social relations increasingly came to be dominated by market forces.

THE RURAL ELITE

The history of the tobacco-growing peasantry in the Villa González region was closely linked to the emergence of a local elite. Cibao society was relatively homogeneous ethnically, but socially it was stratified. The small elite was called *gente de primera*. Its members considered themselves direct descendants of the Spaniards. Some families could trace their roots directly back to the "old" colonial aristocracy. However, most elite families acquired their status only in the nineteenth century. Possessing land was the principal symbol of social status, but mercantile wealth became increasingly important toward the end of the century. Many members of native elite families married well-to-do immigrants who settled in the country around the turn of the century. In this way a new and rejuvenated elite came into existence in the final decades of the nineteenth century.[35] This occurred on a national scale, but the process was especially significant in the Cibao, where the regional merchants benefited from growth of the export sector. This regional elite consisted of large landholders, well-to-do merchants, and intellectuals. It was regularly replenished by successful entrepreneurs but in general was a fairly closed social group. Wealth was important in the acceptance of newcomers, but education, cultural characteristics, and racial features were no less important. In this way a closed, self-conscious, and close-knit regional elite came into existence.

Relations between elite and peasantry were quite ambiguous. The elite in the Villa González region lived close to the peasant producers and, in order to procure their labor, established various sorts of personal relations with individual peasants. On the other hand, the elite was clearly distinguished from the peasantry by its social position, material welfare, and superior education. The majority of the regional elite lived in the cities, preferring Santiago, but many of the elite lived in the countryside. Continuing dependence on agricultural production gave the Cibao elite a definitely rural character. According to Pedro Batista, this gave the region a specific character. People used to draw an imaginary circle around Santiago with a radius of some ten miles, where urban and rural societies coexisted. This area was called *La Campiña*: "Among the masses of peasants and workers, small and large proprietors . . . were also very urban people who lived, however, on farms, haciendas, and rural shops; but because of their similar customs, ways of living, social and family status, education, and economic position, they were closely linked to the city, resembling the principal families in Santiago."[36] The clearest material expression of the social and economic superiority of the

elite was its housing. In a period when the majority of the peasant population lived in *bohíos* and slept on beds made of wood covered only by hides,[37]
the elite possessed large wooden houses with several rooms, comfortable
beds, and furniture. They may have been somewhat shabby and primitive
by the standards of the European elite of the day, but their luxury was sufficient to express great social inequalities.[38] The technological advances which
shook the world at the end of the nineteenth century and the increasing
supply of luxury goods in the country allowed the elite to express its social
superiority through other material possessions as well. We may obtain an
impression of the lifestyle of this rural elite in the early decades of the
twentieth century by citing an observer who wrote in 1917: "The people of
the Santiago countryside are normally civilized and wealthy persons, who
regularly travel abroad and like to surround themselves in their well-con-
structed houses with all the comfort customary in the cities. They are lovers
of music: the luxurious piano, the melodious pianola, or the enchanting
gramophone provided with the best pieces of the musical repertory. The
culture of the Santiago countryman allows him to frequent the most aristo-
cratic social centers of the city."[39] The piano and the record player, then,
served to affirm the social status of the rural elite. In the 1920s, the car
became its most outstanding status symbol. Everyone in Villa González, rich
and poor, remembers the day that Don Manuel González first drove around
in his new car. Traveling abroad was another privilege of the elite in the
days before "Nueva York" became a mythical paradise for many poor Dominicans. Hoetink stresses the fact that a journey through Europe was "the
crowning moment of education" for the Dominican elite in the nineteenth
century. It confirmed the high social status of the person involved.[40] When,
in the twentieth century and especially during the U.S. occupation, North
American culture became dominant in the country, the United States became just as attractive. Until the 1960s, freedom of travel remained a distinct privilege of the wealthy.

Despite this emphasis on style and status, most elite families in the region were self-made, and their wealth was the result of hard work. Much
attention was given to the education of children. They often received their
primary education privately and then were sent to schools in Santiago or
Puerto Plata or sometimes abroad. On the other hand, the rural elite had a
great preference for a practical state of mind and sometimes disdained too
much education.[41] As important a member of the rural elite as Augustín
Espaillat (born in 1883) could, for example, take some pride in his lack of

Figure 12. Deserted house of one of the elite families in the Villa González region. Built around 1900. Photograph by Michiel Baud.

formal education.[42] An active role in the family business often was valued more highly than a prolonged education. Such a stance could lead to a repudiation of the urban way of life and of intellectual education.

Elite families constituted extensive social and economic networks under the direction of a father-entrepreneur.[43] The head of the family ruled with virtually unlimited patriarchal authority in business and family affairs. Each member of the family had her or his assigned place in the family hierarchy, although every family had its occasional "black sheep" who did not want to play according to family rules. The role of the women is not easily judged by outsiders. Normally, women remained in the background, secluded from public view behind imposing male figures. Still, it is probable that many women held important positions in the family empire and fulfilled important tasks behind the scenes.[44]

Boys started to assist their fathers at a young age. They cared for the animals, bought tobacco, checked the crops, and kept in contact with the peasantry. When a boy reached adolescence, he started a business of his own or continued to work for his father. It is interesting to note that most successful entrepreneurs of the 1930s stress their humble beginnings. Some even affirm that they were "poor" at the start of their business careers. Apart from the fact that this self-image fits neatly with the ideal of the self-made man, it probably suggests a key element of rural elite ideology. Like young peasant men, young elite males had to demonstrate an ability to secure their own livelihoods. The elite man could take advantage of his education or family name and might even receive some material support, but thereafter he had to prove that he was able to stand on his own feet. The "poverty" in which such a youngster started adulthood was of course relative, but it was sincerely felt. Such a "rite of passage" was a symbol of independence and a proof of having grown up.

> We may obtain a idea of the life cycle of a member of the Cibao elite by examining the life of Francisco Javier Espaillat, who in 1925 was portrayed in *La Información* as an "outstanding farmer and successful man." According to his own information, Francisco Javier was born—"poor"—in 1881, a child of Augustín Espaillat and Magdalena Jiménez. As an adolescent he began working in a "casa comercial" and later worked in a *pulpería*. As a fifteen-year-old boy, he worked on the *conuco* of his mother and bought his first land with the proceeds of this work. Profits from corn and tobacco he cultivated on this land he used to buy more land in Hoya del Caimito. When he was eighteen, he married a niece of Francisco Antonio Jiménez, "persona principal" in this zone. Gradually, he acquired knowledge of buy-

112

ing and selling (*compra y venta*) tobacco, and when he was thirty, he bought his first tobacco in partnership with Emilio Almonte. He continued to invest the profits of his enterprises in land and possessed six thousand tareas in 1925, of which he cultivated two hundred tareas himself. Approximately half of his property was planted with tobacco, which was expected to gain him some forty thousand pesos. In addition, he bought twenty-five thousand *serones* of tobacco for a German export house in 1924. He was doing well in 1925. He showed this by driving around in an eight-cylinder Packard.[45]

Leisure was not greatly appreciated in the *progresista* ideology of the time, and the diversions of the elite were not very exclusive. In many respects they were the same as those enjoyed by the mass of the rural population. Male members of the elite participated in cockfights, liked to play with guns, and did their share of hunting in the abundant forests. One of the few signs of social difference may have been that a hunting party of the elite was mentioned in the regional press.[46]

Social distinctions played an important role in social activities, however. Under the tutelage of wealthy members of Las Lagunas, a building for the "Sociedad Instrucción y Recreo" was constructed in 1909. To announce the initiative and possibly also to raise funds, a "corrida de sortijas" was organized by "the well-known group of worthy citizens who are fighting for development and progress with all their energy." During the spectacle, that group's wives and daughters were seated in the *tribuna de las damas*, spatially affirming the social distance between classes and sexes.[47] In other activities, too, such as the construction of a church in 1907 or the organization of a nationalist meeting in 1923, the Villa González elite played a decisive role.[48]

It could well be a proof of its consolidation as a class that the rural elite around Santiago became more culturally sophisticated in the 1920s. In 1923 we find the first mention of a literary evening (*velada literaria*), organized by the Hermandad Nacionalista de Damas and obviously meant to foster the nationalist cause.[49] In the following years many such *veladas líricos-literarias* were held in the houses of the wealthy. Usually the ladies were in charge of these meetings, at which poems were recited, songs sung, and music played.[50] The music was not, of course, *merengues*, which were held in very low esteem, but nocturnes of Chopin and other examples of "high" culture.[51] These evenings fostered the rural elite's self-image as a culturally superior and distinguished class that had raised itself above the illiterate masses.[52] The evenings emphasized the "social distance" that has been so characteristic of Dominican society.[53]

This social distance was, above all, however, an ideological construct meant to counter the consequences of daily contact between classes in the countryside. In Cibao rural society, a contradiction existed between an ideology of distance and a reality of proximity. The emphasis on cultural exclusivity within the rural elite may well have been a direct consequence of the daily contact between the elite and the peasantry.[54]

PATRONS AND PATRIARCHS

One of the most remarkable aspects of rural society in the Villa González region was the close co-existence of the different classes. Rich landowners lived side by side with poor peasant families and were in daily, and sometimes intimate, contact with members of peasant society. Elite children often maintained friendships with peasant age peers, which could establish a basis for lifelong mutual esteem between members of the two classes. This ambiguity shaped relations between elite and peasantry. It showed itself most clearly in the long-lasting paternalistic interdependence between the two groups.

Peasants and landowners were linked by a complex set of rights and obligations, and patron-client relations proliferated in Cibao rural society. The mutual dependency and vertical bonds between rural elite and peasantry originated in the insecure Dominican political situation in the nineteenth century. The authority of political leaders depended on the loyalty and support of the peasant population. On the other hand, peasant cultivators needed protection against the abuses and constant incursions into their property to which they were exposed. One of the principal threats to peasant society was the forced recruitment of its men. It was very difficult to avoid enlistment, especially when it was national army was "detailing groups of soldiers with orders to seize any youths they found in passing."[55] Many peasants cleared their *conucos* as far from the roads as possible, in the hope that roving bands of soldiers would not notice them.[56] The peasants tried to secure protection by entering into vertical relationships with the elite.[57] An influential patron could help one evade expropriation or involuntary recruitment. The paradox, of course, was that one would be expected to fight *for* the patron when he himself got into political trouble.

When the agrarian export economy of the Cibao expanded around the turn of the century, enterprising landowners extended and modified the existing system of patronage and used it to further their commercial interests. With the commercialization of Cibao agriculture in the twentieth century, regional patron-client relations became more extensive. Instead of eradicating personal and "pre-capitalist" relations of production, the market economy gave new significance to such institutions as *compadrazgo* and other systems of personal loyalty, and sometimes even helped form them.[58] The paternalistic ties created by the region's agricultural transformation became crucial features permeating all aspects of rural Cibao life and society. Reflecting the masculinist ideology that underlay Dominican thought and was shared by all classes, these ties were based on silent contracts between the powerful and the powerless and between men and women. In exchange for loyalty and obedience, weaker individuals could count on the paternalistic support and protection of stronger ones.

Such understandings were very clear in the squatting arrangements between landowners and peasant producers. To obtain access to land, the producers became dependent on the benevolence of the landowners. Old peasants often recall that, until the 1920s, landowners demanded no compensation for the use of a patch of land. A cultivator would simply go to one of the landowners and normally would be assigned a piece of land. As long as the applicant was *decente* and *cristiano*, permission to clear a *conuco* was never refused. This implicit condition suggests the dormant inequality of power in these squatting arrangements. The landowners gave permission as an act of individual generosity and so reinforced vertical, paternalistic ties between themselves and the peasant. Squatting on someone's land in fact implied a range of obligations for the peasants. They were expected to offer their labor to the landowner, sell their tobacco to him, and obey his family. The more authoritarian landlord might even interfere in the private lives of "his" peasants, meddling in the education of their children, arranging or at least consenting to their marriages, and censuring inappropriate conduct of individuals. The dependent peasant producers were expected continually to reconfirm their loyalty. When they were "sent for" by their patron, they had to go or at least send a son. In 1907, Manuel de J. González took the initiative to build a church in Las Lagunas. We may be certain that most peasants who "spontaneously" cooperated in the construction did not have much of a choice.[59] The essence of the rural elite's social dominance was that it was informal and unpredictable. At any time, the benevolence and protection of the patron could turn into rage and loss of favor.

Listening to elderly peasants, one cannot but conclude that peasant producers were aware of the conflicts of interests between the different social groups. Many peasants tell stories about illicit land usurpations by local potentates.[60] Numerous examples exist of conflicts over land boundaries or divisions of *comunero* lands.[61] Yet the patriarchal authority of the landowner was hardly questioned. Open opposition to the landowning class or a stubborn defense of acquired rights seem to have been absent in the region.[62] This remained true even after land had acquired unprecedented value, and squatting relations were replaced by sharecropping systems that were very unfavorable to the peasantry. Many peasant producers confirm that this development meant a crucial deterioration in the conditions of peasant agriculture, but they add that personal relations with the landowner could mitigate its worst consequences.

The replacement of squatting by sharecropping was an important factor in the introduction of capitalist relations of production in the countryside. Still, peasant producers continued to judge their relationships with landowners from a personal perspective. Just as "giving" pesos was the rural description of credit, so peasant producers often designate sharecropping as "working with" a certain landowner. Today, most cultivators condemn the "media" system as a system of exploitation. Talking about their own experiences, however, they tend to stress the personal characteristics of the different landowners. The patron's willingness to help the sharecropper's family in times of distress was more important than the structural exploitation to which the latter was exposed. It is remarkable that C. D., mentioned above, who paid very low prices for tobacco and was known to have cheated more than a few producers, is still remembered within peasant society for his generosity— buying a coffin for a poor widow, giving milk to children, or buying medicine for a destitute family. Other landowners were severely criticized for not helping old tenants who had been sharecropping on their land all their lives but could no longer work.

PATRIARCHALISM WITHIN PEASANT SOCIETY

It is easy to see what the value of these relationships was for the powerful, but what were the advantages of this continuing paternalism for the peasants? Clearly, landowners could grant access to land and credit. Too, the political and economic vulnerability of peasant producers made protection and security under the wing of a powerful member of rural society an important asset. But why was there so little resistance to the pressure of paternalism in a period when the landowners expanded their agricultural enterprises and increasingly monopolized access to land?

One answer to this question is that rural paternalism was, in fact, far from uncontested and that its conditions formed a continuous field of negotiation. The balance between rights and obligations depended on the outcome of these negotiations and were always open to change. The squatting arrangements in the first stage of agricultural development in the region were the consequence of the peasantry's "strong" negotiating position, while the introduction of sharecropping demonstrated the increasing dominance of the larger landowners. Continual commentaries about the behavior of patrons in peasant discourse are another indication of the peasantry's attentive scrutiny of those patron-client relations in which they participate.[63]

On the other hand, peasant society itself was imbued with a strong sense of hierarchy, based upon differences in economic power, social status, and manliness. Distinctions in social status pervaded all relations among adult men. This characteristic of peasant culture was related to the masculinist sensibilities often viewed as characteristic of Mediterranean culture. Men had to prove their manhood, to show that they had "balls" (cojones), or their social status diminished.[64] Masculine prestige was based not only upon physical courage, however; it depended also upon social responsibility and ability to take care of one's family. The "serious husband" and the man who "honored" his promises was esteemed. Peasant society thus reproduced patriarchal ideology in both its essential sides: an assumed male superiority and social responsibility.

The consequence of this hierarchical ideology was a strict set of rules for "decent" behavior. Respect should be shown by younger to elder, by female to male, by poor to rich.[65] It is significant that the unwritten codes of daily behavior for the three subordinate groups were very similar. Peasants with their landlords, women with their men, children with their parents—none might initiate a conversation, none might show curiosity, all must "civilize" their language. Children had to kneel down along the road and wait for the benediction of an adult. Women had to submit to the whims of their men. Peasants had to approach large landowners as father figures towering high above the humble peasants, all-knowing in their advice, always to be respected. In exchange, they received protection, help in difficult times, and, in some cases, a fraternity transcending class differences and approaching friendship. Thus, the existence of patriarchal relations *within* peasant society functioned to sustain the landowning elite's patriarchal authority.

On another level, patron-client relations were instrumental in sustaining a degree of peasant autonomy. These relations were based on the implicit idea that clearly separate and unequal social spheres existed. Despite ethnic and cultural similarities between landowners and the peasantry, the social distinctions never were in doubt. Patron-client relations thus implicitly

117

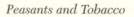

Figure 13. Although preparing tobacco for the *rancho* is considered women's work, men often help. Photograph by Michiel Baud.

confirmed the existence of a separate peasant society which had its own logic and lay outside the control of the landowners. It is significant that in daily life the peasantry tended to emphasize these distinctions, as if aware of their importance in protecting the autonomy of peasant society. This led to a very formal acting out of the social hierarchy. Peasants approached with a great deal of deference people who were considered socially superior. The latter were addressed with the honorary title *Don* or *Doña* and were treated with great courtesy. Similarly, children had to behave with utmost deference toward their godfathers. People from outside the community also were approached with extreme courtesy. Unexpected visitors were received with reverence and hospitality. It was the duty of the housewife to offer something to drink or eat to each visitor.[66]

Nowadays, rural inhabitants describe elite life and urban society as belonging to a different world, unrelated to rural society and governed by distinct rules and values. Rural inhabitants often refrain from judgment of elite behavior or urban life with the excuse that "there" people act differently and so can only be judged according to other values. Eduardo García Tamayo considers such an attitude, which is often accompanied by self-denigrating references to the peasants' own illiteracy or ignorance, to be part of the survival strategy of the peasant population.[67] His analysis coincides with the ideas of Pitt-Rivers, who has stressed the double edge in the extreme respect shown to visitors by the peasantry. To act respectfully and hospitably toward strangers was part of rural culture. "Yet," writes Pitt-Rivers, "its analysis would not be complete if one were not to point out that it is also a means whereby the community defends itself against outside interference."[68] Peasant producers usually eschewed open confrontation. An appearance of submissiveness often proved much more effective in safeguarding to some degree the autonomy of peasant society.[69] Adopting a submissive attitude toward outsiders was a method of fending off peasant society. As long as their behavior was flawless—*decente* or *cristiano*—rural inhabitants might escape problems or unfavorable attention.

The emphasis on social distinctions between the peasantry and the rural elite thus enabled the peasant producers to protect specific elements of their social and cultural organization and to avoid outside interference. This was even more important because of centrifugal tendencies always latent within peasant society. Peasant producers competed for the same resources, and there was always the potential for conflicts between individual peasant households, especially in a society experiencing multiple processes of differentiation. Peasant society therefore sustained social and cultural codes geared toward counteracting centrifugal tendencies. This may explain the importance attached to ritual trust relationships—to mutually maintained and valued relationships between two persons. To place confidence in (*estar en confianza con*) a person meant that, at any moment in one's life, one could appeal to this solidarity and support. Active participation in such relations was a basic strategy to guarantee the material and immaterial survival of a peasant household. It is clear that this relationship depended on a mutually felt responsibility, even an obligation, to help each other when needed. The idea of obligation (*compromiso*) implied an almost sacred responsibility to comply with the implicit and explicit requirements of a trust relationship. While peasant consciousness accepted certain acts of cheating and fraud toward outsiders, to do the same with friends or family was seen as treason (*traición*) and was considered unacceptable. Although such *traicioneros* were not immediately kicked out of the family, as often happened in more formally organized rural kin groups elsewhere, such behavior could irremediably shatter existing mutual trust.

The distinction between peasant society and the outside world, then, was essential. In spite of the peasant population's apparent submissiveness, peasants commonly accepted, and even admired, cunning, treachery, or evil (*maldad*) in relations with the outside world. Open rebellion was uncommon, but the peasantry was not unsympathetic to men who successfully defied the authorities.[70] As we have seen, many peasants tried to offset low tobacco prices by cheating the merchants. They put stones and branches in the tobacco or hid badly fermented tobacco with good-looking leaves. Such actions can be interpreted as examples of this attitude. Many observers may have condemned these tricks, but the peasants considered them justified retaliations against a hostile environment.

AN ILLUSION OF DISTANCE: SEXUAL RELATIONS IN THE COUNTRYSIDE

The ambiguity of relations between the rural elite and the peasantry showed itself clearly in one other feature of rural life. Sexual relations belong to the intimate sphere of human existence and in many respects defy social analysis. At the same time, they are a key arena of social life. Mating and marriage are essential for establishing social relations and often determine patterns of social mobility, inheritance, and power.

Sexual relations in Cibao rural society were not confined to members of the same class, despite the great ideological emphasis placed on distance between the classes. It was generally accepted that elite men might have sexual relations with women of lower social status. It may be argued that this acceptance was a direct consequence of the social differences and the patriarchal ideology in which they were embedded. Whereas elite females were kept under close watch and the virginity of daughters jealously guarded, male adolescents were allowed to acquire sexual experience with girls of poor families.

Both in adolescence and later, sexual relationships outside marriage were easily accepted within the rural elite. Three "model cultivators" were interviewed by *La Información* in 1925, and all stated proudly that their one "vice" was their attraction to the female sex. Don Ramón de Jesús Henríquez was described thus: "As a good countryman, who is reared and educated in the fullness of nature, he is dominated by the eternal female." Francisco Javier Espaillat boasted that "the spell cast on him by the skirts has led him to make four conquests in one year." The two men speculated that they had some thirty and sixteen children, respectively, "behind the palm tree" (*por detrás de la palma*).[71] This behavior—not only the sexual relations, but also the boasting—fit perfectly with the masculinist ideology that pervaded Dominican society. The idea that men could have many sexual relations was also accepted in peasant society. Within elite ideology, such an assumption was complemented by a class-based sense of superiority toward the poor. Elite males often used their social superiority to seduce peasant girls. Even today, mothers warn their daughters against the sweet talk and persuasiveness of rich men. Many do not want their daughters to live as maids in the houses of the rich because of the danger of pregnancy. An admonition often heard is this: "They promise paradise, but leave you with a baby."[72]

Despite such interclass sexual relations, members of the elite *married* only social equals. I know of only one case in Villa González in which an affair between a rich man and a peasant woman led to a formal marriage. This occurred when the persons involved were already of advanced ages and the first wife of the man had died. It is astonishing to observe the frequency of marriages between members of the few influential families. For instance, in the beginning of the century, two of the most influential families of the region were related by three marriages.[73] At the same time, however, many illegitimate children were born as a result of short affairs between members of the rural elite and young peasant girls. Even when these interclass relations lasted longer, they were hardly ever formalized.

J.M. exemplifies this pattern of multiple sexual affairs. This man belonged to the region's landowner elite at the beginning of the century. He possessed several thousand tareas, which he used for agriculture and cattle. He married a girl of one of the other elite families and had a number of children with her. Simultaneously, he had children with two other women of the region. He took care of these children but did not recognize them legally. His amorous relations with their mothers were common knowledge, just as was his paternity of the children. It was only when, advanced in age, he took a young mistress that people started to frown upon his behavior, but even then it was not the relation in itself, but the "male foolishness" of getting involved with a woman so much younger, on which people commented.

Extramarital relations could be serious love affairs and sometimes resulted in the transfer of property to peasants, but they did not threaten the position of the elite. Men were expected to take care of their illegitimate offspring. Because many men did not live up to this expectation, those who fulfilled this responsibility were admired and praised in popular discourse for doing so. The girl or her parents might receive some sort of allowance when the child was born, which might be continued until the child was grown. Some fathers paid for the education of their children, secured a job, or made available a piece of land on which they could live with a family.[74] Illegitimate children could not, however, assert any claim to the possessions of their father, let alone enter the paternal family. Although men often publicly supported their illegitimate children, access to the father's social class was out of the question for mother and children. The father's support depended exclusively on his generosity and had no legal basis. The preservation of elite family capital and class cohesion were first priorities and precluded admission of illegitimate children to the family.[75] The extramarital children of the elite swelled the ranks of the peasantry. They usually ended up in the social class of their mother and shared her poverty.

A.M. is the illegitimate son of the above-mentioned landowner J.M. He bears the surname of his father because the latter, on his deathbed, decided to recognize his son. During his youth, the father supported his mother financially. When the father died, everything changed. Because of his delayed recognition, he was cheated out of the inheritance. He received only a few tareas around his mother's house. When he reached adolescence, he worked in many different jobs. As a wage laborer he traveled to various places in the country; he delivered milk in the neighborhood for three pesos a month; and he worked in the tobacco storehouses. At an advanced age, he started to cultivate tobacco as a sharecropper, first alone

and later in cooperation with his son. In his house, some luxurious arti-
facts—a silver watch, a black suit, a painting—remind of his origins. When
he rides his mule with dignity through town, there is something of the
grandeur of his father's family in his posture. However, in general, he always lived the simple life of a poor peasant. While his legitimate brothers
and sisters all live in Santo Domingo and New York, as an old man he has
no savings and is supported by his children.[76]

It may be obvious that illegitimate children conceived in these sexual relations did not threaten the coherence and material superiority of the rural
elite. On the contrary, they contributed to the growth of the peasantry and
swelled the ranks of the poor rural population. At the same time, however,
this social mechanism reinforced and perpetuated intimate relations between the classes. Extramarital affairs could not break through the social barriers of Cibao society, but often they generated affective ties across class
lines. Even though the material benefits were few, blood relationships with
members of the elite could be advantageous for individual peasants. The status of a rich father might shadow his illegitimate offspring, subtly helping
him to find work or loans. It may be significant that so many rural inhabitants today still trace their descent to important (European) families. These
sexual relations, which transcended class boundaries, suggest one dimension
of the contradictory nature of elite attitudes toward the peasantry. The rural
elite did all it could to maintain and even increase the social distance sepa-
rating it from the peasantry, but it was unable, and partially unwilling, to give
up many of the customs that linked it to the peasant population.

The microscopic focus on a small region such as the Villa González area may
help us to understand the history of the Cibao countryside and above all the
changing position of the peasantry. This chapter has provided a specific example of the transformation of rural society in the Cibao in the twentieth
century. Railroad construction and an upward surge in the international market gave new dynamism to the regional economy. Entrepreneurs acquired
large tracts of land and gradually restricted the tobacco-growing peasantry's
access to land. The emerging landowning elite came not only to control access to land, but also to play a crucial role in the tobacco trade. Taking advantage of their close relations with urban merchants, many landowners cap-
tured a share of the rural tobacco trade. These two elements allowed the
rural elite significant control of the local peasantry.

This did not mean, however, that local landowners completely controlled
the peasantry in the period 1870–1930. The owners allowed the majority of

tobacco growers to continue their subsistence orientation. Scott and Kerkvliet have rightly pointed out that the one service dear to a rural elite, which cannot be extracted by force, is the active loyalty of the peasantry. These authors suggest viewing legitimacy as a service the peasant potentially can give the elite: "The more the patron needs the active loyalty of his clients, the more likely [it is] that he will avoid using force."[77] In addition, tobacco cultivation did not conflict with the entrepreneurial dynamism of a new landowning elite. On the contrary, the cultivation of tobacco provided a cheap way of clearing virgin lands, and the tobacco trade proved a very profitable activity for many of these landowners.

The fact that elite and peasantry shared the same rural environment and were ethnically hardly distinguishable had important consequences for social relations in the countryside. The most conspicuous results of physical proximity were the vertical relations between local landowners and the peasantry, and the frequent occurrence of sexual relations between members of the two classes.[78] These day-to-day relations between landowners and cultivators did not lead to social fusion. On the contrary, they tended to reaffirm social differences while disguising them in a complicated and opaque web of loyalties and obligations.

The regional elite formed a buffer between peasant society and outsiders, most notably representatives of the national government. Local landowners' economic and political power allowed them to manipulate, and if necessary evade, state intervention and legislation. Such power could result in unrestricted exploitation of the peasantry, or its protection from an obtrusive state. In the Villa González region, the latter situation seems to have prevailed, resulting in strong paternalistic relations between the elite and the peasantry. The elite benefited from these relations by securing a political clientele and a labor force. To the peasants it guaranteed the continuation of their household economy and protection against external threats.

The increasing dominance of the market gradually transformed peasant society. One conclusion we can draw from the evidence gathered in Villa González is that the influence of the market provoked new forms of differentiation within peasant society, creating a gap between more market-oriented cultivators and the majority who remained geared toward subsistence. This differentiation could be a stealthy, hardly distinguishable process, difficult to capture, even for the historical actors themselves. Reciprocal help was gradually replaced by wage labor, and personal loyalties gave way to impersonal market forces. The basis of peasant agriculture, free access to land, slowly eroded, and peasant existence grew more precarious and dependent on the vagaries of the market.

PART III

Outsiders and the Peasant Economy

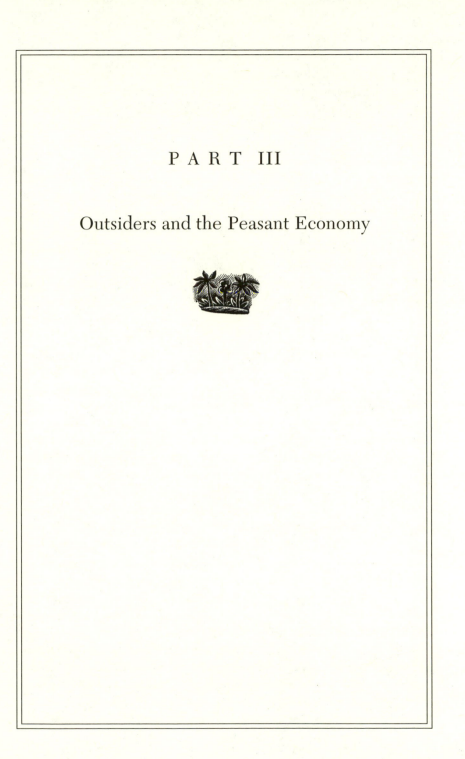

7

Tobacco as an Export Crop: Urban Merchants and the Regional Economy

There is the irritating circumstance that our exporters are debtors of
the merchants of Hamburg, to whom they are required to consign the
tobacco in order to sell it. This situation makes everybody eager to sell
rapidly in order to collect their advances, interests, and commissions.

—*El Noticiero,* 1908

Despite the economic hegemony of the southern sugar sector and the political dominance of Santo Domingo, the strength and political influence of the
mercantile elite of the Cibao have become proverbial in Dominican political
discourse. The self-conscious, chauvinistic character of the Cibao elite was
often contrasted with the prevalence of expatriate interests and foreign values in the southern part of the republic.[1] This is somewhat surprising, when
we observe that the prosperity and economic activities of the elite were
strongly dependent on the support of foreign capital. Until 1914, the regional
merchants were servants of the German market, and they could hardly do
any business without credit from German importers. This dependency diminished in subsequent years, but trading companies from various European
countries and the United States continued to play an important role in the
regional tobacco economy.

This chapter focuses on these large-scale merchants, who were responsible for exporting tobacco. They represented the world market in the region and as such occupied a crucial place in the tobacco economy. Their
commercial behavior determined the development of the tobacco market
and, in this way, of the region. It will be argued that the Cibao tobacco merchants' dependence on the world market was double-edged. On the one
hand, it resulted in an unpredictable and erratic market situation.[2] On the
other, the regional merchants used their relations with European importers

to become the most important economic group in the region. The European market provided them with opportunities to accumulate capital and to build a regional power position. They distributed the money that poured into the region with the beginning of the tobacco harvest, and they controlled the imports. It is an interesting aspect of the Cibao economy that the merchants did not derive their powerful position from monopolizing land or from exerting direct control over the cultivators. The organization of production, and peasant society in general, remained largely outside their control.

The commercialization of tobacco was not the only source of capital accumulation in the region, but in the central Cibao it certainly was the most important. An analysis of the tobacco trade therefore not only is essential for understanding the tobacco sector but also may increase our understanding of the social, economic, and political position of the Cibao elite in general. The social and economic stratification of Cibao society was a direct reflection of the hierarchy within the tobacco trade. At the top of the pyramid stood an elite of regional merchants who in general lived in the urban centers of the region, but who in time acquired land and became linked to rural elite groups. The expansion of tobacco production and the establishment of a regional tobacco industry led to a consolidation of this commercial elite's economic superiority in the twentieth century. We must therefore ask ourselves: What was the basis of the social and economic power of the urban tobacco merchants? How did their position change in the period under study? And, most important, how did their changing position within the regional economy influence the viability of peasant production?

Cibao Tobacco and the International Market

The year 1890 promised to be a very profitable year for the Dominican tobacco sector. The rains had come at the appropriate time, and there had been no hurricanes or revolutionary unrest. Moreover, the tobacco was going to be of excellent quality. The newspapers and the trading community were in high spirits. Was the "aromatic leaf" going to spread its benevolent radiance over the Cibao again? Everyone remembered the heavy rains that had destroyed the 1889 harvest, and many people hoped that the victims of that disaster would now be recompensed. The eyes of the men who stood talking in front of the rural *pulperías* or the warehouses went to the sky more often than usual. One hailstorm or hurricane could dash local hopes. The peasants frequently were seen wandering through the green fields, only their heads showing above the large tobacco plants. They looked for the treacher-

128

ous *gusanos*—caterpillars that could destroy a crop overnight—and ascertained that no diseases were attacking the tobacco. Large landowners and traders suddenly seemed to possess extraordinary amounts of free time and dawdled on the porches of their tenants' dwellings or talked with the men who assembled at the *pulperías* after a hard day's work. The upcoming harvest was the only topic of conversation.

Everyone was convinced of the excellent quality of the tobacco. "The best tobacco in twenty years," rejoiced the *Eco del Pueblo* when the harvest was in full swing in April. However, the journal warned against too much optimism. The fate of tobacco was determined not only by the quality of the leaf, but also by market conditions and, more specifically, by the attitudes of the German merchants. The newspaper admonished: "Now the only thing that must be avoided is that the German Gentlemen do as they please [*hagan de las suyas*] and determine a price for our tobacco which is to their advantage and which, because they are financially superior, we cannot contest. How long will we be at the mercy of so many speculators who rob us of one of our best export products?"[3] Indeed, the optimistic mood gradually gave way to a recognition that the high quality of tobacco did not result in high prices. The tobacco was easily sold, but prices were just as low as in preceding years. The hopes of the Cibao population dissolved in anger and frustration.

In the following years, the story was repeated. High-quality tobacco was produced, but prices did not rise. Everyone was convinced that dependence on the German market was the principal explanation of this phenomenon: "The German purchaser *takes advantage* of the precarious situation of our exploited commerce, which, because it has to repay its debts and other commitments, is forced to accept the sales and auctions that are there decided by the privileged group which has been accumulating its millions upon the backs of all the Dominican producers for so many years."[4] The most obvious characteristics of the Cibao mercantile class in the late nineteenth century indeed were its financial weakness and its dependence on German credit. Until the beginning of the twentieth century, the commercial fortunes of Santiago were closely tied to conditions in the German market and to the behavior of the German importers, who often operated from the Danish free port of St. Thomas. In the nineteenth century, usually up to 90 percent of Dominican tobacco was sold in Bremen and Hamburg. The position of the German importers went practically unchallenged, as it was based on the low customs duties of these cities. A cheap, dark tobacco like the Dominican product could be sold only when duties were low. For that reason, Dominican tobacco never could gain access to the British and North American markets, where low-grade tobacco was subject to a relatively high duty.[5]

The strong position of the German importers and the permanence of their monopoly was based upon their access to credit. Interest rates in Latin America remained high as long as local capital was scarce and political unrest made investments risky. In most of the Latin American republics, it was not uncommon to pay 12 to 15 percent on good real estate mortgages, and 25 to 30 percent on personal security loans.[6] The credit that Dominican President Heureaux obtained from the Spanish firm Font & Co. in the 1890s bore an annual interest of 24 percent plus 2.5 percent commission.[7] The rates in the European countries normally varied between 3 and 10 percent. This difference gave the European mercantile houses a strong hold over foreign trade. If local merchants in any Latin American country wanted to order goods from abroad, they could hardly avoid buying through a European middleman, because banking houses would not give them credit. The *Eco del Pueblo* wrote in 1891, "It is well known that the lack of sufficient capital of many of our merchants is the reason that they see themselves forced to endure the attitude of the German importer."[8]

Dominican merchants traded by way of a two-sided credit from the German importers, with the tobacco harvest as pawn. They received money to finance the purchase of tobacco and at the same time ordered European consumer goods. This was a very speculative undertaking and formed the most insecure stage of the tobacco trade. The German money gradually was distributed in the countryside. The merchants had their money "on the street," as they say today, and could only wait for the tobacco to pour into their storehouses. It must have been this type of commerce that gave the urban merchants their local name, *especuladores*. The anxiety and insecurity of the mercantile sector was reflected in the Santiago newspaper, *El Eco del Pueblo*, every year. The urban merchants were sticking their necks out, risking bankruptcy. The rewards of the trade could be high, of course. Much of the commercial wealth in the region derived from the tobacco trade.

The German market directly influenced the organization of tobacco cultivation and trade in this period. The German importers really were not interested in a high-quality tobacco. They needed a cheap, strong-tasting tobacco that could be used as filler in German cigars. In 1888, Abad commented: "This influence of the Hamburg market has been decisive and fatal for our leaf, which has had no stimulus for improvement. The Dominican purchasers, as agents for the German houses, do all they can to obtain as much weight and quantity as possible. Therefore the cultivators opt to cultivate tobacco on virgin, very dark, and rich lands. In this way they obtain a large amount of tobacco of low quality."[9] Other tobacco experts, such as M. C. Grullón and Pedro M. Archambault, expressed similar opinions at the beginning of the twentieth century.[10]

THE CIBAO TOBACCO EXPORTERS

The Dominican export sector in the late nineteenth century was the domain of a relatively small group of merchants. Only a few export firms had direct contact with the European market. The two most important firms in the closing decades of the nineteenth century undoubtedly were Ginebra Hermanos and G. W. Heinsen. Unfortunately, we know little about their commercial position or about the end of their dominance. It is clear, however, that they had close commercial ties with German importers. Their leading position in the Cibao commercial community was, above all, the consequence of their access to German credit.[11] But they were not the only important merchants at this stage of the tobacco trade. José Battle y Cía. and José M. Glas were powerful merchants in Santiago. The same was true of Juan Isidro Jiménez in Monte Cristi, Zoilo García in La Vega, and Gregorio Rivas in Moca.[12] Alongside these men, smaller-scale merchants did business, but their enterprises were less stable and their commercial activities irregular. Often they were only part-time traders and derived their local status from large landholdings. As landowners, they dedicated as much time to agriculture as to trade.[13]

Because tobacco was the only important commercial product in the region before the 1880s, many firms suspended their activities when the tobacco harvest proved small. Five times between 1865 and 1889, smaller commercial firms closed their doors and did not conduct business for four or five months.[14] Municipal records of the period demonstrate the instability of urban commerce in the late nineteenth century. Businessmen came and went, and many names disappeared from the records after a few years. Bankruptcies were regularly reported.[15] All this attest to the very precarious financial bases of all but the largest firms. As their names indicate, they were generally individual undertakings. Any setback on the economic, political, or personal level could be enough to force a merchant out of business.

The commercial crisis which hit the region as a result of the German protective measures of 1879 caused a realignment of the commercial sector. Its consequences were twofold. First, many of the smaller and financially more vulnerable firms of Santiago disappeared or merged with other enterprises. Most traders who survived the crisis emerged with a stronger financial basis than they had had before. Competition was sharply reduced, and profits were shared with only a few competitors. Second, most of the larger enterprises started to diversify their commercial activities in an attempt to reduce their exclusive dependence on tobacco. Diversification was facilitated by the emergence of coffee and cocoa as important export crops.

This reorganization of the commercial sector enabled the Cibao merchants to consolidate their positions and heralded a new period in the export trade. New crops, especially cocoa, and the improved (railroad) connections to the seaports provided Cibao commerce with more business opportunities. At the turn of the century, then, a well-established mercantile sector emerged in the Cibao. Tulio Cestero's booklet *Por el Cibao*, published in 1901, gives a detailed account of commercial activity in the Cibao.[16] The scale of many enterprises was still small compared to businesses in other Latin American or European countries, but the signs of an emerging native bourgeoisie are undeniable. Santiago hosted some thirty commercial firms; in Puerto Plata, more than twenty firms were engaged in the import-export trade. Other towns in the Cibao also had a considerable number of commercial establishments.

One of the principal firms in Santiago was Augusto Espaillat Sucesores, the shareholders of which were described in 1903 as "the most patriotic and progressive persons of this valiant Province." The firm, which represented capital of more than 100,000 pesos and employed more than forty people during the tobacco harvest, was associated with the Puerto Plata firm A. S. Grullón & Co. It possessed a steam-driven sawmill, an ice factory, and a cigar factory. It also ran the largest store in Santiago, the "Bazaar Parisién."[17] Other important merchants were C. Sully Bonelly Cía., which employed more than sixty people during the tobacco harvest; José Battle y Cía., with forty employees; Tomás Pastoriza; Manuel de Js. Tavárez; J. M. Marchena; the Cuban Nicolás Vega; Toribio Morel Co.; and Enrique Pou.[18] The largest factory of cigars—one year before the establishment of "La Habanera"—was "La Matilde," owned by Simón Mencia.[19]

A monthly statistic of exported products, published by the *Boletín Municipal* of Santiago in 1905, gives a rare glimpse of the volume and yearly cycle of Santiago commerce.[20] It shows that the companies of José Battle and Nicolás Vega were the two largest tobacco exporters. They were responsible for 30 and 20 percent, respectively, of the tobacco exported that year. They were joined by four more large exporters: Augusto Espaillat Sucs., T. Pastoriza & Cía., V. F. Thomén, and Perelló & Cía. These six enterprises exported more than 4.5 million kilos of tobacco in 1905, almost 90 percent of the total exported.[21] All of these mercantile firms did business in more than one town and were engaged in the exportation of many products.[22] After tobacco, cocoa was the most important export product. This is not surprising, since 1905 fell in the middle of the cocoa boom of the first decade of the twentieth century. The statistics also show the strictly seasonal character of the tobacco trade. Exports began in May and hardly existed after September.

In the early decades of the twentieth century, many successful merchants bought land around the cities, above all around Santiago. In this way a number of merchants came to reside in the rural areas and became agricultural producers themselves. Mario Fermín Cabral was such a man, "one of the principal buyers of the prosperous commercial enterprise of Sucs. de José Battle" and "one of the most powerful buyers of the Cibao."[23] The landowners in the Villa González region also belonged to this class of powerful merchants who bought tobacco for the exporters.[24] These entrepreneurs belonged to the same social class as the urban merchants and shared the latter's social and political prestige. Although the urban merchants normally disposed of more capital, the advantage of the rural elite was that it lived in the rural environment and was linked to the tobacco-producing peasantry through bonds of patronage and dependence.

A Changing World Market for Dominican Tobacco

The market position of Dominican tobacco remained quite insecure until the first two decades of the twentieth century. Profitable years alternated with commercial depressions or poor harvests. The influence of the German market remained great. The large 1909 harvest could be sold only slowly and at low prices, because the German importers still had stocks and new customs duties were pending.[25] The same thing happened in 1912, "demoralizing" the commercial class in the Cibao.[26]

The problem of the Dominican exporters was that there was no guarantee that better quality tobacco would procure higher prices. Not so much the quality of the tobacco, but the situation of the world market determined the fate of the Dominican tobacco. The competition of other areas of tobacco production, such as Brazil and the Dutch East Indies, increased. The German importers did not hesitate to use the weak market position of Dominican tobacco to bring down prices. Hamburg and Bremen remained the most important market for Dominican tobacco until 1914, and complaints about "the monopoly that they have held from time immemorial" were numerous.[27] Anger toward the Germans continued to lead to bitter accusations.

El Diario in 1910 called the German merchants "the blood-suckers who suck up our spirit, and make all the profits."[28] *Listín Diario* wrote in 1919 about "the octopus that strangles all the energy of our Cibao tobacco cultivators."[29]

Yet, when the German monopoly was broken, the Cibao merchants were unprepared. As a consequence of the outbreak of the First World War in 1914 and the U.S. occupation of the Dominican Republic beginning in 1916, commercial relations with Germany were severed, and there was an immediate need to find new tobacco markets. Only a few regretted the closing of the German market. Alternative markets appeared promising, and, initially, optimism reigned in the Cibao. All provincial governors of the Cibao received a letter from the Ministry of Agriculture in March 1915 indicating that France was interested in buying the Dominican tobacco that could not be shipped to Germany because of the war. According to the letter: "France is interested in establishing a regular trade between the two countries and wants to replace Germany once and for all as tobacco buyer."[30] In the same year, the Dominican consul in Madrid tried to open up the Spanish market. Rumors circulated in the Cibao that a representative of the Spanish tobacco monopoly had left Spain "with the intention of buying all the remaining tobacco of the Cibao."[31] Two years later, M. de Flores de Cabrera analyzed the prospects of finding alternative markets for Dominican tobacco. After once again denouncing "the capitalists on the other side of the Rhine," he showed great optimism about the Spanish and French markets. Access to them would enable the Dominican merchants to sell their tobacco "without the intervention of any *trust*."[32] However, the Spanish *Tabacalera* refrained altogether from buying on the Dominican market, and the French remained hesitant buyers.[33]

These frantic attempts to find outlets for Dominican tobacco reflected the serious problems World War I caused for Dominican exporters. As the war escalated and the U.S. became involved, shipping became increasingly difficult. The U.S. government created a list of nonessential goods, including tobacco, whose transport had low priority. Thus tobacco export was greatly hampered.[34]

The war also had positive effects for the exporters. It increased the prices of commodities such as tobacco, and made for speculative profits. Such effects intensified during the "Danza de los Millones" that occurred when the war ended. Prices skyrocketed, causing a boom in tobacco export. Producers who, in response to high food prices, had switched to food crop production in the first years of the war, returned to tobacco cultivation. This went so far that the president of the Chamber of Commerce in Santiago, Luis Carballo, felt the need to warn cultivators: "With great sorrow and considerable fear we see that the Province of Santiago is not producing the food-stuffs necessary for its inhabitants at this moment, due to the fact that our cultivators are dedicating all their energy to the cultivation of tobacco, to the neglect of other crops." Carballo was especially worried about the cultivators' reaction to the high prices of the preceding year: "It is incredible what has been happening this year, as our cultivators have been consumed by a real tobacco mania (*furia de tabaco*). I have seen with my own eyes how peasants were destroying prosperous fields of sweet potatoes, ready to be harvested, in order to sow tobacco."[35]

The optimism of the mercantile circles in the Cibao was shattered when the Dance of the Millions turned into a commercial crisis in 1920. In an effort to deal with the low prices and decreasing European demand in the 1920s, the Cibao tobacco exporters tried to convince the U.S. government to grant Dominican tobacco preferential access to the U.S. market. In their opinion, this would solve the commercial problems of the region and guarantee the future of Dominican tobacco in one stroke. The city councils of the Cibao in October 1919 asked the Military Government for "certain privileges in the U.S. which permit the importation of Dominican tobacco to that market with stimulating advantages for the cultivators and merchants in the Republic."[36] However, the U.S. officials could hardly grant such a privilege. Trying to modernize a semicolony was one thing; promoting measures that might stimulate competition with production at home was quite another. As an official dryly remarked, such a policy was doomed because of "the antipathy that any tendency to favor a competitor would provoke in the ranks of the American tobacco cultivators."[37]

Nevertheless, the Military Government could not ignore the tobacco problem. Never had the demand for Dominican tobacco been so small or prices so low.[38] The government therefore asked the advice of the Chamber of Commerce of Santiago. A delegation traveled to the Dominican capital in September 1920 and set out the problems of the tobacco market. As a result, the Military Government agreed to guarantee a minimum price of four pesos per bale for all the tobacco of the 1920 harvest. In practice this meant that the U.S. government committed itself to buy the entire tobacco crop for a fixed price. The merchants of Santiago had actively promoted state intervention, but they were not allowed to play the central role they had envisioned for themselves.[39] The collective buying was to be coordinated by the mercantile house of the Sres. Divanna, Grisolia & Co. in Puerto Plata, which would buy the tobacco from the producers on behalf of the government.[40] The capital was furnished by the International Banking Corporation in New York.[41]

Problems arose immediately. The 1920 harvest was an unusually large one, in part due to energetic activities on the part of the peasantry, and in part due to good weather. It was estimated at 375,000 *bultos* (of approximately 60 kilos each). By April 1921, only half the 1920 harvest had been bought and paid for. And, as the Chamber of Commerce of Santiago warned, the 1921 harvest was already pending.[42] The government could do nothing but continue its policy for another year, buying the 1921 harvest as well.

A second problem was the international marketing. The accumulated tobacco sold slowly and often at not very profitable prices. At the end of 1922, the government still possessed more than 100,000 *bultos*.[43] Even the concerted efforts of Dominican diplomatic representatives in Italy, England, and Spain, who were allowed to offer a 120-day credit, could not accelerate commercial activity.[44] In view of the capital invested and the deteriorating economic position of the U.S. government in the Dominican Republic, the policy was revoked. In January 1923, the Chambers of Commerce of the Cibao towns received a letter in which the government informed them that "the financial position of the government at the present time is such that it cannot possibly undertake new purchases of tobacco."[45] A more graphic illustration of the difficult market position of Dominican tobacco would be hard to find!

THE CIBAO EXPORT SECTOR IN THE 1920S

The recovery of European economies in the 1920s stimulated regional and international trade. Increasing sophistication was evident above all in the organization of trade and of tobacco processing. From 1923 on, Belgium, Germany, France, and Holland were among the four largest buyers of Dominican tobacco. Tobacco companies from these countries established themselves in the Cibao and became economically and politically important in the region. The U.S. occupation had also attracted a number of U.S. companies. Representatives of the Tropical Tobacco Company started doing business in Santiago in 1918. This firm was established in New York and gradually expanded its activities in the Dominican Republic, acquiring interests in the "Compañía Anónima Tabacalera" and starting to manufacture its own cigarettes in Santiago.[46] The Dutch firm "Curaçaose Handelsmaatschappij" (Curaçao Trading Company) started to buy large quantities of tobacco in this period. Another Dutch merchant, Hugo Scheltema, representing the "Compañía Dominicana de Tabacos" in Santiago, played an equally important role in Dominican tobacco export. Every year during the harvest, the mother firm in Holland sent two Dutch employees to the Cibao to help him organize the purchase and sale of tobacco.[47] The Spanish "Tabacalera" also started to buy Dominican tobacco on a regular basis and had a permanent representative in the Cibao.[48] The representative of the French "Compagnie Générale des Tabacs," Albert Oquet, became the most influential and best known trader in the Cibao in the late 1920s. In 1925, his firm bought and exported approximately 100,000 *bultos* (more than 5 million kilos). Together with the Santiago firm of V. F. Thomén, he determined the prices and set the market trends.[49] Only two representatives of the German importers remained: the company Schulze and Lembcke, which had already been an important buyer of tobacco before 1914, and the German merchant C. Peters, who bought tobacco for the firm of G. A. Luening in Hamburg.

The increased capital outlay of the mercantile firms meant, in effect, that the international market moved *into* the Cibao. They bought and processed the tobacco within the region and often shipped it directly to the purchaser. They brought capital into the region, introduced modern tobacco processing techniques, and in general modernized commercial practice. An anonymous observer wrote in 1925: "The tobacco trade has been changing for the better . . . because the purchasers now come to our market and buy directly and for ready money from merchants from different regions, contrary to the former system, under which Dominican commerce of a earlier generation was dependent on the German importer and sent its tobacco to that market to repay the credit which it received there."[50] There can be no doubt that the tobacco trade indeed progressed and was consolidated in the 1920s. It became more professional and did not show the instability and extreme variations so characteristic in the nineteenth century.

Another important change in the tobacco sector was the establishment of regional cigarette production. As a result of this new industry, the use of tobacco as raw material within the region dramatically increased in the first decade of the twentieth century. We have already seen that the cigarette factory "La Habanera," later called "Compañía Anónima Tabacalera," gave a major impetus to tobacco cultivation and trade in the Cibao. The factory became a large purchaser of Dominican tobacco and rapidly extended its activities to the realm of production and trade. Its principal innovation was that it did not limit itself to buying tobacco, but instead started an intensive program of supervising cultivators. The company bought land of its own and hired peasants to cultivate the tobacco according to company wishes. The firm also distributed seeds, experimented with new methods of cultivation, and gave technical advice. Together with the educational efforts of the authorities, this active policy had a tremendous impact, especially since the company pursued this policy to its logical conclusion and paid high prices for good quality tobacco.[51]

Many native merchants attached themselves to these newcomers, resulting in a number of solid firms well provided with capital. Most Dominican exporters were linked directly to the foreign companies, sometimes as independent traders, sometimes as paid employees. A number of the larger Dominican firms extant at the beginning of the century were consolidated in this way. They formed a "new generation" of real capitalist entrepreneurs, who made significant investments and were tied closely to the world market. The firm "Hermanos Bonelly" possessed four storehouses in 1925 and employed 125 persons during the harvest. The firm of Victor F. Thomén, with offices and storehouses in Santiago, was connected to important European and U.S. importers and also traded directly on the principal markets. This firm was viewed as "the regulating force for market prices of coffee, cocoa, and tobacco" and exercised a decisive influence on the Santiago commodities market.[52] Other important urban traders were R. A. Echevarría, Manuel Battle, Javier Espaillat, Jorge Hermanos, Octavio Patxtot, and José María Benedicto. In the rural areas, many individual merchants bought large quantities of tobacco on account with the exporters.[53]

More care was now given to the tobacco before it was exported. Repacking, classification, selection, and fermentation became the normal practice in the storehouses of the tobacco merchants. By far the majority of the tobacco was now classified and prepared in the Cibao. The exporters employed large numbers of laborers during the harvest. *La Información* in 1928 called these new practices a "transformación completa" of the tobacco trade. The careful preparation of the tobacco by the actual exporters stood in glaring contrast to old ways: "In former times the Dominican exporter was interested only in sending large quantities, in order to obtain and repay credit available on the German buyer market. When buying fever set in, the tobacco was sent away in the worst condition. Then came the quotations determined by the foreign speculator . . . and ruin was certain." The newspaper concluded, exaggerating somewhat, that "there is not one of these old tobacco merchants who still has a cent."[54]

The picture was not all rosy, however. Some observers voiced misgivings. First, the innovations did not always guarantee good market prices, and dependence on a uncontrollable world market continued. Second, the innovations were for the most part limited to olor tobacco, that used in local in-

dustry. The *criollo* tobacco meant for export continued to receive less attention. Much of this tobacco was shipped in unsatisfactory condition. As late as
1929, German importers formulated devastating judgments about the Dominican tobacco. One of them wrote: "The selection and packing of the
Domingo tobacco has not improved. It still suffers from the same defects.
The tobacco is selected badly and often packed when it is still much too humid. . . . There is no standard whatsoever. Good- and bad-burning tobacco,
damaged and undamaged leaves are packed in the same bale, large and small
mixed together. In addition, tobacco leaves from different production regions
are packed together."[55]

The establishment of expatriate firms in the region also robbed the Dominican merchants of part of their commercial autonomy. They could only
survive (and, to be sure, make profits) by associating with foreign companies. A letter written in 1932 by the Chamber of Commerce of Santiago
stated that only three Dominican firms continued to export tobacco on their
own account: Javier Espaillat, Victor F. Thomén, and R. A. Echevarría.[56] The
nationalist *La Información* wrote in 1930: "Foreign capital, methodical and
farsighted, is lord and master of our commercial realms—the ailing and
painstaking routine of our Dominican merchants was followed and overcome
triumphantly by the fertile and positive practices of the foreign merchants'
hard cash."[57] This statement was exaggerated—Dominican merchants continued to be responsible for the majority of the commercial process. However, the newspaper correctly stressed the changes in the tobacco trade as
results of the foreign presence. Most Dominican merchants were denied access to the international market and became intermediaries between the local market and the urban exporters. They bought and processed the tobacco
in the Cibao and then sold it to the exporters, who shipped it to European,
North American, and, increasingly, North African markets.

MERCHANTS AND POLITICS

It would require another book (a very interesting one, to be sure) to analyze
the political power structure of the Cibao. Here we can only try to give a
rough and incomplete sketch of the social and political position of the mercantile elite in the urban centers of the Cibao. The commercial elite of the
Cibao was a relatively small but politically important group. It had to share
its position with landowners, businessmen, military officials, and politicians
(one person often combined several of these functions). Socially, this political establishment formed a fairly closed group, although individuals from

lower echelons of society might be admitted. Politically, this group was often divided into various contending factions. This ambiguity between social cohesion and political (and sometimes economic) competition determined the merchants' behavior.

We have seen that Dominican merchants had very little influence on the international market in the late nineteenth century. This must have been the principal reason for the venomous attacks on the German monopoly in the regional press. To compensate for their powerlessness, the merchants tried to control the commercial process and minimize their commercial risks *within* the region. The obvious strategy for insuring each merchant a comfortable profit was to decrease competition and to make deals to keep tobacco prices down. In its most inconspicuous form, this diminution of competition led to the formation of mercantile organizations. Already in 1883, the Progress Society (*Sociedad "El Progreso"*) was founded, "consisting of respectable citizens," most of them members of the mercantile class of Santiago. Its most important feat was the invitation in the same year of a number of Cuban tobacco planters.[58]

Toward the end of the century, cooperation between the merchants intensified. Their dependence on the German market and their weak commercial position diminished profit margins and provided sufficient motives to close ranks and keep prices on the regional market as low as possible. In a sense, they were mere intermediaries for the German importers, and their only interest was to maintain a profitable difference between the price they paid to the peasantry and what they received from the German importers.

Informal agreements became more frequent in the early twentieth century.[59] In 1907, the "Unión de Especuladores y Compradores de Tabaco" was established. The union was composed of the important merchants of Santiago, and its goals were "defending the interests of the union and maintaining harmony between producer and purchaser."[60] It is probable that this cooperation was mainly intended to counter plans in Puerto Plata to charge exported tobacco an extra duty.[61] However, it also showed that the few merchants who had survived the post-1879 crisis were conscious of the advantages of some degree of cooperation. In the Chamber of Commerce of Santiago, which was founded in 1904, the tobacco merchants had already established another forum for informal consultation.[62]

It can be no coincidence in that this same period we find the first indications that the urban merchants made formal agreements to keep down the prices of tobacco and other regional export products. In 1899, the merchants of La Vega agreed on a maximum price for tobacco and cocoa. Zoilo García, the town's most powerful businessman, wrote in a private letter to José Battle: "With this agreement, this commerce has given a clear demonstration of its sincere willingness to cooperate in regulating commercial operations as much as possible with respect to the export of products."[63]

With the consolidation of the tobacco trade in the beginning of the twentieth century, cooperation among the merchants became more regular. In June 1918, *La Información* carried a leading article on the low prices paid for tobacco and the absence of commercial activity in the region. This was the season of the year when tobacco buying and selling normally was at its height. The newspaper wrote: "It appears that there exists a determined attempt to keep the price of tobacco low. And, to reach that goal, there has been no lack of agreements and combinations (*combinaciones*) among the high commercial class."[64]

This is the first time that the word *combinación* is used to indicate that the mercantile class was consciously manipulating the market. From then on, denunciations of price manipulations and secret agreements became a regular feature of the tobacco trade. As we have seen, the urban merchants used such agreements to strengthen their positions vis-à-vis the intermediaries and the peasantry. They monopolized information about the international market and always tried to excuse low tobacco prices by referring to the low prices paid by European importers.[65]

One of the most obvious way to manipulate the market was to divulge incorrect information about the situation of the European market, with the purpose of pushing down prices. This was done frequently. Sometimes foreign exporters tried to use the same trick in a different way, divulging false information in the European market in order to bring prices down. The most notorious case occurred in 1928. The Dutch merchant, Scheltema, published a report on Dominican tobacco in one of the best-known German tobacco journals, advising European purchasers to refrain from buying Dominican tobacco that year. He asserted that the price of stocks of Dominican tobacco remaining in Europe was lower than that of the new tobacco in the Dominican Republic itself.[66] This incident also demonstrated the fragility of mercantile cooperation. Scheltema had tried to play a trick not only on the producers, but also on the other merchants. This produced a furious reaction from the region's commercial community.[67]

Another strategy of the mercantile community to diminish its commercial risks was to acquire political influence. Representatives of the mercantile sector often ran for office or accepted state appointments. In this way, many people close to the mercantile community held crucial positions within

141

the regional government. These public functions guaranteed good relations with the regional authorities. A tobacco merchant, Mario Fermín Cabral, even became provincial governor in the late 1920s.[68] A rare insight into this use of political influence for commercial purposes is seen in his correspondence. In a private letter to a business friend in Puerto Plata, Cabral stressed two elements: "The most important importers of this city [Santiago] maintain long-established relations with the consigning companies of Puerto Plata and are linked to them through family ties or friendship. The other point is that they have been receiving certain favorable conditions [*condiciones de comodidad*] with respect to the payment of customs duties on their imports."[69] We can only guess as to the nature of these *condiciones de comodidad,* but we may be sure that they implied a (probably unlawful) reduction in customs duties.

Many merchants cooperated with the authorities in their attempts to promote technological changes in peasant agriculture. It was the merchant Máximo Grullón who imported the first plows into the Cibao in 1875.[70] From then on, continuous cooperation existed between members of the merchant class and government officials. The commercial houses of José Battle, Nicolás Vega, and Pastoriza & Co. made a gift in 1905 of "a good number of axes, spades, and machetes" to the provincial authorities of Santiago. It is impossible to avoid the impression of hand-in-glove relationships among mercantile sector, provincial authorities, and local leaders, when we read that these utensils "were given to the rural authorities who had most distinguished themselves in the fulfillment of their duty and their agricultural efforts."[71] In the 1920s, many merchants assisted the Chamber of Commerce in its attempts to advance the harvest season and to have cultivators start sowing at an earlier date. The largest mercantile companies planted seedbeds for distribution among the cultivators.[72]

Sometimes there were direct rewards for close cooperation with the government. Because of bad commercial prospects, the tariffs for transporting tobacco to Puerto Plata by the (government-owned) Ferrocarril Central were reduced by 25 percent in 1910 and 1913.[73] The minister of finance and commerce reported in his annual report (*memoria*) for 1910 : "In view of the unfavorable circumstances and low prices of tobacco exports, it was necessary to come to the aid of that sector with a bonus of 50 percent of the [FCD railroad] fares. Therefore, 39,326.02 pesos were returned to the exporters."[74]

These examples of cooperation within the mercantile sector and between merchants and the authorities should not blind us to numerous instances of friction. Despite the social homogeneity and frequent agreements of the mercantile elite, competition was never absent among its members. Uncertainty often existed as to the volume of the crop, and individual merchants had to fulfill their contracts and buy a certain amount of tobacco. Commercial agreements therefore were charged with suspense and lasted only until the moment when one of the merchants broke the pact and tried to buy large amounts of tobacco for a slightly higher price.[75]

A similar situation can be seen in the relations between merchants and the state. The commercial sector supported government initiatives only when they were advantageous to its business interests. Measures which threatened its commercial position were systematically opposed. The matter of customs duties was an eternal point of friction. The majority of the revenues of the Dominican government came from import-export duties. Although even the merchants accepted the necessity of some taxation, they were bent on making it as low as possible. This struggle could take on political overtones, especially given the contrast between the Cibao and the southern part of the country. Tax evasion then could become a justifiable act of regional chauvinism against a parasitic government.[76]

But also on a regional and more mundane level, friction easily flared between the authorities and the mercantile community. This is what happened in 1911, for instance, when the Cáceres government seriously tried to control tobacco cultivation and to standardize (*unificar*) the quality of the Dominican tobacco. In his yearly *memoria,* Minister of Agriculture Rafael Díaz complained: "The same people who on various occasions have proposed this, have been the first ones to fight it . . . making propaganda against it among our simple cultivators; and the problem is not that they do not understand the damage they do . . . ; no, they restrain themselves because the majority are themselves speculators, who forget everything in the frenzy of an unorganized speculation."[77] A similar commercial attitude was visible at moments when the government attempted to interfere in the commercial process. The merchants vehemently opposed governmental measures that regulated the shipping of the tobacco.[78] When the government decreed on various occasions in the twentieth century that tobacco inspection was obligatory, this aroused furious mercantile protests. The inspection of export crops by the Santiago authorities in 1902 was resisted by many merchants. When the government decreed a new law and organized a better equipped inspection agency in the late 1920s, the mercantile community indulged in contortions to evade this interference.[79] Some merchants tried to evade inspection altogether.[80] Others attacked the inspection on formal grounds, implying that it contravened the freedom of commerce.[81] The underlying motive for this attitude was a mercantile aversion to regulation. The mercantile community did not hesitate to take advantage of legislation, but it bitterly protested what it saw as infringements on the freedom of commercial activity.

The problem encountered by the authorities was that the mercantile elite represented a formidable economic force in the Cibao. Faced with unfavorable legislation, the elite was able to sabotage or delay implementation of a law. Often merchants looked down upon government officials who attempted to control their business activities. For instance, in 1934 Emilio Almonte, the general inspector of produce (*inspector general de frutos*) in Santiago, had to answer to his superiors for his decision to declare a load of tobacco unfit for shipment. This measure had provoked the wrath of one of the merchants. In his own defense, Almonte wrote, "When I observe something irregular, I report it, and it makes no difference to me if it is not well received, because they look down upon me as a subordinate."[82] It is obvious that government officials were sometimes treated contemptuously by the mercantile community. This attitude was clearly visible in the late 1920s and 1930s, when the authorities developed a growing interest in the cultivators and a concern for their unfavorable market position. When officials such as Luis Carballo and Emilio Almonte started to side with the cultivators against the merchants and sometimes advised them not to sell their tobacco yet, because they expected the prices to rise, the mercantile community was indignant. This conflict between the state and the mercantile community in the Cibao intensified in the 1930s, when the Trujillo regime tried to take control of the tobacco trade.

Dominican merchants started out in the nineteenth century as intermediaries for German importers. This trade could be quite profitable and allowed some Cibao merchants to acquire considerable fortunes.[83] European advances enabled the merchants to obtain a dominant position in the region. On the other hand, dependence on the German market gave the tobacco trade a particularly erratic and unpredictable character. The regional economy underwent recurrent commercial crises in the late nineteenth century, making the position of the Cibao commercial elite insecure.

In the twentieth century, the commercial sector consolidated. The exclusive dependence on tobacco decreased, and the financial bases of the merchants improved. The weakest firms disappeared, and the remaining merchants prospered in the shadow of the international tobacco market. Some of the family firms that had been established around the turn of the century developed into full-fledged capitalistic enterprises. The commercial mo-

nopoly of Germany disappeared after 1914. From then on, Dominican tobacco was exported to various European countries. This development increased competition and stimulated European importers to establish themselves in the region. Some regional firms started to work for these foreign
companies, while others succeeded in maintaining their independence. In
general, the tobacco trade in the region became more competitive in the
1920s. Although the mercantile firms tried to decrease competition by se-
cretly establishing maximum tobacco prices, competition often prevailed in
the end. This was also the result of a more independent (and nationalist)
press, which was prone to denounce these schemes.

The dominant economic position of the Cibao merchants was based
principally on their access to credit.[84] Their position as intermediaries between the regional economy and the world market was essential to their regional hegemony. The establishment of foreign merchants in the region in
the 1920s somewhat restricted its commercial monopoly, but did not
threaten its social and political hegemony in the region.

The relationship between the mercantile elite and the government was
quite ambiguous. When it seemed profitable, the Cibao merchants did not
hesitate to take advantage of public initiatives. They often worked with the
authorities in efforts to improve the market position of regional commodities and to gain control over the peasantry. However, more often than not,
the two groups pursued different goals. The regional elite resented state interference in regional affairs and, above all, in its commercial activities. The
weak Dominican government often could not enforce its policies in the independent and chauvinistic Cibao, where the regional elite tenaciously defended its regional privileges. As we will see in the next chapter, it was only
in the 1920s that the state succeeded in breaking the regional autonomy of
the Cibao elite. Then it implemented a more interventionist policy and
sometimes even sided with the agricultural producers.

This position of the Cibao mercantile elite suggests some reasons for
the persistence and resilience of peasant production in the region. Without
a doubt, the urban merchants were the superior force in regional society.
However, they could never establish an *exclusive* hegemony in the region. In
the late nineteenth century, they were dependent on German credit. Simultaneously, they had to compete with a dynamic sugar sector and an indiffer-
ent, if not hostile, national government. In the twentieth century, the commercial elite had to share its regional hegemony with foreign firms (now
established *within* the region) and with a national government that it could
not control. The commercial elite's financial weakness in the nineteenth

century and the political competition in the twentieth prevented it from completely subordinating the peasantry. Their dominant position allowed the Cibao merchants to control prices and dominate the market. They did not hesitate to defend their interests collectively with price agreements or other kinds of commercial cooperation. However, they were not intent on changing the scale of cultivation or eliminating the peasantry. Commercial practices in the Cibao continued to depend on small-scale production. The specific organization of the urban export trade thus provided social and economic space for the persistence of peasant tobacco production in the Cibao.

8

Ideologies of Progress:
State Intervention and Rural Society

People lived satisfactorily in those days. Cultivators who owned a small plot of land, which they called *conuco*, felt themselves to be rich, when in reality they were poor, since they lacked aspirations and initiative toward progress and civilization.

—Governor Fermín Rodríguez of La Vega, 1906

Work with love and order, while your feet and hands are well. Others, who have more money than you, work with their feet and hands, but they need not be better off than you. Why can't you do the same? Do not be lazy. Do not gamble. Do not drink. These three things will make you poorer than you already are. Cultivate with energy and take care of what you have sown. When possible, do not buy on credit. And when you have to, pay it back as a honest man. AND WHEN YOU DO SO, PEASANT, YOU WILL NOT BE POOR ANYMORE.

—J. Cardona Ayala, 1922

The second half of the nineteenth century saw the emergence of a new kind of Latin American government. In this period of liberalism and positivism, when "order" and "progress" were considered sacred goals, the state assumed a new and active role. Liberal ideology may have pursued the free development of economic forces and preached the state's nonintervention in economic matters, but most liberal reformers accepted the idea that Latin American society was not yet prepared for restrained government.[1] On the contrary, they were convinced that Latin American governments had to take responsibility for creating the preconditions for economic growth and progress. It was the ultimate paradox of Latin American liberalism in this period that so much state intervention was required to bring about the free interplay of economic forces and to promote economic growth.

The situation in the Dominican Republic was not much different. Although the weakness of the Dominican state prevented it from taking a leading role in the economic development of the country, entrepreneurs and observers expected it to create the legal and political preconditions for a transformation of the country's economy. State policy in the Dominican Republic was geared essentially toward increase in agricultural production and expansion of export agriculture. Many people considered the idleness of so much land, labor, and resources in the Dominican Republic unacceptable. Did not the Dominican intellectual José Ramón López write in 1896, "No nation has the right to take possession of a piece of land and then leave it unproductive for civilization, for progress"?[2]

The principal purpose of state intervention in rural society was to increase the use of the country's natural resources and to stimulate economic growth. State policy was most crucial in the matter of landholding. Capitalist agriculture needed a situation in which land was a commodity, as well as an unequivocal system of land tenure. As had been the case during the so-called "liberal reforms" in mainland countries such as Mexico and Colombia,[3] regulation of the system of landholding was the most prominent example of state intervention in the Dominican Republic. However, state policy also touched other aspects of agrarian society, such as the relation between cattle raising and agriculture, the problem of deforestation, and the agricultural methods, deemed irresponsible and backward, that were employed by the rural population.

The modern state envisioned by Dominican politicians was dependent on regular public income, and this could only come from increasing exports.[4] Import-export duties provided the principal source of state revenues in the Dominican Republic, and, if the state was to become an active agent in the development of the country, these revenues had to increase. On the other hand, it was considered necessary to attract foreign investment. Taxes therefore were reduced to a minimum, and private enterprises hardly contributed to the government's finances. Gregorio Luperón complained in 1880 that "our fertile land is too cheap, and landowners pay nothing to the State. Our agrarian laws are full of exemptions, and, because of that, our most important agricultural products contribute hardly anything to the public treasury."[5] The insolvent government needed to stimulate productivity in order to acquire the financial means to promote such growth! This circularity explains the hesitant and at times contradictory character of state intervention in the Dominican Republic, especially before 1914, when the insolvency of the state was proverbial.

A second paradox of Dominican state intervention was even more important. Its basic premises were formulated at the time when the southern sugar sector underwent its first phase of dramatic expansion. Rather than initiating economic reform, the Dominican state could often do no more than regulate or legalize the practical consequences of uncontrolled growth of the sugar plantations. Under President Heureaux, the Dominican state became the loyal servant of the sugar interests. The majority of state measures was inspired by the situation in the sugar regions. The problem was that the agricultural situation in other parts of the country was completely different from that of the plantation-dominated southern region. Laws designed for the regions where sugar plantations were dominant, often were unsuited to other areas.

A third problem was the relation between the national state and the Cibao region. On the one hand, the state really was an external factor in the Cibao. The center of governmental power was Santo Domingo, and the majority of the social groups controlling the government originated in the southern part of the country. On the other hand, many members of the Cibao elite also held important government posts, and a considerable number of Dominican presidents came from this region. This puzzle is difficult to solve analytically. Still, it seems clear that most legislation, regulations, and public programs were conceived quite independent of the realities of rural life in the Cibao. They were usually provoked by the interests of the powerful sugar industry or, to a lesser extent, by the fiscal needs of the state. The Cibao elite appears normally to have been unable (or too uninterested) to influence public policies directly. However, within the region, they were the ones charged with their execution. This enabled them effectively to protect their interests. They simply ignored or, if necessary, disobeyed unfavorable government measures.

This chapter analyzes how the Dominican government tried to remodel rural society from the end of the nineteenth century on. The key questions that this chapter tries to answer are: In what ways did this legislation affect the regional economy of the Cibao? What were the consequences of a series of laws designed to foster expansion of large-scale plantations, in an economy based primarily on small-scale agricultural production? And to what extent was this legislation used and manipulated by different social sectors in the region? As we shall see, the results of many measures were determined more by the dynamics of rural society than by the intentions of the legislators.

149

THE STATE AND AGRARIAN CHANGE

Modernization of Dominican society was the shared and virtually unanimous desire of Dominican elite groups and state authorities alike, but many differences of opinion existed as to what this transformation should look like and how it might be induced. A basic contradiction existed between "plantationists" on the one hand, and the "peasantists" (*campesinistas*) on the other. Despite the fact that a number of people argued for a harmonious coexistence between the two models, this basic opposition structured public discussion in the Dominican Republic around the turn of the century. It gained further relevance after the U.S. invasion of 1916, when national identity became an important political issue. Many critical observers began to see the sugar plantations as the bearers of foreign influence, whereas the peasantry became the national symbol of Dominican identity (*dominicanidad*).

The second question—*how* had society to be transformed?—was answered in equally conflictual ways. There was no doubt in the minds of the Dominican elite that progress could be accomplished only by further integration of the rural population. If the latter was not prepared to cooperate in this sacred project of modernization, it had to be forced. In Dominican rural society, there always remained a certain ambivalence in elite ideology, however, reflecting different social and economic interests. On the one hand, the scarcity of labor demanded the dissolution of rural society and the creation of a class of wage laborers; on the other, there was a desire to keep rural society intact and to accustom the peasantry to modern society only gradually.

The historical development of state intervention and the discussion of rural society in general may be divided into three episodes, represented by the governments of Ulises Heureaux (1882–99), Ramón Cáceres (1906–11) and Horacio Vásquez (1924–30). These three governments symbolized the changing perspective on rural change within Dominican society.

The government of Ulises, "Lilís," Heureaux marked the beginning of a central state in the Dominican Republic. Although Heureaux was a Cibao native, his power base was in the South, where the sugar entrepreneurs enjoyed virtually unlimited freedom of enterprise and received numerous tax benefits in exchange for their loyalty. Benefiting from improvements in infrastructure and communications, Heureaux succeeded in creating a more or less stable and clearly national state.[6] The price the country had to pay for this accomplishment was twofold. Most important was the subservience of the government to the sugar companies. The economic policy of the president was completely geared toward facilitating the expansion of the plantation sector. The financial survival of his government depended on the financial support of all members of the commercial elite, to be sure, but it rested above all on the credit derived from the sugar entrepreneurs. This situation formed the backdrop for Heureaux's famous, although perhaps apocryphal, remark that he himself was not the real president of the country, but Juan Bautisto Vicini, owner of several sugar plantations and the government's main creditor.[7]

A second consequence of Heureaux's long reign was a certain atrophying of intellectual discourse. Although discussion concerning the future of the country never ceased completely, the president's dictatorial and populist regime was hardly favorable to the expression of liberal and democratic ideas. Not for nothing did the influential Puerto Rican liberal Eugenio María de Hostos leave the country in 1889 after having lived there for almost a decade, only to return in 1900, after Heureaux had been assassinated.[8]

The lack of political freedom was reflected in the field of state policy. Legislation during the Heureaux government was scant and often amounted to no more than grants of concessions to entrepreneurs. The only substantial law of the period with respect to the organization of rural society was an 1895 law on cattle raising, which was—as we shall see later—in effect one more concession to the sugar plantations. Most high officials under Heureaux distinguished themselves more by their military vigor and loyalty than by their sophisticated ideas on economic policy. The only people who managed to affect agrarian policy were clever entrepreneurs such as Gregorio Rivas and Casimiro de Moya, but the best part of their influence was directed toward their own business success. In short, the Heureaux government supported the expansion of the sugar sector and other capitalist undertakings and was hardly interested in other spheres of the Dominican economy. At best it disregarded the peasant sector, but often it showed a strong disdain for the peasant way of life. Writings of this period reflect a deeply felt conviction that rural society was characterized, above all, by passivity and backwardness. Governor Emilio Cordero of Puerto Plata wrote in 1898: "The character of our peasants is—as is well known—obedient, but they are prone to routine as far as their work is concerned; they do not have real knowledge about the cultivation of certain plants. This makes it necessary for our country people not to waste their time in the continuous festivities in which they indulge themselves daily. . . . The care and maintenance of a *conuco* requires constant work and, above all, order."[9] Of course, these ideas were not exclusive to the Dominican Republic. Nor did they

disappear with the death of Heureaux. However, the end of his regime ush-
ered in a revival of intellectual debate in Dominican society, and dissenting
opinions could be expressed more easily.

The government of Ramón Cáceres may be considered the product of
this new freedom and of the deeply-felt urge among the Dominican elite to
transform society. The Cáceres government has been the subject of extremely divergent judgments. Some observers express unconcealed admira-
tion for the efficiency of the Cáceres government and for its technocratic
character, which allowed it to benefit from favorable economic circumstances
and enlist the support of many gifted individuals. Others hold that the ac-
complishments of this government were possible only at the expense of
bringing the country's economy and politics under U.S. domination.[10] It is
clear that, under the Cáceres government, a coherent agrarian policy took
shape for the first time.[11] Support for the plantation sector continued to form
the basis of state policies, but the authorities directed their attention to other
sectors of the economy also. Their principal purpose was to modernize peasant agriculture. Educational activities aimed at the native cultivators were
expanded, and, for the first time, attempts were made to intervene directly
in peasant agriculture. These activities still did not show much respect for or
comprehension of the daily existence of the peasantry and were often extremely authoritarian, but, as attempts to incorporate peasant agriculture
into the modernizing project of the state, they were innovative.

The changing role of the government was confirmed during the U.S.
occupation (1916–24). In the field of legislation, this period was very fertile.
The Military Government really tried to change the organizational founda-
tions of Dominican society, but its efforts were stymied by the resistance of
the Dominican population and the financial problems of the occupational
forces after 1921.[12]

The government of Horacio Vásquez brought state intervention in rural
society to its logical conclusion, especially between 1926 and 1929. The
Vásquez government could take advantage of the nationalist consensus that
existed in the country after the departure of the U.S. Marines. This national-
ism created an atmosphere which saw native, small-scale agriculture as an
important vehicle for creating a national identity, as opposed to the "imperialist" sugar plantations. Peasant production was seen with new eyes and
started to receive more attention. Agricultural extension workers were appointed, and some interest emerged in the logic and organization of peasant
production. Capable ministers, such as Rafael Espaillat and Rafael Díaz, succeeded in organizing their departments and gave some coherence to the di-

vergent activities of the state.[13] Many aspects of the agrarian policy of the Trujillo regime, such as the so-called "campaigns" (*campañas*) to propagate the use of the plow or improve the cultivation of corn or tobacco, in fact were initiated under the government of Horacio Vásquez.

On the surface these governments may seem not so different. All of them were primarily interested in modernizing the Dominican economy and all intended to foster development of the productive forces in the country. However, they differed in their approaches to the problem of development. While the Heureaux regime opted for an exclusively plantation-based road to modernization, subsequent governments gradually dedicated more attention to peasant production. While in the late nineteenth century most Dominican intellectuals and politicians favored plantation-based modernization,[14] in the twentieth century the peasant (*campesinista*) perspective gradually gained ground.[15] This shift was partly the result of nationalist sentiments created in reaction to U.S. dominance of the country.

THE TERRENOS COMUNEROS

Access to land has been seen principally as a function of the ratio of people to land and of demographic growth in general. However, recent research has emphasized that access to land was conditioned also by social and political factors.[16] The "openness" of land resources was conditioned as much by state intervention and the usurpation of land by rural elites as it was by the growth of the rural population. It is therefore important to understand the policies that have affected the organization of landownership and the smallholders' access to land.[17]

The Dominican system of landownership contained many uncertainties. Boundaries were vague, and many transactions were not recorded properly or legalized by the presence of a third party. In the nineteenth and early twentieth centuries, discussions of the landholding system invariably singled out the *terrenos comuneros* as the source of the backwardness of Dominican agriculture.[18] Confusion about land entitlements was seen as an obstacle to further commercialization of land and expansion of export agriculture. In the *comunero* system, land was not physically divided. All co-owners possessed a certain number of shares (*acciones* or *pesos*). Each of them could take what he needed from the land as long as he did not take more than his shares entitled him to and he did not infringe on the rights of a co-owner.[19]

The government's essential objection to the *comunero* system was its legal uncertainty. *Comunero* lands were not divided; that was the reason they were often called *indivisos*. The number of co-owners could amount to several hundred, each of whom could assert a rightful claim to part of the property.[20] This situation was an irritant to liberal reformers and entrepreneurs who were convinced that individual property rights were indispensable for economic modernization. The fact that the *comunero* system prevented individuals from knowing the exact extent of their properties was considered archaic and unacceptable. The famous liberal intellectual, José Ramón Abad, observed in 1888: "Our social situation is contrary to any system of communism."[21] And in a series of important articles published in the *Listín Diario* in 1910, Félix Rodríguez wrote: "Our *terrenos comuneros* are a remnant of the barbarous customs of the feudal period in Europe."[22] Like liberal reformers in other Latin American countries, Dominican politicians aimed at the privatization of land. This would, they believed, facilitate the commodification of land and create a land market: "It is imperative, from any point of view, to give land a real and quantitative value in direct relation to its qualitative value. . . . The State must survey the agricultural land and give anyone what by reason and right belongs to him."[23]

We have already seen that the Heureaux government did not produce much agrarian legislation.[24] The solution of the land question was left to the parties involved. This in practice meant that the sugar companies in the southern part of the country could expand their properties, often through illicit means, without any opposition of the authorities.

With the end of the Heureaux regime in 1899, previous state policy began to be criticized. The extreme subservience of the government to the foreign sugar companies became a focus of debate. Many observers protested the way in which sugar enterprises past and present exploited the confusion over land rights. The governor of Santo Domingo reported problems experienced by a number of landowners in his province who, due to expansion of the Vicini estate, "were encircled by a net of surveyed land which prevented them from expanding their agriculture and initiating other works." The governor permitted these landowners to expand their cultivation because the prior surveying had been "unlawful and illegal." He declared that "only the arbitrariness which ruled [during the Heureaux regime] could have silenced the rest of the co-owners."[25]

In 1907, a land law was issued which made surveying a condition before a land transaction could take place. This law was hardly effective, however. The problem of the *comunero* lands was squarely confronted for the first time under the Cáceres government. In 1911, the *Law of the Division of Common Lands* (*Ley sobre división de terrenos comuneros*) was accepted by the Dominican Congress, which declared the division of the *comunero* lands "in the public interest" (*de utilidad pública*).[26] It required the surveying and division of *comunero* lands by official surveyors when one or more co-owners asked for it. In 1912, such an official survey was made obligatory whenever a transaction involving landed property took place.[27] The survey had to be paid for by the owners of the land. When they did not have the money to do this, they were to relinquish part of their land. The law provided virtually no protection for poor co-owners of collective property. Some politicians therefore raised their voices in support of the peasantry. They feared that the unlimited expansion of a few large enterprises would eliminate smaller-scale Dominican undertakings. In the Senate, José Ramón López proposed a tax on land which was kept only as an investment and left fallow, "with the purpose of preventing the poor Dominicans from falling victim to land usurpations and speculations."[28]

Indeed, the sugar companies proved amazingly eager to have their land surveyed. Many of the official surveyors were even paid by the companies— a clear indication of the advantages for the sugar plantations of obligatory surveying. Many sugar plantations, which had acquired shares in collective property, forced their co-owners to have the property surveyed, and many smallholders lost part of their land in this way.[29] Large enterprises were prepared to use devious means to acquire land. U.S. Consul Russell reported to his superiors in 1911: "It can easily be seen how, by gradually extending their operations, the most influential inhabitants soon came to control the largest share of the communal land. . . . It is commonly stated that at least 80 percent of the large landholders in Santo Domingo are merely "squatters" and hold their land by the force of a fence and influence with the central government."[30] Some people publicly denounced the proliferation of false titles that were sweeping away the small proprietors. It was common knowledge that fraudulent land titles were produced by the thousands. False titles could easily be converted into legal entitlements by means of a land survey.[31] The surveyor Vicente Tolentino wrote in 1917: "The honest observer is alarmed when he listens to the righteous protests of the poor country people against the avalanche of false or dubious titles." He therefore requested measures "which will put an end, once and for all, to the evil which threatens the right of the poor peasant who almost always is ignorant, pious, and devoid of means and therefore prefers acquiescing in the loss of part of his legally obtained land, rather than starting a judicial procedure."[32] One of the leading lawyers of the Dominican Republic, Manuel Troncoso, wrote afterward: "I have never been happy with the 1912 law because it was ineffective in preventing the manufacture of illegal titles. In fact, there has been an increase in this activity, which has inundated the country with false papers."[33]

The advantage of the confusing system of land ownership for the peasant producers was that it enabled them also to usurp land on a small scale. Many cultivators did not possess land titles and took possession of lands of which the ownership was unclear. The *comunero* system enabled them, in this way, to maintain access to land and continue their agricultural production. San Miguel quotes some peasant producers in the Cibao, who opposed the demarcation of their land, as stating that they would "continue living in community (*en comunidad*), as they have lived up to date, because it is so convenient to their interests."[34] This shows that among the peasantry there existed an awareness of the importance of the *terrenos comuneros* for the perpetuation of their economic system. The quotation also suggests another explanation for the state's assault on the *comunero* lands. Whatever its origins and legal implications, it *was* a system of communal landholding that required a minimum of cooperation and agreement. Even when this cooperation was minimal, it at least provided a common ground around which the co-owners could rally when their interests were threatened. Archival sources from the period suggest that resistance to the expanding plantations and mobilization of the peasantry in general often were organized as a collective action by co-owners of *comunero* land. Such activities were seen not only in the southeastern part of the country, but also in the Cibao.[35]

It may be argued that without this legislation capitalist transformation would have changed the position of the Dominican peasantry anyway, but the laws on land registration certainly put small landholders under increasing pressure. Although these laws were presented as means to increase agricultural production, implicitly they aimed at making land a commodity that could be bought and sold on a free market. The real intent of these laws may best be understood from an open letter by a group of co-owners, or shareholders (*codueños*), in *El Diario,* in support of a proposed law on the *terrenos comuneros* in 1909. The letter stated that it was necessary to end the situation in which "any co-owner of two pesos can clear land every year in order to turn it into *botado* ("fallow") and leave it fallow the next year. When this law is passed, the value of the *tierras comuneras* will be double the current value."[36] The legislation thus supported tendencies toward social differentiation within rural society and laid bare the conflicting interests of more market-oriented, richer cultivators and the majority of the subsistence-oriented peasantry.[37]

Public Lands

Added to the problem of the *comunero* lands was the contradictory policy of the Dominican government with respect to public lands. Until the 1920s, state action moved simultaneously in two opposing directions. On the one hand, it tried to clarify the size of public possessions and to obtain more control over them. On the other, it continued to distribute lands without any formalized control.

Theoretically, all land not legally possessed by private owners belonged to the state. However, no central institution or land registry office existed in the country, and there was no certainty whatsoever about the dimensions of public lands. It was on a lower, municipal level that the realities of the confused land situation were clearest. The town councils possessed their own land resources, the so-called *ejido* lands, which formed a circle around the towns. These were used for public buildings and rented out as sources of revenue. In many cases, the municipal authorities were not able to enforce their rights, however. When the towns were still small, the assigned territory was large enough, but when they started to grow, they needed more land, and then it was often impossible to evict obnoxious squatters. In the 1870s, many municipal councils wrote despairing letters to the central government complaining about illegal occupation of the *ejido* lands.[38] Most municipal councils lacked the manpower and strength to impose their will on these squatters. Without the support of the central government, the municipal authorities were powerless to enforce their legal rights. It proved impossible to collect even small rents.[39] The mayor of Santiago complained bitterly in 1927, "For the last several years, the municipal council has been struggling with numerous persons who have taken possession of municipal land without any authorization and without documents. . . . Extraordinary efforts have been made to dislodge these people, but to no avail."[40]

Not only were the municipalities not supported, but state intervention often was the direct *cause* of the problems of the lower authorities. In its feverish urge to generate economic development, successive Dominican governments were prepared to grant extensive privileges to private entrepreneurs. In the 1876 *Law Concerning Free Grants of Public Lands* (*Ley sobre la concesión gratuita de los terrenos del Estado*), no conditions were specified for taking possession of government lands other than that the land should be used for export agriculture.[41] In later versions of this law, land could be obtained only when the production was large enough and exceeded some minimum established by the law. This procedure favored large-scale

157

agriculture. The *Law Concerning Public Land Concessions* (*Ley sobre la concesión de terrenos del Estado*) of 1905 and the *Law Concerning Agrarian Concessions* (*Ley sobre franquicias agrarias*) of 1911 were instrumental in enabling foreign corporations to take over large tracts of land.[42]

The Dominican government sometimes tried to attract foreign investors by emphasizing the possibilities for obtaining cheap—almost free—land. In a 1906 brochure, the Dominican government even invited foreign investors to take advantage of the *comunero* system to acquire land for almost nothing: "Sometimes, when a request is made for the survey and division of a property, the latter is so large that a few shares can entitle the owner to several hectares of land. . . . In no other American country is it as easy to become a landowner as in Santo Domingo."[43] Such a stance weakened the position of the lower authorities. It also prevented government officials from regulating landholding in the Dominican Republic. Foreign companies which acquired large tracts of land in the southern part of the country were far too powerful to be lectured by local government officials.

Calder indicates that it was only during the "imperialist" occupation of the country by the U.S. that the government somehow succeeded in controlling the large sugar plantations, which were, for the most part, U.S. owned.[44] In its push to modernize the country and stimulate the spread of capitalist relations of production, the U.S. authorities tried to rationalize the legal system and increase government control.[45] As outsiders, they gave the Dominican state a certain independence from civil society. Ignoring sensitivities within Dominican society, the U.S. government passed laws which gave the state more control of the country's system of land tenure. The first thing the Military Government did was to appoint land surveyors with the explicit task of mapping the country. To settle the land question, it issued a new law in 1920, the *Land Registration Law* (*Ley de registro de la propiedad territorial*). This law built on, and improved, previous land laws. It determined the organization of partition, measurement, and registration of land property and established several land courts in the country. Every province got a land court (*tribunal de tierras*); the highest such judicial institution was located in Santo Domingo.[46] Although many parts of the country were hardly affected by the law until the late 1930s, the law formed the basis for legal discussion on the land issue in the decades to come. More important, the law created an organizational infrastructure, which for the first time made general registration of land practical.

The new land law was preceded by another, much more controversial, law of 1919, the *Law Concerning Property Tax* (*Ley de impuesto sobre la propiedad).* This law, which imposed a direct tax on land property, caused a wave of protest, especially in the Cibao. The modest attempt to tax real estate became the focus of anti-American sentiments among the Cibao elite and became a test of its strength. The property tax law decreed an annual tax on land property which ranged from 0.5 to 2 percent of its value, according to its size.[47] The initial complaints about this tax came from the sugar companies, who even protested directly to Washington.[48]

When a commercial crisis hit the country in 1920, the landowners raised their voices, complaining that it was impossible to pay the tax and asking for postponement. Agitation in the Cibao increased, and the land tax became a major issue in the nationalist campaign which started to gather strength in this period. It was reported that in the second half of 1920, "the Junta Patriótica of Santiago had sent men through the province stirring up agitation against the land tax and calling on them as a patriotic measure not to pay such taxes."[49] These activities were most notable in the tobacco-growing areas where the crisis hit hardest, but cocoa growers in the Espaillat province also asked for suspension of the law because of the low cocoa price.[50] Resistance to the law was almost general in the Cibao. In December 1920, the treasurer of the Dominican Financial Department predicted that it would be very difficult to collect the tax and to quell the agitation if more human and legal resources were not placed at the disposal of the authorities.[51] In the following year it was reported: "It seems the *políticos* are becoming even more enthusiastic than usual in opposing the collection of property taxes; even municipal officers are worried, upon seeing that people do not pay the tax."[52] The concerted opposition to the land tax made it virtually impossible to collect. In 1927, the Horacio Vásquez government issued a weaker version of the 1919 law, and in 1935 it was finally abrogated. Calder concludes that "the boycott had fatally crippled the land tax."[53]

This episode clearly demonstrates the limits of state power in this period of transformation. The U.S. authorities were less than respectful of regional sensibilities and tried to impose their own brand of modernity on Dominican society. They wanted to create a modern, centralist state that was financially independent. Rich citizens too should contribute to the financial solvency of the Dominican state. The property tax was a direct expression of these ideas. The successful opposition to the land tax showed the strength of the Cibao landowning elite. The latter made use of the nationalist banner as a means of legitimizing its own interests, but its success was based on its dominant position in regional agriculture and trade and on its political strength. It was only during the Trujillo regime that the limits of this elite's regional power became apparent. The landowners in the Cibao were no match for the strong and ruthless "criollo" dictatorship of Trujillo.

In spite of this failure to *tax* landed property, the laws on land registration succeeded in *regulating* land. From the 1920s on, property rights were clearly defined, and communal landholding was virtually eradicated. This was not the result of legislation alone, however; other factors, such as population growth and the expansion of export agriculture, also were important. Gradually, the nineteenth-century system of land ownership made way for the strict and impersonal claims of the market. In retrospect, this process seems to have been inevitable, but its uneven and ambiguous nature must not be ignored. Land conflicts continued, and remnants of the *comunero* system caused legal complications well into the 1940s and even later.[54] After the Trujillo regime was firmly established around 1935, resolution of the land question proceeded hand in hand with enormous usurpations of land by the Trujillo clan. This gave a new tinge to the land debate, reflecting the authoritarian character of a despotic state.

CATTLE VERSUS AGRICULTURE

The dominant place of land in discussions of agricultural development in the Dominican Republic must not obscure other aspects of state intervention. Land legislation was only one element in a series of political interventions aimed at promoting market-oriented agriculture and further expansion of capitalistic enterprise. An important issue, for instance, was the so-called *crianza libre*, unfenced cattle raising. With the growth of agricultural activity, complaints about this practice proliferated. Many people advocated the protection of Dominican agriculture. Abad noted that cultivators needed to build a "Chinese wall" around their *conucos* to protect their crops.[55] In the eyes of the governor of Santo Domingo, loose cattle grazing "not only hinders, but makes almost impossible the prosperous and rapid development and growth of small agricultural enterprises."[56]

The protection of the smallholding cultivator was often mentioned as the principal motive to restrict and regulate the holding of animals. It was true that a clear tension existed between agriculture and the existence of free-roaming pigs, goats, and cows, which always threatened to destroy crops. However, cattle raising was not restricted to large landowners; it was also a vital part of the smallholder economy. The subsistence agriculture of the peasants normally was supplemented by loose cattle grazing—which, in the more remote parts of the republic, often resembled a type of hunting.[57]

160

When the municipal council of San Pedro the Macorís tried to restrict cattle raising in 1870, a group of small-scale sugar-cane cultivators protested in ungrammatical Spanish: "We let you know that in this place, I and other individuals, we have a number of oxen, because we have fields of sugar cane, and necessarily we must grind the cane with oxen; and we have a few milk-cows which are very necessary, both to save sick people and to consume in the houses, because we do not keep pigs here."[58] Most tobacco-growing peasant families also held pigs and poultry and sometimes cows or goats. These animals were not held and fed in restricted areas, but roamed around in woods. It was no coincidence, therefore, that in the discussion on this topic, often a direct connection was made between cattle raising and the *comunero* system.[59]

In 1895, a law passed that was meant to determine the relation between cattle raising and agriculture, the *Law Concerning Raising Domestic Animals in Pasture (Ley sobre crianza de animales domésticos de pasto)*.[60] The purpose of this law was to protect Dominican agriculture against animals not properly fenced in and which hence posed a severe danger to crops in the fields. The law on *crianza libre*, as it was commonly called, aimed at goals very similar to those of the land laws: the promotion of commercial agriculture, the protection of private property, and the modernization of rural society in general. This law superseded the prior initiatives taken on a municipal level to control cattle raising.

The law was based on two premises. First, cattle raising, like agrarian production, could be allowed only when it was based on possession of land. Second, in the conflict between the agricultural and the cattle interests, the latter were to be responsible for avoiding damage. This stance was a strong rupture with previous practice. In the *Law Concerning Urban and Rural Police (Ley de policía urbana y rural)*, which had regulated these matters before 1895, the cultivator had been responsible for protecting his crops.[61]

Neither of these two basic premises was pursued to its logical conclusions, however. Cattle raising continued to be permitted on *terrenos comuneros*. The law prescribed only the maximum number of animals allowed on a piece of property. Enforcement of this element of the law was practically impossible as long as the exact extension of *terrenos comuneros* was uncertain. The second principle, too, was pursued halfheartedly. The agricultural interests of the cultivator were protected only in the so-called *zonas agrícolas*, regions explicitly designated for agriculture. The decision to designate an agricultural region was to be taken by the municipal authorities or by the National Congress. The law did not stipulate conditions that had to be met for a region to be labeled "agricultural." The real intentions of the legislators became apparent in article 24 of the law, which reads: "Every individual who possesses a piece of fertile land that is more than 750 hectares and is his exclusive possession, in regions not zoned for cattle raising, and who wants to dedicate this land completely or partly to agriculture, has the right to request the municipal council to declare this property *agricultural land,* as long as half the property is dedicated to agriculture."[62] This article simply meant that any large-scale agricultural entrepreneur could demand state protection against animals trespassing on his property. Obviously it was not the cattle of large landowners that were affected by this law, but the few animals possessed by every peasant family. This article in particular benefited the sugar plantations in the southern part of the country. The land laws guaranteed their titles, and the law on cattle raising further legitimized the enclosure of the peasant economy. J. B. Vicini, for example, successfully appealed to article 24 of the law. When his property was declared "zona agrícola," he immediately sued the smallholders of the neighborhood and told them that after a period of twelve months he would kill all animals invading his property.[63] Since Vicini was one of the most powerful men in the Heureaux regime, it is not unreasonable to conclude that the law was designed to favor the business interests of the large landowners who supported Heureaux.

Such considerations also must account for the immediate abrogation of the law after the assassination of Heureaux. A new decree in 1900 preserved the distinction between agricultural and cattle regions but diminished the opportunities for abuse.[64] Another law restricting the freedom of cattle raising was passed in 1907,[65] but it was hardly effective. The commentary of the governor of Santiago is worth noting: "The *Ley de Crianza* gave rise to some discontent among the cattle growers, but later they became convinced that this law, instead of hurting their interests, would favor them, *because they are also agriculturalists.*"[66] This was a clear acknowledgment of the dilemma posed by restrictions on cattle raising. Many cattle growers were at the same time agricultural producers.

Attempts to protect agrarian producers against cattle continued to engage the attention of the authorities. In 1912, *crianza libre* was still viewed as "the major obstacle and the worst enemy of agriculture and industry."[67] When the U.S. Military Government decided to put a definitive end to free cattle raising in 1918, it became clear how widespread this practice was, especially in the western regions of the country. Hundreds of petitions were sent by peasants in the northern and western parts of the country to the responsible U.S. official, Holger Johansen. Although the initial reaction of the military authorities was strict and uncompromising, eventually they had to budge. Johansen wrote to his superiors in September 1918: "In our opinion, there are reasons, in the places where free cattle raising is most abundant, to concede some delay so as not to harm the cattle raising. We have on various occasions advised proceeding cautiously in this matter."[68]

Evidence from the Villa González region suggests that here the large landowners themselves circumvented restrictions on cattle raising, using their newly acquired, uncleared land for cows. Since the use of their land by smallholders depended on the good will of the large landowners, the latter could with impunity continue the old practice that the law was designed to eliminate. Peasants confirm that, well into the twentieth century, they were obliged to fence their *conucos* against wandering cattle. The issue lost importance only in the 1930s and 1940s, as a result partly of legislation and partly of the expansion of export agriculture, which definitively tipped the scale in favor of the agricultural interests.

The Suppression of Slash-and-Burn Agriculture

Another aspect of rural society that became the object of legislation was the slash-and-burn agriculture of the Dominican peasantry. In the twentieth century, criticism of this shifting cultivation became a routine part of official discourse. Protection of the thinning forest (today we would say ecological control) became a growing concern of commentators and government officials. This concern did not affect the large landowners or sugar plantations that had deforested immense tracts of land, but was directed exclusively against the small-scale cultivators. Slash-and-burn agriculture was considered an unacceptable waste of natural resources. In 1875, the president of the Development Council (*Junta de Fomento*) in La Vega wrote: This type of cultivation "accustoms the majority of the peasants to idleness and vagrancy. That is the reason why there are so many people without farms, and why the majority of those who cultivate something do so without rule or order. They clear a piece of land, sow a little tobacco, and abandon the *conuco*. The next year they clear another piece of land, which they also abandon. And this goes on, year after year, without taking further advantage of the extremely fertile land."[69] These complaints were repeated more insistently in the twentieth century. The Minister of Agriculture wrote in 1912: "Our forests are destroyed these days in order to clear *conucos* which are abandoned after two or three years; and trees do not grow back on the fallow land (*botados*) that remains once the land is abandoned."[70] The director of agriculture during the U.S. occupation, Holger Johansen, reported in 1918: "During my trip

163

through the country I have noticed that much forest land is being cut down to procure room for "conucos," the native Dominican housefarm. This is a very praiseworthy effort, but carries with it an imminent danger that many of such *conucos* are being cultivated for but a short time and then left to grow up in secondary growth and exposed to erosion."[71] Due to these observations, state officials tried to curb the unlimited *tumba* ("land cleaning") of the peasant producers. In 1910, it was proposed that peasants be required to get permission before opening a new *conuco*.[72] Annual reports (*memorias*) of the Ministry of Agriculture evince ongoing concern with deforestation and erosion. Such concern led in 1920 to the *Forest Law* (*Ley forestal*), which meant to "put an end to the relentless destruction of forests on the mountain slopes."[73] Legal remedies were also expanded, and in the 1920s cultivators were sometimes brought to court.[74]

The legislation did not show much comprehension of the actual situation in the Dominican Republic, however. The entire system of peasant agriculture was based upon the continuing access to virgin lands. This was true for the cultivation of both food and cash crops. In the cultivation of tobacco, this condition was even more important because the use of virgin lands gave the specific quality and aroma to the Dominican tobacco, and basically determined its position on the world market.

In addition, the forest cut down by the peasantry was only a minute portion of all logging done. The sugar plantations had destroyed the forests of the southern plains in the last decades of the nineteenth century. Lumber companies were doing the same in other parts of the republic. These activities not only disturbed the ecological balance of the rural areas, but they also posed a direct threat to peasant agriculture, which was dependent on access to forest resources. Indeed, sometimes the cultivators themselves protested against the unfettered destruction of the forests. *La Información* reported in 1919, "The peasants of the place called 'La Isla' protest against the extensive cutting of trees done by persons who live by selling firewood to the electrical company. Immense parcels of land stripped of trees are left fallow, and they are not used for the cultivation of useful crops."[75]

Although the peasant producers were not oblivious of the necessity for ecological control, legislation could not put an end to their shifting cultivation. First of all, the peasantry was aware that its contribution to the problem of deforestation was minimal. Second, slash-and-burn agriculture had a number of advantages for the peasantry. It generated a high level of production and did not require investment of money. The silent support of merchants, large landholders, and even government officials was another important reason for its persistence. Agricultural production was the peasants' primary objective. They were not prepared to sacrifice this objective because of the abstract danger of erosion. Slash-and-burn agriculture eventually decreased as a result of restricted access to land. In the central area of the Cibao, this happened in the first decades of the twentieth century; in the Villa González region, in the 1940s and 1950s.

THE GOVERNMENT AND PEASANT SOCIETY

As we have seen, many people believed that the principal explanation for the backwardness of Dominican agriculture was the innate conservatism of the peasantry. For instance, *El Porvenir* wrote in 1873: "One of the principal causes of the evil which we lament here is the indolence and the notorious apathy of the rural people, who limit their agriculture to the utmost minimum of land and satisfy their needs as cheaply as possible, and therefore do not feel the least stimulus to increase and improve their production."[76] There is no doubt that widespread disdain for and neglect of the rural dwellers lay at the root of many government policies. The wish to modernize the Dominican economy caused impatience with the peasantry, which held onto its own system of production. Government intervention therefore explicitly aimed at disrupting peasant society and forcing it to adapt to the market. An unknown observer stated in 1926: "Here people do not work to eat, acquire shoes or clothes, because, save for rare exceptions, the poor people do not need either the one or the other. It is therefore indispensable to augment the needs of the worker, to force them to eat, dress, and shoe."[77] These ideas were expressed most bluntly—almost tragicomically—by a U.S. official:

> The Dominican will not work unless he wants something that can be had only in exchange for money, which he must work to obtain, therefore we must create in him an appetite for things that he must purchase with money. We must get those who deal in such things to take them right into the country and show them to the bushmen and their families, who will first desire, then work, then buy; what they acquire through work they will doubtless stay home and guard; the more they own, the more liable they are to remain at home and behave themselves. We must do all we can to make them own things; the more and the heavier they are, the better.[78]

However, Dominican officials also were convinced that it was necessary to take strong measures to force the peasants to give up "the stale routine in which they find themselves immersed," as the *Voz de Santiago* put it.[79]

When the peasants did not want to cooperate, force had to be used. As happened in many other countries in the world, government policy in the Dominican Republic gave rise to a series of vagrancy laws. If Dominican society was to be modernized, every citizen had to cooperate. In this perspective, the indolence and passivity of the peasant population became akin to criminal offenses.

Considering that the first postcolonial period of export-oriented economic growth occurred during the Haitian occupation, it may come as no surprise that the first of these vagrancy laws was proclaimed during that period.[80] With the expansion of capitalist agriculture and renewed pressure for development on the part of the Dominican elite, legislation proliferated from the 1870s on. The second article of the 1870 *Law Concerning Repression of Indolence and Vagrancy* (*Ley sobre la represión del ocio y la vagancia*) reads: "The rural inhabitants who do not have cultivated fields or pastures, nor dedicate themselves to the holding of cattle or small animals, of their own or other people's, and who are not rightfully incapacitated to work and do not have agriculture according to their capacities, will be punished according to the judgment of the officials of the rural police."[81] This law was the first in a virtually endless series of laws and ordinances which obliged the individual peasant to dedicate himself to agriculture and cultivate a minimum amount of land. Many municipalities made it a criminal offense for a rural dweller to cultivate less than ten tareas.[82] Rural dwellers who were suspected of not fulfilling their duty could be forced to work for the government or to do military service.[83]

Repressive state policies were clearest under the Heureaux regime. For many officials, the peasantry became synonymous with backwardness and laziness. The governor of El Seybo reported in 1896, "With the cooperation of the *alcaldes pedáneos* and the agricultural inspectors . . . I have tenaciously persecuted the idleness and vagrancy which have had such a pernicious influence on the development and growth of agriculture."[84] This policy initially was meant to force rural dwellers to look after the sustenance of themselves and their family. As the pursuit of economic development intensified and the southern sugar showed the Dominican elite the potential for large-scale agriculture, the content of the laws gradually changed. The vagrancy laws no longer were directed exclusively at insuring the sustenance of the rural population, but also came to contain more general condemnations of the laziness of the peasantry and of its unwillingness to place its labor at the disposal of progress. The cultivators had not only to increase their agricultural production, but they also had to provide capitalist enterprises and the government with labor. In 1897, the governor of Puerto Plata called vagrancy (*vagancia*) a "terrible evil and one of the principal obstacles to the development of the agriculture . . . And I have been so energetic in this respect, that I have decreed that vagrants and idlers who have not cultivated at least ten tareas within the fixed term of six months, will be brought to justice in accord with the law."[85]

The governor of Santiago, José Dolores Pichardo, took this attitude a step further, when he wrote in 1889: "Vagrancy occurs principally in the countryside. Groups of men without work, who are always prepared to cause disorder and live from thieving, assemble in the rural stores and along the public roads."[86] It was clear that, in the eyes of the authorities, even walking along the road could amount to an antisocial activity. Did it not mean an expensive waste of precious time which could be more fruitfully dedicated to agricultural production?[87] In the expanding Dominican economy, the opportunity costs of leisure dramatically increased, and the elite did all it could to emphasize this message.

THE STATE TURNS PATERNALIST

The Dominican elite faced a basic dilemma. It favored capitalistic transformation of the Dominican economy, but simultaneously it was worried about the resulting disruption of rural society. All members of the Dominican elite subscribed to the idea of progress, but no one knew exactly what it meant and how one might judge its consequences. Some people had always expressed doubt about the desirability of progress based on large-scale plantations and forced proletarianization.[88] There was little doubt that the sugar refineries (*ingenios*) in the south had resulted in economic growth, but what about the dispossession of Dominican landowners and the lawlessness in boom towns such as San Pedro de Macorís, where prostitution and crime abounded?[89]

Gradually, then, in the first decades of the twentieth century, a reappraisal of peasant production took place. Small-scale production, with its disadvantages of inefficiency and technological backwardness, often seemed a lesser evil than the uncontrollable southern plantations and their attendant social upheavals. This reevaluation entailed, too, a different vision of peasant agriculture. Most defenders of peasant agriculture in the nineteenth century had been inspired by a conservative vision of an unspoiled countryside, where social harmony had not (yet) been destroyed and where every person had his assigned place. Someone like José Ramón López even favored some sort of social segregation between town and countryside, with young people assigned to the latter so as not to spoil "the innocent purity of their love for the rural life."[90] With the reappraisal of peasant agriculture, support for the peasantry lost its conservative, nostalgic character and became part of the *progresista* ideology of the Dominican elite. This also explains the increased concern for technological instruction of the peasantry. If peasants would change their habits and accept new agricultural methods, they could make a useful contribution to the country's wealth.

In this period, the idea that lack of education was the main obstacle to "emancipation" of the peasantry became generally accepted. Such beliefs were strongly colored by the positivist educational ideas of Eugenio Maria de Hostos, which were very influential among the Dominican elite.[91] It was asserted that only education could save the country.[92] Enlightened members of the elite and public instructors had to guide the peasantry forward. When the elite became aware that leisure and social and ritual obligations took away time which the cultivators otherwise might dedicate to agriculture, a campaign was begun to curb these unproductive activities. Thus the elite began to interfere with many different aspects of peasant culture.

An important part of this criticism pointed at the pernicious effects of alcohol consumption in the countryside. Many people saw the *ventorillos* as the principal villain in this respect: "the cancer which destroys our agriculture," corrupting the rural population and hindering agricultural progress.[93] The governor of Espaillat Province, C. Ma. de Rojas, wrote in 1891: "In this province, most damage to agriculture is done by the great number of *ventorillos*, which obtain a license for a mere five pesos. They are supposed to sell provisions, but they do nothing other than sell liquor under the counter. In every one of them, one sees ten or twelve vagrants daily."[94]

Halfhearted attempts were made to put an end to alcohol consumption in peasant society, with little result. Many people pointed to the *vicio de alcohol* as the principal defect of the peasantry. Nevertheless, a consistent campaign against the use of alcohol, such as was initiated by the socialist movement in Europe and later supported by many governments, never got off the ground in the Dominican Republic.[95] It is probable that the economic interests involved in alcohol production and retail trade precluded its effective prohibition.[96] The elite was not interested in the *moral* problem of the use of alcohol, but only in its *economic* consequences. As a logical consequence of this attitude, the consumption of alcohol was not to be prohibited, but rather restricted so that it did not affect agricultural production or interfere with the workday.

Concern about the noneconomic aspects of peasant society led to increasing restrictions on rural festivities, designated together under the name *fandangos*. These celebrations usually were organized by rural entrepreneurs, who arranged the music and made a small profit on the sale of drinks. These occasions often featured "the terrible and disastrous passion" of gambling, another activity frowned upon by many nineteenth- and twentieth-century observers.[97] In the 1880s in Moca, rural dances were assessed a tax of four pesos in an attempt to increase municipal income and restrict the occurrence of these events. Other municipalities rapidly followed suit.[98] Not long after the imposition of these taxes, restrictions were issued concerning when these festivities could be held. In Santiago, from 1891 on, they were permitted only on "the eve of Sundays and national or religious holidays."[99]

These measures demonstrate that state intervention gradually tended to become a "civilization offensive." Coercive measures were supplemented by more paternalistic forms of state intervention, intent on educating the rural population and destroying remnants of a "barbaric" past. In the discourse of the Dominican elite, gambling, drinking, and idleness now were lumped together and became the symbolic antithesis of the poor, decent, and hardworking cultivator. *La Información* admonished: "It is necessary that these men who live a life of continuous parties, drink too much, dedicate themselves to gambling, and provoke fights, etc., be corrected."[100]

It is interesting that cockfights were hardly criticized in this context. It must be assumed that the Dominican elite, or at least its masculine half, was itself too fond of this diversion to include it in reform activities. In the rare instances when cockfights were mentioned, the fights themselves were not deplored, but rather the "irresponsible" amounts of time the peasants spent in and around the cockpits. *El Diario* called this waste of time a "calamity," writing in 1907, "When two individuals who are devoted to cockfights meet each other on the road, they can be seen talking long hours about the fortunes of their respective cocks who have been fighting and those they plan to use in the next fight."[101]

It was only during the U.S. occupation that cockfighting became a serious point of discussion, obviously because the North Americans saw it as a primitive, unnecessary, cruel remnant of the past. As an anonymous official remarked: "Cockfighting appeals to the lowest instincts of human nature, and develops the worst qualities in men."[102] The military authorities preferred to see this sport replaced as soon as possible by a more civilized amusement, such as baseball, but even they understood that they had to act cautiously with respect to such a generally accepted pastime.[103] Although baseball became very popular in the Dominican Republic, the efforts to restrict cockfighting were futile and led to no more than a public discussion.[104]

169

All aspects of peasant society which tended to take away time from productive activities and could produce disorderly conduct (*desordenes*) came under attack, including spheres of rural life far removed from production, such as social events and religious rituals. Apart from some isolated measures, the efforts to curtail or even suppress undesirable elements of popular culture began in the first decade of the twentieth century. It may be that the lower-class origin of former President Heureaux had prevented earlier attempts of this nature. It is also possible that the transformation of Dominican society and the consolidation of capitalist relations of production were causes. It is significant that 1900 was the year in which the struggle against the peasantry's gambling habit acquired new dynamism.[105] This was the beginning of a new assault on peasant culture, especially those elements considered incompatible with modern discipline.

Government efforts were directed especially at popular rituals which consumed a lot of time. Especially condemned were the *velorios* lasting seven days and nights when someone had died.[106] Similar reunions, called *baquinís*, were held when a baby died within a week, "innocently." These were more festive occasions because the child was believed to go straight to heaven to become an angel. Apart from the wasted time, disorder caused by alcohol consumption elicited complaints from officials. The various restrictions concerning peasant culture were put together in the "Order of the Corps" (*"Orden de Cuerpo"*) of the Guardia Republicana, issued in 1908 by its "Supreme Commander" (*jefe superior*), Manuel de J. Tejera. First it prohibited such "normal" practices as gambling and holding festivities on workdays. It then continued: "The so-called 'velorios de angelitos' or 'baquinís,' when the body of a child is left unburied for several days and nights as a pretext for organizing unlicensed parties and dances, will not be permitted. Neither will be permitted the wakes, last prayers, mourning nights, and other similar acts which are unauthorized religious practices and which in reality are highly irreligious and savage acts and occasions for drunkenness and improper diversion."[107] We thus see that the state intervention reached into far corners of peasant existence.

But it was not only popular religion that came under fire. In this period, criticism was also directed at elements of religion that were actively fostered by the official church. The great many religious holidays already had caused complaints by many observers in the late nineteenth century.[108] Some sugar entrepreneurs now began to criticize the conduct of the local priests, who were drawing their laborers away from the work in the fields. The *Ingenio Italia* complained in 1910 that cane-cutting could not continue, because the priest had told the laborers not to work; and, "since these people easily leave work and believe the words of the priests to come from God, they have not presented themselves today to cut sugar cane." The meaningful question was posed: "Is it the constructive mission of the priest, the representative of the religion of Christ, to preach laziness?"[109]

In the Cibao, too, some opinions critical of the role of the official church were heard. The observer in *El Diario*, whom we already encountered venting his opinion on cockfights, identified another "calamidad" thwarting the development of Cibao agriculture: "This is caused by the religious festivities celebrated at rural shrines. When there is a religious service in 'Reyna de los Angeles,' 'Santo Cerro,' 'La Torre' etc., enormous masses of peasants go there, attracted by the gambling they are sure to find in these centers during the nine days that the festivity lasts."[110] These sentiments, which were shared by many members of the liberal elite, did not, however, lead to a formal anti-religious policy such as those that came into being in other Latin American countries. On the contrary, most people considered the Church a necessary ally in educating the rural population. One of the most devoted modernizers of the Cibao in the late nineteenth century, for instance, Gregorio Rivas, was actively involved in the ordination of priests in the province of Samaná.[111] In 1918, the archbishop of Santo Domingo wrote to the authorities that "our parish priests work with love and enthusiasm to convince the peasants of the necessity and importance of increasing their agricultural production."[112] And a priest in Altamira wrote to the Ministry of Agriculture in 1927: "I am stirring up the cultivators of the entire region. When they are assembled in the Church, they will receive the seeds from my hands after we have solemnly celebrated the Holy Sacrifice of the Mass and after I, with my modest words, have indicated that they must work and that agriculture produces great benefits for their families and for their fatherland."[113]

The Chamber of Commerce of Santiago understood the importance of this spiritual support. It stated in 1924 that "it will be of utmost importance to accustom all peasants to go to church, where the priest will admonish them every Sunday to keep away from gambling."[114] This attitude may have been the result of the influence of the specific brand of liberalism practiced by Eugenio María de Hostos, which was not principally anti-religious.[115] On the other hand, it also shows that the Dominican elite was prepared to tolerate religious intervention as long as it did not place obstacles on the sacred path to modernity.

171

The dramatic social and economic changes experienced by Dominican society from the end of the nineteenth century on forced the Dominican elite to elaborate new ideas about economic growth. Initially, the peasantry was seen as a major obstacle to the expansion of agricultural production. The large-scale southern sugar plantations provided a model of rapid economic growth that seemed to ensure the country a bright future. Under the Heureaux government, the state did all it could to support the plantation sector, to the point that the government practically became subordinate to private capital.

Although "ideologies of progress" continued to prevail after the death of Lilís and many politicians continued to advocate large-scale plantations as the favored model for agrarian growth, a gradual reappraisal of peasant agriculture took place. Government officials and elite groups appreciated the fact that modernization was impossible without somehow incorporating the rural population. This subtle change could be seen in the policies of the government of Ramón Cáceres, but it became stronger in the 1920s, during the government of Horacio Vásquez. Through legislative measures and practical support, the state tried to stimulate agrarian production and to modernize the rural economy. Government intervention became less repressive, and increasing legislative activity reflected new interest in rural society. State measures were characterized by a new paternalism that was geared toward educating as well as disciplining the rural population.

Nevertheless, the majority of the legislative activity of the various Dominican governments had little influence on rural society. The laws on cattle raising were effective only in the few places where agriculture had already won the struggle against loose cattle, such as in the central part of the Cibao. In other regions, the state was unable to restrict cattle raising. The land laws allowed the plantations to accumulate immense properties but did little to clarify the system of land tenure in the rest of the country.

In spite of this official impotence, legislation reinforced existing tendencies to open the country for the market, promote commercial agriculture, and individualize ownership of landed property. In the long run, the legislation was instrumental in the commodification of land and the incorporation of rural society into the market economy. Many peasants still remember the impact of the 1920 law which decisively changed their agricultural practice. Most did not have money to survey their land and gave part of it to the surveyors in exchange for their services. Others sold their land. If we believe old peasants, some did not even bother to claim all the land they were entitled to and surveyed only the part they needed for their immediate use.

As happened in many other countries, the Dominican state was caught between its desire to transform rural society and its practical inability to do so.[116] Although governmental presence in rural society increased, the government showed remarkable weakness in its attempts to effect social change. This weakness was partly a function of the insolvency and deficient organization of the government apparatus, but, above all, the ineffectiveness of government intervention was due to the economic and political strength of the regional elites.[117] The Dominican state before the Trujillo dictatorship was neither autonomous nor the expression of a single class, and it therefore depended upon continuous accommodation to local circumstances and to the wishes of regional elites. Legislation was filtered through the regional elite, and the government had few possibilities to intervene directly in rural society. Only gradually did it create instruments to circumvent the power of regional elites and establish relationships directly with the peasantry. This was done, above all, by intervening in the organization of peasant production and by implementing programs of agricultural education, both treated in the next chapter.

9

The Struggle for Technology:
Improving the Quality of Dominican Tobacco

> Scientific instruction in agricultural knowledge has been largely
> neglected in Santo Domingo. It has been forgotten that, given the
> spirit of progress and evolution which is characteristic of the modern
> world, everything which does not go ahead, goes backward.
>
> —Emilio Tejera, Minister of Agriculture and Immigration, 1909

As we saw in the preceding chapter, government interventions affected many aspects of rural society. Despite the sometimes arbitrary and ineffective nature of these interventions, the motives underlying them were unequivocal. In fact, Dominican agricultural policies were guided by two objectives. In the first place, agricultural production for the market had to be improved, quantitatively and qualitatively. To reach this goal, peasant production had to be brought under control. The second public policy objective, therefore, was to attain control over the peasantry and end the autonomy of peasant agriculture. Only through official intervention could the peasant producers be drawn out of their agricultural conservatism and technological ignorance. This conviction, an essential part of the modernizing ideology of the period, led to considerable interference in agricultural production and brought peasant producers increasingly in contact with government representatives. This began under the Heureaux government, accelerated in the first two decades on the twentieth century, and reached its apogee with the Vásquez government.

The urge to change agricultural technology was obvious in the tobacco sector. Politicians and state officials were convinced that, in order to strengthen the market position of Dominican tobacco, it was necessary to improve cultivation methods. Both government officials and merchants tried to put an end to what they perceived as the peasantry's backward or archaic cultivation techniques and constantly propounded new methodologies. These efforts were always presented in strictly technological terms, often carefully couched in *campesinista* rhetoric. However, technological innovations and new techniques were by no means socially and politically neutral and could have important consequences for peasant society. Jewsiewicki rightly states: "Every technological innovation is, sooner or later, an intervention which questions . . . a given equilibrium of political forces. To the extent that the technological innovation modifies the life of a society in an important manner, its prestige is appropriated by politics because it is an important factor in the reproduction of the legitimation of power."[1] The different parties involved in Dominican tobacco production held different and often conflicting opinions on agricultural innovation in the tobacco sector. The merchants and the government tried to introduce new methods of production which would increase government control over peasant production and which could strengthen the market position of Dominican tobacco. Since these modernizing efforts were prompted by a desire to increase commercial profits and state income, rather than by real interest in peasant production, they tended to be authoritarian and unfavorable to the direct interests of the majority of the peasant producers. In many cases they even represented a direct attack on the logic of peasant agriculture.

This chapter analyzes government efforts to influence peasant tobacco cultivation. It is important to understand the tools available to the authorities in interfering with the production process and the ways in which cultivators could benefit from new technology or avoid undesirable outside interference. As tobacco is a crop with specific botanical characteristics and consumption patterns, it is necessary to examine some technical aspects of tobacco cultivation. This discussion will establish a basis for describing changes in tobacco technology in the Cibao in the nineteenth and twentieth centuries.

The last part of this chapter explores the social and political context of technological change, arguing that agricultural technology was an important instrument by which outsiders might interfere in the peasant economy. At the same time, then, agricultural technology was an essential issue in the peasantry's struggle for autonomy. An understanding of the continuities and changes in techniques of Dominican tobacco cultivation may provide valuable information about relationships between the peasantry and the government or the market economy.

Changing Methods of Tobacco Cultivation

Tobacco is a crop which is not necessary to human survival. It is normally consumed by inhaling the smoke of the burning tobacco leaf. This particular mode of consumption underlies any discussion of the methods of tobacco cultivation. First and foremost, the taste and the aroma of the burned leaf must be pleasant. When, in the nineteenth and twentieth centuries, the perception of "pleasantness" changed, this had important consequences for the discussion of tobacco cultivation.[2] Second, the "burn" of the tobacco is of crucial importance. Tobacco which burns too quickly or too slowly is of little use to the tobacco industry.

Commercial cultivation of the tobacco plant entails several stages. Seeds are sown; the plant matures; the leaves are picked, dried, fermented, and, finally, sold. While this sequence of stages is invariable, at every stage the cultivator faces a range of alternative methods. He may experiment with certain innovations and abandon them when the results are disappointing. Too, outsiders may try to influence particular stages of the cultivation process.

The first objective of government intervention was to regulate and standardize the cultivation process. Officials and merchants especially tried to stabilize the harvest season. As long as the peasantry continued to wait for the rains before sowing the tobacco, the harvest season could vary between February and June. To diminish the insecurity of the tobacco harvest, pressure on the peasants increased to change their cultivation methods. The use of seedbeds (*semilleros* or, in the local vernacular, *canteros*) was particularly recommended. The advantage of seedbeds was that they decreased dependence on climatological conditions. Tobacco was to be sown in a small patch of (virgin) land, where the seeds could germinate under continuous care and irrigation. When the small tobacco plants (*posturas*) were strong enough, they were transplanted to the field. This innovation limited the long delays caused by faltering rains. From the 1870s on, agronomists and politicians wrote numerous leaflets and newspaper articles trying to convince the peasants that the seedbeds were "the soul of tobacco cultivation" (*el alma de las cosechas*).[3] This technique was presented as an important—probably even the only—instrument for securing the future of the Dominican tobacco sector.[4]

The success of these educational campaigns was very meager until the 1920s. The tobacco growers did not see the advantages of a method which did not raise the price of tobacco but required much extra work. Many elderly peasants in the 1980s still did not seem to understand the advantages of seedbeds: Land was so fertile and "ferocious" that tobacco prospered anyway, and seedbeds were a waste of time. Only during extremely dry years were seed-beds generally used. They allowed the peasant producers to take advantage of climatic differences between valley and mountains and thus to maintain tobacco growing at such times. Cultivators went into the mountainous areas around the Cibao Valley to prepare the small tobacco plants, which they later brought down to be transplanted. In April (*sic*) 1919, for instance, it was reported that "with the advent of the rains, the peasant producers have started, albeit late, to sow tobacco, carrying the plantlets out of the mountains."[5]

The peasantry's skepticism about the advantages of seedbeds was not surprising. Use of seedbeds undeniably was a methodological improvement—in all larger-scale, market-oriented farms it was customarily used—but it clashed with the logic of the peasant economy. Transplanting the tobacco plants almost doubled the growers' work. Nor was the use of seedbeds a guarantee against disaster; hail or heavy rainfall could destroy the seed-beds in one afternoon. Moreover, using seedbeds implied greater emphasis on tobacco monoculture. It required growers to cease intercropping tobacco with food crops such as yucca or corn.[6] Intercropping was the basis of subsistence agriculture. It was also a method of preventing diseases and insect plagues in the tobacco. A tobacco disease such as the "Blue Mold" (*Moho Azul*), which was to wreak so much havoc in modern times, did not exist in the nineteenth century.[7] The same could be said about the worm (*gusano*) that feeds on tobacco leaves and was to become one of the fiercest enemies of tobacco in the twentieth century.[8] It was only in the 1920s, with their increasing integration into the market and with active support by the government, that most tobacco growers came to use seedbeds.

The discussion of tobacco sowing was only an insignificant overture to the fierce debates on harvesting and preparation of the tobacco leaves. It is difficult for outsiders to understand the intensity of this discussion, which filled the pages of newspapers, weeklies, and government reports around the turn of the century. Still, it is not all that surprising that the end stages of the tobacco cultivation process received so much attention. It was at these moments in the productive cycle that the actual commodity "tobacco" took its final shape. These stages immediately preceded transfer of the tobacco to the merchants, and mercantile interest in the product increased accordingly. In addition, these were the most delicate stages of tobacco production, in many respects decisive for the quality of the tobacco. The tobacco leaf had to be picked, dried, and fermented before it could be handled and prepared for smoking. In the nineteenth century, these three stages generally took place on the farms themselves. Here the fate of the tobacco was decided and the struggle for technology was keenest.

Figure 14. Man selecting and piling tobacco in the *rancho*. Photograph by Michiel Baud.

Poor construction of the drying sheds (*ranchos*) was one of the principal objects of merchants' and authorities' complaints.[9] Many growers, because of the work involved in the construction of these sheds, seem to have built them too small. When the tobacco harvest was abundant, the leaves hung too close to each other, resulting in inadequate drying and even putrefaction. This occurred, above all, when a lot of rain was falling during the drying season. A report on the tobacco harvest in 1891 stated that "the excessive rains have caused the putrefaction of two-thirds of the tobacco harvest in the drying sheds."[10] On other occasions, the *ranchos* were not ready in time or had defective roofs.[11] Under such conditions, the peasants had to hang their leaves in the open air, praying that no sudden rainfall would destroy their crop.

The *juntas,* by means of which the peasants banded together to harvest the tobacco crops, were much criticized. Merchants and other urban observers saw this traditional cooperative mechanism as an important cause of negligent, hurried picking of the tobacco, which diminished its quality. It is significant that, even for the sympathetic Bonó, the *junta* was a symbol of the ignorance and inefficiency of peasant production. In his famous 1882 essay on the Dominican working classes, he tried to explain the decreasing acceptance of Dominican tobacco in the international market: "A continuous series of *juntas gratuitas,* by nature lazy, undisciplined, inefficient, and hungry, devoured entire months' worth of food for the cultivator's family in two or three days, and produced a badly classified and even worse packed tobacco, which when it arrived in Europe was very humid and dirty and in this way discredited itself."[12] Such criticism ignored the importance of communal labor for the continuation of peasant tobacco agriculture. Labor exchange was a convenient response to a situation in which money was scarce and food crops were cultivated by everyone and therefore did not represent exchange value. In addition, this system reaffirmed horizontal personal relations and cemented peasant society, which was always liable to break apart into individual households.[13]

It was a sign of the weakness of the Dominican commercial class that the very delicate process of fermentation was done on the farms. Most observers therefore stated that it would be possible to improve the market position of the tobacco only when peasants *and* local merchants changed their ways. Criticism was directed at the merchants as well as the producers. M. C. Grullón wrote in 1918, "The carelessness with which our peasants cultivate the leaf is fully justified by the custom, established by the traders some time ago, of buying the tobacco without previous examination and limiting themselves merely to checking whether the tobacco is putrefied or not."[14]

Figure 15. Inside and outside views of tobacco hanging to dry in a *rancho*.
Photographs by Michiel Baud.

Figure 16. When there is not enough space in the *ranchos*, cultivators may hang surplus tobacco anywhere—here, on the side of their house. Photograph by Michiel Baud.

Many people believed that the intermediaries who had established themselves between the cultivator and the urban merchants were responsible for the problems of the Dominican tobacco sector. As we have seen, the *corredores* and *comines* frequently were blamed for the inferior quality of Dominican tobacco.[15] They were accused of being responsible for deficient methods of tobacco cultivation and preparation. The tobacco growers were pressed to pay their debts to the merchants and tried to sell their tobacco as soon as possible.[16] As a U.S. official indicated, "The *comín* has the product watered by the grower, who with an insane logic easily sees how each pound of water makes a pound of tobacco, and pours it down without measure. It seems as if farmer and *comín* are in competition to injure the tobacco and fool each other."[17]

The exporters also were to blame for this situation. If they continued to export the tobacco to Europe without so much as a look into the *serones*, they could not complain about the low profits and bad reputation of their product. *El Diario* wrote in 1909, "The trade is done with such hurry and so little knowledge that it can be stated that a fourth or fifth part of the exported tobacco is putrefied and badly classified."[18]

Many people argued that the merchants should do the final classification and fermentation before exporting the tobacco. Eventually, that came to pass.[19] The first attempts to increase the responsibilities of the mercantile sector occurred in the 1880s, in response to the new import tax in Germany, which decreased the profitability of exporting inferior tobacco.[20] However, these efforts came to naught because, in the subsequent decades, prices for Dominican tobacco continued to be low. The consolidation and expansion of tobacco as an export product in the early decades of the twentieth century gave new impetus to mercantile interference in the preparation of tobacco. This increased the paternalistic supervision of peasant producers by the mercantile sector.[21] Nevertheless, as late as 1917, a majority of the tobacco was exported in *serones* filled by peasants, without any interference from the merchants.[22]

The problem of improving the quality of Dominican tobacco was as much a social and economic as a technical problem. Most people agreed that the peasants in general knew how to process the tobacco leaves and that much of their negligence was a direct reaction to the low prices and their unfavorable market position. As *El Eco del Pueblo* said in 1882, "The problem is not that our cultivators do not know how to grow the leaf—they have proven the contrary at other times. No, we have to search in a different direction to find the real motive of this neglect, which is, if you like, *conscious*."[23]

The peasants felt that they were not compensated appropriately for better quality tobacco. Most peasants tried to obtain as much tobacco as their *conuco* would yield, irrespective of its quality. They also preferred their own *criollo* tobacco varieties, which gave a high yield but one reputedly of worse quality. Despite severe criticism, they fiercely resisted attempts at eradicating the cultivation of *criollo* tobacco.[24] The governor of Santiago wrote in 1908: "The majority of the cultivators will continue to grow bad quality tobacco, because they know that a piece of land produces a greater quantity of this kind than of good quality tobacco. And they do not understand that the latter, harvested and processed according to the scientific prescriptions, will bring them higher profits."[25] The Cibao tobacco grower José J. Díaz estimated that, whereas a good quality harvest produced two quintales per tarea, most growers in the Cibao aimed at a yield of three to four quintales.[26]

The growers used many tricks to add weight to their loads of tobacco. Experts agreed that only the leaves springing directly from the stem should be picked during the first harvest. Some advocated not picking the other leaves at all; others recommended a second harvest (*retoño*), when the (small) leaves that grew after the first harvest could be picked.[27] Everyone agreed that the leaves of the topsuckers (*bayonetas* or *banderas*) should not be picked because of their bitter taste and low quality. However, most cultivators ignored these suggestions and increased the weight of their tobacco by adding these leaves. For the same reason, they sometimes also included immature leaves (*tabaco nuevo*). These leaves contained a great deal of humidity and therefore could add significantly to the weight of the crop, but they never could be adequately dried and used for smoking.[28] To impart a yellow, quasi-mature color to the leaves, the growers sometimes made a small incision in the stem.[29] Another way to add weight, repeatedly denounced, was to insert stones and branches into the tobacco. More serious, some peasants added too much water. Water had to be sprinkled over the tobacco before it could be manipulated, but too much of it initiated an uncontrollable process of fermentation and putrefaction.

Only in the 1920s did a clear division of responsibilities between cultivator and merchants come into existence. The peasants made a rough classification in the field, while hanging the leaves in the *ranchos*. The merchant took care of the tobacco when it was in piles (*trojas*) fermenting. In their storehouses, the tobacco was cleaned and classified by women laborers and passed through a final fermentation. Then it was packed in bales (*pacas*) made of textile or jute, which gradually replaced the *serones*.[30] Interestingly, the merchants took over not only part of the work of the cultivators, but also the preparation, which traditionally had been done in Europe. This shift came as part of the larger process by which European houses established themselves in the Cibao in the 1920s and started exporting Dominican tobacco directly to consuming countries.

Tobacco technology and the choice of agricultural methods thus produced a continuous debate in Dominican society. For every stage of the production process, improvements were suggested. There is no doubt, however, that the last stage, when the tobacco was prepared for sale, provoked the most debate. Mercantile groups and politicians were involved in this discussion, often in pursuit of quite different goals. Merchants were interested in a cheap tobacco that they could sell easily. Many tobacco experts and politicians sincerely believed in technocratic solutions to the problems of Dominican agriculture and wanted to improve peasant agriculture. They were often frustrated by the historical conspiracy between producers and merchants, which blocked their efforts at agricultural modernization. Their misfortune was that they were first of all intellectuals, who expressed their ideas in written form and therefore could expect to have only a limited impact on actual events. Moreover, the cultivators held onto their own methods of cultivation and resisted outside interference, which ran contrary to their interests.

LEGISLATION AND THE TOBACCO SECTOR

Many people expressed strong opinions on tobacco technology, but it was the government that somehow had to formulate and regulate their implementation. Despite all its weakness and inefficiency, the state became the principal instigator of technological change and the vehicle of increased pressure on peasant society. It was not always that officials chose to play such roles, but rather it was as if all of Dominican society expected them to do so. Many members of the mercantile class also held political positions and therefore had a double interest in improving the market position of Dominican products. Another incentive for state intervention in the tobacco sector was its financial dependence on export agriculture. Until the 1920s, however, a systematic agrarian policy was absent, and, especially in its practical aspects, public policy was extremely erratic. Ideas and suggestions for improving the quality of Dominican tobacco were abundant, but most remained confined to paper; when laws were decreed, they often were ineffective. To be sure, the various ideas are interesting in themselves, as they reveal the ambiguities and paradoxes inherent in formulating a consistent and effective agrarian policy in a poor country with a weak governmental structure.

The first concrete government measure to improve Dominican agricultural production was to establish rewards and premiums for outstanding agricultural performance. Under the active González government (1873–75), free tools were promised to farmers who cultivated a certain number of plants.[31] In 1903, honorary awards were given to exemplary farmers.[32] It is not surprising that, in the highly stratified society of this period, large landowners and other members of the rural elite took most advantage of the premiums. These measures were probably meant to have a stimulating effect on agricultural production, but sometimes it is difficult to avoid the impression that they were designed primarily to favor the rural elite. They enabled the latter to reconfirm its social and political hegemony in the countryside and resulted in a redistribution of state income in favor of the rural elite.

The state tended to use somewhat more force and authority in its efforts to influence the tobacco-producing peasantry. Occasional paternalistic expressions of support and sympathy for the producing class were often accompanied by compulsive measures. The government's peasant-oriented policy originated in the tobacco crisis of the 1880s. The carelessness and the drudgery (*rutina*) of peasant production generally were seen as the principal reason for the low prices and faltering demand on the world market. The solution to the crisis was sought in the transformation of the peasant sector.

Many observers expected that the new German tariffs and low prices would be enough to bring about a change for the better. Just the opposite happened. Merchants were anxious to maintain their profit rates and paid lower prices to the producers. These responded by paying even less attention to their tobacco and by withdrawing labor from tobacco agriculture. They sold their tobacco as quickly as possible, with the result that their tobacco contained more un-fermented and humid leaves and received even lower prices in Germany.

The government realized that Dominican tobacco could remain competitive only if its quality improved. As early as 1880, a decree had been issued referring to the "weight, conditions, and inspection of tobacco loads" and specifying proper conditions for tobacco exportation.[33] In the same year, so-called Agriculture Councils (*Juntas de Agricultura*) were created to supervise this decree. They were, in general, intended to improve the cultivation and commercialization of Dominican export crops.[34] In the following decades, numerous national and municipal decrees were issued in attempts to control the tobacco trade and prevent tobacco from being shipped prematurely.[35] They usually implied prohibitions on shipping tobacco before a certain date. The problem with these measures was that cultivation was still so dependent on the climate that it was very difficult to design straightforward laws. In 1888, tobacco which was exported before a certain date was burdened with an extra tax. Each quintal exported was taxed 1.50 pesos from March to June but only 0.75 the rest of the year.[36] Within two years, the law was withdrawn at the request of the merchants, "because the tobacco is liable to loss of quality when it is stacked in the storehouse awaiting its shipment in July."[37] Later measures encountered similar difficulties related to the irregularity of the tobacco harvest and the preparation methods.[38] In 1905, after the failure of one of these later versions, which again prohibited the export of tobacco before a certain date, the *Revista de Agricultura* commented: "In this way these measures have been discredited and are going out of use, although they stay on the books."[39]

In 1894, the Santiago municipal government issued a resolution requiring that tobacco be bought and sold under rigidly defined conditions.[40] This resolution probably formed part of a discussion in the Dominican Congress about a decree concerning "sowing, cultivation, and exportation of tobacco, coffee, and cocoa." This discussion perfectly exemplifies the problems of government intervention. Although the decree dealt with the three "traditional" export crops, the organization of the tobacco sector was the focus of discussion.

Much attention was devoted specifically to the need for a standardization (*unificación*) of tobacco seeds. The unreliability and diversity of Dominican tobacco was seen as the sector's main problem. It was argued that only government-enforced cultivation of one type of tobacco could insure the market position of Dominican tobacco. The National Congress devoted three sessions to this topic.[41] Deputy Román was the fiercest defender of the proposed decree, which he saw as "the only way to save" the tobacco sector. Citing the European tendency to protect its markets and the Dominican dependence on the German market, he concluded that "the only way to prevent the ruin of our tobacco is to use the seed that is best for exports." Arguing that the Sumatra and Cuba seeds were not suited to the Dominican environment, he proposed designating the so-called *punta de lanza* variety as the favored seed, because "nowhere does this tobacco give better results than here."[42]

A dissenting voice was that of Deputy Pierret, who shared Román's concern but argued in favor of the superior Sumatra and Cuba seeds. If these seeds were not the ones selected by the government, he did not see the utility of any unification at all. If the "punta de lanza" variety were made the only legal seed, the use of even better seeds would be prohibited—an absurd situation. He warned that the cultivators would not obey such a decree anyway. Dominican tobacco does not have a bad reputation, he stated, "because of a diversity of types of tobacco, but because of bad cultivation methods." Another deputy supported Pierret, expressing great doubt about the capacity of the municipal government to implement the decree, "poor" as they generally were.

The deputy representing the Cibao, Isaias Franco, raised a more principled, "liberal" point, when he questioned the legitimacy of state intervention. Expressing his endorsement of the idea "that governments can and must support the cultivators, offering premiums to those who obtain excellent products by their dedication," he severely criticized the decree's authoritarianism with regard to the agricultural practice of the peasantry: "It amounts to *forcing* the cultivator to grow only one variety of tobacco." This was, in his eyes, "a direct attack on the freedom that everyone has, and must have, to cultivate the crop which suits him best." Moreover, force was unnecessary, because if better tobacco were rewarded with a higher price, the cultivators would not hesitate to improve their methods: "There is not one cultivator who is not going to grow the best seed and who is not going to treat his tobacco well, when he sees that the traders pay a fair price after having weighed the tobacco honestly." Franco took this matter so seriously that, when several municipal commissions in the Cibao began implementing the decree, he felt he could no longer represent his province and resigned.

The discussion pointed up the problems of state intervention, and, in the end, the law enacted was only a watered-down version of the original proposal.[43] Virtually nothing remained concerning unification of the seed. It was left to every individual municipality to decide which seed suited it best. The tone of the law was still severe and the sanctions rigorous—if the tobacco was not in "perfect condition," it would be burned. The principal result of the law was an increase in the power of municipalities in their confrontations with the cultivators.

The *Law on Crops* (*Ley de Frutos*), as the decree was generally called, had only limited success. Pedro Ma. Archambault in 1901 wanted it strengthened, arguing that its results had been positive in Santiago. However, he also indicated that it had failed in other places and needed to be reinstated.[44] After Isaias Franco had explained his ideas on this matter once again,[45] Mario F. Cabral made clear why the Santiago merchants were so worried about the law. He argued that it paralyzed the city's mercantile activity, while in other places such as La Vega and Moca "they laugh at the law, buying tobacco as usual: in a disorderly fashion." He added bitterly, "The current law gives good, very good, results—so good that these days all the tobacco and cocoa which should have been sold here are being taken to Moca and La Vega, where there are no such laws to force the cultivators to do twice as much work *for the same price.*"[46]

We have treated this discussion in some detail because it clearly illustrates the ideological and practical dilemmas surrounding state intervention in agriculture in this period. The absence of technological consensus, the government's inefficiency and poverty, ambivalent and conflicting ideologies, and, not least of all, the obstinate realities of recalcitrant peasants, uncooperative merchants, and regional competition—all these conspired to bring about the failure of state intervention and regulation of the tobacco sector.

AGRICULTURAL SUPERVISION

Many people gradually became aware that it would be possible to change tobacco cultivation methods only when the daily practice of the producers was taken into account. The first decades of the twentieth century saw the emergence of a more active and efficient state policy, based on better comprehension of peasant agriculture. The emergence of this policy was accompanied by increasing enclosure of the peasantry in the 1920s and eventually led to a more dominant state presence in the countryside and more successful state intervention in agricultural technology.

Public instruction was an obvious way of influencing the peasantry. Despite the fact that a large majority of the rural population was illiterate, most of this agricultural instruction was presented in written form. Reflecting a wish on the part of the Dominican elite for agricultural modernization, articles on tobacco cultivation filled the Dominican press around the turn of the century. The urgency of this need to educate the agricultural producers resulted in the establishment in 1905 of the *Revista de Agricultura,* the first government publication of this kind.[47] Government activities received a further boost when, in 1909, a Ministry of Agriculture and Immigration was established.[48] This marked the inception of more active public efforts to accomplish agricultural improvements.

In the case of tobacco cultivation, governments at various levels attempted to improve technological instruction by appointing expert agronomists. Cuban advisors had been brought to the area twice in the late nineteenth century, but results had been negligible because the Cubans were more interested in establishing their own farms than in instructing the Dominican cultivators.[49] State instruction took a new turn with the appointment of Albert Michels as undersecretary of agriculture (*subdirector general de agricultura*) in 1911. This German agronomer became responsible for the improvement of Dominican tobacco. He took charge of an experimental station (*campo de experimentación*) of thirty-six tareas, which was rented for two years from a local landowner in Jacagua (El Ingenio). This experimental farm had several goals: to convince the Dominican cultivators of the advantages of technological modernization and "scientific" cultivation; to produce seedlings and seed for interested peasants; and to experiment with new seeds and techniques. The ultimate goal was "to obtain a special variety of tobacco" which could compete with similar varieties in other countries.[50]

It did not take long for Michels to find out that state farming was not all that easy. It was almost impossible to find laborers to work on the farm for a monthly wage of 12 pesos. It was just as difficult to find people who could execute the more demanding tasks. Michels had a hard time finding people and animals to plow his land and at long last had to hire a Spaniard.[51] The project also suffered from the previous failures of state intervention. Michels noted a "pessimism" among the cultivators as the result of the low prices and "the efforts made before by people without the necessary competence, who incurred expenses without an increase in results." He perceived, as another problem, that tobacco cultivation was for the most part "in the hands of people with little knowledge and even less financial means."[52]

In the beginning of 1912, Michels' just-transplanted seedlings were subjected to "a terrible drought" (*una seca tremenda*) and had to be watered every day, at a cost of 30 pesos a week, while the construction of the *ranchos* had not even started.[53] We do not have the farm's production figures, but they must have been disappointing.[54] In October 1912, plans were published to introduce Puerto Rican seeds, which promised good results. Thus, it was added somewhat meekly, the experimental farm had not been a failure after all, as some people had suggested.[55] Michels remained active in the Cibao until the 1930s, but this project died a silent death after the assassination of President Ramón Cáceres in November 1912. The tobacco merchant Ramón Asensio diagnosed dryly: "I think it is fair to say that Dr. Michels is more a theoretical than a practical man."[56]

The U.S. occupation reactivated state intervention in tobacco cultivation. A Puerto Rican (or Cuban?) expert, José L. Amargos, was appointed as "instructor assigned to tobacco" (*instructor encargado del tabaco*) in 1917. He resumed the well-known methods of instruction, writing pamphlets and articles, organizing meetings, and traveling around telling farmers what to do. It may be that he reflected a more general neocolonialist U.S. attitude.[57] In any case, he took a very authoritarian posture and fulminated continuously against Dominican customs. His articles were interspersed with exclamation marks and underlinings.[58] His impatient condemnation of local practices must have prevented Amargos from having much success. This was clear in the case of the *ranchos*. Time and again he raged against the open ranchos used in the Cibao but never was successful in his endeavor to have them replaced by closed barns.

In 1920, the Military Government committed itself to buy the entire tobacco harvest. In consequence, government officials became more interested in the tobacco sector and in the concrete practice of peasant agriculture. Again they tried to increase control over the production, processing, and marketing of tobacco. The produce inspectors (*inspectores del fruto*) who had been installed under the Cáceres regime functioned very unsatisfactorily. In Santiago, only two officials were available to check all the incoming tobacco, and most of the tobacco never was inspected at all. In addition, inspection was a great nuisance to the peasants. They often had to wait long days to obtain their certificate, and when they had the bad luck to be ordered to open their serones, they had to repack the tobacco in the middle of the street.[59]

Therefore, in 1920 a new law was enacted which ordered the cultivators to classify their tobacco before they were allowed to sell it. This law, which was reissued in 1924, was formulated in very authoritarian terms and gave detailed rules for the processing and classification of the tobacco. Cultivators and merchants who did not obey the law would be fined fifty pesos, and their tobacco would be seized. The last paragraph read: "Every government inspector who is rightfully appointed can inspect the tobacco at any time, give a fine for violation of this order, and confiscate the tobacco when it does not meet the required conditions."[60]

When this law was effectively enforced, it elicited much protest. The focus was not so much the assault on peasant autonomy as the impact on urban employment. Many women who had found work in the storehouses classifying tobacco lost jobs as a result of the new law. Moreover, the classification done on the farms was deficient, and the cultivator was not paid for his extra effort. The most important reason for the rejection of this law, however, must have been that it affected not only the producers, but also the mercantile class in the Cibao. As we have seen, the merchants had no use for government inspections. They looked to the government for help but wanted no restrictions on their commercial freedom. Repeal of the law was repeatedly requested, but to no avail.[61] This was the period when military officials were in conflict with the Cibao elite over a land tax, and they had no intention of budging.

State intervention was more successful when it coincided with the wishes of the tobacco growers. In 1920, the Department of Agriculture rented ninety-six tareas near Santiago, exclusively for the cultivation of tobacco plants to be distributed in the region.[62] The project had two goals: to convince the peasantry to use semilleros, and to foster cultivation of a uniform type of tobacco throughout the region. Preparation of seedbeds in different areas of the Cibao diminished the risk that a harvest might completely fail. Free distribution of plantlets grown on state farms turned out to be an effective instrument to influence peasant agriculture. The peasants reacted favorably to this initiative, and thereafter the distribution of *posturas* remained a common practice in the Cibao.[63] Together with other changes occurring in the peasant economy, these state efforts tipped the balance in favor of the use of seedbeds. This probably first happened in the central Cibao as a consequence of the increasing scarcity of land. In the Villa González region, use of seedbeds began more recently. It is not clear whether some peasants prepared seedbeds for commercial purposes.

Under the government of Horacio Vásquez, government interest in the agricultural sector intensified. Improved infrastructure also facilitated government intervention in the Cibao. The first initiatives of the Vásquez government were geared toward implementing extant laws and institutions. Inspection of tobacco became more effective. Badly fermented tobacco was turned down or sometimes confiscated. The Department of Agriculture wrote a letter to its inspectors in May 1927, emphasizing that tobacco inspection had to be a serious activity. It was even suggested that police support would be invoked when necessary: "We cannot accept disobedience, nor can we be weak in the carrying out of our duty."[64] Some two months later, Minister of Agriculture César Pérez reiterated that he wanted "the most complete control of the movement of tobacco."[65] This effort at control was not directed exclusively at the peasant producers; small-scale traders who took the tobacco from the countryside to the urban merchants were also targets.[66]

In other areas of technical control and assistance, too, new energy was displayed. Government-controlled seedbeds were extended, more seed was distributed (the *amarillo parado* variety was now selected); and again premiums were established.[67] For the first time, systematic attention was paid to use of the plow.[68] Here we see a new effort to implement an unified agricultural policy dealing with both cultivation and marketing of the tobacco.

Luis Carballo and a New Tobacco Policy

In February 1914, a young Costa Rican agronomer, newly hired by the prestigious Santiago firm, Manuel de Js. Tavárez y Compañía, arrived in Santiago. His name was Luis Carballo Romero, and he was to have a decisive influence on the Cibao tobacco sector in the years to come.[69] He integrated easily into the Santiago elite and became the best-known tobacco expert of the region. As general secretary of the Chamber of Commerce of Santiago, he symbolized a new era of active government intervention. He became a key figure in the implementation of agricultural policies that emerged during the Vásquez government.[70] Especially after 1926, when the presidency of Horacio Vásquez was consolidated, state intervention acquired a new, more efficient face.[71] Results of the tobacco campaigns were published in monthly newsletter (*informes*). Seed distribution and maintenance of public seedbeds became accepted activities, and many of the technological innovations proposed in preceding decades came to seem merely commonsensical.

A man like Luis Carballo epitomized the new contradictions of state intervention in rural society. On the one hand, he evinced curiosity about peasant agriculture and comprehension of its underlying logic—attitudes unthinkable only a few decades earlier. Such interest was principally the result of a technocratic attitude that sought the concrete knowledge necessary for technological change.[72] More than his predecessors, Carballo related his technical advice to the social and economic structure of the countryside. He did not try to solve the technical problems of tobacco production in isolation, but understood that they were related to food production and other elements of the peasant economy.[73] On the other hand, however, the effects of Carballo's activities showed how a better understanding of rural society and its associated system of agricultural production could be instrumental in restricting peasant autonomy and intensifying government intervention. Public policy thus became better adapted to the logic and methods of peasant production, and this enabled the government to obtain a greater hold on rural society.[74]

The most sweeping change in rural policy brought about by Carballo was acceptance of the fact that tobacco was a peasant crop. He was intolerant of easy armchair denunciations of the indolent peasants and believed that agricultural improvements would be possible only when they were adapted to the logic of peasant production. In his agricultural advice he took the daily reality of peasant production as a starting point. Two facts—that "the tobacco harvest is the only one which moves our commerce," and that it was produced by smallholders—gave agricultural experts the responsibility of adapting their technological suggestions to the needs of the peasantry.[75] Carballo's agricultural activities therefore were designed to be immediately useful to the peasantry. Under his direction, free distribution of plantlets was extended, financed partly by the mercantile sector.[76] Carballo directed a series of intensive "tobacco campaigns" aimed at improving tobacco cultivation. The campaigns started in 1928 under the Vásquez administration and were continued under the Trujillo regime.

The first of these campaigns was announced in September 1927.[77] The press lent its wholehearted support to the initiative, and some enthusiasm also existed in mercantile circles.[78] An important goal of these campaigns was to begin the tobacco season earlier. After conducting an investigation of the rainfall in the Cibao, Carballo had concluded that the tobacco season had to begin some two months earlier. The custom among the cultivators had been to transplant the small tobacco plants in January or February. Carballo argued in favor of transplanting the tobacco in November and tried to convince the cultivators that "our sermons for early sowing are based on our extensive experience." He showed the cultivators that this change did not cause more work and that it would diminish the dangers of the droughts that occasionally occurred in February and March.[79] He also emphasized that the quality of tobacco would improve when it was sown early. His admonitions began in 1928,[80] but they became more insistent in the 1930s. Carballo himself reported initial "strong resistance among the cultivators," but by 1931, according to his report, this had turned into "great enthusiasm."[81]

A second focus of the campaigns was the condition of the tobacco *ranchos*. Inadequate *ranchos* were seen as a principal cause of the low quality of the Dominican tobacco. Carballo was convinced that it would be impossible to improve the quality of Dominican tobacco if the tobacco could not dry properly: "All work done to increase tobacco production and to improve its quality is in vain, given the unquestionable fact that most cultivators are not able to build *ranchos* adequate to a large harvest without financial help."[82] Carballo therefore took charge of securing cheap credit that would allow the tobacco cultivators to build more and better *ranchos*. In the early months of 1928, credit assistance was offered to cultivators who planted more than twenty-five tareas. They could construct a *rancho* with a government loan that they could pay back after the harvest. In March, 528 cultivators had received such a loan. The railroad companies, which were frequently accused of being too expensive, joined the action and transported the material for the *ranchos* free of charge.[83] Two months later, the credit program seemed to have become the latest in a long list of failures. Tobacco prices remained low, and rumor had it that many cultivators could not pay back their debt.[84] The final report of the campaign was not too bad, however. Carballo even called the campaign "a resounding triumph": 81.5 percent of the cultivators had paid their debts without problems, 9 percent had been slow, and only 8.6 percent of the debts had been collected "by juridical means." According to Carballo, the conclusion could be drawn that "our agriculturalists are ready to receive small short-term loans."[85]

The turbulent years 1929 and 1930 did not allow for any government programs, but in 1931 the credit system was revitalized. The new Trujillo regime dedicated twenty thousand pesos to financing tobacco *ranchos*. Everyone was now eligible for such a loan, and the required minimum of twenty-five tareas of cultivated land was canceled. This time 1,015 cultivators received a loan, while the amount of land involved increased only from 21,878 to 26,767 tareas. Many of the loans were very small, often less than ten pesos.[86]

Carballo's technocratic attitude is demonstrated by his flat refusal to use the credit for political purposes, as had been suggested when the results of the 1928 credit program were evaluated. A local official wrote, "I have received information that the majority of [the remaining debtors] are followers of Horacio Vásquez and that a large part of them are not able to pay at this moment." He suggested taking political advantage of this situation: "I consider that, whatever their political affiliation, this is a good occasion to attract those who cannot pay by remitting their debts in the name of the government."[87] A similar proposal in 1931 in relation to problems in Janico also met with Carballo's disapproval, because forgiving debts in this manner would imperil future credit programs.

Carballo believed that the state had to teach peasant producers the value of money and the logic of the market economy. In the 1930–31 harvest, an interest of 1 percent was charged to pay for "inspection costs," but also "to accustom the peasant producers to the idea that it takes money to make money."[88] When, a few months later, problems arose about the repayment of loans taken out by a number of cultivators in Janico, he wrote privately to Minister of Agriculture César Tolentino: "It is necessary to accustom the cultivator to making sacrifices in order to live up to his commitments; that is the education that I am giving them right now. No one gets one day of respite, and I assure you that not one of the persons who up to this moment have paid, have paid with money resulting from the sale of tobacco; everyone is selling animals, etc., and they have even sold land, because when we act weakly, the peasant becomes accustomed to seeing his duties as unimportant things."[89] In practice, his attitude was more pragmatic. Carballo acknowledged that low tobacco prices were an important reason for the financial problems of the peasantry. He wrote, "Tobacco has become a thing of charlatans (*charlatanería*), and for the first time I understand that the merchants are ABUSING the poor peasants, because they are paying only 1.50 pesos for a quintal of the very best tobacco."[90] He therefore in the same letter proposed leniency when the cultivators really could not repay their loans. This alternation between harsh paternalism and sympathy toward the cultivators showed a basic ambivalence in the attitudes of these new technocrats. Agricultural experts such as Luis Carballo and Emilio Almonte had to maintain a difficult equilibrium between the interests of the cultivators and those of the merchants. These men's activities in favor of the growers often strained their relations with the merchants. In 1928, Carballo had stated that it was necessary to liberate the cultivators from "the clutches of the speculators."[91] In his monthly reports he often rejoiced that the cultivators held firm and refused to sell their tobacco for unfavorable prices.[92] It may be that this prudent, technocratic identification with the cultivators' interests was the greatest change in agrarian policies during this period.

Gradually a complete infrastructure, primarily meant to support the tobacco sector, came into being. Although we must doubt that the practical influence of this government support was always great, the new attention to the peasant producers was not insignificant. Modernization and civilization continued to be the two principal goals, but the methods gradually changed. Through its influence in the bureaucracy and the press, a new group of public officials and technicians was able to spread a more realistic, less prejudiced image of the peasantry. These people tried to improve the quality of

Dominican tobacco by strengthening the position of the tobacco growers. They also tried to improve the latter's market position by giving them detailed information about the market. It is enough to compare the 1919 booklet of M. C. Grullón, written entirely from a merchant's point of view, with the correspondence of Luis Carballo or Emilio Almonte in the late 1920s to become immediately aware of this difference. It is also reflected in the writings of Amado Bidó and Ramón Emilio Jiménez, which present a romantic "folkloristic" image of the peasantry.[93]

We can say little about the reaction of the peasant producers. The written sources suggest that they took a fairly pragmatic attitude toward the increasing state presence. My fieldwork in the Villa González region did not yield much information about the subject of technological change, but it seems evident that government intervention played an important role in the differentiation within peasant society. The more market-oriented cultivators took advantage of the opportunities presented by state support. However, as we have seen in the case of the credit program, this could turn against them when they could not repay their loans. Most cultivators seem simply to have ignored the activities of the state. It may be significant that, in their stories about cultivation methods in the past, the activities of agronomers or state officials play no role at all. They are well aware of the technological changes within agricultural production but do not give much credit to state intervention. They tend to emphasize their own experiments and innovations. The best example is the selection and improvement of seeds. Although I do not know if we can speak of a "national sport" such as that identified by Richards in connection with continuous experimentation with rice seeds in Sierra Leone,[94] it is undeniable that the Dominican cultivators demonstrated great interest in seed improvement. This interest has led to the development of specific Dominican seeds, some, such as the famous Chago Díaz variety, named after their inventors. Usually the cultivators experimented on a small scale, trying to improve their seeds over the years. In the Villa González region, a number of peasants prided themselves on the advantages of their own varieties of tobacco: greater resistance to drought, bigger leaves, better smoking characteristics, etc. This pride in variety and in the specific qualities of a given tobacco stands in glaring contrast to the state officials' and merchants' wish for uniformity and predictability.

State intervention was directed at two principal goals. First, it tried to introduce new techniques and methods of cultivation via technological instruction of the peasant producers. Second, it tried to increase political control over rural society and to restrict the autonomy and legal space of the peasant producers. The problem was that the Dominican state did not have the power or the money to perform this role effectively. State intervention in peasant agriculture therefore had to rely on persuasion, instruction, and legislation, which often were ineffective. A clear inconsistency existed between the weakness of the state and the authoritarian and centralist nature of most legislation. The result was that many laws went unenforced.

The ineffectiveness of government policy was the consequence of a complete ignorance of, or disdain for, the logic of peasant agriculture. This attitude led to the neglect of peasant expertise and local knowledge. State intervention became more successful when the rural situation and the logic of peasant production were taken as points of departure for policy formulation. This happened in the late 1920s, when local politicians and merchants with greater comprehension of rural society in the Cibao took charge of agricultural instruction. With the cynical logic of social change, it was precisely this better understanding of peasant society that facilitated the eventual control and transformation of peasant society.[95]

The importance of local knowledge was clearly demonstrated by the failure of some experiments with large-scale tobacco agriculture in the Cibao. The farm established in 1889 by the Dutchman W. C. van Veen is a good example. Despite huge capital investments and modern management, the project failed dramatically. The cases of the Cuban tobacco experts and the German agronomer Michels in the twentieth century were similar failures. Michels tried to establish state farms in 1911–12 and in 1933, but neither attempt succeeded. His correspondence is full of lamentations concerning the disasters befalling his tobacco. When his harvest in Mao failed again, he concluded, "It is my opinion—and the opinion of many people—that this region is not suited for the cultivation of tobacco."[96] But, of course, tobacco could be cultivated in Mao. It was only necessary to adapt to local circumstances and to choose appropriate methods. Cibao landowners such as M. C. Grullón, José J. Díaz and Zoilo García proved that tobacco growing could be done very well on a larger scale. Their knowledge of local ecological and socioeconomic conditions enabled them to increase and improve their tobacco production. These local entrepreneurs managed successful farms for a long time.

The attitude of the peasant producers themselves is difficult to ascertain directly. The struggle for technology is best understood by way of its practical outcome. Many technological changes were eventually adopted. Seedbeds became an accepted part of tobacco cultivation, new tobacco varieties came into use, the harvest season was pushed forward, and the fermentation and classification of the tobacco were improved. Impressive indeed. But in many other cases, government pressure failed completely. Closed *ranchos* never were adopted in the Cibao; the making of *sartas* with palm leaves instead of thread continues to this day; and intercropping tobacco with food crops always has remained a favorite system of many peasants.

When doing my first fieldwork in the Dominican tobacco region, an old peasant showed me a small knife which long ago he had used to cut the tobacco leaves instead of breaking them off, as has always been, and still is, the custom. He told me that "formerly" experts and merchants had insisted on the use of such a knife. Tobacco Institute personnel and I could hardly believe what he told me, because we never had seen any indication of such a way of harvesting. However, in the following weeks other peasants confirmed his story, saying that in the 1920s they had had to harvest the tobacco leaves with a knife. Much later I even found written evidence of this long-forgotten practice.[97] This example, in itself insignificant, shows the erratic and uneven character of technological change. Innovations were introduced and abandoned in a complicated trial-and-error process, in which many different parties and interests were involved. Technological innovation was clearly a matter of "give and take," depending on its effectiveness and on the balance of power between producer and the state. It is therefore important to be aware not only of methodological innovations and improvements, but also of possible technical regression and loss of technological sophistication.

We have no proof of open defiance of the authorities by the peasants, but reading the reports of frustrated agronomic instructors and state officials, we must assume that the Dominican peasants skillfully employed the ultimate weapon of the weak: ignoring the authorities or, in the words of Eric Hobsbawm, "working the system to their minimum disadvantage."[98] It is significant that many observers emphasized that peasant resistance to technological innovation was a premeditated, conscious reaction. It was not their *rutina* or indolence that induced the peasantry to maintain a distance from labor-intensive innovations, but the unsuitability of these innovations to the peasant economy in a deteriorating market situation.

Hidden behind the screen of an ongoing discussion of the quality of Dominican tobacco, the peasants themselves experimented and innovated. Unfortunately, we know little about the extent and the course of peasant experimentation. Often it was hardly recognizable as independent action, in the complicated relation between external instruction and agricultural practice. Present-day peasant agriculture in the Cibao suggests that many peasants have been experimenting continuously with methods developed by themselves or offered to them by outsiders. Today, if one listens to the heated discussions among peasant producers concerning the best moments to fertilize, irrigate, and harvest their tobacco; and if one sees the continuous adaptations made by peasants and the small but significant differences among individual cultivators, it is impossible to doubt that this spirit of innovation and this discussion also existed in an earlier period.

It is typical of the structure of the tobacco sector and the diverging interests of various actors within it that the mercantile sector always has been very critical of these experiments. The merchants wanted a uniform, reliable leaf and were not at all pleased with the diversity of Dominican tobacco production, which resulted from peasant experimentation. This attitude highlights the subjective and political element in the discussions of technological innovation. It was not technological improvement as such that was at stake; rather, it was a question of *who* exactly was to effect *what* kind of innovation. The intensity of the discussion of technological improvement can be understood only by taking into account the dependence of the Dominican elite on the export of agricultural commodities. Against the decentralized and autonomous nature of peasant production, simply called *la anarquía* by *La Información* in 1926,[99] stood the wish of the merchants and the state to obtain a uniform, standardized tobacco leaf for the international market.

PART IV

Conclusion

10

The Cibao Peasantry in Comparative Perspective

Twentieth-century discussions of peasant production have gravitated toward two related themes: the viability of peasant production in a period when capitalist relations of production have reached the farthest corners of the globe, and the dynamics of peasant societies, their potential for sustained growth, and their capacity to alleviate the problems of poverty in the so-called Third World.[1]

The underlying question is whether small-scale peasant agriculture has a place in the modern world. This question has provoked widely differing answers. From the debate between Narodniks and Bolsheviks in pre-Revolutionary Russia to contemporary differences between *campesinistas* and *descampesinistas* in Mexico, advocates and opponents of peasant production have engaged in heated debates.[2] As we have seen, such discussions also took place in the Dominican Republic. This last chapter attempts to see if the history of the Cibao tobacco sector can make a useful contribution to this debate.

THE RESILIENCE OF PEASANT PRODUCTION IN THE CIBAO

The Cibao tobacco sector shows clearly how a regional export sector can be based on peasant agriculture. The production of thousands of smallholding families linked the region to the world economy and allowed regional elite groups to accumulate substantial wealth. Although this form of small-scale production for the world market is often presented as a temporary deviation of the "normal" pattern, in many other regions in the world, too, peasant production for the market developed and persisted over long periods. In Latin America, the comparison with Costa Rican and Colombian coffee production is obvious. These cases have become famous because of the place they have acquired in the nationalist ideology in these countries. In addition, they have been subjects of extensive historical research. Latin American history contains many more examples of small-scale production for the world market that have not yet been thoroughly investigated. To give only one example, we are still awaiting the first monograph on the very important tobacco sector in Bahia, Brazil, and on peasant production in the Andes, Mexico, and Central America.

In the cases we know, we find evidence that the opposition between peasant producers and the market is less clear-cut than is often assumed. Many peasant producers seem to have seen the market as a support for their subsistence economy, rather than as a threat. The tobacco growers in the Cibao had been accustomed to the market and the money economy since the colonial period, and it was never necessary to force them to produce for the market. On the contrary, they often actively sought access to the market and integrated the production of tobacco with their subsistence agriculture. Although in Africa the presence of the market is a more recent phenomenon, the history of African peasant production shows some interesting similarities with the Cibao situation. In many African countries, governments tried to "break open" peasant societies for the market in the late nineteenth and twentieth century. The rural population was often subjected to forced cash crop production and compulsory labor in order to produce commodities for the (colonial) market. However, many peasantries did not have to be forced. They eagerly accepted the opportunities of the world market in the second half of the nineteenth century. They used the advantages of household production, traditional mechanisms of labor recruiting, and access to land to bring about a rapid increase in cultivation of cash crops for the (international) market. Ranger and others have emphasized that, despite a hostile ideological climate and an intervening (colonial) state, autonomous peasant agriculture often increased dramatically.[3] Large-scale agriculture could often not compete with the small producers. Export agriculture sometimes even became the monopoly of smallholders.[4] Even in the areas of Africa where settler agriculture was predominant, peasantries were so successful that they competed with settler production and became a threat to the social status quo. This led to the paradoxical situation that in some British colonies in Africa the government *prohibited* cash crop production by peasant producers or excluded them from technological innovations.[5]

On the other hand, we must not close our eyes to the changes taking place within peasant society. The resilience of small-scale tobacco production in the Cibao did not mean that peasant society was immune to change. It is easy to see that rural society in the Cibao underwent profound changes in the period 1870–1930. The expansion of capitalist relations of production and the increasing dominance of the market were reflected in the organization of peasant tobacco production. Work that had been done by family or community labor started to have a price; production techniques which were adapted to the use of family labor came under fire from merchants and state officials; and the peasantry's autonomy eroded under influence of new market relations. The most obvious result of the changing relations of production was an increasing differentiation within the peasantry. Some peasant producers succeeded in taking advantage of these developments and accumulated capital or acquired secure land titles. Others experienced upward social mobility in the cities. Less fortunate members of peasant society, often belonging to the same families, were caught in a downward spiral from which they could not escape. They gradually lost control over the means of agricultural production and could only continue to exist as agricultural producers by relegating part of their produce to landowners or merchants. They ended up as sharecroppers or landless laborers. A number of cultivators managed to continue the traditional slash-and-burn agriculture by migrating to the agricultural frontier in the mountains.

This stratification within peasant society is a complicated historical process only touched upon lightly in this book. However, the cases of the Cibao tobacco growers and the Colombian and Costa Rican coffee producers point to a factor that is often neglected: the ethnic homogeneity of the population. That is, peasants and the elite belonged to the same ethnic group. For one thing, this ethnic homogeneity was the basis of nationalist romanticizing of the peasantry, so characteristic of political elites in these three countries.[6] On a more practical level, the homogeneity seems to have strengthened vertical patriarchal relations between the social classes and in this way tended to mitigate the ugliest consequences of the social stratification taking place in these societies. This is not to say that there was no social inequality, but this factor gave the peasants more space for negotiation and to some degree facilitated upward mobility. It may also explain the absence of peasant rebellion in times of economic distress. The ethnic factor in the historical analysis of class relations, especially in a rural setting, deserves future study.

One of the most important conclusions of this book is that the Cibao peasantry, despite its long history of market production, succeeded in maintaining a high degree of autonomy and independence. The Cibao tobacco growers utilized a variety of instruments to protect themselves from unfavorable outside interference. They used their market participation as a means to safeguard their peasant agriculture and to maintain their independence. Although it can be argued that this participation in the market implanted germs that eventually would lead to the eradication of their independence in the second half of the twentieth century, this strategy was the underlying cause of the resilience of the tobacco-growing peasantry in the period 1870–1930. It is possible to understand the continuing peasant production in the region only if this continuity is interpreted as a result of adaptations within peasant society in the context of its changing place in wider society. The nature and success of this adaptive strategy on the part of the tobacco-growing peasantry in the Cibao depended on various factors.

We must start with the *crop* itself. Many observers have commented that tobacco is a crop favoring small-scale production and an equitable distribution of material prosperity. They stress the constant attention required by the plant during the period that it is in the field. The labor needed for the harvest and preparation very well can be provided by the peasant family. In addition, the tobacco plant requires only two months to mature, and thus it provides peasant families with ample opportunity to cultivate food crops in the remainder of the year. From this perspective, the botanical aspects of the tobacco plant favor independent small-scale agriculture.[7]

This analysis seems to be supported by the fact that no large-scale plantations came into existence in the Cibao. Only a few large landowners succeeded in cultivating tobacco profitably themselves. The nineteenth-century German merchants never even tried to extend their activities to agricultural production itself. They probably learned their lesson from the Dutch project in 1889–90, which signally failed in its attempt to cultivate high quality Sumatra tobacco in the Cibao. The native entrepreneurs who bought large tracts of land in the beginning of the twentieth century normally dedicated the majority of their property to cattle raising.

However, the nature of tobacco production in the Cibao also points to the limitations of too rigid crop determinism. In this region, tobacco was not a high-quality, labor-intensive cash crop. Rather than by its meticulous preparation, Cibao tobacco was characterized by the *restricted input of labor and technology*. The Dominican elite turned its back on the production of tobacco in the final decades of the nineteenth century, when prices declined persistently on the German market. Tobacco cultivation existed in the shadow of the more remunerative production of sugar cane and cocoa. Only peasant families were prepared to continue producing tobacco for the market. It can even be argued that the peasant sector was saved by the tobacco crisis of the 1880s and by the failure of the Dutch plantation experiment. It is not inconceivable that the peasant producers would have been pushed aside by avid settler farmers had tobacco production been more profitable in this period. It would probably not have been difficult to "capture" the peasant producers—to bind them firmly to the market and the state— had prices been consistently higher. However, the mercantile class in the region either was not prepared or simply was unable to raise the prices. The Cibao tobacco sector was founded upon very cheap production of the tobacco leaf.

This characteristic of regional tobacco production enabled the tobacco growers to resist outside interference. Frederick Cooper is right when he writes that "the cheapness [of peasant-produced commodities] was difficult to separate from the autonomy."[8] As long as access to agricultural resources was open, the relative autonomy of the peasantry was the price the merchants had to pay for their cheap tobacco. This autonomous position of the tobacco-growing peasantry was strengthened by the structure of the market. The existence of an *internal market* created a secure demand that made it easier for the peasants to weather world market crises. The fact that much tobacco was processed locally in the form of cigars and *andullos* further decreased the producers' dependence on the international market. Thus, several factors together—botanical characteristics of the plant, the social structure of the region, and its economic linkages to the world market—determined that a major portion of Dominican tobacco would be produced by peasant families.

An important explanation of the resilience of peasant production in the Cibao tobacco sector can be found in the peasants' *continuing access to land*. The low man/land ratio and traditional systems of landholding guaranteed every cultivator a piece of land. This practically free access to land has been the crucial element of Cibao agricultural history. The existence of the *terrenos comuneros* and the lack of an effective land registration system were essential for the peasantry's independence. With the transformation of the Cibao economy and the expansion of capitalist relations of production, access to land became more restricted, but land prices remained low. Although land and labor were definitively converted into commodities in the twentieth century, peasant agriculture was not destroyed or marginalized. In contrast to the situation in Cuba and Puerto Rico, for instance, in the Villa González region the landowning elite was even instrumental in maintaining the peasantry. The landowners allowed peasant producers to squat on their lands in exchange for labor and loyalty. This system enabled the elite to exploit their properties despite the absence of a regular wage labor force. They were able to control the rural population without destroying the basis of peasant production or resorting to open coercion. That social responsibilities and political obedience to local leaders were prices of this access did not alter the fact that the peasant family maintained its access to land.

Conclusion

The resilience of peasant production in the Cibao thus also was a function of the *complementarity* of peasant production and of a native rural capitalism. In general, the landowners were smalltime capitalists who lacked the capital to pay wage labor. By allowing peasants to squat on their land, they obtained access to peasant labor. This attitude fostered strong vertical relationships between the landowners and the tobacco cultivators, relationships that we have studied in the Villa González region. Although it can be argued that the tobacco growers had to pay for the land with their labor and thus were subject to exploitation and surplus extraction,[9] they were able to continue their subsistence-oriented agriculture and maintain a degree of economic autonomy. At the same time, the continuation of tobacco production in general was secured. The system thus was mutually advantageous for the tobacco cultivators and the landowners.[10] Clearly, the existence of large landholdings does not always entail destruction of peasant production. The interests of large landowners and peasant producers can (temporarily) coincide. As long as landowners allow peasant producers to continue small-scale agriculture on their properties, peasant production can be sustained indefinitely. In many respects, we can compare the Cibao peasantry to the so-called "squatting" peasantry in South and East Africa in the first decades of the twentieth century.[11] In these regions, a large and prosperous peasantry came into being which did not have formal land rights. These peasants were allowed to squat on the property of white landowners in exchange for occasional labor services. The same situation existed in Puerto Rico during a short period of time in the first half of the nineteenth century, when squatting *agregados* were privileged compared to landless laborers and even small landholders.[12] The strength of the landowning class lay in its social and political dominance. The crucial position of the Cibao elite between the state and the cultivators also strengthened its political position in the region. As in the African examples, the Cibao landowners were in charge of the marketing the peasant crops.[13] This economic dependence on the tobacco trade forged strong links between rural landowners and the tobacco growers.

The *weakness of the Dominican public sector* was another factor in the resilience of peasant production. The political and financial impotence of the Dominican government precluded closure of the agricultural frontier and definitive "capture" of the peasant producers. Centralist legislation and authoritarian rhetoric could not conceal the fact that most attempts at intervention in the agricultural sector were utterly ineffective. A number of explanations of this weakness have been mentioned. State formation began relatively late in the Dominican Republic. Personalism and regional divisions continued to restrict the achievements of the central government. The latter's weak financial position was another cause. This position was partly a consequence of the country's dependence on external economic and political forces. The country's economic weakness allowed foreign corporations to dominate. The growing influence of the US eventually resulted in its military occupation of the country. In the tobacco sector, European importers wielded extraordinary power in determining tobacco prices. When the government started to become interested in peasant society in the twentieth century, agricultural policies continued to be out of touch with the concrete situation in rural society. Decisions were taken in Santo Domingo, far from the rural production areas; little comprehension existed of the logic of small-scale production; and profound differences of opinion existed as to the preferred road to agricultural modernization.

These factors, important as they may have been, still are not sufficient to explain the relative autonomy of the tobacco cultivators. Weakness in the international market frequently has led to great internal coercion. Why, then, did the Dominican state allow so much autonomy to the tobacco sector in general, and to the tobacco cultivators in particular? The answer to this question must be sought in the fact that the modern Dominican state originated in a period when the newly established sugar plantations attracted all attention. The majority of state revenues were linked in one way or another to the sugar sector, and all eyes were fixed upon the increasing sugar production. In this way, the establishment of large sugar plantations in the southern part of the country deflected state attention from the peasant sector. This hypothesis is confirmed by historical developments in other countries. In his analysis of African peasantries, René Lemarchand writes, "Where peasant production plays a relatively small part in the transfer of revenue to the State, chances are that the rural networks will operate under fewer constraints and with greater flexibility in patron-client exchanges."[14] He suggests that, in such circumstances of *benign neglect,* peasant production may thrive.

On a regional level, this aloofness was reinforced by strained relations between the government and the Cibao elite. Many people in the Cibao considered the national government an obstacle to, rather than a support for, economic development. The new entrepreneurial groups that engaged in commercial and productive activities were ambivalent toward the state. On the one hand, they expected it to create conditions favorable for their activities; on the other, they preferred to do business and run their enterprises without outside interference. These attitudes were augmented by a strong regionalism, which tended to see the national state as a predator, taking money out without giving anything in return. These feelings often led to *elite opposition to state intervention*. Protection of the regional elite was an important factor in the continuing viability of peasant production. The shared interests of cultivators and elite, and the symbiotic relation of the two economic systems, could go so far that landowners sided with the peasants when they came under attack by the national government. Recent discussions of the lack of effectiveness of state intervention in the Third World increasingly have focused on the tenacity of rural patrons and on their networks of political and economic loyalties. Joel Migdal sees fragmented social and political control, an outgrowth of these vertical relations, as the principal explanation for the weakness of states in Africa, Asia, and Latin America.[15] The situation in the Cibao seems to confirm this analysis. The alliance between the rural elite and the cultivators often limited the effectiveness of state intervention. It is significant that state intervention in rural society became more or less effective only when, in the late 1920s, the regional elite and rural patrons allied themselves with the state and became integrated into government efforts to control rural society.

The history of the Cibao tobacco growers provides interesting perspectives for Latin American historiography. The debate in Latin America has often led to a dead end: a simple opposition between *latifundios* (large estates) and *minifundios* (small landholdings). Peasantries have been studied only in their confrontation with expanding plantations or with a strong landlord class. The dynamics of peasant agriculture in Latin American history often have been neglected. This makes Hyden's "uncaptured peasantry" and Ranger's notion of peasant agriculture as an "option" particularly interesting for Latin American (and Caribbean) historiography. These two perspectives emphasize the potential autonomy of peasant societies and indicate their specific laws of motion. In spite of the unequal exchange and the increasing pressure of the state, subsistence agriculture gave peasant producers opportunities to influence the historical development of rural society. They did not have social or political power, but they were able to take advantage of fissures in the system and so defend their interests.

Another point that emerges from our study of the Cibao peasantry is the idea that no simple contradiction exists between peasantries and the market (or capitalism in general). We have seen that the Cibao tobacco growers had a long history of market participation. It can even be said that during many periods they were eager participants in the market. It is true that increasing differentiation among the peasant producers resulted in different market behaviors, but market participation was an accepted part of the peasant economy. It is the *limits* on market penetration which constitute the interesting aspect of Cibao history.

Many observers have neglected the existence of successful peasant producers. Many of these, at one point or another, abandoned agriculture and directed their energies to other, often commercial, activities.[16] On the other hand, "success" was visible not only in terms of taking advantage of the market. Peasant producers who managed to hold onto their land could very successfully withstand pressure from the market or the state and had to make few if any concessions to the market economy. They were able to maintain an economic autonomy which made them very "successful" in terms of a subsistence economy and practically invulnerable to outside pressure.

Much more research must be done in order to explain and analyze these different examples of peasant behavior, but these squarely opposed forms of "success" are living proof of the contradictory and uneven penetration of capitalism in rural society. Their simultaneous existence was symbolic of the peasantry's position in the Dominican Republic until the 1930s. Many pressures existed outside the control of the peasantry, but these could not completely eradicate the autonomy of the peasant producers. Peasant producers gradually were integrated in the market, but space remained to continue (parts of) their subsistence economy. The continuation of peasant agriculture was related to uncontrollable market forces, but also to the attitudes and behavior of peasant producers themselves. Our study of the Cibao tobacco growers makes clear that "peasant victories" on the market were rare, but they were not entirely absent.

Peasant producers thus were able to retain some autonomy within a changing society by taking advantage of the market or by resisting its influence. The specific position of the tobacco cultivators, especially their subsistence base, allowed them to vary their market participation. The mercantile class could not extend its socially dominant position into the peasant household, and the cultivators retained options as to the degree of their market dependence. Such observations bring us directly to the issue of power relations in rural society. The peasantry obviously was a socially and politically weak class, and it could maintain a degree of autonomy only so long as it could play different elite factions off against each other. Even a weak government such as that of the Dominican Republic could have subordinated the peasantry had no contending force existed. This contending force was the regional elite of the Cibao. Old and new landowners needed the peasantry's help in the cultivation of their land. This need softened the effects of an increasing concentration of landownership in the twentieth-century Cibao. For their part, the merchants depended on continuing production of cheap tobacco by small-scale cultivators for the maintenance of their commercial activities. The converging interests of the elite and the peasantry resulted in a formidable obstacle to state intervention in the regional economy. The alliance delayed improvements in the quality of Cibao tobacco. The mercantile class sometimes even openly opposed state efforts to innovate in agriculture.

Thus, these elite groups were the peasantry's potential allies (as well as its potential oppressors). Peasant producers, and poor people in general, are not in a position to be fussy about their friends. The Cibao peasantry took advantage of conflicting interests within the regional elite and between the national state and the regional elite. This enabled the peasantry to prevent the destruction of its agricultural system while avoiding open confrontation. It is notable that oral testimonies of peasant producers concerning the first decades of the twentieth century refer to, but do not passionately express resentment of, the loss of land to new landowners. Terence Ranger describes a similar phenomenon in the case of Zimbabwe, which he explains by the fact that "despite the very extensive land alienation, it was possible in this period to create a viable peasant economy."[17]

The Dominican state became more efficient and more powerful in the 1920s. When government projects became better adapted to peasant agriculture, the state became a more important force in rural society. Some peasant producers now tried to take advantage of its presence, just as they were trying to do with regional elite groups. State support sometimes could help them to counteract the destructive tendencies toward land concentration in the region and offer them help in thwarting the commercial manipulations of the merchants. At the same time, such state support accelerated the erosion of peasant autonomy. Especially when the Cibao elite joined the state in its efforts to control peasant society, the maneuvering space of the tobacco growers decreased rapidly. Technological education and political integration then became part of the new survival strategy of a peasantry that gradually was losing ground to capitalist entrepreneurs. This is only one more argument for the basic supposition of this book: it is only possible to understand rural change when an analysis is made of the dynamics and adaptive strategies of the peasant producers themselves.

The Cibao Peasantry in the Twentieth Century

The tobacco-growing peasants of today no longer are the independent, volatile, and relatively autonomous producers of the nineteenth century, nor are they the patronized clients of the 1920s. The poverty that characterizes their lives and the exploitation from which they suffer have made the peasantry a symbol of backwardness and oppression. This image of hopelessness is shared by both Left and Right, and most observers do not see a future for the Dominican peasantry. How is it possible to reconcile this image of hopeless poverty with the picture of a poor but self-conscious and relatively autonomous peasantry presented in this book? What happened in the past sixty years to cause such a dramatic change in the social and economic position of the Dominican peasantry? Or must we assume that it is not so much a changing rural society as a different perspective on the place of the peasantry in Dominican society that explains this new image? Let us try to shed some light on these questions.

Two simultaneous historical events shaped the development of the Dominican economy in the second half of the twentieth century. Rafael Leonidas Trujillo came to power in 1930. At the moment of his ascent, the first effects of the economic world crisis were already being felt in the Dominican Republic. The world crisis caused a restructuring of the Dominican economy. The prices of Dominican commodities fell dramatically, and imports diminished accordingly. Government revenues, heavily dependent on import-export duties, declined so rapidly that even under the government of Horacio Vásquez, expenditures had to be cut by 30 percent.[18] Indeed, Roberto Cassá suggests that the ascent of Trujillo was occasioned partly by the economic crisis.[19]

The weakness of the export-oriented economy explains why agricultural self-sufficiency on a national scale became one of the basic tenets of the Trujillo ideology. When Trujillo had secured his power base, he set himself the task of increasing production of daily consumption goods such as rice, meat, and dairy products. Native industries producing hats, *serones*, leather, etc., were also fostered by the dictator. To bring about these changes in economic production, the Trujillo regime extended the policy of earlier governments. The infrastructure was further improved, bringing remote areas within reach of the market and—not to be forgotten—of state control. Formerly isolated regions on the border and in the mountain areas were integrated into the market economy.[20] Simultaneously, the relations of production underwent changes. In the Cibao, large-scale irrigation projects were

211

undertaken, financed by private and state capital. The Trujillo regime tried to reconcile two objectives in its policy toward rural society and agricultural production. On the one hand, it aimed at keeping rural society intact, promoting small-scale agriculture, and even proclaiming a guaranteed access to ten tareas of land for every peasant family. On the other hand, the regime stimulated the penetration of capitalist relations of production in the countryside and did all it could to free labor for government and private projects.[21] These apparently contradictory objectives could be harmonized temporarily because of the rapid demographic growth in this period and the abundance of uncultivated land. The Trujillo regime could force the rural population to work on government projects without endangering the agricultural subsistence base of the peasantry. More than that, the regime allowed the growing rural population to occupy uncultivated land and so secured the survival of the peasant population. This policy explains the fact that, during the Trujillo regime, capitalist relations of production expanded, while, at the same time, the number of minifundios increased dramatically. From a total of 200,000 in 1940, their number increased to 345,000 in 1960. Approximately half these landholdings comprised less than fifteen tareas.[22] The process of peasantization thus continued and even intensified, while state intervention in rural society increased. The social and economic autonomy of the peasantry was reduced, and the agricultural sector was brought under government control.[23] While their number increased, not much was left of the autonomy of the peasant producers by the end of the Trujillo period.

The tobacco producers were not unaware of these developments. But the organization of the tobacco sector gave a specific edge to their insertion in the national and international economy. There is no agreement on the relative position of tobacco. The tobacco sector was hard hit by the world crisis, as prices decreased to an all-time low. Cassá states that the tobacco and cocoa sectors were the sectors of the Dominican economy most affected.[24] Contemporary reports suggest that tobacco production maintained itself well, however, and that it recovered rapidly. It benefited from the existence of a national tobacco industry, and prices rose in the mid-1930s.[25] Peasant producers diminished their production in the first years of the crisis but quickly resumed their cultivation of tobacco. The dictatorial state tried to use the crisis to obtain control over the tobacco sector, but Trujillo's attempts to establish a tobacco monopoly in 1934 failed. The Trujillo regime never was able to obtain more than a remote control over the sector's organization.

It is undeniable that the processes of change and the reduction of peasant autonomy which were beginning in the 1920s became more pronounced in the 1930s and 1940s. Access to land became restricted and had to be paid for. Sharecropping half and half (*a media*) became a generally applied practice. As *medianeros*, cultivators often had to accept interference in the actual agricultural process, but for landless peasant cultivators, these contracts were the only way they could obtain access to land. In the valley region in the 1950s, most tobacco was cultivated under sharecropping arrangements. So general was this system in the tobacco sector that in present-day Dominican agriculture, sharecropping arrangements and tobacco growing have become almost synonymous. It was said in the 1970s that "sharecropping is more important in the case of tobacco than in any other crop."[26] It is an interesting question why tobacco production has been so susceptible to this system. Various factors seem to have played a role. In the first place, for many landowners sharecropping must have been the only way to generate income from their landed properties. They did not have the capital or the labor to make their land productive themselves and so took advantage of the increasing scarcity of land to appropriate part of the peasant production. Later, in the 1940s and 1950s, sharecropping was used to introduce capitalist relations of production into tobacco production. Larger landholders and the urban middle class tried to take advantage of rising prices on the tobacco market by way of sharecropping. It seems evident that this had to do with the nature of tobacco as a cash crop. The seasonal need for labor in tobacco cultivation and its unstable position on the world market precluded the formation of capitalist farms. It was more profitable for landowners to use the labor of the free peasant household.[27]

However, it was not only a "capitalist" logic which forced tobacco growers into sharecropping arrangements. They themselves seem often to have preferred sharecropping. Despite radical restrictions of peasant autonomy, the majority of tobacco cultivators continued to be subsistence-oriented. The sharecropping system at least enabled them to safeguard the household organization of peasant production and to maintain partial autonomy in agricultural decisions. Sharecropping also allowed for the continuation of vertical relationships in the countryside, which brought some security to peasant families as access to land became closed. Their personal contacts with the landowner guaranteed them protection and formed a buffer against the insecurities of the market economy.[28] This may also explain the fact that many sharecropping contracts existed between smallholders and their relatives.[29]

Agricultural technology did not change much, either. The fate of the tobacco harvest remained largely a function of climatological conditions. Apart from the few places that could be irrigated, cultivation of tobacco remained strongly weather-dependent. Indeed, tobacco was a favored crop in unirrigated areas because it always rendered something, even in the driest years. Irregular production figures for these years indicate that agricultural technology was still rather rudimentary.

Differences within the peasantry became more marked in the 1950s and 1960s. More research is needed on the differentiation within peasant society. My research in the Villa González region suggests that the impoverished part of the peasantry continued growing during and after the Trujillo period. Some cultivators managed to improve their positions through a combination of commercial and agricultural activities. They became what could be called a rural middle class, which made regular use of local wage labor. The majority of the increasing population of smallholders and sharecroppers experienced increasing difficulty in meeting its subsistence needs. Some landless cultivators migrated to the *sierra*. Often they continued to use slash-and-burn techniques to bring new land under cultivation. In this way the agricultural frontier expanded into the mountains. While tobacco agriculture in the valley region gradually became a monocultural export sector closely supervised by the government and the tobacco industry, more independent and technologically primitive tobacco production continued in marginal frontier regions. As late as the 1980s, clear differences existed between tobacco cultivation in the Villa González region and the mountainous Limón area—a distance of only ten miles.

The irreversible consequences of the Trujillo period became apparent in the 1970s and 1980s. Indeed, they were rendered even more poignant by the fact that many landowners took advantage of the chaotic post-Trujillo period to usurp large tracts of land. The net closed around the peasant producers. The price that had to be paid to obtain access to land went up, undermining the viability of the peasant sector. Sharecropping contracts and unfavorable market conditions restricted peasant producers in the allocation of their produce. Many producers lost their land to creditors. Demographic growth aggravated pressures on agricultural resources. For the first time in Dominican history, land became a scarce commodity. Many landless cultivators now were unable to secure access to a piece of land which could maintain their families. Subsistence agriculture no longer functioned as a self-evident safety net for the peasant family. The enclosure of the peasant cultivators destroyed their economic independence. It was no coincidence that the Instituto del Tabaco was founded in 1962 (under the supervision of Luis Carballo!). The peasantry was "ripe" for agricultural advice in the 1960s. Elderly peasants may have held onto the old ways and continued to intercrop tobacco with food crops, but the majority of cultivators could no longer reject technological innovation or evade state intervention. Carlos Dore has stressed the increasing number of *microfincas* of less than eight tareas in the 1970s, which no longer could sustain a family. Thus the peasant population was forced to engage in wage labor during part of the year.[30] In the tobacco sector, cultivators who cultivated less than thirty-two tareas (two hectares) produced 34 percent of the entire tobacco crop in 1972, but they had been surrounded by large landholdings. While these small farms occupied a total of 37.17 tareas, seventy-six large enterprises that were, among other things, engaged in tobacco cultivation, together possessed 177,520 tareas.[31] Few tobacco growers owned the land they cultivated. According to Ferrán, only 40 percent of the tobacco fields of less than eighty tareas (five hectares) were owned by the person cultivating it in 1971.[32] Peasant society could survive only by expelling part of its population. The "voluntary" wage labor of former times turned into a necessity, and migration became an integral element of peasant society.[33] Many youngsters migrated to the cities, often extending their journey on to New York. The remaining rural population tried to eke out a living on its small pieces of land.

The agrarian policy initiated by the Balaguer government in 1972 must be seen in the context of this rapidly deteriorating situation of the agricultural producers. It was clear that it would be impossible to guarantee a sufficient supply of foodstuffs to the urban population and maintain a steady export of agricultural commodities if the rural population did not get access to land. In addition, there was fear that the increasing rural poverty might lead to social unrest and radicalization of the rural population. These considerations resulted in halfhearted government initiatives to alleviate the problems of rural poverty. In 1972, a project was presented to distribute land among the peasant producers. Resistance by the landowning classes was great, and, in the end, only public lands were distributed under tight state control. Another state initiative aimed at improving the situation of the sharecroppers in the country was hardly more effective. The so-called *Law 289* was never enforced and, until the 1980s, tobacco cultivators of the Villa González region had to accept very unfavorable sharecropping conditions that were explicitly prohibited by the law.[34]

The most obvious result of these 1972 laws was that the peasantry became more conscious of the causes of rural poverty. In the following years, a number of peasant unions was formed. In many parts of the country, groups of peasant producers organized land invasions. In the areas of tobacco cultivation, cooperatives were established to improve the market position of the producers. These initiatives accelerated in the post-1978 period, after twelve years of Balaguer's government. For the majority of the peasant producers, these developments did not offer a viable solution. Its poverty continued to increase dramatically in the 1980s. Some cultivators tried to get access to land via local networks or (illegal) squatting. Many people despaired, and the exodus of the younger generations out of the countryside intensified during the last two decades.

A visitor to the Dominican Republic's rural areas can clearly observe the results of the transformation the country has undergone. Changes have been rapid and decisive. Elderly people still remember the introduction of the first cars by wealthy entrepreneurs in the 1920s or the construction of the first electric plant in the village, but they have now accepted these things as facts of life. The old man who refuses to ride in a car and still travels to Santiago on horseback generally is considered an eccentric, and the rest of his generation quietly squeeze into the minibuses responsible for regional transport. In tobacco cultivation, complex changes are also visible. More or less illiterate tobacco growers heatedly discuss the pros and cons of different types of insecticide or fertilizer. One can hear peasant producers talk about having spent thousands of pesos for labor or fertilizer, while their children are sent to the shop for one egg or ten centavos of salt or butter. Sales in most rural shops are so small that it is almost impossible to change a low-value bank note in the countryside. On the outside, the lives of tobacco-growing families are not much different from the lives of their predecessors. At dawn, men and women can be seen walking to their *conucos* in work clothes. As the day progresses, children carry food and coffee to workers in the fields. In the afternoon, smoke curls up from the outdoor kitchens where women prepare dinner on a small log fire. In the late afternoon, men walk back to their houses, bathed in perspiration, clothes dirty. They often linger in front of the small stores or talk with their friends at the roadside.

It is only on closer observation that the difficult position of the peasant producers becomes apparent. They can no longer cultivate virgin lands and need to invest in fertilizer and insecticides. The *juntas* have disappeared, and labor now must be compensated. Many cultivators, even when they have access to land, work as day laborers on other people's land. Boys and girls earn some money in the harvest season, working in the *ranchos* or selling *sartas* that they make at home. The money economy has penetrated all levels of rural society, and it is virtually impossible to name activities in which no monetary expenses are involved. The low labor costs that supported peasant agriculture for so long have gradually vanished. Cultivators nowadays often are obliged to pay their adolescent children for their work.[35] The possibility of emigration and the disdain for agricultural work which is one of its consequences have increased the opportunity costs of rural wage labor in general. Despite the rural unemployment, cultivators have often difficulty finding laborers. This situation has led many small-scale cultivators to revitalize the old custom of recruiting labor via personal networks. The tobacco cultivator who visits his friends at night to summon their (paid) help for the next day is doing something very similar to calling a *junta*. Dependence on the situation of the world market has made the situation of the tobacco growers very insecure. In recent years, many producers have completely turned away from tobacco cultivation.

Rural families wage a daily struggle to survive. A running account at the local store is an absolute necessity, and often the income from tobacco production is insufficient to pay off the family's debts. In this way, many cultivators have now become "the condemned ones of tobacco" (*los condenados del tabaco*).[36] They go on cultivating tobacco because they see no alternative. Others have recently changed to more promising cash crops such as tomatoes, sorghum, or flowers. Some peasants, especially the older ones, continue to defend the rural way of life and the beauties of small-scale tobacco production, but their voices are increasingly muffled.

A popular *merengue* of the 1980s, about the situation of the Dominican peasant, sings: "At night your weeping is heard in the village, when you are comforting your family because there is no food" (*De noche se oye en el pueblo tu llanto, cuando estás consolando toda tu familia porque no hay comida*). And its chorus says: "No longer he feels like going on."[37] This text quite accurately reflects the image of the peasantry in today's Dominican society. It must be seriously asked if this process of fragmentation of peasant society must not be stopped.[38] Many politicians, development experts, and academic observers seem unaware that the hardship of the Cibao tobacco growers has not always existed and that the loss of their economic independence occurred relatively recently.

Appendix 1

Export Figures and Prices
of Dominican Tobacco, 1870–1930

Export Figures

Reliable statistical material for Dominican history is notably scarce. Figures for the tobacco sector are particularly problematical because of the specific characteristics of the crop. During the process of drying, fermentation, and transport, the tobacco leaves lose weight. This loss even affected the use of units of weight. A *quintal* is the equivalent of 100 pounds of 0.46 kilo (46 kilos). A *bulto* or *serón* generally was considered to contain one quintal of tobacco and was counted as such in the statistics. Because of the expected weight loss, however, they were made much heavier. No merchants accepted (or accepts today) a serón of tobacco weighing less than 60 kilos.

Production and export figures were gathered intermittently, causing three problems. First, not all tobacco was exported; some tobacco remained on the island to be consumed locally or exported (outside the statistics) to Haiti. An increasing amount of tobacco was used in the national tobacco industry. Second, tobacco usually weighed less at the moment of exportation than when it was harvested or brought to the storehouses in the city. Third, tobacco which was produced in one year often was exported in the next year. This factor is especially significant for nineteenth-century statistics, as shipping capacity then often was limited. These factors account for widely varying production and export figures in the statistics reproduced below. Figures for tobacco exports, then, must be viewed with extreme caution. This is certainly true for the nineteenth century, but even the more consistent statistics of the twentieth century cannot always be taken at face value.

Tobacco production of the Dominican Republic in the 1870s oscillated around the 100,000 *bultos*, or five million kilos. Steady growth began in the first decade of the twentieth century. Tobacco production reached a peak of 22 million kilos in 1925. A structural upward trend is obvious in this period; tobacco production more than quadrupled in sixty years. Nevertheless, these

Appendices

Table 2
Dominican Tobacco Exports, 1870–1900 (in quintales)

Year	El Mensajero (1888)	De Tabaksplant (passim)	Gaceta Oficial (1891)	Boletín Municipal (1902)
1870	120,000			
1871	125,000			
1872	125,000			
1873	160,000	107,000		
1874	170,000	132,500		
1875	134,000	112,000		
1876	71,000			
1877	97,000			
1878	116,000			
1879	45,000			
1880	31,000	30,000		
1881	75,000	65,000	62,000	
1882	119,000	55,000	81,000	
1883	83,000	75,000	127,000	
1884	110,000	60,000	109,500	
1885	96,000	96,000	112,500	
1886	114,000	95,000	114,500	170,000
1887	175,000	117,000	175,500	132,000
1888		127,000	118,000	130,000
1889		50,000	52,500	62,000
1890		72,000	89,000	72,000
1891		92,000	89,000	101,000
1892		149,000	128,000	155,000
1893		155,000	166,000	154,000
1894		75,000		77,000
1895		43,000		43,000
1896		75,000		71,000
1897		70,000		69,000
1898		157,000		180,000
1899		90,000		88,000
1900				175,000

Sources: *El Mensajero* 6, no. 116 (11 June 1888); *De Tabaksplant,* passim; *Gaceta Oficial* 18, no. 857 (24 Jan. 1891); *Boletín Municipal* 14, no. 381 (5 Apr. 1902).

clean production figures for single years are deceiving. Production figures showed extreme variations from one year to the next. The low level of agricultural technology and the absence of irrigation made tobacco cultivation strongly weather-dependent. This, added to the fact that tobacco is an annual crop, made for wide variations in production figures. In 1889, for example, the harvest amounted to hardly more than 50,000 *bultos*, while it had tallied 127,000 in the previous year. A similar sudden decrease occurred in 1894, when exports to Germany were 75,000 *bultos*, compared with more than 150,000 in each of the two previous years. When the technology improved and state control increased in the twentieth century, the variability of the tobacco crops tended to diminish, but significant year-to-year variations still occurred in the 1920s. See the patterns in figure A1.

Prices of Dominican Tobacco

There is a paucity of detailed information about changes in prices paid to cultivators, let alone about changing values of the Dominican peso and the inflation rates in the period 1870–1930. Prices of Dominican tobacco were

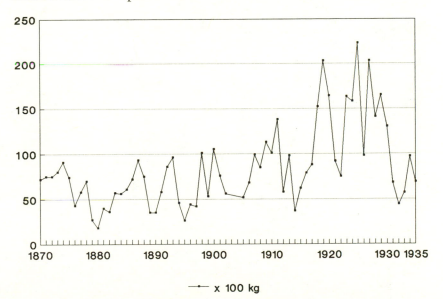

Figure A1. Average exports of Dominican tobacco, 1870–1935. Source of data: For 1870–1900, totals are derived from table 2. For 1900–1935, data are taken from Mutto, "La economía de exportación de la República Dominicana, 1900–1930," *Eme Eme Estudios Dominicanos* 3, no. 15 (Nov.–Dec. 1974): 107.

high until the 1870s. Place mentions prices between 14 and 20 pesos per quintal in 1849, paid at the farm level.[1] In the 1870s, prices gradually decreased, partly as a result of the unstable political situation. A report on the 1876–77 harvest, for instance, observed that warfare "paralyzed business transactions until April."[2] Prices hovered around 7 pesos in the late 1870s, reaching a high of 12 pesos, and went down to 4 to 5 pesos in the 1880s. The three classes were priced as follows in this period: primera, superior: 5 pesos; primera, inferior: 3.50 to 4 pesos; segunda: 2.50 pesos.[3] In the 1890s, prices increased somewhat.[4] In those years, an average of 7, 6, or 5 pesos was paid for the three classes. Prices went down again in the first decade of the twentieth century. In 1909, it was reported that the three classes yielded no more than 3, 2, and 1 pesos, respectively. In 1917, prices had gone up to 5, 4, and 3 pesos. During the boom years of 1918–19, prices rose to 8 pesos. They stabilized between 4 and 6 pesos in the 1920s. Only in 1924 did they rise again to more than 7 pesos.[5] This long period of more or less stable prices may explain the shock experienced by producers when they suddenly received no more than 50 centavos for their tobacco in the 1930s.

A very general summary for these years would look like figure A2. For prices on the world market, better serial data are available, as shown in figures A3 and A4.

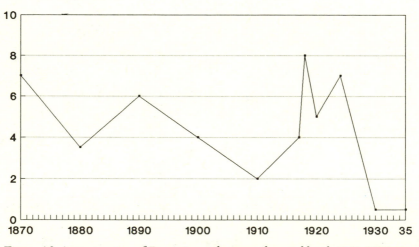

Figure A2. Average prices of Dominican tobacco at the rural level, 1870–1935 (pesos per quintal).

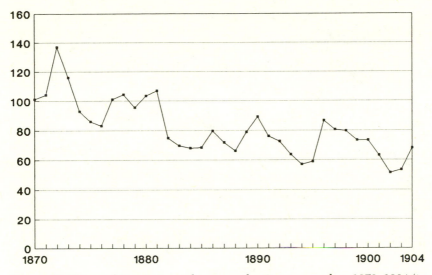

Figure A3. Prices of Dominican tobacco on the German market, 1870–1904 (in German marks per 100 kilos). Source of data: *Gaceta Oficial* 23, no. 1735 (3 Nov. 1906).

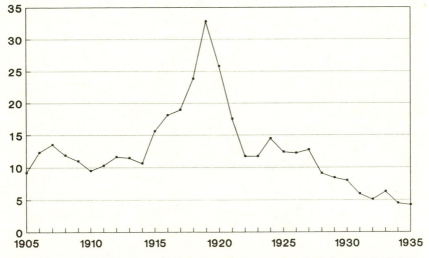

Figure A4. Prices of Dominican tobacco on the international market, 1905–35 (in U.S. dollars per 100 kilos). Source of data: Mutto, "La economía de exportación de la República Dominicana, 1900–1930," *Eme Eme Estudios Dominicanos* 3, no. 15 (Nov.–Dec. 1974): 107.

APPENDIX 2

A Note on Dominican Tobacco, 1870–1930

Classification of tobacco is a hazardous undertaking. Botanists, producers, and merchants use different criteria and names. A certain type of tobacco, such as "Burley," may be considered "light" in one context, and "dark" in another. Every production region has its own nomenclature, and only a botanical expert can discern differences between one kind and another.[1] If we limit ourselves to the *Nicotiana tabacum*, a first distinction can be made between light and dark tobacco. Akehurst writes: "Broadly, light colour is synonymous with mildness and cigarette manufacture; dark colour with strength and mainly non-cigarette manufacture."[2] We may add that the dark tobaccos generally are found in older production regions where archaic production techniques prevail, while the lighter tobacco is a new and often semi-industrial crop in many regions of the world. The cultivation of light tobacco requires substantial capital investment, sophisticated techniques, and a market orientation.

Specific classification thus is a complex matter, especially because names with a geographical connotation, such as Virginia or Turkish tobacco, refer to types of tobacco that are found all over the world. Anastasia distinguishes four principal types of tobacco: Havanensis, Brasiliensis, Virginica, and Purpurea.[3] Many other classifications have been proposed, but none has found general acceptance. This led Goodspeed to express doubt about the utility of any general classification. Akehurst suggests considering *Nicotiana tabacum* as representing a wide range of continuously variable material with the ability to produce a collection of different products under various environmental conditions.[4] A fixed nomenclature is possible only in a regional context.

The Dominican tobacco, with which we are concerned here, consists exclusively of dark tobaccos and is divided in two types: *criollo* and *olor.* The lighter tobaccos (mainly "Burley") only found general acceptance in the

1960s. *Criollo* is the "traditional" Dominican tobacco. This implies that it developed over the course of many years of cultivation and adaptation, without any systematic effort to improve the plant through conscious seed selection.[5] According to Zaldívar, the denomination *criollo* today refers not so much to specific characteristics of the tobacco as to its commercial purpose and use in cigarettes. It usually is of a lower quality than the *olor* tobacco. Low quality *olor* may be called "criollo," and good *criollo* may be sold as "olor."[6] Originally the *olor* tobacco must have been imported from Cuba, probably when Santo Domingo was still under Spanish rule. In the beginning of the nineteenth century, *olor* tobacco was known also as *tabaco de la Habana* or *semillas de Cuba*.[7] Gradually, both *criollo* and *olor* became native tobaccos, with *criollo* geared toward export and *olor* generally consumed within the country.

CRIOLLO TOBACCO

Criollo tobacco has always been meant exclusively for export. It had some very distinct characteristics: "The leaf is rather fine, small, and pointed, with the veins very close to the stem. After being well fermented, it takes a dark brown color. It has a good burn, is resistant, and possesses a light but not unpleasant aroma."[8] Until well into the twentieth century, two types of *criollo* tobacco were dominant in the country: *amarillo parado* and *amarillo punta de lanza*. How complicated it is to establish the origin of a certain type of tobacco and to reach a formal nomenclature may be shown in connection with the *punta de lanza* variety. Everyone agreed that it was one of the *criollo* tobaccos, but also that its seeds had been imported from Cuba very recently.[9] Sometimes a third name can be found, *amarillo planchado*, but it is not clear whether this was a separate type.[10] In the 1930s, people also distinguished between *amarillo corriente* and *amarillo especial*.[11] The *amarillo* type of tobacco easily found a market in Europe. *El Orden* wrote in 1875: "According to information from Europe, the tobacco varieties *amarillo parado* and *amarillo punta de lanza* are the ones that people there prefer."[12] In 1926, these varieties were described by one of the most renowned tobacco merchants in the Cibao, the Frenchman Oquet: "*Amarillo parado* has a oval leaf, oblique veins, more or less curved like the veins of 'criollo'. . . . Its leaves are normally large, very healthy, uniform and with a clear brown, almost yellow color." *Punta de lanza* possessed large leaves also, "very pointed and with a lighter color than the *criollo* tobacco after fermentation."[13] Around 1900, a new type of tobacco emerged in Guayacanes, called

ranchero or *olor ranchero*. Although connoisseurs judged its smoking qualities very negatively,[14] it gained some popularity among growers because of
its rapid growth and copious yield.[15]

In the countryside, many other types were distinguished: *jaquito, hojas
de cal, lengua de vaca, rabo de mula,* etc. These were "varieties with very
narrow and pointed leaves with very little commercial value." In commercial
discourse, these names became symbolic of the technological backwardness
of the peasantry and synonymous with inferior quality and low prices.[16]

Each of these types had its special characteristics, which determined the
opinions of the cultivators and merchants. Not surprisingly, the evaluations
of these groups did not always coincide. Many peasants preferred to grow
the so-called "inferior" types of tobacco, since these plants usually were well
adapted to the environment and strong enough to endure droughts and ex-
cesses of rain. Moreover, they normally produced large quantities of leaves.[17]
Such considerations also applied to the more sophisticated types of tobacco.
The *amarillo punta de lanza* found a somewhat better reception in Germany
at the end of the nineteenth century, but the plant was not so strong or well
adapted to different ecological conditions.[18]

In the 1920s, state officials chose *amarillo parado* as the tobacco preferred for the state seedbeds. It was probably for that reason that the
amarillo parado type emerged as the predominant *criollo* tobacco in the
twentieth century.[19] For cultivators, its advantage was a favorable balance
between the quality and quantity of its yield and its great capacity to survive
heavy rainfall.[20] The leaf of this plant was generally large and, after fermentation, took on a light color. It was eagerly accepted in the German market.
However, many cultivators continued to prefer the traditional types of tobacco, in part because they preferred them for their *andullos*. In 1963, the
director of the Tobacco Institute, Luis Carballo, still felt the need to write:
"We expect that amarillo parado will soon replace such undesirable varieties
as 'Amarillo punta de lanza,' 'Lengua de vaca,' 'Rabo de mula,' etc., etc."[21]

Olor Tobacco

Olor tobacco was already known early in the nineteenth century, but it acquired popularity with the emergence of a national cigar-producing sector at
the end of the nineteenth and beginning of the twentieth centuries. In 1849,
the French agronomer Victor Place noted that, "because it is much juicier
and stronger than other tobaccos, it is consumed almost entirely within the
country."[22] Three varieties were known in the first half of the twentieth cen-

tury: *el hatero, el olor pequeño,* and *Quin Díaz.*[23] At the end of the nineteenth century, seeds of Sumatra were introduced into the country. These
also usually were classified as *olor.* According to Luis Carballo, they formed
the basis for what later was called *Quin Díaz.*[24]

The leaf of *olor* was smaller than the leaf of *criollo* plants, but it was
preferred because of its "light color and good aroma."[25] According to Oquet,
the plant "has elastic leaves, a more or less dark cinnamon color, and a penetrating, slightly chocolate-like aroma. The leaf is oval and very large and
has veins which are almost perpendicular to the stem." The plant was somewhat more vulnerable to adverse weather conditions and epidemics. It therefore required closer attention and greater investment in capital and labor.
When the leaf was well tended, it could be used as a binder and even as a
wrapper (*capa*) and so obtained higher prices. Oquet states that in quantitative terms, it produced only two-thirds of the *criollo* tobacco but normally it
obtained 50 percent higher prices than the rest.

With the expansion of the tobacco manufacturing industry in the twentieth century, more *olor* tobacco was cultivated. Some of the factories actively promoted cultivation of this type of tobacco. In the period under investigation here, the great majority of Dominican producers cultivated
criollo tobacco, and only a small group of wealthier cultivators occupied
themselves with olor.

In commercial practice, other names often circulated. They were used
not so much to indicate a *type* of tobacco as to designate the region where
the crop was grown, and sometimes the grower or merchant with whom the
tobacco had originated. Zoilo García, the famous cultivator and merchant
from Moca, had his own tobacco. The mark "ZG" was everywhere acknowledged as indicating excellent quality. Other merchants also used their own
tobacco insignia.[26]

Regional circumstances could cause important differences in tobacco
characteristics and quality. In the nineteenth century, the German importers
always considered the so-called *tabaco de Samaná* to be the best Dominican
tobacco. It was observed in 1887 that "this tobacco [comes] from a specific
part of the Cibao, Jaigua, Cotui, Almacén de Yuna, Macorís, Moca, etc." The
writer confessed that no one understood why this tobacco should be better.
Perhaps it was its processing (*acondicionamiento*) that produced a type of
tobacco called *La Mocana.*[27] Later this tobacco received the name *Moca* and
had a very good reputation. Inspector Especial de Agricultura Emilio
Almonte observed in 1933:

The tobacco indicated by *Zona de Moca* is harvested not only in the prov-
ince of this name, but also in the regions Hoya del Caimito, Pontezuelo,
Don Pedro, Guazumal, Tamboril (in the flat parts), Sabana Grande, Licey,
Cruz de Ysalgue, La Javilla, Limonar, Las Palomas, Monte Adentro y
Uveral, which belong to the province of Santiago.[28]

The tobacco cultivated in particular regions often was considered to be of
superior quality, but no consensus existed, and some commercial rivalries
centered on this issue.[29] The well-known tobacco cultivator José Joaquín *Díaz*
stated in 1908 that tobacco well suited for consumption was produced in Hato
del Yaque, Palmarejo, Arroyo Hondo, Jacagua, El Ejido, Jicomé (de Esperanza),
La Grimosa (Valverde). He probably was referring only to *olor* tobacco.[30]

Several times in the 1920s merchants were accused of selling tobacco
from other regions under the name *Moca.*[31] When such practices were reported, it was usually coastal tobacco (the so-called *tabaco de la Costa*) that
was involved. This tobacco, which originated in the Linea and the northern
coastal area, had a very bad reputation. Félix Ma. Nolasco in 1904 called the
coastal tobacco "the object of ruinous manipulations and the effective cause
of the poor reputation of our tobacco in foreign markets." Its bad quality
was revealed only after some time, when it was affected by "a white dust"
that the cultivators called *suitre,* "a natural product of the sea winds."[32]

The classification of Dominican tobacco continued to be problematical. This
difficulty was due in part to both the plant's botanical characteristics and the
commercial practices of cultivators and merchants who tried to upgrade their
lots of tobacco by mixing different types. The most important reason for the
confusion, however, must have been the cultivators' constant experimentation. Many cultivators selected and crossbred their own seeds, ignoring merchants' complaints. The difficulty of a strict classification becomes clear when
we read a letter written in 1934 by the agronomer Albert Michels, who had
dedicated more than twenty years of his life to improving the quality of Dominican tobacco. Reporting a new variety of tobacco cultivated near Janico
by Emilio Jorge, called *Digallagua,* Michels adds in parentheses, "I don't
know how it is written." Michels wrote enthusiastically, "This tobacco constitutes a superior variety which will be fit for wrapping cigars and will undoubtedly be able to compete with the best varieties from Java."[33] It would not be
surprising if this tobacco were a *criollo* variety, but the letter is telling enough
in itself. It was, in 1934, still possible for an agronomer who had been working in the region for more than twenty years to "discover" a new variety of
tobacco with promising qualities but an unknown name!

Notes

Abbreviations

AGN	Archivo General de la Nación, Santo Domingo, Dominican Republic
AHN	Archivo Histórico Nacional, Madrid, Spain
A/I	Ministerio de Agricultura e Inmigración, AGN
BM	*Boletín Municipal* (Santiago, Dominican Republic)
BO	*Boletín Oficial* (Santo Domingo, Dominican Republic)
CSSH	*Comparative Studies in Society and History*
DC	Distrito Catastral, Tribunal de Tierras, Santiago, Dominican Republic
EdlO	*El Eco de la Opinión* (Santo Domingo, Dominican Republic)
EdP	*El Eco del Pueblo* (Santiago, Dominican Republic)
F/OP	Ministerio de Fomento y Obras Públicas (Ministry of Development and Public Works), AGN
GdStD	*Gaceta de Santo Domingo* (Santo Domingo, Dominican Republic)
GM	Archives of the Gobierno Militar (U.S. Military Government), AGN
GO	*Gaceta Oficial* (Santo Domingo, Dominican Republic)
Hac/Com	Ministerio de Hacienda y Comercio (Ministry of Financial Affairs and Commerce), AGN
HAHR	*Hispanic American Historical Review*
IP	Ministerio de Interior y Policía (Ministry of Home Affairs and Police), AGN
JPS	*Journal of Peasant Studies*
LARR	*Latin American Research Review*
LD	*Listín Diario* (Santo Domingo, Dominican Republic)
LIN	*La Información* (Santiago, Dominican Republic)
RdA	*Revista de Agricultura* (Santo Domingo, Dominican Republic)
SEA	Secretaria de Estado de Agricultura, AGN

UASD   Universidad Autónoma de Santo Domingo, Dominican Republic
UCMM   Universidad Católica de Madre y Maestra, Santiago, Dominican
          Republic
VdS   *Voz de Santiago* (Santiago, Dominican Republic)

All non-English citations in the text have been translated into English by the author. Citations in the notes are reproduced in the original language.

1. ABOUT THIS BOOK: SOCIAL AND HISTORIOGRAPHICAL CONTEXT

1. For this period, see two books by Frank Peña Pérez: *Antonio Osorio: Monopolio, Contrabando y Despoblación* (Santiago: UCMM, 1980), and *Cien Años de Miseria en Santo Domingo, 1600–1700* (Santo Domingo, Dominican Republic: Universidad APEC, [1986]). Also see Michiel Baud, "A Colonial Counter-Economy: Tobacco Production on Española, 1500–1870," *Nieuwe West-Indische Gids/New West Indian Guide* 65, nos. 1–2 (1991): 27–49.

2. Engel Sluiter, "Dutch-Spanish Rivalry in the Caribbean Area, 1594–1609," HAHR 28, no. 2 (May 1948): 165–96.

3. In Costa Rica, the same thing happened with cocoa beans. See Mitchel A. Seligson, *Peasants of Costa Rica and the Development of Agrarian Capitalism* (Madison: Univ. of Wisconsin Press, 1980), 17.

4. "Memoria de Mariano Torrente," 6 Jan. 1853, in AHN, Papeles de Santo Domingo, Parte II, Siglo XIX, box 3524, no. 66.

5. *Eco de Pueblo* 4 (17 Aug. 1856).

6. "Disertación sobre tabaco leída por el señor Luis Carballo," 16 Aug. 1934, in SEA, box 194.

7. *Gaceta de Santo Domingo* 4, no. 177 (25 June 1877), and following issues.

8. J. Fred Rippy, "The Initiation of the Customs Receivership in the Dominican Republic," HAHR 17 (1937): 419–57. Also see the leaflet by sugar entrepreneur William C. Bass, "Reciprocidad" (Santo Domingo: Cuna de la América, 1902).

9. For this episode, see Bruce J. Calder, *The Impact of Intervention: The Dominican Republic during the U.S. Occupation of 1916–1924* (Austin: Univ. of Texas Press, 1984).

10. See José Del Castillo, "La inmigración de braceros azucareros en la República Dominicana, 1900–1930," *Cuadernos del Cendia* 262, no. 7 (Santo Domingo, Dominican Republic: UASD, 1978).

11. On some early industrial activity in Santiago, see "Industria Nacional," *El Orden* 1, no. 35 (4 Apr. 1875). Esp. in the early years of the U.S. occupation, important changes occurred within Dominican society. José del Castillo and Walter Cordero, *La economía dominicana durante el primer cuarto del siglo XX* (Santo Domingo: Fundación García-Arévalo, 1979), 52, describe this period as "un

movimiento general de modernización de la sociedad dominicana, consistente en la reorganización de los servicios públicos, dotándolas de sistemas de funcionamiento más eficientes, en la apertura de nuevas vías de comunicación, construcción de escuelas, realización de obras de infraestructura urbana, etc."

12. This characteristic is generally accepted as the central element of peasant economies. Teodor Shanin, in *The Awkward Class: Political Sociology of Peasantry in a Developing Society, Russia, 1910–1925* (Oxford, England: Clarendon Press, 1972), 28, e.g., writes: "The nature of peasant households seems to constitute the most significant single characteristic of the peasantry as a specific social phenomenon . . . A peasant household is characterized by the nearly total integration of the peasant family's life with its farming enterprise." The double function of the household as unit of consumption and production is analyzed in A. V. Chayanov, *The Theory of Peasant Economy*, ed. D. Thorner et al. (Homewood, Ill.: Irwin, 1966). See also Eric R. Wolf, *Peasants* (Englewood Cliffs, N.J.: Prentice-Hall, 1966), 14–17.

13. This is the basic assumption in Goran Hyden, *Beyond Ujamaa in Tanzania: Underdevelopment and an Uncaptured Peasantry* (London: Heinemann, 1980). Also see William Roseberry, *Coffee and Capitalism in the Venezuelan Andes* (Austin: Univ. of Texas Press, 1983), 99ff.

14. For a general appraisal of this problem, see Teodor Shanin, "The Peasantry as a Political Factor," in Shanin, *Awkward Class*, 203–18. For the Dominican history, see Michiel Baud, "The Struggle for Autonomy: Peasant Resistance to Capitalism in the Dominican Republic, 1870–1924," in *Labour in the Caribbean: From Emancipation to Independence*, ed. Malcolm Cross and Gad Heuman, 120–40 (London: Macmillan, 1988).

15. Fernando Ortiz, *Cuban Counterpoint: Tobacco and Sugar* (1940; rpt. New York: Random House, 1970), 30–31.

16. See, e.g., Karl J. Pelzer, *Planter and Peasant: Colonial Policy and the Agrarian Struggle in East Sumatra, 1863–1947* ('s-Gravenhage, Netherlands: Martinus Nijhoff, 1978).

17. Good monographs on coffee production are much more numerous than those on tobacco: Laird W. Bergad, *Coffee and the Growth of Agrarian Capitalism in Nineteenth-Century Puerto Rico* (Princeton, N.J.: Princeton Univ. Press, 1983); Carolyn Hall, *El café y el desarrollo histórico-geográfico de Costa Rica* (San José: Editorial Costa Rica, 1978); Thomas Holloway, *Immigrants of the Land: Coffee and Society in São Paulo, 1886–1934* (Chapel Hill: Univ. of North Carolina Press, 1980); Marco Palacios, *Coffee in Colombia, 1850–1970: An Economic, Social and Political History* (Cambridge, England: Cambridge Univ. Press, 1980); Fernando Picó, *Amargo café (Los pequeños y medianos caficultores de Utuado en la segunda mitad del siglo XIX)* (Río Piedras, Puerto Rico: Huracán, 1981); and Roseberry, *Coffee and Capitalism.* Interesting also is the discussion in *Revista de Historia* (Costa Rica) 14 (July–Dec. 1986), with contributions by L. Gudmundson, C. LeGrand, W. Roseberry, and E. Kuznesof. See, too, William Roseberry, "Beyond the Agrarian Question in Latin

America," in Frederick Cooper et al., *Confronting Historical Paradigms: Peasants, Labor, and the Capitalist World System in Africa and Latin America* (Madison: Univ. of Wisconsin Press, 1993), 318–68, esp. 352–57.

18. Catherine LeGrand, "Comentarios sobre 'La Costa Rica cafetalera en contexto comparado,' de Lowell Gudmundson," *Revista de Historia* 14 (July–Dec. 1986): 41–52, esp. 44.

19. Pedro F. Bonó, "Apuntes sobre las clases trabajadoras dominicanas" (1881), in *Papeles de Pedro F. Bonó,* ed. E. Rodríguez Demorizi (Barcelona: Editorial M. Pareja, 1964), 190–245. Also see H. Hoetink, "El Cibao, 1844–1900: Su aportación a la formación social de la República," *Eme Eme Estudios Dominicanos* 8, no. 48 (May–June 1980): 3–19. On the ideas of Bonó, see Raymundo González, "Bonó, un intelectual de los pobres," *Estudios Sociales* 18, no. 60 (Apr.–June 1985): 65–77.

20. "La agricultura en el Cibao," EdlO, no. 1741 (2 Sept. 1893). Rafael Abreu Licairac (1850–1915) was a liberal opponent of Heureaux. See Rufino Martínez, *Diccionario biográfico-histórico dominicano, 1821–1930* (Santo Domingo: UASD, 1971), 21.

21. In the 1920s, the Cibao intellectuals Amado F. Bidó and Ramón Emilio Jiménez voiced such opinions. Jiménez later became an ideologue of the Trujillo dictatorship. See, e.g., his *Trujillo y la Paz* (Ciudad Trujillo: Impresora Dominicana, 1952). For similar constructions of peasant producers as the bearers of national identity in Puerto Rico, see Bergad, *Coffee and the Growth,* 60–62. For Colombia: Charles Bergquist, *Labor in Latin America: Comparative Essays on Chile, Argentina, Venezuela, and Colombia* (Stanford, Calif.: Stanford Univ. Press, 1986), 274–81.

22. E.g., Franc Baez Evertsz, *Azúcar y Dependencia en la República Dominicana* (Santo Domingo: UASD, 1978); Jacqueline Boin and José Serulle Ramia, *El proceso de desarrollo del capitalismo en la República Dominicana, 1844–1930,* 2 vols. (Santo Domingo: Editorial Gramil, 1979 and 1981); Roberto Cassá, *Historia social y económica de la República Dominicana,* 2 vols. (Santo Domingo: Alfa y Omega, 1977 and 1980); José Del Castillo et al., *La Gulf + Western en República Dominicana* (Santo Domingo: Taller/UASD, 1974); Wilfredo Lozano, *La dominación imperialista en la República Dominicana, 1900–1930* (Santo Domingo: UASD, 1976).

23. See, e.g., Boin and Serulle Ramia, *El proceso de desarrollo,* 2:194: "El proceso de descomposición del campesinado tiene lugar paralelamente al proceso de expansión de la economía monetaria en detrimento de la economía natural." However, these ideas were not exclusive to Marxist thinking. See, e.g., S. J. Gonzalo Arroyo et al., *El campesino dominicano: Un estudio de marginalidad* (Santiago de Chile: Centro para el Desarrolle Económico y Social de América Latina, [1966]). The authors of this study stress "la falta de cohesión del campesinado como grupo social" and therefore "el escaso potencial real de participación en las decisiones relativas a su incorporación al desarrollo global, que tiene el campesinado dominicano" (2).

24. David B. Bray, "Dependency, Class Formation, and the Creation of Caribbean Labor Reserves" (Ph.D. diss., Brown Univ., 1983); Patrick E. Bryan, "The Transfor-

mation of the Dominican Economy" (Ph.D. diss., Univ. of London, 1978). In this context we could also mention Luis A. Crouch, "The Development of Capitalism in Dominican Agriculture" (Ph.D. diss., Univ. of California, 1981), although he places more emphasis on the destructive tendencies of world capitalism.

25. Kenneth E. Sharpe, *Peasant Politics: Struggle in a Dominican Village* (Baltimore, Md.: Johns Hopkins Univ. Press, 1977); Bryan, "Transformation of the Dominican Economy." Also see Pedro L. San Miguel, "The Dominican Peasantry and the Market Economy: The Peasants of the Cibao, 1880–1960" (Ph.D. diss., Columbia Univ., 1987). This approach is also apparent in numerous essays by H. Hoetink, collected in *Santo Domingo y el Caribe. Ensayos sobre cultura y sociedad* (Santo Domingo: Fundación Cultural Dominicana, 1994).

26. Fernando I. Ferrán, *Tabaco y sociedad: La organización del poder en el ecomercado de tabaco dominicano* (Santo Domingo: Fondo para el Avance de las Ciencias Sociales, 1976).

27. They are published in Paul Mutto, "La economía de exportación de la República Dominicana, 1900–1930," *Eme Eme Estudios Dominicanos* 3, no. 15 (Nov.–Dec. 1974): 67–110.

28. "Nuestra cosecha de tobacco," LIN 12, no. 3107 (6 Oct. 1927). In this year the tobacco trade suddenly ceased, because the crop size was 300,000 quintales instead of the predicted 500,000.

29. Michiel Baud, "La gente del tabaco: Villa González en el siglo veinte," *Ciencia y Sociedad* 9, no. 1 (Jan.–Apr. 1984): 101–37.

30. For an evaluation of this type of historical fieldwork, see Michiel Baud, "Para oír a los sin voz: Posibilidades y limitaciones de la historia oral," *Ciencia y Sociedad* 10, no. 4 (Oct.–Dec. 1985): 451–71. About my fieldwork material, see "Essay on Sources" in this book.

31. David W. Sabean, *Power in the Blood: Popular Culture and Village Discourse in Early Modern Germany* (Cambridge, England: Cambridge Univ. Press, 1984), 2.

2. TOBACCO AND THE CIBAO, 1870–1930: THE REGIONAL ECONOMY

1. Victor Place, "Memoria sobre el cultivo, la cosecha y la venta de los tabacos," in Boin and Serulle Ramia, *El proceso de desarrollo,* 1:194.

2. See, e.g., "Sobre los billetes de la Junta de Crédito," *El Monitor* 3, no. 101 (10 Aug. 1867): "Las provincias de Cibao, mantienen en movimiento durante su cosecha de tabaco más de un million de duros."

3. "El Tabaco y el Cibao," EdP 4, no. 198 (10 Mar. 1886).

4. This idea of an integrated regional system was, of course, first expressed by P. F. Bonó in his "Apuntes sobre las clases trabajadoras dominicanas" (1881). See Rodríguez Demorizi, *Papeles de Bonó,* esp. 196–201.

5. For the 1863 figures, see José Ramón Abad, *La República Dominicana: Reseña general geográfico-estadística* (1888; rpt. Santo Domingo: Banco Central, 1973), 87. For 1920: *Primer Censo Nacional de República Dominicana, 1920* (1923; rpt. Santo Domingo: UASD, 1975), 142. Part of this increase was the result of immigration. For a well-documented overview of groups of immigrants: José Del Castillo, "Las emigraciones y su aporte a la cultura dominicana (finales del siglo XIX y principios del XX)," *Eme Eme Estudios Dominicanos* 8, no. 45 (Nov.–Dec. 1979): 3–43.

6. The population of the provinces of Santiago and Monte Cristi was said to have been 40,000 in 1875: "Apuntes históricos de Santiago," EdP 9, no. 290 (7 Apr. 1891). If we hold onto the figure of 90,000 for the entire region in 1863, it is evident that the majority of the population lived in the region east of Santiago.

7. All these figures are estimates. The limits of the Cibao region were unclear, and the figures can be compared only with great caution. The 1863 figure is from an ecclesiastical count. See Abad, *República Dominicana,* 87. To obtain the figures for 1908 and 1920, the population figures of the provinces Monte Cristi, Santiago, Pacificador, y Espaillat are taken together: Frank Moya Pons, "Nuevas consideraciones sobre la historia de la población dominicana: Curvas, tasas y problemas," *Eme Eme Estudios Dominicanos* 3, no. 15 (Nov.–Dec. 1974), 26.

8. The pattern of population growth in Santiago rose from 5,482 inhabitants in 1874; to 8,140 in 1893; 9,398 in 1898; 10,921 in 1904; 14,774 in 1916; and 17,152 in 1920. From *Censo de población y datos históricos y estadísticos de la ciudad de Santiago de los Caballeros (terminado el 31 de Diciembre de 1916)* (Santiago: La Información, 1917), 76; *Primer Censo,* 126. In comparison, the figures for La Vega were 5,547 in 1909 ("Censo de Población de la Ciudad de La Vega," Anexo de Memoria de Interior y Policía, 1909, AGN) and 6,564 in 1920 (*Primer Censo,* 126). See also H. Hoetink, *The Dominican People, 1850–1900: Notes for a Historical Sociology* (1972; Baltimore, Md.: Johns Hopkins Univ. Press, 1982), 43–44.

9. Samuel Hazard, *Santo Domingo: Past and Present with a Glance at Hayti* (1873; rpt. Santo Domingo: Editorial de Santo Domingo, 1982), 316–25.

10. From the 1960s on, when many foreign companies had offices in Santiago and took care of the tobacco buying themselves, an inverse situation sometimes occurred. Foreign exporters lent money on the local capital market. Although interests were higher than in Europe, they economized on transfer costs.

11. E.g., "Grave Cuestión," EdP 10, no. 293 (3 June 1891). Also see Abad, *República Dominicana,* and Hoetink, *Dominican People,* 84–87.

12. Hoetink, *Dominican People,* 69–87.

13. This is well documented for the sugar-cane plantations in the southern part of the country, but it also happened on the fruit and cocoa plantations, e.g., the Bay Fruit Co. and "Evolución" in Sabana de la Mar: "Letter Ayuntamiento Sabana de la Mar," 16 Dec. 1894, in IP, box 148, folder 14.

14. Letter from Gov. J. V. Núñez of Santiago, 14 Dec. 1870, in IP, box 11. The same

situation had occurred in 1854 when the start of the Crimean War in Europe resulted in low tobacco prices: *El Porvenir* 4 (29 Oct. 1854).

15. See the list in Dr. A. Llemas, "Apuntes históricos y estadísticos acerca de Santiago de los Caballeros," EdP 9, no. 290 (7 Apr. 1891). Santiago was besieged in 1866; 1867; during the "Combate de 5 agosto" (1873?); 1875; 1878; and 1886. Also there were "terribles combates" in 1889. With respect to the climate, famine scourged the Cibao in 1872 due to a prolonged drought.

16. "La situación actual," *El Porvenir* 1, no. 50 (28 Dec. 1872).

17. See, e.g., a report on the consequences of the German tariff policy on the Cibao tobacco sector, in the Dutch tobacco journal *De Tabaksplant* 7, no. 334 (23 Sept. 1879). It observed "great distress" (*groote ellende*) in the region and wrote that "some of the larger farmers have substituted tobacco for sugar or coffee."

18. Antonio Lluberes, "La crisis del tabaco cibaeño, 1879–1930," in Antonio Lluberes, José del Castillo, and Ramón Albuquerque, *Tabaco, azúcar y minería* (Santo Domingo: Banco de Desarrollo Interamericana, 1984), 3–22. See also appendix 1 in the present volume.

19. "Caminos!," VdS 2, no. 64 (12 June 1881).

20. EdP 1, no. 35 (3 Dec. 1882).

21. "La cosecha de 1886," EdP 4, no. 204 (9 May 1886).

22. For the figures, see our app. 1. The tobacco was packed in *serones*, also called *bultos*, which were supposed to contain a *quintal* of 100 pounds of 0.46 kilogram but usually contained some 60 kilos.

23. See the list given in Dr. A. Llemas, "Apuntes históricos y estadísticos acerca de Santiago de los Caballeros," EdP 9, no. 290 (7 Apr. 1891). Santiago was besieged in 1866, in 1867, during the "Combate de 5 agosto" (1873?), in 1875, in 1878, and in 1886. Also there were "terribles combates" in 1889. With respect to the climate, a famine scourged the Cibao in 1872 due to a prolonged drought.

24. "Ramo de Estadística (I)," EdP 2, no. 68 (22 July 1883).

25. See "Bremen, 1894," *De Tabaksplant* 12, no. 1131 (22 Jan. 1895).

26. E.g., between the years 1920–21 and 1925–26. See our app. 1.

27. "Informe mensual de la Cámara de Comercio de Santiago, Julio 1928," in Gobernación de Santiago, box 7.

28. E.g., "Sobre tabaco, III," *El Diario* 7, no. 2018 (5 May 1909): "Mientras no se mejore el cultivo del tabaco y su acondicionamiento . . . hay que luchar sin tregua por disminuir a todo trance la cantidad de este fruto en nuestro mercado. Si el tabaco no vale porque no sirve, ¿para qué estimular su siembra con precios superiores a su valor?"

29. The figures of Mutto, "La economía de exportación," and the general picture that emerges from the sources indicate such a trend. Also see "Llegando al colmo: Especulaciones usurarios," LIN 3, no. 741 (1 Sept. 1918), in which the merchants were warned that crisis was imminent: "Si las ganancias obtenidas en las cosechas anteriores, i que les han permitido hecharse el lujo de instalarse palacialmente en la

ciudad i gastar manos llenas de dinero en continuos i espléndidos festivales, no les basta para satisfacer sus aspiraciones de sibaritismo." Of course, some bad periods occurred, esp. after the termination of the Dance of the Millions.

30. See chap. 7 of the present volume, "Tobacco as an Export Crop."

31. "Cuestión Tabaco: A los habitantes del campo," *El Orden* 1, no. 9 (4 Oct. 1874).

32. These letters can be found in the "Epistolario Noel," AGN—examples include letters from Dubocq, Arroyo Blanco, 12 Aug. 1859: I–D, no. 33, and 6 Aug. 1860: I–D, no. 38.

33. A number of these contracts are reproduced in Julio C. Rodríguez J. and Rosajilda Velez C., *El precapitalismo dominicano de la primera mitad del siglo XIX, 1780–1850* (Santo Domingo: UASD, 1980), 161ff.

34. See "Cuestión Tabaco," *El Orden* 1, no. 9 (4 Oct. 1874): "También tenemos entendido que en aquella época hacían poco caso del tabaco malo, o segunda, y así lo hacen aún varios cosecheros, como el general Sosa, de Canca." Also see M. C. Grullón, *Sobre nuestro tabaco* (Santo Domingo: Montalvo Hermano, 1919), 25. José Díaz and Zoilo García held a comparable position in the twentieth century.

35. Emilio Rodríguez Demorizi, ed., *Papeles dominicanos de Máximo Gómez* (Ciudad Trujillo, Dominican Republic: Editorial Montalvo, 1954), 31.

36. "¡Importante asunto! Mejora del cultivo de tabaco," EdP 7, no. 255 (30 Sept. 1889) The cultivated area was reported to be some thousand tareas (16 tareas equals 1 hectare).

37. "Memoria del Gobernador Civil y Militar de Santiago [José D. Pichardo?], 1889," in AGN; and "Memoria Ministerio de Fomento y Obras Públicas, 1889," GO 17, no. 816 (12 Apr. 1890).

38. Consul-General Tweedy to Home Office, 8 May 1893, cited in Bryan, "Transformation of the Dominican Economy," 138, n56.

39. "Congreso Nacional, 27-3-1889," GO 16, no. 778 (20 July 1889). Diputado Castillo remarked, "Ahora mi parecer es dejar ésta [a decrease in the export duties on tobacco] en beneficio del pueblo, y no quitarla al pueblo para cederla a particulares." Also see *El Orden* 3, no. 84 (22 June 1889); and Hoetink, *Dominican People,* 9.

40. The origins of the cocoa sector are vividly depicted in "Corresponsal de La Vega," VdS 1, no. 12 (13 June 1880).

41. "Tabaco en Santo Domingo," *El Diario* (14 May 1908). Some large-scale cocoa farmers are mentioned in "Fincas de cacao establecidas desde 1879," GO 9, no. 418 (17 June 1882).

42. See Mutto, *La economía de exportación,* esp. 108. In a number of years at the beginning of the twentieth century, the value of cocoa exports exceeded that of sugar exports.

43. Cited in Antonio Lluberes N., "El tabaco dominicano: De la manufactura al monopolio industrial," *Eme Eme Estudios Dominicanos* 6, no. 35 (Mar.–Apr. 1978): 5–8.

44. Lluberes, "El tabaco Dominicano," 12.

45. Michiel Baud, "German Trade in the Caribbean: The Case of Dominican Tobacco, 1844–1940," *Jahrbuch für Geschichte von Staat, Wintschaft und Gesellschaft Lateinamerikas* 25 (1988): 83–115, esp. 102. See also chap. 8 of the present volume, "Ideologies of Progress."

46. "Nuestra industria," LIN 3, no. 755 (16 July 1918).

47. "Destilería del Yaque, C. por A.," LIN 12, no. 3109 (8 Oct. 1927). Also see "Noticias de Villa González," LIN 13, no. 3088 (16 Mar. 1928).

48. "Hablando con el Presidente de la Compañía Agrícola Dominicana," LIN 15, 4807 (24 Dec. 1929). United States, Dominican Customs Receivership, *Report of the 23d Fiscal Period, Calendar Year 1929* (Washington, D.C.: U.S. Government Printing Office, 1930), 10. Further analysis of this enterprise, which was an important factor in rural society of the Cibao in the 1930s, falls outside the scope of this study.

49. For an example of a more traditional type of landowner who used his land principally for cattle, compare Manuel María Ventura, who possessed 22,552 tareas in the eastern Cibao in 1903: GO 20, no. 1514 (10 Oct. 1903).

50. See chap. 5 of the present volume, "Peasants and the Market."

51. Michiel Baud, "La huelga de los tabaqueros, Santiago, 1919: Un momento de la lucha obrera en la República Dominicana," *Estudios Sociales* 23, no. 81 (July–Sept. 1990): 3–19.

52. See, e.g., "Reglamentando la mendicidad," LIN 4, no. 1064 (9 Sept. 1919): "Ha sido i es costumbre de nuestro comercio, disponer una suma semanal para limosnar, que se reparte los sábados, cuando la doliente caravana de los mendigos en procesión pedigüeña recorre de puerta en puerta los tiendas i oficinas." About child shoeshiners: "Limpiabotas," LIN 2, no. 393 (19 Apr. 1917).

53. See, e.g., *Eco del Cibao* 1, no. 101 (11 Mar. 1905).

54. "Congreso Nacional, 14-6-1889," GO 16, no. 797 (30 Nov. 1889). In EdP 1, no. 21 (27 Aug. 1882): "Se entretienen en los almacenes en la preparación y empaque, un número regular de hembras y mujeres entendidos en la materia."

55. See, e.g., Tulio Cestero, *Por el Cibao* (Santo Domingo: Imp. Cuna de America, 1901), 77 (for Augusto Espaillat Sucs.), 81 (for Enrique Pou).

56. "Los Pobres y la Cosecha," LIN 8, no. 1928 (18 Dec. 1922). See also H. A. Franck, *Roaming through the West Indies* (New York: Century, 1921), 202: "The tobacco comes in great bales wrapped in *yagua*. . . . Women and boys are constantly picking these bales apart and strewing their contents about in various heaps."

57. "El Mercado de Tabaco en Santiago," LIN 10, no. 2163 (23 Apr. 1925).

58. Rodríguez Demorizi, *Papeles de Bonó*, 199.

59. "Congreso Nacional, 14-6-1889," GO 16, no. 797 (30 Nov. 1889).

60. "Rápida visita a Janico y San José de las Matas," EdP 3, no. 152 (23 Mar. 1885).

61. See Fco. Gregorio Fondeur, "La paralización de la industria del serón ocasiona una considerable merma en los beneficios del campesino nacional," LIN 14, no. 4713 (30 Aug. 1929): "Desde hace unos dos años se viene practicando y gradualmente generalizándose el empaque en diversos almacenes de nuestros

tabacos, con señalado menoscabo de la industria de serones, hilos, y del consumo de yaguas." In the 1930s, some initiatives were taken to protect this sector but to no avail. The serones were too heavy and therefore increased transportation costs, and European buyers did not like them. See Luis Carballo to Manuel Evertz, 9 Jan. 1931, in SEA, box 169.

62. E.g., E. Rodríguez Demorizi, *Papeles de Bonó*, 203–4, n. 50. Also see Hoetink, *Dominican People*, 48–50.

63. See letter from Gov. J. V. Núñez of Santiago, 3 Sept. 1872, IP, box 16.

64. "Cuestión recuas," *El Orden* 1, 50 (18 July 1875): "Es innegable que cierto número de *recueros*, con el objeto de apropiarse lo ageno o de hacer mas ligeras las cargas, abren los serones de tabaco, deshaciéndolos por la costura del fondo, y volviendo a coserlo habilmente, luego que han extraído una parte de su contenido."

65. "Sesiones del Congreso: Sesión del 3 de mayo de 1867," *El Monitor* 2, no. 97 (13 July 1867). GdStD 4, no. 179 (9 July 1877), celebrated the 10th anniversary of the cigar factory "La Esperanza" of Santiago N. Acevedo in Santo Domingo.

66. To name just a few: "El Paquete" and "La Esperanza" in Santo Domingo; "La Garantía," "La Unión," and "La Cibaeña" in Santiago: *La Patria* 1, no. 27 (13 Oct. 1877), and VdS 1, no. 37 (5 Dec. 1880).

67. Rodríguez Demorizi, *Papeles de Bonó,* 200.

68. Amado Franco Bidó, "Las Tabaquerías," LIN 9, no. 2325 (20 Feb. 1924): "En las fábricas de cigarros y cigarrillos muchos niños pobres que sus padres no pueden enviar a la escuela en el día por la escasez de recursos económicos, ganan allí el pan cotidiano para ayudar a su familia."

69. "Cámara de Diputados, 22-3-1911," GO 28, no. 2199 (10 June 1911). In "Cuestiones economicas," *El Diario* (30-3-1912), the following year wrote about "la reducción de la industria tabacalera a muy escaso número de fábricas."

70. Amado Franco Bidó, "Las Tabaquerías," LIN 9, no. 2325 (20 Feb. 1924).

71. Countless press reports dealt with this matter. Examples: "Dos cigarrerías clandestinas sorprendidas," LIN 10, no. 2292 (22 Sept. 1925); "Otra cigarrería clandestina sorprendida," LIN 10, no. 2294 (25 Sept. 1925); "Fabricadores clandestinos de cigarros sometidos a la justicia," LIN 11, no. 2581 (14 May 1926).

72. Many people still remember the *gavilleros*, cigars produced illegally and sold during the Trujillo era. The organization of the tobacco industry merits a study of its own. For such a study of the Cuban tobacco industry, see Jean Stubbs, *Tobacco on the Periphery: A Case Study in Cuban Labour History, 1860–1958* (Cambridge, England: Cambridge Univ. Press, 1985). On the situation in the Cibao, see Baud, "La huelga de los tabaqueros."

73. Cited in Ian Bell, *The Dominican Republic* (Boulder, Colo.: Westview, 1981), 136–37. Schomburgk alleged that one had to pay eight Spanish dollars for one load. Also see Hazard, *Santo Domingo,* 382–83.

74. "No se nos olvide," EdP 3, no. 111 (18 May 1884). An animal was valued at 50 pesos.

75. See also Jaime de J. Domínguez, *La dictadura de Heureaux* (Santo Domingo: UASD, 1986), 103–9.

76. Otto Schoenrich, *Santo Domingo: A Country with a Future* (New York: Macmillan, 1918), 207–14. The construction of the two Cibao railroads is treated in more detail in Michiel Baud, *Historia de un sueño: Los ferrocarriles públicos en la República Dominicana, 1880–1930* (Santo Domingo: Fundación Cultural Dominicana, 1993).

77. See, e.g., W. Figuero, "Memoria del Secretario de Estado de Interior y Policía," GO 15, no. 712 (14 Apr. 1888), stating that the district of Puerto Plata "que ve en peligro los intereses de su antigua preponderancia."

78. "Memoria Hacienda y Comercio, 1910," GO 28, no. 2178 (29 Mar. 1911).

79. Compare, for Navarrete, the speech of Diputado Acevedo: "Congreso Nacional, 13-3-1909," GO 26, no. 1993 (21 May 1909): "Navarrete sirve de punto donde van a establecerse durante la cosecha de esta hoja [de tabaco] muchos especuladores que compran por cuenta de comerciantes de Santiago, Moca, La Vega y Puerto Plata."

80. See F. J. Vásquez, "Memoria Fomento y Obras Públicas, 1905," AGN. It describes Altamira as "floreciente territorio."

81. See "Memoria Hacienda y Comercio, 1912," GO 30, no. 2453 (19 Nov. 1913): "La empresa [FCD] sufrió algunos deterioros extraordinarios en 1912. Fué incendiado el depósito de Puerto Plata, perdiéndose en valor del edificio y materiales almacenados $54,275. Dos estaciones más fueron también incendiadas; puentes fueron derribados, y las lluvias también ocasionaron algunos daños. Un tren fué asaltado en Barrabas, y la mayor parte de la carga que conducía se perdió."

82. Letter Ayuntamiento de la común de Moca (Manuel Cabrera hijo), 3 Feb. 1915, in F/OP, box A, 1915. Telegram from Cámara de Comercio de Santiago (Rafael Espaillat), 15 Jan. 1916, in F/OP, box B, 1917: "Empresa ferrocarril muy mal servicio. . . . Comercio sufre perdidas y terminará por ruina. Como 5,000 toneladas carga en Puerto Plata. Aquí como 50,000 bultos productos."

83. R. A. Delgado Carbonell, "Santiago se muere . . . ," LIN 8, no. 2104 (25 July 1923).

84. "El FCD frente a un problema," LIN 8, no. 2033 (8 May 1923).

85. "El FCD," LIN 12, no. 3041 (14 Nov. 1927).

86. E.g.: "Otra campanada: Ferrocarril de S a S": LIN 2, no. 478 (10 Aug. 1917): "La queja contra el elevado costo de fletes del ferrocarril es unánime. La Empresa Escocesa que tantas ventajas obtuvo a trueque de emprender la construcción del camino de hierro, muéstrase dura en conceder lo que reclaman de consumo la agricultura, la industria, y el comercio cibaeños."

3. Peasants and Historians: A Theoretical Survey

1. See, e.g., G. L. Beckford, *Persistent Poverty: Underdevelopment in Plantation Economies of the Third World* (Oxford, England: Oxford Univ. Press, 1972); José A. Benítez, *Las Antillas: Colonización, azúcar e imperialismo* (Havana, Cuba: Casa de las Americas, 1977).

2. Julian Steward et al., *The People of Puerto Rico* (Urbana: Univ. of Illinois Press, 1956).

3. A number of these articles were collected in Sidney W. Mintz, *Caribbean Transformations* (Chicago: Aldine, 1974).

4. See Ciro F. S. Cardoso, *Escravo ou camponês? O protocampesinato negro nas Américas* (São Paulo: Editora Brasiliense, 1987).

5. Mintz, *Caribbean Transformations*, 132–33; italics in original.

6. A study of the Jamaican peasantry that remains important and was written independently of Mintz's ideas in this period is G. Eisner, *Jamaica, 1830–1930: A Study in Economic Growth* (Manchester, England: Manchester Univ. Press, 1961); see esp. chap. 12, "The Growth of the Peasantry," 210–36. In an important monographical study on Guyana, *A History of the Guyanese Working People, 1881–1905* (Baltimore, Md.: Johns Hopkins Univ. Press, 1981), Walter Rodney rejects the term "peasants" but brilliantly describes the existence and struggle of a Caribbean peasantry; see esp. chap. 3, "Crisis and Creativity in the Small-Farming Sectors," 60–89. On Dominica: Michel-Rolph Trouillot, *Peasants and Capital: Dominica in the World Economy* (Baltimore, Md.: Johns Hopkins Univ. Press, 1988). On Trinidad: D. Harrison, "The Changing Fortunes of a Trinidad Peasantry," in *Peasants, Plantations and Rural Communities in the Caribbean*, ed. Malcolm Cross and A. Marks (Guildford, England: Univ. of Surrey; Leiden, Netherlands: Dept. of Caribbean Studies, Royal Institute of Linguistics and Anthropology, 1979): 54–85.

7. See, e.g., the somewhat idiosyncratic essay by Peter Fraser: "The Fictive Peasantry: Caribbean Rural Groups in the Nineteenth Century," in *Contemporary Caribbean: A Sociological Reader*, ed. Susan Craig, 1:319–47 (Maracas, Trinidad and Tobago: College Press, 1981).

8. Compare: H. Hoetink, review of *Papers in Caribbean Anthropology*, ed. I. Rouse and Sidney W. Mintz, in *Caribbean Studies* 1, no. 2 (July 1961): 23–25. Mintz answered, in his "The Question of Caribbean Peasantries: A Comment," *Caribbean Studies* 1, no. 3 (Oct. 1961): 31–34. The Cibao peasantry qualifies Mintz's statement that "those segments of the peasantry that can subsist without selling their own or their families' labor off the farm have always been tiny minorities in Caribbean history": Sidney W. Mintz, "From Plantations to Peasantries in the Caribbean," in *Caribbean Contours*, ed. Sidney W. Mintz and Sally Price (Baltimore, Md.: Johns Hopkins Univ. Press, 1985), 139.

9. He writes: "The urban-rural dichotomy [in Puerto Rico] is intertwined with the plantation-counterplantation tension in Caribbean cultural history. The *cimarrón* or runaway social formation involved two related aspects: the (economic) opposition to slave work and the (political) opposition to State rule." Angel G. Quintero Rivera, "The Rural-Urban Dichotomy in the Formation of Puerto Rico's Cultural Identity," *Nieuwe West-Indische Gids/New West Indian Guide* 61, no. 3–4 (1987): 129.

10. Trouillot, *Peasants and Capital*, 18–23 and passim. Sidney W. Mintz, "Slavery and the Rise of Peasantries," *Historical Reflections* 6, no. 1 (1979): 213–53.

11. For a similar historiographic interpretation, see Frederick Cooper et al., *Confronting Historical Paradigms: Peasants, Labor, and the Capitalist World System in Africa and Latin America* (Madison: Univ. of Wisconsin Press, 1993).

12. Trouillot, *Peasants and Capital*, 21. Also see Mintz, "Slavery and the Rise of Peasantries," 223.

13. The problems involved in formulating new insights may be demonstrated by the fact that an influential collection of articles, Teodor Shanin, ed., *Peasants and Peasant Societies* (Harmondsworth, England: Penguin, 1971), recently has been re-edited (rev. ed., Oxford, England: Basil Blackwell, 1987). For a negative assessment of this new edition, see William Roseberry, review of *Peasants and Peasant Societies* in JPS 16, no. 4 (July 1989): 631–34.

14. The influence of crops on social structures was one of the essential points of Steward's "cultural ecology" approach. See, e.g., R. D. Manners and J. H. Steward, "The Cultural Study of Contemporary Societies: Puerto Rico," *American Journal of Sociology* 59 (July 1953–May 1954): 129–30. They write: "The data suggest that under a system of production for profit and in the multiple context of a dependent, class-structured society, which participates in the world market, certain cultural forms and productivity arrangements tend to be associated in special ways with the crops cultivated. Thus, the nature of the crop . . . may favor the predominance of holdings within a certain range of size; may dictate the general patterns of inheritance and the rate of turnover in landholdings . . . and affect the nature of the family, the local clan structure, and the religious and political attitudes of the people." This idea was, of course, also the background of Ortiz, *Cuban Counterpoint*, and the work of Pedro F. Bonó. The case of sugar cane may warn us against too much crop determinism. Sugar was, and is, grown by peasant families all over the world, but as a food crop, satisfying part of the family's need for sucrose. At the beginning of the nineteenth century, sugar cane was considered "el pan de los pobres" in the Dominican Republic. The municipal council of Samaná tried to prohibit sugar-cane cultivation within town limits in 1891. Many people cultivated a patio with cane for their own consumption. See letter from Rodríguez Díaz, Samaná, 20 June 1891, in IP, box 130.

15. This situation formed the basis of the work of A. Chayanov; see his *Theory of Peasant Economy*.

16. See, e.g., A. Macfarlane, *The Origins of English Individualism: The Family, Property and Social Transition* (Oxford, England: Basil Blackwell, 1978), 24ff, 73.

17. See, e.g., the Peruvian case: J. Ossio Acuña and O. Medina García, *Familia campesina y economía de mercado* (Lima, Peru: Centro Regional de Estudios Socio-económicos, 1985), 77: "Un patrón común en la historia laboral de los campesinos, antes de establecerse en forma más o menos definitiva en sus comunidades, es la migración temporal a uno o varios lugares del territorio nacional."

18. Merilee S. Grindle, *Searching for Rural Development: Labor Migration and Employment in Mexico* (Ithaca, N.Y.: Cornell Univ. Press, 1988), 38. Also see

Florencia E. Mallon, *The Defense of Community in Peru's Central Highlands: Peasant Struggle and Capitalist Transition, 1860–1940* (Princeton, N.J.: Princeton Univ. Press, 1983), 247–67.

19. When Dominicans living in New York send dollars home today, they continue the pattern established by nineteenth-century migrant laborers, who sent home cash and goods. See Patricia R. Pessar, "Kinship Relations of Production in the Migration Process: The Case of Dominican Emigration to the United States," Occasional Papers No. 32, New York Univ., New York, 1982.

20. James C. Scott, *The Moral Economy of the Peasant: Rebellion and Subsistence in Southeast Asia* (New Haven, Conn.: Yale Univ. Press, 1976). He borrowed the term from E. P. Thompson. See the latter's "The Moral Economy of the English Crowd in the Eighteenth Century," *Past and Present* 50 (Feb. 1971): 76–136.

21. Scott observes, in *Moral Economy,* 176: "There is strong evidence that, along with reciprocity, the right to subsistence is an active moral principle in the little tradition of the village." About the responsibility of the rulers, see also Barrington Moore, *Injustice: The Social Bases of Obedience and Revolt* (New York: M. E. Sharpe, 1978), 21–31.

22. Hyden, *Beyond Ujamaa,* 18. Hyden speaks only of the internal organization of the peasant community. Contrary to the situation in Asia and Latin America, the position of "landlords" was insignificant in Africa.

23. See René Lemarchand, "African Peasantries, Reciprocity and the Market: The Economy of Affection Reconsidered," *Cahiers d'études africaines* 29, no. 113 (1989): 33–67. The problems of a simple dichotomy between "traditional" peasant production against "modern" capitalism come to light in Michael Taussig, *The Devil and Commodity Fetishism in South America* (Chapel Hill: Univ. of North Carolina Press, 1980).

24. Compare David Levine, *Reproducing Families: The Political Economy of English Population History* (Cambridge, England: Cambridge Univ. Press, 1987), 22–23. For an analysis of class struggle within peasant communities, see Frans J. Schryer, *Ethnicity and Class Conflict in Rural Mexico* (Princeton, N.J.: Princeton Univ. Press, 1990).

25. See esp. Brian Juan O'Neill, *Social Inequality in a Portuguese Hamlet: Land, Late Marriage, and Bastardy, 1870–1978* (Cambridge, England: Cambridge Univ. Press, 1987); and Jack Goody, Joan Thirsk, and E. P. Thompson, eds., *Family and Inheritance: Rural Society in Western Society, 1200–1800* (Cambridge, England: Cambridge Univ. Press, 1976). Also see Macfarlane, *Origins of English Individualism,* and Levine, *Reproducing Families,* 27 and passim.

26. Nola Reinhardt, *Our Daily Bread: The Peasant Question and Family Farming in the Colombian Andes* (Berkeley: Univ. of California Press, 1988), 7–8 and passim. Also see Daisy Dwyer and Judith Bruce, eds., *A Home Divided: Women and Income in the Third World* (Stanford, Calif.: Stanford Univ. Press, 1988), and G. Elwert and D. Wong, "Subsistence Production and Commodity Production in the Third World," *Review* 3, no. 3 (Winter 1980): 501–22, esp. 505.

27. N. Kasfir, "Are African Peasants Self-Sufficient?," *Development and Change* 17, no. 2 (Apr. 1986): 335–57, esp. 351.

28. An example of this kind of research is Sara S. Berry, *Fathers Work for their Sons: Accumulation, Mobility, and Class Formation in an Extended Yoruba Community* (Berkeley: Univ. of California Press, 1985).

29. Roseberry, *Coffee and Capitalism*, 197.

30. It may be significant that Eric Wolf, who in his *Europe and the People Without History* (Berkeley: Univ. of California Press, 1982) tries to present a global history without losing sight of the specifics of local societies, seems to avoid the word "peasant" consciously, using it very seldom.

31. Trouillot, *Peasants and Capital*, 19–20.

32. See, e.g., Rodney Hilton, "Introduction," in Paul Sweezy et al., *The Transition from Feudalism to Capitalism* (London: Verso, 1978), 9–30, esp. 27. Also see Catharina Lis and Hugo Soly, *Poverty and Capitalism in Pre-Industrial Europe* (Brighton, England: Harvester, 1979); although it tends to stress the uniformity of the process of impoverishment, the book is a vivid description of variations in the subordination of the European peasantry.

33. Hyden, e.g., writes in *Beyond Ujaama*: "One major political consequence of the dominance of the peasant household economically, and the familial mode socially and culturally, is indifference, sometimes active resistance, to operating in a framework of impersonal rules" (17).

34. For modernization theorists, peasant production will be superseded by the inevitable benefits of "progress," read as capitalism. The Marxist position is more complicated. The basic idea is that it was in the relation with the market that surplus value was extracted from the peasant economy. Where land had not (yet) been monopolized and the importance of land rent therefore was limited, commerce was considered instrumental in the process of "primitive accumulation." Surplus value was extracted from the producers without structurally changing pre-capitalist relations of production. Often a distinction is made between "peasant" production and "simple commodity" production. It is argued that the latter form of domestic production is only one step away from capitalism, while the former must still be considered purely pre-capitalist. In this point of view, peasant production was organized according to noncapitalist principles. Simple commodity production is supposed to be organized according to capitalist principles except for the use of domestic, nonwage labor. Gavin Smith, e.g., writes: "Under SCP all moments of production but one, the use of domestic labor, are expressed through commodities, while peasants engage in production through the use of many institutions that allow them access to resources and to labor *unmediated by the commodity form*" (italics Smith's). Gavin Smith, *Livelihood and Resistance: Peasants and the Politics of Land in Peru* (Berkeley: Univ. of California Press, 1989), 156–57. Also see J. M. Chevalier, "There Is Nothing Simple about Simple Commodity Production," JPS 10, no. 4 (1983): 153–86.

35. On Brazil: Roderick J. Barman, "The Brazilian Peasantry Reexamined: The Implications of the Quebra-Quilo Revolt, 1874–75," HAHR 57, no. 3 (1977): 401–24. Also see David Lehmann, "Introduction: Andean Societies and the Theory of Peasant Economy," in *Ecology and Exchange in the Andes,* ed. David Lehmann (Cambridge, England: Cambridge Univ. Press, 1982), 1–26. For a classical African example, see Polly Hill, *The Migrant Cocoa Farmers of Southern Ghana* (Cambridge, England: Cambridge Univ. Press, 1963). Also see Sara S. Berry, *Cocoa, Custom and Socio-Economic Change in Rural Western Nigeria* (Oxford, England: Clarendon Press, 1975); and J. Boesen and A. T. Mohele, *The "Success Story" of Peasant Tobacco Production in Tanzania* (Uppsala, Sweden: Scandinavian Institute of African Studies, 1979).

36. This is one of the key elements in the "revisionist" interpretation of Andean *enganche* labor in the work of Michael J. Gonzales; see his *Plantation Agriculture and Social Control in Northern Peru, 1875–1933* (Austin: Univ. of Texas Press, 1985), and his "Capitalist Agriculture and Labour Contracting in Northern Peru, 1880–1905," *Journal of Latin American Studies* 12, no. 2 (1980): 291–314.

37. This was written in a review of the work of Robert Brenner by Terence Ranger, "Recent Discussion of African Peasantries: A Survey" (Keynote Paper for Conference of African Studies Association of the United Kingdom on "Recent Changes in Development Theory and Africa," Manchester, England, 1980), 15.

38. Terence Ranger, *Peasant Consciousness and Guerrilla War in Zimbabwe* (London: James Currey, 1985), 31.

39. Compare Diana Wong, *Peasants in the Making: Malaysia's Green Revolution* (Singapore: Institute of Southeast Asian Studies, 1987), 20–21.

40. Ibid., 25.

41. Here I refer, of course, to Samuel L. Popkin, *The Rational Peasant* (Berkeley: Univ. of California Press, 1976), attacking Scott's idea of a "moral economy." He had precursors in Latin American anthropology, such as Sol Tax, *Penny Capitalism: A Guatemalan Indian Community* (1953; rpt. Chicago: Univ. of Chicago Press, 1963). Scott and Hyden are clear exponents of the contrary opinion. For a more recent emphasis on the opposition between a precapitalist peasant economy and the market, see Taussig, *The Devil and Commodity Fetishism.*

42. In Latin America, Claude Meillassoux, *Femmes, greniers et capitaux* (Paris: Maspero, 1975) is best known. However, this book still depicts a capitalism that is all-dominant, irresistably undermining and destroying all its adversaries. It is uneven development, and the active influence of local populations in capitalist development, that needs to be stressed. See, e.g., Peter Geschiere, *Village Communities and the State: Changing Relations among the Maka of Southeastern Cameroon since the Colonial Conquest* (London: Kegan Paul International, 1982). For the Dominican Republic, Crouch, in "Development of Capitalism in Dominican Agriculture," goes a long way in this direction.

43. Wolf, *Europe and the People Without History,* 75–77 and passim.

44. See, e.g., P. Singelmann, *Structures of Domination and Peasant Movements in Latin America* (Columbia: Univ. of Missouri Press, 1981), 55–57. Also Alain De Janvry, *The Agrarian Question and Reformism in Latin America* (Baltimore, Md.: Johns Hopkins Univ. Press, 1981).

45. In the Andean region, where the peasant population had not lost its access to land, this struggle for labor control was particularly intense. The interpretation of this struggle has led to a major debate in Bolivian historiography. See Erwin P. Grieshaber, "Survival of Indian Communities in 19th-Century Bolivia: A Regional Comparison," *Journal of Latin American Studies* 12 (1980): 223–69. For the Peruvian Andes: Norman Long and Bryan Roberts, *Miners, Peasants and Entrepreneurs: Regional Development in the Central Highlands of Peru* (Cambridge, England: Cambridge Univ. Press, 1984), 82–83.

46. Mintz, "Slavery and the Rise of Peasantries," 220. For the Cuban case, see Robert B. Hoernel, "A Comparison of Sugar and Social Change in Puerto Rico and Oriente, Cuba, 1898–1959" (Ph.D. diss., Johns Hopkins Univ., 1977), 61.

47. A general overview: Ciro F. S. Cardoso and Héctor Pérez Brignoli, *Historia económica de América Latina*, 2 vols. (Barcelona, Spain: Editorial Crítica, 1979), esp. chap. 4, "La transición al capitalismo periférico (Siglo XIX)." It is well known that Dominican President Trujillo ran many of his enterprises with this kind of conscript labor.

48. I agree completely with the critique of Steve Stern on the world-system theories of Immanuel Wallerstein. He writes: "In Wallerstein's big picture, the imprint of the laboring poor of Latin America and the Caribbean . . . shrinks to futile resistance to the external force, on terms that do not change in any meaningful way the course of the world-system's impact on economic life and social relations in the American corner of the world. The contours of popular struggles, successes, and failures are so determined by the world-system's framework the historical 'agency' shrivels up." Steve J. Stern, "Feudalism, Capitalism, and the World-System in the Perspective of Latin America and the Caribbean," *American Historical Review* 93, no. 4 (Oct. 1988): 896. The same issue contains Wallerstein's "Reply" (873–85) and Stern's "Reply: 'Ever More Solitary'" (886–97). See also the essays in Charles Bright and Susan Harding, eds., *Statemaking and Social Movements: Essays in History and Theory* (Ann Arbor: Univ. of Michigan Press, 1984).

49. In the Andes, hacendados often protected "their" colonos from military service or abuse by state officials. In many parts of Latin America, rural elites organized armed peasant bands to resist state intervention. See, e.g., Lewis Taylor, *Bandits and Politics in Peru: Landlord and Peasant Violence in Hualgayoc, 1900–1930* (Cambridge, England: Cambridge Univ., Centre of Latin American Studies, 1988).

50. Compare Roseberry, *Coffee and Capitalism*, 107, who stresses that capitalism was introduced through private persons "who were pursuing their own interests, interests that cannot be reduced to, and might be in conflict with, those of 'capitalism' or the 'world system.'" For Puerto Rico, see Bergad, *Coffee and the Growth of Agrarian Capitalism*, 181–83.

51. For these different situations, see, e.g., Joel S. Migdal, *Peasants, Politics, and Revolution: Pressures toward Political and Social Change in the Third World* (Princeton, N.J.: Princeton Univ. Press, 1974), 33–45. Also see Jeffrey M. Paige, *Agrarian Revolution: Social Movements and Export Agriculture in the Underdeveloped World* (London: Macmillan, 1975).

52. This attitude could also lead to open rebellion against the state. See, for the Andes, Taylor, *Bandits and Politics in Peru*. Also Carlos Aguirre and Charles Walker, eds., *Bandoleros, abigeos y montoneros: Criminalidad y violencia en el Peru, siglos XVIII–XX* (Lima: Instituto de Apoyo Agrario, 1990).

53. For an erudite discussion of this system, see Stephen Gudeman, "The *Compadrazgo* as a Reflection of the Natural and Spiritual Person," in *Proceedings of the Royal Anthropological Institute of Great Britain and Ireland* for 1971 (London, 1972), 45–71. For a case study intelligently exploring the complexities of these relations, see Jeffrey L. Gould, *To Lead as Equals: Rural Protest and Political Consciousness in Chinandega, Nicaragua, 1912–1979* (Chapel Hill: Univ. of North Carolina Press, 1990).

54. This is, e.g., suggested in Seligson, *Peasants of Costa Rica,* 153–69. Marco Palacios suggests the same thing for the Colombian situation, in his *Coffee in Colombia,* 80–83 and passim.

55. See, e.g., Palacios, *Coffee in Colombia,* 154–57.

56. Compare S. H. Alatas, *The Myth of the Lazy Native: A Study of the Malays, Filipinos and Javanese from the Sixteenth to the Twentieth Centuries and Its Function in the Ideology of Colonial Capitalism* (London: Frank Cass, 1977).

57. Taussig, *The Devil and Commodity Fetishism*; Gould, *To Lead as Equals,* 28–31.

58. Michael Adas, "From Avoidance to Confrontation: Peasant Protest in Pre-Colonial and Colonial Asia," CSSH 23 (1981): 217–47; James C. Scott, *Weapons of the Weak: Everyday Forms of Peasant Resistance* (New Haven, Conn.: Yale Univ. Press, 1985).

59. The metaphor is from Witold Kula, *An Economic Theory of the Feudal System: Toward a Model of the Polish Economy, 1500–1800* (1962; rpt. London: New Left Books, 1976), 67.

60. Goran Hyden, "The Resilience of the Peasant Mode of Production: The Case of Tanzania," in *Agricultural Development in Africa: Issues of Public Policy,* ed. Robert H. Bates and M. F. Lofchie (New York: Praeger, 1980), 218–43, esp. 223.

61. See, e.g., the critique in Kasfir, "Are African Peasants Self-Sufficient?" Also Peter Geschiere, "La paysannerie africaine est-elle captive?," *Politique africaine* 14 (1984): 13–34.

62. Scott, *Weapons of the Weak,* 348.

63. Ibid., 346. This is also the essential idea in Wolf, *Europe and the People Without History*.

4. The Tobacco-Producing Peasantry in the Cibao: The Logic of Small-Scale Agriculture

1. See chap. 3 of the present volume, "Peasants and Historians: A Theoretical Survey," for a discussion of these theories.

2. Bonó, "Cuestiones sociales y agrícolas" (1880), in Rodríguez Demorizi, *Papeles de Bonó*, 263. I presume that where Bonó writes *emigrantes*, today we would write *inmigrantes*.

3. See, e.g., "Los beneficios de la irrigación," LIN 11, no. 2614 (21 June 1926); "El éxito de la irrigación en Mao," LIN 12, no. 2990 (8 Mar. 1927); "El canal de irrigación," LIN 13, no. 4008 (11 Apr. 1928).

4. Hoetink, "El Cibao, 1844–1900," esp. 6–7, also stresses the frontier character of Cibao society, but sees the "fronteras internas" gradually disappearing in the nineteenth century.

5. Some of them also lived in more isolated parts of the region. What they shared was their dependence on agricultural activity. They often also did some simple handicraft and sometimes possessed a *trapiche* to grind sugar cane. The logic of peasant production becomes clear in a description of a Catalán farmer and his family, who was encountered by another British traveler near Guayabín in 1830: "He cultivated a little coffee, some cotton, sugar-cane, which he ground with a small mill worked by two horses, and vegetables. He manufactured sugar, syrup, and tafia. . . . In short, though poor, they were independent, and possessed all that they could desire in a genial climate and a productive soil." C. MacKenzie, *Notes on Haiti Made during a Residence in that Republic*, 2 vols. (1830; rpt. London: Frank Cass, 1971), 204–5.

6. R. Kiszling, *Beknopt handboek van de tabakskennis, tabaksteelt en tabaksfabricage* [*Short Handbook of the Knowledge, Cultivation and Manufacture of Tobacco*] (Amsterdam: Kuilenburg, Blom & Oliviers, 1907), 19.

7. Johannes Wilbert, *Tobacco and Shamanism in South America* (New Haven, Conn.: Yale Univ. Press, 1987), 87.

8. Manuel Llanos Company, "Evolución de las técnicas para el cultivo del tabaco en las colonias hispano-americanos," *Anuario de Estudios Americanos* 40 (1983): 469–96, esp. 472. Also see C. O. Sauer, *The Early Spanish Main* (Berkeley: Univ. of California Press, 1966), 56–57.

9. P. Gisquet and H. Hitier, *La production du tabac* (Paris: Ballière, 1961), 25. They speak of some 60 classes.

10. This contrast may warn us again against too strong a crop determinism. On the other hand, the accepted image of the Cuban tobacco producer, which is reflected here and which is based principally on the work of Fernando Ortiz, may obscure the fact that in Cuba, too—esp. in the Oriente—the "Dominican" type of subsistence-oriented tobacco cultivation occurred.

11. See Iturbides G. Zaldívar L., *Producción y comercialización del tabaco negro en la República Dominicana* (Santiago: UCMM, 1979), 8–9.

12. See, e.g., the Colombian case: John Parker Harrison, *The Colombian Tobacco Industry from Government Monopoly to Free Trade, 1778–1876* (Bogotá: Centro de Estudios Sobre Desarrollo Económico, Universidad de los Andes, 1969). Also see William P. McGreevey, *An Economic History of Colombia* (Cambridge, England: Cambridge Univ. Press, 1971). Climate is of less importance. Although tobacco originates in a (sub)tropical environment, it grows wherever a summer with sufficient sunshine exists. Tobacco was cultivated in Europe in places as far north as Holland and northern Germany. It is still an important crop in the Canadian lake region around Toronto. Akehurst emphasizes the flexibility of the plant, which easily adapts to different environmental circumstances and has developed into an endless series of types, subtypes, and varieties. B. C. Akehurst, *Tobacco* (London: Longmans, 1968), 28.

13. E.g., Abad, *República Dominicana*, 297. See also Baron de Candia, "Temas agrícolas," LD 21, no. 6250 (19 Apr. 1910): "El procedimiento de nuestros campesinos es harto conocido: tumban un monte virjen, lo cercan, y hacen sus siembras de frutos menores luego de practicadas la quema y el hábite."

14. For the introduction of the plow, see *El Orden* 1, no. 51 (25 July 1875). Hoetink dates the introduction of the plow in the Cibao to 1898: Hoetink, *Dominican People*, 5.

15. Abad, *República Dominicana*, 297.

16. Letter of Gov. J. Rodríguez of La Vega, 17 Sept. 1872, in IP, box 15, 1872.

17. See, e.g., Abad, *República Dominicana*, 317. This theme is treated more extensively in chap. 9 of the present volume, "The Struggle for Technology."

18. Louise Fresco, *Cassava in Shifting Cultivation: A Systems Approach to Agricultural Technology Development in Africa* (Amsterdam: Royal Tropical Institute, 1986), 134. For the Cibao: "A los cultivadores del campo," RdA 1, no. 5 (Aug. 1905): 83.

19. See Augusto Ortega, "Breves apuntes acerca de la psicología Dominicano, etc., de Santiago, 20-3-1922," in Emilio Rodríguez Demorizi, ed., *Lengua y folklore de Santo Domingo* (Santiago: UCMM, 1975), 142. Compare also Louise Fresco's discussion of farming practices in Zaire, where women (farmers) observe that "if a man wants to be nice to his wife, he opens up a new field for her"; Fresco, *Cassava in Shifting Cultivation*, 134.

20. See, e.g., the opinion of José Gabriel Aldebot in "El tabaco dominicano," *El Diario*, 4 Apr. 1924.

21. Letter from Junta de Fomento, La Vega, 9 June 1875, in F/OP, box 2, folder VII.

22. Informant 30. This logic of the family economy still existed in 1935. See the description of Mayor Rafael Espaillat of Santiago: "Cada familia, generalmente, tiene su conuco i si el tiempo es favorable nunca falta el alimento en la familia. Cuando se prolonga un estado de sequía, la situación cambia completamente; se agotan los 'viveres,' como llaman ellos. Lo único que perdura en el terreno es la yuca; las gallinas no se pueden mantener por falta de maiz; hai que vender el puerquito que se tenía para el engorde." Rafael Espaillat, "Datos sobre el costo de la vida," 1935, in Sección de Comercio, box 40, no. 268.

23. See, e.g., "La cosecha en este año se ha reducido a la mitad de lo que se esperaba fuese, a no haber faltado las lluvias en los días de resiembra," EdP 3, no. 155 (12 Apr. 1885). Also *El Diario* 5, no. 1352 (31 Jan. 1907): "Buena parte de la actual cosecha de tabaco se ha perdido, debido a la prolongada seca que reina en estas comarcas."

24. The newspapers of the period abound with information about these problems. To give just one example: the harvest of 1885 produced only 25 percent of the expected amount of tobacco due to "la prolongada seca." "Efectos de la seca," EdP 4, no. 174 (6 Sept. 1885).

25. "Cultivo del tabaco, II," GdStD 4, no. 360 (26 Jan. 1865).

26. H. A. Allard and H. F. Allard, *Tobacco in the Dominican Republic*, Foreign Agricultural Report No. 30 (Washington D.C.: U.S. Dept. of Agriculture, 1948), 12. Instructor Encargado del Tabaco J. L. Amargos, Report to the Dept. of Agriculture on "Usos del citrato de hierro amoniacal en el cultivo del tabaco," 30 June 1923, in Sección de Agricultura, 7. In 1977, only a third of the tobacco-growing peasants in the Villa González region used fertilizer; Baud, "La gente del tabaco," 115.

27. Grullón, *Sobre nuestro tabaco*, 21.

28. E. C. Enklaar, *Volledige handleiding voor de teelt en verdere behandeling van den tabak* [*Complete Manual for the Cultivation and Preparation of Tobacco*] (Amsterdam: J. Noorderdorp, 1858), 15.

29. Sometimes the entire plant was cut down and hung to dry. Complaints about the export of low-quality *barresuelos* leaves indicate that most cultivators picked their tobacco in subsequent rounds.

30. Bundles of two or three tobacco leaves were plaited into two of these strings, which then were hung in the drying sheds.

31. The Frenchman Victor Place mentions the junta in his 1849 report on the Dominican tobacco sector: Place, "Memoria sobre el cultivo," 189.

32. For a comparative approach: Charles J. Erasmus, "Culture, Structure, and Process: The Occurrence and Disappearance of Reciprocal Farm Labor," *Southwestern Journal of Anthropology* 12 (1956): 444–69.

33. See also the report of E. García Santelises, 22 June 1922, about the situation in the countryside of Puerto Plata: "La persona que trata de efectuar [la junta] convida entre los habitantes de la región que habita y las circunvecinas a sus amigos quienes se reunen el día indicado en las primeras horas de la mañana y empiezan el trabajo entonando cantos rústicos. Por lo regular, trabajan hasta la 1 P.M. hora en que todos se reconcentran debajo de los árboles o en los *ranchos* para tomar los alimentos que les prepara el dueño de la *junta*, que consisten en *salcochos* [*sic*], dulces de batata y como aperitivo, abundantes tragos de ron"; in Rodríguez Demorizi, *Lengua y folklore de Santo Domingo*, 275.

34. For a sympathetic description, see A. Jiménez, "Informe sobre la psicología, etc., de los habitantes del Distrito Escolar (Común de Salcedo), 10-10-1922," in Rodríguez Demorizi, *Lengua y folklore de Santo Domingo*, 208: "Se reunen todos los

trabajadores vecinos, familiares, amigos, y compadres, hoy aquí, mañana en otra parte, se trabaja alegremente hasta acabar y luego, a falta de remuneración de otra naturaleza, el dueño ofrece una gran comilona y bebida en abundancia."

35. Allard and Allard, *Tobacco in the Dominican Republic,* 16.

36. In an article in *La Información,* different terms were used in connection with the fermentation: *matules, sartas, manillas,* and *gavillas;* LIN 6, no. 2181 (24 June 1921).

37. "Informe del Consul General in Hamburg, Eduardo Soler," *Producción Nacional* 15 (10 Dec. 1901): "Nuestro tabaco llega *especialmente quemado* a este puerto, a causa de la humedad que contiene."

38. M. R. Ruiz Tejada, *Estudio sobre la propiedad inmobiliaria en la República Dominicana* (Santo Domingo: UASD, 1952). Also see Abad, *República Dominicana,* 261.

39. This same process occurred in Cuba. See R. Guerra y Sánchez, *Sugar and Society in the Caribbean: An Economic History of Cuban Agriculture* (New Haven, Conn.: Yale Univ. Press, 1964).

40. See, e.g., Frank Moya Pons, "The Land Question in Haiti and Santo Domingo: The Sociopolitical Context of the Transition from Slavery to Free Labor, 1801–1843," in *Between Slavery and Free Labor: The Spanish-Speaking Caribbean in the Nineteenth Century,* ed. Manuel Moreno Fraginals, Frank Moya Pons, and Stanley L. Engerman (Baltimore, Md.: Johns Hopkins Univ. Press, 1985), 181–214.

41. "Law on the Free Transfer of State Lands," *Colección de Leyes,* 1876, no. 1548, 89–90. Also see *Colección de Leyes,* 1883, no. 2143, 478–80. It must be stressed that these laws were esp. meant to favor the larger, more market-oriented cultivators.

42. Melvin M. Knight, *The Americans in Santo Domingo* (1928; rpt. New York: Arno, 1970), 46.

43. Rodríguez Demorizi, *Papeles de Bonó,* 82.

44. Cestero, *Por el Cibao,* 117.

45. San Miguel, "Dominican Peasantry," 223–24; see also chap. 8, "Ideologies of Progress."

46. Informant 36.

47. This would be comparable to the public land question in other Latin American countries. E.g., Catherine LeGrand, *Frontier Expansion and Peasant Protest in Colombia, 1830–1936* (Albuquerque: Univ. of New Mexico Press, 1986), esp. 10–18.

48. This could be an example of an "invention of tradition." See Eric Hobsbawm and Terence Ranger, eds., *The Invention of Tradition* (Cambridge, England: Cambridge Univ. Press, 1983).

49. See Baud, "La gente del tabaco," 101–37.

50. Bray, "Dependency, Class Formation," 81–83. In his emphasis on the difference between peasant and proletarian migration, Bray overstates, in my view, the monetization of mountain society.

51. For these possible alternative historical processes, see E. J. Domar, "The Causes of Slavery or Serfdom: A Hypothesis," *Journal of Economic History* 30 (1970): 18–32.

52. See, e.g., "Sobre nuestro tabaco," LIN 4, no. 114 (10 Nov. 1919). In the Villa González region, many elderly people have participated in such processions.

53. "La situación actual," *El Porvenir* 1, no. 35 (14 Sept. 1872), reported on the long drought: "Hay lugares en que no hay agua para beber y familias enteras tienen que abandonar sus casas y labranzas por ampararse en secciones mas afortunadas."

54. Rafael Espaillat, "Datos sobre el costo de la vida," 1935, in Sección de Comercio, box 40, no. 268.

55. "Hacia el campo," LIN 9, no. 1968 (25 June 1924).

56. An observer described in 1922 how cultivators in the *sierra* still had a lot to do when they came home after a hard day's work on the conuco: "Es preciso aún *jalar* nuevamente, *respañar* y limpiar el andullo; es decir, despojarlo de la hojas y filamentos podridos o malsanos que puedan luego comprometer su pureza; hay que tejer los serones; dar los últimos amarres de solidez a los aparejos y enjalmas . . . ; mientras la esposa, con el recién nacido *al anca,* prepara el *sancocho.*" José Medina P., "Informe acerca de la raza, etc., de los habitantes del 36 distrito escolar comunes de Sabaneta y Monción (12-4-1922)," in Rodríguez Demorizi, *Lengua y folklore de Santo Domingo,* 240.

57. Rodríguez Demorizi, *Papeles de Bonó,* 200. Also Cestero, *Por el Cibao,* 53, writes about Jarabacoa: "Principal industria es el 'anduyo' (tabaco prensado o hueva)."

58. Amiama Gómez, "La unificación de la semilla del tabaco," RdA 5, no. 5 (Aug. 1909): 127–28.

59. Diputado Andrew, "Congreso Nacional, 14-6-1889" in GO 16, no. 797 (30 Nov. 1889). In 1891 more than 23,000 pack animals entered the city of Puerto Plata. See "Estado demostrativo del movimiento de pasaportes de recueros," in IP, 134.

60. Amado Franco Bidó, "El cosechero de tabaco," LIN 9, no. 2294 (12 Jan. 1924). Rpt. in Bidó, *Páginas sencillas* (Santiago, 1927), 74. This connection between cash crop harvest and marriage can be seen elsewhere also. E.g., Peter Boomgaard, *Children of the Colonial State: Population Growth and Economic Development in Java, 1795–1880* (Amsterdam: Free Univ. Press/Center for Asian Studies, 1989), 145.

61. Compare also: Reinhardt, *Our Daily Bread,* 58–60.

62. Bray, "Dependency, Class Formation," 93.

63. For more information on this subject, see chap. 6 of the present volume, "The Transformation of Rural Society."

64. Compare the story of General Corona told to José Martí in 1895. The general had 13 children, "pero no de la misma mujer," "poique eso sí tengo yo, que cuando miro asina, y veo que voi a tener que etai en un lugai má de un mé o do, enseguía me buco mi mejó comodidá." When he had to leave, "la dejo en su casita y con aigunos cuartos: poique a mi mujer legítima poi nada de este mundo le deberé faitai." Martí continues: "A ella vuelve siempre: ella le guardó la hacienda cuando se destierró, le pagó las deudas, le ayuda en todos sus trabajos." José Martí, "Páginas de un diario," Feb. 1895, in *Martí en Santo Domingo,* ed. Emilio Rodríguez Demorizi (Barcelona, Spain: M. Pareja, 1978), 230–31. See also Hoetink, *Dominican People,* 202.

65. A 76-year-old man (J. V.) told: "Me negaron los amores a los 18 años de edad y mi mamá me prohibió casarme con mi primera novia. Mis padres me eligieron la esposa que tengo." Many elderly people tell similar stories. They stress that a young person "no se pertenecía."

66. Sherri Grasmuck and Patricia R. Pessar, *Between Two Islands: Dominican International Migration* (Berkeley: Univ. of California Press, 1991), 140ff.

67. M. A. Monclus, "Informe acerca de las costumbres, etc.," Monte Plata, Dec. 1921, in Rodríguez Demorizi, *Lengua y folklore de Santo Domingo,* 95. Also see Hoetink, *Dominican People,* 196–98.

68. Rafael Espaillat, "Datos sobre el costo de la vida," 1935, in Sección de Comercio, box 40, no. 268.

69. Also see Michael Kearney, "From the Invisible Hand to the Visible Feet: Anthropological Studies of Migration and Development," *Annual Review of Anthropology* 15 (1986): 331–61.

70. On social mobility, see Hoetink, *Dominican People,* 169–70.

71. Letters from the governors of Santiago and La Vega, 21 Oct. 1870, IP, 1870–71, box 39.

72. Compare Martí's observations: n. 64 above.

73. Mallon, *Defense of Community.*

74. The complaints of the entrepreneurial class were similar to those in other parts of the world where colonialism tried to transform rural societies. E.g.: Alatas, *Myth of the Lazy Native.* Cooper stresses the need for "predictability" intrinsic to imperialism, in his "Peasants, Capitalists, and Historians: A Review Article," *Journal of South African Studies* 7, no. 2 (1981): 284–314, esp. 304.

75. U.S. Consul in Puerto Plata, Dominican Republic, to U.S. Secretary of State Hunter, 28 May 1884, in microfilm series T662, no. 1.

76. As late as 1926, it was written that, in order to modernize Dominican society it was "indispensable aumentar las necesidades del obrero": Dr. J. Jover, "El fracaso de muchas empresas se debe en parte a la poca necesidad del peón Dominicano," *El Anuncio* (San Francisco de Macorís), 26 June 1926; see also chap. 8, "Ideologies of Progress."

77. A. M. in Palmar.

78. Serious research on this aspect of Dominican peasant society is still lacking. This is regrettable since it could provide us with insights concerning present-day migration to the U.S. For a very interesting beginning, see Pessar, "Kinship Relations of Production in the Migration Process." Also the essays in José Del Castillo and C. Mitchel, eds., *La inmigración dominicana en los Estados Unidos* (Santo Domingo: Universidad APEC, 1987).

79. For a similar analysis, see Muriel Nazzari, *Disappearance of the Dowry: Women, Families, and Social Change in São Paulo, Brazil, 1600–1900* (Stanford, Calif.: Stanford Univ. Press, 1991), 44–46

80. Reinhardt, *Our Daily Bread,* 59, also suggests this twofold explanation for the wanderlust of young males—escape from patriarchal control and their own identities as incipient patriarchs.

81. Pessar, "Kinship Relations of Production in the Migration Process." See also Hoetink, *Dominican People,* 170ff.

82. See, e.g., Geschiere, "La paysannerie africaine est-elle captive?," and Kasfir, "Are African Peasants Self-Sufficient?"

83. Luis Carballo R., *Informe Mensual, Cámara de Comercio Santiago,* Oct. 1931, in Sección de Agricultura, box 9, no. 201.

5. Peasants and the Market: Organization of the Rural Tobacco Trade

1. See, e.g., the exaggerated attack on C. Girault's analysis of the Haitian coffee market in Mats Lundahl and Y. Bourdet, "Haitian Coffee Marketing Revisited" (Paper presented at the 46th International Congress of Americanists, 1988). For a creative application of neoclassical economic theory, see Robert H. Bates, *Essays on the Political Economy of Rural Africa* (Cambridge, England: Cambridge Univ. Press, 1983).

2. Kula, *Economic Theory of the Feudal System,* 43. In this English translation, it is called "obligation to commercialize."

3. This is also the opinion of the Dominican economist Carlos Dore, who sees land distribution among peasant producers as "un retroceso histórico." See Carlos Dore y Cabral, *Reforma agraria y luchas sociales en la República Dominicana, 1966–1978* (Santo Domingo: Taller, 1981), 92–93.

4. Lemarchand, "African Peasantries," 57–58. For a similar view of the Andes region, cf. Tristan Platt, "The Role of the Andian *Ayllus* in the Reproduction of the Petty Commodity Regime in Northern Polos (Bolivia)," in *Ecology and Exchange,* ed. Lehmann, 27–69.

5. Sidney W. Mintz, "Internal Market Systems as Mechanics of Social Articulation," *Proceedings of the 1959 Annual Spring Meeting of the American Ethnological Society* (Seattle: Univ. of Washington Press, 1959). Also see his "Peasant Marketplaces and Economic Development in Latin America," Occasional Paper No. 4, Graduate Center for Latin American Studies, Vanderbilt Univ., Nashville, Tenn., 1964.

6. Eric R. Wolf, "Types of Latin American Peasantries: A Preliminary Discussion," *American Anthropologist* 57 (June 1955): 452–70, esp. 462–63, adds: "It would seem advisable to beware of treating production of subsistence and production for the market as two progressive stages of development. Rather we must allow for the cyclical alternation of the two kinds of production within the same community."

7. This type of relation has sometimes been designated by the term *interlocking factor markets.* Such multistranded relationships between economic agents encompassed several markets, particularly those of land, labor, and credit. See Pranab K.

Bardhan, "Interlocking Factor Markets," in Pranab K. Bardhan, *Land, Labor, and Rural Poverty: Essays in Development Economics* (London: Oxford Univ. Press, 1984). Also see Mintz, "Internal Market Systems" and "Peasant Marketplaces."

8. As Bardhan, "Interlocking Factor Markets," writes: "Different participants enjoy differential access to markets outside their village, and this is clearly reflected in the highly unequal bargaining power of agents in a given submarket" (158).

9. Bonó, "Apuntes sobre la clases trabajadoras dominicanas," 194.

10. Trade in the twentieth century often shows astounding similarities to his description. See, e.g., Ferrán, *Tabaco y sociedad.*

11. See ibid., 113–30 and passim. Ferrán calls the *corredor* "una de las figuras más enigmáticas de la industria criolla del tabaco" (113).

12. Grullón, *Sobre nuestro tabaco,* 30.

13. A. Oquet, "Los tabacos de Santo Domingo," LIN 11, no. 2610 (16 June 1926).

14. E.g., "Educación industrial," LIN 2, no. 420 (21 May 1917): "Debe sepultarse el rutinario y vicioso molde de enseronar y empacar el tabaco al mismo tiempo y tal como nos lo traen de los campos."

15. This system, which was also practiced in the coffee and cocoa sectors, was called "venta a la flor."

16. L. Cristóbal Perello, "Causas que se oponen al desarrollo de la riqueza pública en las comarcas cibaeñas," *El Diario,* 5, no. 1353 (1 Feb. 1907). For a more general condemnation, see "Memoria Santo Domingo," 1893, AGN.

17. The observations of the Santiago tobacco merchant V. F. Thomén in 1928 seem to contradict this absence of interest: "Cuando el comercio daba dinero a los campesinos, lo hacía a algunos individuos que servían como agentes y que, aunque no pagaban ningún interés al comerciante, prestaba a los necesitados con alta prima y por eso, aunque botaban una parte, siempre podían devolver algo de lo que cojían," V. F. Thomén to Ministro de Agricultura e Inmigración Rafael Espaillat, 12 Feb. 1928, in SEA, box 64 (1928). I believe, however, that he also refers to the interest implicit in the tobacco trade.

18. L. Cristóbal Perello, "Causas que se oponen . . . ," *El Diario* 5, no. 1353 (1 Feb. 1907): "Los menos garantes toman según la época del año a 100% de interés, a 50%, y a 25%."

19. Luis Carballo, "Informe Mensual de la Cámara de Comercio, etc., de Santiago," Feb. 1928, in Gobernación de Santiago, box 7 (1928).

20. San Miguel, "Dominican Peasantry," 168. It is not completely clear how he computes his figures. If a cultivator gave a 90-peso harvest as guarantee for a loan of 50 pesos, it is not self-evident that the remaining 40 pesos were the intermediary's profit.

21. "El Cibao y el tabaco," EdP 4, no. 209 (15 Aug. 1887).

22. "El comercio y los arrieros," EdP 4, no. 193 (24 Jan. 1886).

23. Grullón, *Sobre nuestro tabaco,* 28.

24. E.g., "La cosecha," EdP 4, no. 163 (7 June 1885). "Tabaco," EdP 10, no. 314 (14 May 1892).

25. See Grullón, *Sobre nuestro tabaco,* 35–37. These classes were also called *primera, primerita,* and *segunda.*

26. One *manilla* weighed one pound. In the colonial period, similar bundles were called *manojos,* but these weighed approx. 4 lbs.

27. Informant R. T. This association tries to sell the tobacco of its members collectively.

28. "Usureros y prestamistos," LIN 10, no. 2100 (5 Feb. 1925). Don Felipe A. Vicini, "Solucionando nuestro problema del tabaco," LIN 14, no. 4699 (12 Aug. 1929). Also: informant 25.

29. Shanin, *Awkward Class,* 114.

30. "La agricultura en el Cibao," EdlO 741 (2 Sept. 1893).

31. "Los Corredores," LIN 8, no. 2030 (4 May 1923).

32. E.g., "Avance sobre el tabaco," LIN 10, no. 2347 (1 Dec. 1925): "De inmenso daño resulta el avance sobre cosechas para los campesinos, porque según el documento que se les hace firmar, se exije como condición única, obligatoria, le entrega del tabaco en todo el mes de Mayo, cualquier sea el precio que exista en ese mes."

33. "Navarreteros (10-6-1917)," LIN 2, no. 433 (18 June 1917).

34. Ferrán, *Tabaco y sociedad,* 120.

35. *Eco de Cibao* (30 May 1905).

36. José Gabriel Aldebot, "El mercado del tabaco," *El Diario* 7, no. 2025 (13 May 1909). In the original, the Spanish expression is translated as "chance price."

37. See "Al Sr. Comisario," VdS 2, no. 69 (17 July 1881). For a later period: "Por el campo y los campesinos," LIN 9, no. 1972 (1 June 1924). For the *comín,* the following adjectives were used: "despiadado, vicioso, corrupto, libidinoso, lascivo"!

38. E.g., "Los corredores en funciones," LIN 8, no. 2065 (8 June 1923).

39. "Solucionando . . . ," LIN 14, no. 4700 (13 Aug. 1929).

40. See "Por el campo y los campesinos," LIN 9, no. 1972 (1 July 1924): "Abandonado en el campo, el pobre agricultor es más luego explotado sin misericordia en las ciudades. Recogidas sus limitadas cosechas, el pulpo de la ciudad lo espera para comprarle por nada sus productos, ofreciéndoles precios insignificantes que no pagan ni la tercera parte de su extenuadora labor de un año."

41. For that reason, the municipal council of Santiago installed a government scale in 1880. However, the peasants had to pay five centavos for each serón they wanted to weigh, and they hardly made use of it. "Nos da pena," VdS 1, no. 12 (13 June 1880).

42. E.g., Félix Ma. Nolasco, "Tabaco de la Costa," *El Diario* (22 Aug. 1904). Also see app. 2.

43. "Notas agrícolas," LIN 5, no. 1779 (24 Jan. 1920).

44. "La baja del tabaco es una maniobra de especuladores locales . . . ," LIN 9, no. 1963 (6 June 1924).

45. J. R. Malagón, "Especuladores de tabaco," LIN 10, no. 2152 (8 Apr. 1925).

46. See, e.g., "El mercado de tabaco," LIN 10, no. 2182 (15 May 1925). It was reported that, although the large-scale merchants were not yet buying, "Los intermediarios, que compran por cuenta propria con esperanza de buenas ventas se mueven con más actividad."

47. See, e.g., "Llegando al colmo," LIN 3, no. 741 (1 July 1918): "Los dos o tres acaparadores de tabaco cibaeño . . . pasan una orden a todos sus compradores, para que desde esta fecha de hoy, el tabaco no sea admitida en sus almacenes sino es al ínfimo, al miserable i ruinoso precio de cinco pesos el serón."

48. Informant 25.

49. San Miguel, "Dominican Peasantry," 131–33. Above all, the urban merchants complained about the fact that many *corredores* were not able to pay back their debts at the end of the harvest. See "El Tabaco," *El Diario* 8, no. 2342 (2 June 1910).

50. EdP 10, no. 295 (4 July 1891). *Quemar* in this context means "selling for a very low price." This statement was almost literally repeated a few months later. Then, the term *regalar* ("give away") was used: "Sobre el tabaco," EdP 10, no. 300 (19 Sept. 1891).

51. In this regard we have already cited Amiama Gómez, "La unificación de la semilla," RdA 5, no. 5 (Aug. 1909). See also Cámara de Comercio, La Vega, to Director, *Listín Diario*, 30 May 1933, in Sección de Agricultura, box 14, in which it was observed that, due to the low tobacco prices, "se está empleando una gran cantidad en andullos."

52. When the prices remained low in the same year, 1891: "Esto ha dado lugar a que partidas de la mejor hoja estén aún en manos de los cosecheros," EdP 10, no. 299 (30 Aug. 1891).

53. In the twentieth century, only a few observations suggest persistence of such an attitude. In 1909, an observer, José Gabriel Aldebot, wrote: "He oído decir a muchos que más vale quemar su cosecha antes de darla por el precio que se les ofrece," in "El mercado del tabaco," *El Diario* 7, no. 2025 (13 May 1909). Also LIN 3, no. 736 (24 June 1918).

54. This theme was discussed frequently in the nineteenth-century press. See, e.g., "El tabaco otra vez," EdP 1, no. 17 (30 July 1882); "El tabaco," EdP 3, no. 125 (24 Aug. 1884); "El comercio y los arrieros," EdP 4, no. 193 (24 Jan. 1886).

55. E.g., "El comercio y los arrieros," EdP 4, no. 193 (24 Jan. 1886). Critics complained that this practice induced cultivators to damage the tobacco. For this reason, Temístocles Herrera Borr wrote in 1926: "Las ventas anticipadas y a determinadas precios, son contratos que deben ser prohibidos por una ley impulsivo," in "La venta del tabaco," LIN 11, no. 2618 (6 July 1926).

56. "Por nuestros campesinos," LIN 3, no. 738 (27 June 1918).

57. "La situación del tabaco Dominicano," LIN 14, no. 4678 (15 July 1929).

58. "Sobre tabaco," *El Diario* 6, no. 1522 (23 Aug. 1907).

59. "Desde Mao," LIN 3, no. 710 (21 May 1918).

60. Prices were as low as 30 and 50 centavos per quintal! Cámara de Comercio, etc., La Vega, to Secretario de Estado de Agricultura y Comercio César Tolentino, 6 May 1931, in Sección de Agricultura, box 9. Also President, Cámara de Comercio, to Secretario de Estado, "Telefonema Oficial," 6 May 1931: "La forma como actualmente se compra tabaco en ésta requiere urgente atención, evitar siga disgusto cosecheros, entre los cuales hay quién lo esté quemando."

61. San Miguel, "Dominican Peasantry," 166–205.

62. Baud, "La gente del tabaco," 108.

63. "Solucionando . . . ," LIN 14, no. 4699 (12 Aug. 1929). The empacadores also sold to the urban merchants, however: "Los comines lo mismo que los empacadores campesinos son los que realizan generalmente la venta del tabaco cibaeño a los exportadores quienes . . . son personas establecidas en los principales centros de población y quienes cuentan con depósitos o almacenes amplios en los cuales acostumbran clasificar, enmanillar, fermentar, y empacar el tabaco."

64. "Breves apuntes acerca de la psicología del pueblo Dominicano, etc. (Augusto Ortega), Santiago, 20-3-1922," in Rodríguez Demorizi, *Lengua y folklore de Santo Domingo,* 134.

65. "Congreso Nacional, 26-5-1906," GO 23, no. 1734 (31 Oct. 1906).

66. Demófilo, "Sobre los jefes comunales" (Dajabón, 20-1-1914), LD 25, no. 7400 (28 Jan. 1914). Compare the similar analysis of José Ramón López: Michiel Baud, "Ideología y campesinado: El pensamiento social de José Ramón López," *Estudios Sociales* 19, no. 64 (Apr.–June 1986), 76.

67. This aspect of rural society has been neglected until now. It is mentioned by Pablo A. Maríñez, *Resistencia campesina, imperialismo y reforma agraria en República Dominicana (1899–1978)* (Santo Domingo: Ediciones Cepae, 1984), 83.

68. José D. Ariza, "Protejamos nuestros campesinos contra los especuladores de mala fe" (Tamboril, 22-8-1917), LIN 2, no. 491 (28 Aug. 1917). For an early expression of the same opinion: "Al Sr. Comisario," VdS 2, no. 69 (17 July 1881).

69. On the relation between gambling and contracting debts: L. Cristóbal Perello, "Causas que se oponen al desarrollo . . . ," *El Diario* 5, no. 1353 (1 Feb. 1907): "Para mayor desgracia, este juego comienza en momentos en que se riega la semilla de tabaco, y con raras excepciones, se puede asegurar que no hay un solo cosechero que no venda y comprometa, más o menos una quinta parte de su cosecha próxima, en un precio ruinoso, para atender a los jugadas que tienen lugar entre lo que ellos llaman 'entre pascua y pascua' o sea del 25 de Diciembre al 7 de Enero."

70. Compare also Bardhan, "Interlocking Factor Markets," 159–61. The suggestion that there can be an occasional desirability in an "unfree" situation is presented for Peruvian sugar workers in Gonzales, *Plantation Agriculture and Social Control.*

71. Temístocles Herrera Borr, "La venta del tabaco," LIN 11, no. 2618 (6 July 1926).

72. Compare James C. Scott and B. J. Kerkvliet, "How Traditional Rural Patrons Lose Legitimacy: A Theory with Special Reference to Southeast Asia," *Cultures et développement* (Summer 1973): 510. They write about intermediary rural leaders: "Nouveaux arrivés with little claim to higher status, their rule is less institutionalized—less culturally sanctioned—than the role of a patron, and their relationship to their men is less diffuse and relies more heavily on coercion and/or material reward."

73. Ferrán, *Tabaco y sociedad,* 120/1.

74. E.g., *El Porvenir* 2, no. 39 (28 Sept. 1873), and Abad, *República Dominicana,* 297.

75. David Lehmann, "Two Paths of Agrarian Capitalism, or a Critique of Chayanovian Marxism," CSSH 28 (1986): 601–27.

76. Eric R. Wolf, "Aspects of Group Relations in a Complex Society: Mexico," *American Anthropologist* 58 (1956): 1065–78.

77. This form of condemnation of middlemen is treated in A. P. Lerner, "The Myth of the Parasitic Middleman," *Commentary* 8, no. 1 (July 1949): 45–51.

78. For a positive interpretation of rural traders, see Mintz, "Peasant Marketplaces," 6: "Such small-scale intermediation is probably the principal way in which the poorest segments of the national population can acquire knowledge of commerce and of entrepreneurialism."

6. The Transformation of Rural Society: Peasants and Landowners in the Villa González Region

1. Most peasant studies see a clear dichotomy between a closed peasant community and the external world. See, e.g., the work of James Scott and Goran Hyden. In Latin America, an image is often created of a mythical peasant community rudely destroyed by the forces of the market. Eric Wolf has been very influential in creating this image, through his writings on the "closed corporate" peasant community. For his second thoughts: Eric R. Wolf, "The Vicissitudes of the Closed Corporate Peasant Community," *American Ethnologist* 13, no. 2 (May 1986): 325–29. One of the advantages of the "Russian School," Marxist (Lenin) and non-Marxist (Chayanov), is that they have taken the peasant household as the unit of analysis. It would be interesting to do a comparative investigation of the origins of scientific "mythologies" concerning the nature of the peasant community. An example of such an approach, done in one country, is Cynthia Hewitt de Alcántara, *Boundaries and Paradigms: The Anthropological Study of Rural Life in Post-Revolutionary Mexico* (Leiden: Univ. of Leide, Leiden Development Studies, 1982).

2. See, e.g., P. Singelmann, *Structures of Domination and Peasant Movements in Latin America* (Columbia, Univ. of Missouri Press, 1981).

3. For a general history of the region, see Baud, "La gente del tabaco." In 1913, inhabitants of the region asked the Ministerio de Interior y Policía to make the region a separate "sección electoral" and allow it representation in the Santiago coun-

cil, "dada la importancia de nuestro poblado": "Petición que el poblado de Las Lagunas, común de Santiago, eleva al Poder Ejecutivo para obtener su seccionamiento electoral" (27 June 1913), in IP, box 291 (1913).

4. Despite the specific location of the Villa González region—near Santiago and the railroad—comparative research in two other regions in the central Cibao suggests that the processes of change in the three regions were similar. Developments in the Villa González region began somewhat later, however.

5. Hazard, *Santo Domingo,* 337.

6. Land prices rose accordingly. See Hoetink, *Dominican People,* 18, 56; and Emilio Rodríguez Demorizi, ed., *Papeles de Monseñor Meriño* (Santo Domingo: Taller, 1983), 89.

7. See the article written at his death: "Las Lagunas," *El Diario* (29 Jan. 1912). Many people attended the funeral "por él haber sido, si no el fundador, uno de los primeros fundadores de aquel floreciente pueblo."

8. See Rodríguez Demorizi, *Martí en Santo Domingo,* 485. Today there is controversy about who founded Villa González. Some people say that Boitel did more for the community than González.

9. Tribunal de Tierras, Santiago, DC 126, Saneamiento parcelas, no. 18.

10. Tribunal de Tierras, Santiago, DC 4, Saneamiento parcelas, nos. 19 and 20.

11. Tribunal de Tierras, DC 4, Saneamiento. The case of Vidal Pichardo is significant. Within a short period (1911–12), he sold almost all of his property in the region. DC 4, nos. 172, 173, 175, 177. This source does not give information about the "old" families who held onto their land. One informant stated that the civil war in the first two decades of the twentieth century enabled some people to usurp land: "La mayoría de los habitantes de esta zona emigraron a la loma con miedo a la guerra de los *bolos* y los *rabuses*. Por lo que dejaron abandonado mucho de estos terrenos, lo cual fué aprovechado por algunas familias que hoy son muy ricas"; interview 23. This story is not confirmed by other sources.

12. This way of selling land was also called "de salida." The land remained in this system "sin cercas u otros signos reparativos." See Tribunal de Tierras, DC 4, "Escrito de defensa, asunto: Apelación de Gregorio Guzmán y Compartes," 28 Junio 1934.

13. This system of land selling has not yet received scholarly attention. All elder peasants are able to explain it in great detail. See also San Miguel, "Dominican Peasantry," 235–39. As a result of this system, the land was divided in long strips of land perpendicular on an imaginary baseline showing remarkable similarities to the European *Strassendorfen.* See Bernard Slicher van Bath, *De agrarische geschiedenis van West Europa (500–1850)* (Utrecht, Netherlands: Spectrum, 1960), 62–67.

14. Reaction on "circular 45" (1895) in IP, box 157.

15. *El Diario* 6, no. 1566 (14 Oct. 1907).

16. *El Diario,* 23 Apr. 1908. In 1899, a cemetery had already been consecrated: BM 11, no. 294 (10 Jan. 1899).

17. E.g., the description of the "floreciente caserío comercial" Navarrete in "Esperanza y Navarrete," *El Diario* (7 Apr. 1909) and "Corrida en las Lagunas," *El Diario* (6 May 1909).

18. In 1930, José Manuel Peña installed an electric plant which generated sufficient power for the entire village. "Luz eléctrica en Villa González," LIN 15, no. 5017 (1 Sept. 1930).

19. "Impresiones de Villa González," LIN 13, no. 3079 (6 Mar. 1928). The mill never functioned quite satisfactorily and lost its usefulness after the construction of an irrigation system in the 1930s.

20. We know very little about this process. It is probable that it refers to the families Torribio, Núñez, García Cruz, and Guzmán.

21. See Bergad, *Coffee and the Growth of Agrarian Capitalism.*

22. This is, e.g., confirmed by former land surveyor (*agrimensor*) of the region, don Camilo Casanova. According to him, surveying land in 1920 cost 10 centavos per tarea, but the minimum was 30 pesos. Interview, 23 May 1981. See also chap. 8 of the present volume, "Ideologies of Progress."

23. The parents of one man (informant 22) possessed two "cordeles" of land, but "tuvieron que venderla cuando ellos enfermaron." The father of another man (informant 24) possessed a "propiedad" of 200 tareas, but "él la vendió por fracaso de un negocio y la última que le quedaba por enfermedad."

24. See, e.g., Wong, *Peasants in the Making,* in which an example is given of a poor peasant girl's becoming a doctor. For a rather eurocentric perspective on this question: Macfarlane, *The Origins of English Individualism,* 69–70.

25. This is M. R. It may be significant that a number of these men had lost their wives. The solitude of old age may have hardened this rejection of modernity.

26. This last method is the principal theme of M. M. Vázquez-Geffroy, "Land Tenure and Resource-Holding Groups in a Dominican Municipio" (Ph.D. diss., Univ. of New Mexico, 1977). Also see San Miguel, "Dominican Peasantry," 230–32. In the Villa González region, it was not common.

27. Crouch, "Development of Capitalism in Dominican Agriculture," 32.

28. This is one of the central themes of Berry, *Fathers Work for Their Sons,* on the Nigerian cocoa farmers.

29. Informants M.R. and M.M. The names used in the text are pseudonyms.

30. This is the basis of the Scott-Popkin controversy. Scott, *Moral Economy of the Peasant,* stresses, among other things, the innate solidarity of peasant communities; whereas Samuel L. Popkin in *The Rational Peasant* focuses on the individualistic and competitive aspects of peasant existence.

31. Wolf, *Peasants,* 80.

32. Compare a notice in *La Información* about a fight between two men in Villa González, "quienes riñeron a causa de los ocultas visitas que el segundo hacía al conuco del primero con ideas poco buenas, pues constantemente salía con sacos

repletos de viveres de los que honradamente cosechaba el laborioso Francisco en su pequeño pedazo de tierra"; "Suceso en las Lagunas," LIN 4, no. 1104 (29 Oct. 1919). Also see Gov. Mario Fermín Cabral of Santiago to Alcaldes Pedáneos, 3 Sept. 1928, about the increase of "robo de animales"; in Gobernación de Santiago, box 8.

33. Labourt probably refers to this when he writes: "Los velorios en los pueblos son escenarios de hechos que servirán de tema de conversación durante varios días. Después de pasadas todas las ceremonias acostumbradas, las comadres (y los compadres también) comentaran si el difunto fue 'gritado como se lo merecía,' si se vió que el difunto 'tenía gente,' y revisarán, en fin, si el velorio quedó 'bueno'"; in José Labourt, *Sana, sana, culito de rana . . .* (Santo Domingo: Taller, 1982), 151.

34. See Ferrán, *Tabaco y sociedad*, 78. Conflicts during velorios were not frequent, however, and normally the rituals of mourning were occasions when social loyalties were reaffirmed, families ties strengthened and quarrels—"on the grave of the deceased"—were solved. On the organization of the velorios: Hoetink, *Dominican People*, 209–10. Compare with Wolf, *Peasants*, 98–99.

35. The best analysis of the Dominican elite can be found in Hoetink, *Dominican People*, 165–71.

36. Pedro R. Batista, *Santiago a principios de siglo* (Santo Domingo: Editorial Panamericana, 1976), 151.

37. See, e.g., the description in *Informe de la Comisión de Investigación de los E.U.A. en Santo Domingo en 1871* (preface and notes by E. Rodríguez Demorizi) (Ciudad Trujillo: Montalvo, 1960), 198: "Las casas [de los campesinos] son de tablas de palma y el techo lo hacen de las hojas del mismo árbol (yagua); el piso es de tierra y a veces le ponen encima un piso de madera. Las casas ordinariamente están divididas en dos habitaciones, una de las cuales se utiliza como dormitorio para las mujeres y que contiene generalmente una cama; la otra es la sala y el comedor, y de noche se convierte en dormitorio para los hombres." See also Rodríguez Demorizi, *Lengua y folklore de Santo Domingo,* 128 and 229.

38. Compare, e.g.: Augusto Ortega, "Breves apuntes acerca de la psicología del pueblo Dominicano, Común de Santiago, 20-3-1922," in Rodríguez Demorizi, *Lengua y folklore de Santo Domingo*, 141.

39. "Día de Santiago" (30 Mar. 1917), folleto in Archivo Municipal de Santiago. In the original, the countryman is indicated as "campesino."

40. Hoetink, *Dominican People,* 163.

41. This preference for a practical education—technical training, rather than studying law and the humanities—resembles "the ideal of the practical" of the Colombian elite, as analyzed in Frank Safford, *The Ideal of the Practical: Colombia's Struggle to Form a Technical Elite* (Austin: Univ. of Texas Press, 1976).

42. "Un agricultor modelo y un hombre de éxitos: Francisco Javier Espaillat," LIN no. 2144 (30 Mar. 1925); Espaillat was reported to have said, "Me hice hombre y siento tener que confesar que me quedé sin escuela."

43. For a detailed case study of such a network in Mexico, see Larissa A. Lomnitz and Marisol Pérez-Lizaur, *A Mexican Elite Family, 1820–1980: Kinship, Class, and Culture* (Princeton, N.J.: Princeton Univ. Press, 1987).

44. No research that I know of has investigated the role of women in the Cibao elite. However, nowadays many of the larger shops in Santiago seem to be run by women.

45. This information can be found in "Un agricultor modelo y un hombre de éxitos: Francisco Javier Espaillat," LIN no. 2144 (30 Mar. 1925).

46. "De Villa González," LIN 15, no. 4975 (11 July 1930) mentioned that a number of "distinguidos jóvenes" had made "una excursión de caza por las regiones maeñas, quiniguieras." Also R. Emilio Jiménez, "Informe acerca de la historia, etc., Mao, 16-5-1922," in Rodríguez Demorizi, *Lengua y folklore de Santo Domingo,* 157: "La diversión cinegética es propia de la gente urbana que toma una partida de caza para recreo de su espíritu. El campesino, en cambio, practica la caza como medio de subsistencia y para defender los frutos."

47. *El Diario,* no. 2018 (6 May 1909). A similar event took place in 1908: *El Diario,* 16 Mar. 1908, 23 Apr. 1908. Many people from Santiago visited these events, traveling by train.

48. For the church building: *El Diario* 5, no. 1353 (1 Feb. 1907) and 16 Mar. 1908. For the meeting: "En Villa González se celebró ayer una gran manifestación nacionalista," LIN 8, no. 2113 (6 Aug. 1923).

49. "Velada en las Lagunas," LIN 8, no. 2206 (27 Sept. 1923). In Santo Domingo, they were organized as early as the nineteenth century. See also Hoetink, *Dominican People,* 205.

50. E.g., the "velada" in Palmar, organized by "la culta dama doña Josefa T. de Rodríguez, actual profesora de instrucción y a quién se debe el adelanto cultural de aquel pintoresco lugar" in 1928: "Noticias de Villa González—Acta Cultural," LIN 13, no. 3088 (16 Mar. 1928).

51. About the disdain for the merengue: Raf. Durán, "De Costumbres," LIN 7, no. 1896 (27 Mar. 1922). Durán criticizes the people who describe the merengue as "costumbre de negro" or "de plebe." He quotes someone who "calificó nuestro merengue de ritmo inmoral y de indigno de ser bailado por la aristocracia."

52. An indication of this gap between cultural forms according to class can be found in "Juego de Gallos," LIN 3, no. 735 (20 June 1918): "Nuestro campesino y nuestro hombre del pueblo, aún no ha apreciado a suplir esta costumbre [el juego de gallos] por otra, como lo ha hecho una gran clase, supliendo el juego de San Andrés con el carnaval; las carreras de San Juan con la gira; las de Cruz con el culto de iglesia."

53. Hoetink, *Dominican People,* 165–66, 176–81.

54. Hoetink has stressed this periodization of social mobility and stagnation, in which a relatively "open" elite gradually solidifies and closes its ranks to newcomers: H. Hoetink, "The Dominican Republic, c. 1870–1930," in *Cambridge History of Latin America,* ed. Leslie Bethell (Cambridge, England: Cambridge Univ. Press, 1986), 5:296.

55. The governor of Santiago wrote in his report for 1905: "Fué siempre

costumbre perjudicial para el rama agrícola ir a los campos en busca de los ciudadanos que habían de formar el efectivo de la fuerza pública. En ello no se hizo otra cosa más que restársele elementos a la agricultura, fomentar la vagancia, y formar, por decirlo así, muchos de los llamados *políticos*. Y convencido de que la salvación de los pueblos está absolutamente vinculada en el trabajo, no he querido en forma alguna molestar para ninguna clase de servicio militar activo aquellos honrados ciudadanos que viven consagrados a las faenas agrícolas." Ricardo Limardo, "Memoria del Gobernador de la Provincia de Santiago," 6 Feb. 1906, in GO 22, no. 1687 (19 May 1906). Also see Hoetink, *Dominican People*, 98–99.

56. Special Inspector of Internal Revenue Irvine I. McManus, Santiago, to J. H. Pendleton, 2 Apr. 1918. This letter is unreliable because of its clear political purpose. A good impression of the insecurity in the Cibao countryside during the revolutions is given in the novel by Juan Bosch, *La Mañosa* (1936; rpt. Santo Domingo: Alfa y Omega, 1984).

57. Scott and Kerkvliet, "How Traditional Rural Patrons Lose Legitimacy," 512, mention "protection" as one of the essential elements of a patron-client relationship: "It means shielding the client both from private dangers (banditry, personal enemies) and from public dangers (soldiers, outside officials, courts, tax collectors)."

58. These ideas are not generally accepted. The explanation of Luis Crouch et al. of the existence of sharecropping arrangements in the "capitalist" Dominican agriculture of the twentieth century goes a long way into the direction proposed here: Equipo de Investigación Socioeconomica, *Desarrollo del capitalismo en el campo dominicano: Política agraria, pobreza rural y crecimiento agrícola* (Santiago: Instituto Superior de Agricultura, 1979), 33–36: "Nosotros sustentamos aquí la tesis de que la aparcería en nuestro país es una relación *esencialmente* capitalista, aún si *formalmente* feudal o semi-feudal."

59. See "Corvée," LIN 5, no. 1353 (1 Feb. 1907): "Hoy llegó a este ciudad un corvée de Las Lagunas encabezados por don Manuel de Js. González, en busca de ladrillos para la fábrica de la iglesia que se construye en aquel poblado." The church was consecrated in April 1908: *El Diario*, 16 Mar. 1908.

60. See, e.g., informants 28 and 33, who recall how large landowners moved the fences of their property when an old peasant producer had died.

61. San Miguel, "Dominican Peasantry," gives many examples.

62. Compare also Scott and Kerkvliet, "How Traditional Rural Patrons Lose Legitimacy," 501: "As long as the peasant sees his relation to agrarian elites as one of legitimate dependence . . . peasant 'class-consciousness' is unlikely."

63. For a beautiful analysis of the negotiable nature of patron-client relations on Ecuadorian haciendas, see Andrés Guerrero, *La semántica de la dominación: El concertaje de indios* (Quito, Ecuador: Editoriales Libri Mundi, 1991). Also see Michael F. Jiménez, "Class, Gender, and Peasant Resistance in Central Colombia, 1900–1930," in *Everyday Forms of Peasant Resistance*, ed. Forrest D. Colburn, 122–50 (Armonk, N.Y.: M. E. Sharp, 1989).

64. J. A. Pitt-Rivers, *The People of the Sierra* (1954; Chicago: Univ. of Chicago Press, 1971), 89–92.

65. Gudeman, *"Compadrazgo* as a Reflection of the Natural and Spiritual Person," 55, suggests a less hierarchical understanding of respect relations.

66. This legendary hospitality was the subject of an early photograph of a peasant woman offering a visitor a drink; see Bernardo Vega, *Imágenes de ayer* (Santo Domingo: Fundación Cultural Dominicana, 1981).

67. Eduardo García Tamayo, "Cultura campesina en la frontera norte," *Estudios Sociales* 17, no. 55 (Jan.–Mar. 1984): 46–47.

68. Pitt-Rivers, *People of the Sierra,* 27.

69. Compare Scott, *Moral Economy,* 193: "There is good reason . . . for holding that rebellion is one of the least likely consequences of exploitation." Also see Adas, "From Avoidance to Confrontation."

70. We have no information about social banditry in the Dominican countryside, but the nineteenth-century bandit Francisquito, who came from La Vega, succeeded in eluding the authorities for 10 years. He was reported to have lived undisturbed in various rural villages before he was finally killed in 1874. "Crónica," *El Orden* 1, no. 6 (13 Sept. 1874). About social banditry: Eric J. Hobsbawm, *Primitive Rebels* (Manchester, England: Manchester Univ. Press, 1959). Also see Gilbert M. Joseph, "On the Trail of the Latin American Bandits," LARR 25, no. 3 (1990): 7–53.

71. "Nuestros agricultores de éxito," LIN 10, no. 2144 (30 Mar. 1925).

72. For an analysis of a much more polarized situation: Jiménez, "Class, Gender, and Peasant Resistance."

73. Interview, Hermanas Peña (Santiago, 23 Dec. 1986).

74. Patricia Pessar, "Kinship Relations of Production," 16–17 and 33, n. 14, also emphasizes the tacit acceptance of these liaisons and the obligations of the father in case of pregnancy.

75. This behavior certainly is not unique. Raymond Smith calls it the "dual marriage system." He considers this system the basis for the British West Indian family system and for the existence of female-headed households. See, e.g., Raymond T. Smith, "Hierarchy and the Dual Marriage System in West Indian Society," in *Gender and Kinship: Essays Toward a Unified Analysis,* ed. Jane F. Collier and Sylvia J. Yanagisako (Stanford, Calif.: Stanford Univ. Press, 1987), 163–96. Compare also the detailed description of elite behavior in a Portuguese village: O'Neill, *Social Inequality in a Portuguese Hamlet.* The tendency to have small "legitimate" families helps prevent fragmentation of family property.

76. Compare also the story of informant 27. He was not an illegitimate child but an "hijo de crianza" of his mother's new husband, "el cual al morir sólo me dejó un solar para vivir, y todo el cordel de tierra que poseía se lo dejó en herencia a los hijos verdaderos."

77. Scott and Kerkvliet, "How Traditional Rural Patrons Lose Legitimacy," 525.

78. The patriarchal system of social relations within peasant culture conveniently

coincided with the ideology of the elite. I hope to demonstrate elsewhere that this belief in male superiority has been very important in establishing an ideological hegemony (in the Gramscian sense) of the ruling classes in the twentieth-century Dominican Republic.

7. Tobacco as an Export Crop: Urban Merchants and the Regional Economy

1. Compare Hoetink, "El Cibao, 1844–1900." Many presidents of the republic also originated in the Cibao.

2. The impotence of Latin American merchants is a central theme of dependencia theories. An extreme example of this perspective is Ronaldo Munck, *Politics and Dependency in the Third World: The Case of Latin America* (London: Zed Press, 1984), 233–60: chap. 8, "Comprador Regimes: Central America." Also: Eugene W. Ridings, "Foreign Predominance among Overseas Traders in Nineteenth-Century Latin America," LARR 20, no. 2 (1985): 3–27.

3. "El tabaco actual," EdP 9, 267 (30 Apr. 1890).

4. EdP 11, no. 318 (24 July 1892).

5. See, e.g., Darrell Wilson, *Report on the Economic, Financial and Commercial Conditions in the Dominican Republic* (London: Dept. of Overseas Trade, 1925), 17.

6. D. C. M. Platt, *Latin America and British Trade, 1806–1914* (New York: Harper and Row, 1973), 147.

7. Solicitud de A. Font y Cía., 27 Sept. 1903, in: AHN, Asuntos Exteriores, H 2382.

8. "Sobre el tabaco," EdP 10, no. 300 (19 July 1891).

9. Abad, *República Dominicana*, 317.

10. Grullón, *Sobre nuestro tabaco*. Pedro M. Archambault wrote a number of articles in the *Boletín Municipal* of Santiago in 1902. See, e.g., "La Escuela de Agricultura," BM 14, no. 380 (21 Mar. 1902) and no. 382 (10 Apr. 1902).

11. *El Liberal* 1, no. 10 (14 Nov. 1878).

12. It would be very interesting to analyze the political affiliations of this local elite. We know that Zoilo García was an avowed supporter of Heureaux. Mukien A. Sang, *Ulises Heureaux: Biografía de un dictador* (Santo Domingo: Instituto Tecnológico de Santo Domingo, 1987), 66. So were Gregorio Rivas and many more members of the Cibao mercantile elite.

13. We do not know much about this group. In Moca, men like Raffin Michel, Manuel Morillo, M. de J. Pichardo, and Adriano Cueto belonged to them. See VdS 1, no. 51, 13 Mar. 1881). José M. Michel, son(?) of Raffin, possessed two fincas in Moca in 1900; see Cestero, *Por el Cibao*, 123. The Villa González region developed later than the central Cibao. It may be that the situation in Villa González, where all larger landowners dedicated part of their time to mercantile activity, reflected earlier patterns of capitalist development in the central Cibao.

14. EdP 10, no. 291 (3 May 1891).

15. Compare, e.g., the records of Santiago: "Patentes," BO 2, no. 75 (31 Sept. 1869); and "Patentes," VdS 1, no. 7 (9 May 1880). For bankruptcies in 1873, see *El Porvenir* 2, no. 36 (7 Sept. 1873); no. 41 (12 Oct. 1873); no. 44 (2 Nov. 1873).

16. Cestero, *Por el Cibao*. A copy of this booklet can be found in the library of the UASD.

17. "Mención honorífica: Señores Augusto Espaillat, Sucesores," GO 20, no. 1512 (26 Sept. 1903). Cestero, *Por el Cibao*, 77–79. *El libro azul de Santo Domingo/Dominican Blue Book* (1920; rpt. Santo Domingo: UASD, 1976). San Miguel, "Dominican Peasantry," 215–17, gives information about the land purchases of this company.

18. In 1900, the first six of the merchants mentioned here "representan los capitales más fuertes del Comercio de Santiago." Mario F. Cabral, "Por el Comercio, II," *El Constitutional*, 3 Dec. 1900.

19. Cestero, *Por el Cibao*, 80–86.

20. *Boletín Municipal* (Organo del H. Ayuntamiento de Santiago), 1905. The first figures were published in BM 17, no. 445 (26 June 1905), and the last in BM 18, no. 478 (31 Jan. 1906).

21. The Dominican Customs Receivership gave the figure of 5,232,164 kilos of tobacco exported in 1905. See Mutto, "La economía de exportación," 107.

22. Large exporters in Puerto Plata were Divanna, Grisolia Co., Sucs. de Cosme Battle Co., Sucs. de C. Klüsener Co. (of German origin), A. S. Grullón, and C. H. Loinaz. Most of these firms were associated with firms of the "interior" or had offices in other Cibao towns. Other important merchants of the Cibao were Fenelón Michel (Moca), Zoilo García (La Vega), Moya Hermanos (La Vega, San Francisco de Macorís), Ariza, Moya & Grieser, and Grullón & Co. (both Sánchez). Some years later, five merchants were characterized as "los principales exportadores": Sucs. Augusto Espaillat, Nicolás Vega & Co., Sucs. de José Battle, Fenelón Michel, and Zoilo García: "La Cuestión palpitante," *El Diario* 6, no. 1520 (21 Aug. 1907). See also N. M. Zeller, "Puerto Plata en el siglo XIX," *Eme Eme Estudios Dominicanos* 5, no. 28 (1977): 27–51.

23. "La cosecha de tabaco," *El Diario* 5, no. 1352 (31 Jan. 1907)."

24. In 1907 Manuel de J. Toribio, Manuel de J. González, Vidal Pichardo, Jorge Carbonell, Rafael Fondeur, and Jesús M. Díaz bought tobacco in the region: "Progreso de Las Lagunas," *El Diario* 6, no. 1566 (14 Oct. 1907).

25. "Párrafos de la importante memoria del Secretario de Estado de Relaciones Exteriores José M. Cabral y Baez," *El Diario* 7, no. 2009 (24 Apr. 1909). German importers were said still to have stocks of 20,000 quintales tobacco from the previous harvest.

26. "La depreciación del tabaco," *El Diario*, 24 May 1912.

27. The quotation comes from "Consulado General de la República Dominicana (Hamburgo, 30-10-1908)," RdA 4, no. 11 (Feb. 1909) 186–87.

28. "El tabaco," *El Diario*, 2 June 1910.

29. "Cosechas y . . . Otros Puntos," LD 30, no. 9033 (1 July 1919).

30. Ministerio of Agriculture e Inmigración to Provincial Governors, Mar. 1915, in A/I, box 4 (1915).

31. Consul of the Dominican Republic to Ministerio del Estado of Spain, 12 Mar. 1915, in AHN, Asuntos Exteriores, H 1457. Miguel Montero (Madrid) to Ministerio of Agriculture e Inmigración, 5 Feb. 1915, in A/I, box 4 (1915).

32. "Porvenir del tabaco," LIN 2, no. 477 (19 Aug. 1917). Italics in original.

33. LIN 5, no. 1952 (6 Sept. 1920).

34. Calder, *Impact of Intervention,* 68–72.

35. Luis Carballo R., "Cuestiones de gran actualidad para los agricultores (El Llano, 2-3-1917)", LIN 2, no. 355 (3 Mar. 1917). Italics from Carballo.

36. Ayuntamientos del Cibao to the Military Government, 20 Oct. 1919, in GM, Hac/Com, box 121.

37. Gobierno Civil de la Provincia de La Vega to Gobierno Militar Thomas Snowdon, 26 Aug. 1920, in GM, Hac/Com, box 13.

38. "San Domingo Seeking Market for Its Tobacco," *Journal of Commerce* (New York City), 10 Aug. 1920, in GM, Hac/Com, box 13.

39. Their proposal had been that the state would guarantee a price of 5 pesos per quintal to the cultivator. The merchants would receive 7.50 when they delivered the tobacco to the government. See "Memorandum que la Cámara de Comercio, etc., de Santiago somete a la consideración del Gobierno Militar," signed by A. Pastoriza, in GM, Hac/Com, box 13. The memorandum is erroneously dated 28 July 1912. This must be 1920.

40. LIN 6, no. 2012 (19 Nov. 1920).

41. RdA 16, no. 9 (Dec. 1920), 278–85.

42. Cámara de Comercio de Santiago to Thomas Snowdon, 25 Apr. 1921, in GM, Hac/Com, box 9.

43. "La venta del tabaco," LIN 8, no. 1925 (14 Dec. 1922). Memorandum by Arthur A. Mayo, 28 Sept. 1921, in GM, Hac/Com, box 9, in which all activities—often frustrated—to sell the tobacco in that period are listed.

44. J. Loomis to Military Government, 28 Feb. 1922, in GM, box 6.

45. Letter from Military Governor of Santo Domingo Robson, 3 Jan. 1923, in GM, Hac/Com, box 9.

46. Other U.S. companies exporting Dominican tobacco were the Southern Leaf Tobacco Co. and the Dominican Tobacco Co. The DTC was a subsidiary of the Pennsylvanian Tobacco Co., later called the "General Sales Company." The latter had its own representative in Santiago (Archibald MacPherson). It bought more than 100,000 bultos which it sold in France; and it traded on the Dominican market only so long as it could take advantage of U.S. government protection. LIN 5, no. 1928 (10 May 1920). Also Nancy L. González, "El cultivo del tabaco en la República Dominicana," *Ciencia* (Dirección de Investigaciones, UASD,) 2, no. 4 (Oct.–Dec. 1975): 27.

47. "El tabaco y sus cuestiones," LIN 10, no. 2233 (15 July 1925). "La situación del tabaco Dominicano," LIN 14, no. 4678 (15 July 1929).

48. This tobacco expert was Edmundo García: "Lo que nos dice don Edmundo García sobre el mercado de tabaco," LIN 9, no. 1965 (9 June 1924).

49. "Nuestro tabaco y su mercado—Conversación con don Alberto Oquet," LIN 11, no. 2552 (19 Apr. 1926).

50. "El mercado de tabaco en Santiago, " LIN 10, no. 2163 (23 Apr. 1925) Also see LIN 10, no. 2233 (15 July 1925): "La presencia de los compradores, representantes, y directores de las casas especuladores en tabaco de Europa y los Estados Unidos, hace menos problemático y azaroso el negocio."

51. See, e.g., Baud, "German trade in the Caribbean," 101–3. Also see Informe de la Provincia de Santiago, 15 Jan. 1912, in GO 29, no. 2286 (10 Apr. 1912).

52. "El mercado de tabaco en Santiago," LIN 10, no. 2163 (23 Apr. 1925).

53. See, e.g., the list of storehouses of the Inspector Especial de Agricultura Emilio Almonte, in his letter to the Dept. of Commerce, 28 June 1933, in Sección de Comercio, box 28, no. 253.

Canca:
> Almacenes de Eliseo y Adolfo Cabrera. Compran por cuenta de la Compañía General de Tabacos francesa (CGT).

Licey:
> Almacén de Enrique Fernández. Compra por cuenta de la Compañía Dominicana de Tabacos (CDT).

Peña (Tamboril)/ Canca de la Piedra:
> Almacén de Capellán Hermanos. Almacén de Israel Tavárez. Ambos compran por cuenta de la CDT.
> Almacén de Alberto Valentín. Compra por cuenta de J. H. Groennou (Curaçao Trading Co.).

Pontezuela:
> Almacén de Javier Espaillat y Co. Compra por su propia cuenta.

Villa González:
> Almacén de Rafael Fondeur. Vende al V. F. Thomen.
> Almacén de José Ml. de Peña y Jorge Carbonell. Compran por cuenta de CDT.

Navarrete:
> José Efres. Compra por cuenta de la CDT.
> Almacén de Arturo Bisonó. Compra por su cuenta y vende a la CDT.
> Almacén de Alberto Oquet.
> Almacén de la CGT.

Laguna Salada:
> Almacén de Ismael Peralta. Compra por cuenta de la CGT.

54. "Estancamiento de la cosecha de tabaco," LIN 13, no. 4123 (29 Aug. 1928). The article stressed, ironically, the continuing difficult position of the Dominican tobacco on the world market.

55. Letter from the firm Jedicke, Dresden, to Dominican consul, 21 Sept. 1929 [translated from German]. Also see letter from Julius Loose ("zigarren-fabrik"), 1 Oct. 1929. Both in A/I, 5. The Dutch tobacco importer A. L. van Beek Hzn., ex-president of the Rotterdam tobacco importing company A. L. van Beek N.V., stresses that in the 1930s Dominican tobacco still was considered a "badly selected," inferior tobacco. Its advantage was its extremely low price. Interview, 2 July 1987.

56. Letter from Cámara de Comercio, etc., de Santiago, 3 Dec. 1932; Sección de Comercio, box 16, no. 31.

57. "Nuestra crasa incapacidad comercial y el auge del comercio extranjero," LIN 15, no. 4981 (19 July 1930).

58. "Progreso del Cibao," GO 10, no. 448 (13 Jan. 1883). Another goal of the society was "la apertura de un camino al litoral": "Camino," La Alborada (periódico independiente) 1, no. 2 (10 May 1883). The editor of this short-lived periodical was Eugenio Deschamps.

59. See, e.g., the 1905 meeting of the largest merchants in the house of V. F. Thomén, intended to regulate the purchase of tobacco: "Tabaco," Eco del Cibao 73 (3 Feb. 1905).

60. El Diario 5, no. 1397 (14 Mar. 1907) and no. 1398 (15 Mar. 1907). The first meeting was held in the storehouse of Mario F. Cabral. It is interesting to note that the largest merchants of Santiago (Augusto Espaillat Sucs., Nicolás Vega, T. Pastoriza, V. F. Thomén) did not attend. Perhaps the union brought together members of the mercantile class who did not have direct access to the world market.

61. See "Congreso Nacional, 24-6-1907," GO 26, no. 1982 (27 Mar. 1909).

62. El Diario 3, no. 621 (31 Aug. 1904). One of the purposes of the cámara was: "Estrechar los vínculos que unen a los comerciantes para la defensa de sus intereses; armonizar éstos con los que puedan parecer antagónicos entre agricultores, industriales, y comerciantes." See "Circular a los comerciantes, agricultores, profesionales, artesanos, i a todos los que pueda interesar," 23 Mar. 1917, in F/OP, box 26 C (1917).

63. Zoilo García to José Battle, 15 May 1899, in Hac/Com, box 57 (1899). It may not be superfluous to note that José Battle became the most important tobacco merchant of the region a few years later.

64. "El tabaco," LIN 3 no. 739 (28 June 1918).

65. This was a general tendency in situations where merchants confronted peasant producers. For the Costa Rican coffee trade, see Hall, El café y el desarrollo histórico-geográfico de Costa Rica, 47: "En general, los beneficiadores se ponían de acuerdo en cuanto a los precios manteniéndolos invariables en cada zona, para evitar rivalidades que pudieran perjudicarles."

66. The article was from Suddeutsche Tabakzeitung. Also "Los precios de compra del tabaco," LIN 14, no. 4688 (27 July 1929).

67. When it became aware of this article, the Santiago press reacted furiously and, despite Scheltema's allegations, prices remained more or less stable. "Maniobras especulativas contra el tabaco Dominicana en el mercado Holandés y Alemán," LIN

14, no. 4678 (15 July 1929). The same thing happened in 1934. See the undated draft of a letter from Alberto Oquet, probably to Ministro de Agricultura César Tolentino: "*Muy confidencialmente* le comunicamos que nosotros hemos sabido de una advertencia que la firma Scheltema, sus casi únicos competidores en la compra, que ellos quieren esforzarse en mantener el mercado lo más bajo posible." In another ("muy confidencial") letter of 11 Apr. 1934, Oquet wrote to César Tolentino that the damage had already been done: "Entiendo que este hombre nefasto para el negocio de tabaco, ha inoculado ya el virus de la propaganda subversiva y defetista en el mercado Europea." Both letters in SEA, box 194.

68. He later became a prominent supporter of the Trujillo regime. See Robert D. Crassweller, *Trujillo: The Life and Times of a Caribbean Dictator* (New York: Macmillan, 1966), 99 and 117.

69. M. F. Cabral to Miguel A. Veloz, 10 Apr. 1928, in Gobernación de Santiago, box 14, "Asuntos particulares."

70. *El Orden* 1, no. 51 (25 July 1875).

71. Miguel A. Román, "Memoria del Gobernador de la Provincia de Santiago," 6 Feb. 1906, in GO 23, no. 1687 (19 May 1906).

72. Luis Carballo, "La Cámara de Comercio de Santiago y la cosecha de tabaco, 1926–27," LIN 12, no. 3038 (5 May 1927).

73. "Memoria de Hacienda y Comercio, 1913," in GO 32, no. 2600 (21 Apr. 1915).

74. "Memoria del Secretario de Estado de Hacienda y Comercio, 1909," in GO 27, no. 2081 (13 Apr. 1910).

75. See, for this competition between the tobacco merchants, Grullón, *Sobre nuestro tabaco*, 38: "Cuando alguno que otro especulador ha querido implantar reformas y un más racional sistema de compra, la mayoría de sus competidores . . . le ha hecho la guerra."

76. This was most conspicuous in the evasion of the land tax, issued by the Military Government in the 1920s. See chap. 8 of the present volume, "Ideologies of Progress."

77. Rafael Díaz, "Memoria que al ciudadano Presidente de la República presenta el ciudadano Secretario de Estado de Agricultura e Inmigración," 27 Feb. 1912, in GO 29, no. 2360 (26 Dec. 1912).

78. See the discussion in the National Congress around such a proposal: "Congreso Nacional," GO 25, no. 1891 (13 May 1908) and no. 1893 (20 May 1908).

79. First they tried to dissuade the authorities from taking unfavorable measures. See, e.g., the meeting between merchants and the agricultural inspectors Valentín y Darío Mañón: "La cuestión del tabaco," LIN 10, no. 2161 (22 Apr. 1925).

80. Letter from Bartolo Amararte [?], Inspector de Frutos de la Provincia Duarte, 25 Apr. 1927, in A/I, box 28 (1927).

81. LIN 13, no. 4051 (31 May 1928); "Se protesta contra . . . una ordenanza sobre frutos." A letter from L. de Pou and Julio de la Rocha in the same issue concludes:

"La experiencia de 23 años en el negocio de frutos nos ha hecho aprender que el mal radica en el productor."

82. Inspector General de Frutos Emilio Almonte to Jefe del Departamento de Comercio, 2 May 1934, in Sección de Comercio, box 30, no. 179.

83. It will be clear that no cultural or mental obstacles existed to prevent the regional elite from occupying themselves with trade, such as Ridings, "Foreign Predominance," 17–18, suggests for other parts of Latin America.

84. For a comparable case, see Roseberry, *Coffee and Capitalism in the Venezuelan Andes*, 96: "The important source of power in the nineteenth-century Boconó economy was not access to *land* but access to *capital*" (italics in original).

8. Ideologies of Progress: State Intervention and Rural Society

1. This ambiguity could also be seen in Europe: Raymond Grew, "The Nineteenth-Century European State," in Bright and Harding, *Statemaking and Social Movements*, 83–120.

2. José Ramón López, *El gran pesimismo dominicano* (Santiago: UCMM, 1975), 62.

3. E.g., Ciro F. S. Cardoso and Pérez Brignoli, *Historia económica de América Latina*, 2:32–63.

4. See Paul Muto, Jr., "The Illusory Promise: The Dominican Republic and the Process of Economic Development, 1900–1930" (Ph.D. diss., Univ. of Washington, 1976); and Carlos M. Vilas, "Notas sobre la formación del estado en el Caribe: La República Dominicana," *Estudios Sociales Centroamericanos* 8, no. 24 (Sept.–Dec. 1979): 117–77, esp. 137–38.

5. "Mensaje de Gral. Gregorio Luperón al Congreso Nacional" (Puerto Plata, 11 July 1880), GO 7, no. 322 (14 Aug. 1880).

6. This emergence of a central state during Heureaux's "criollo" dictatorship is the central theme of Hoetink, *Dominican People*.

7. I do not know who quoted this statement first. It can be found in Juan Bosch, *Composición social dominicano: Historia e interpretación* (Santo Domingo: Alfa y Omega, 1979), 215; and Hoetink, Dominican People, 74–75.

8. See Emilio Rodríguez Demorizi, ed., *Hostos en Santo Domingo*, 2 vols. (Ciudad Trujillo: García Sucs., 1939); and Eugenio M. de Hostos, *Obras* (Havana, Cuba: Casa de las Américas, 1976), 20–25.

9. Memoria del Gobernador de Puerto Plata, Emilio Cordero, 1898, AGN.

10. Roberto Cassá even describes the Cáceres government as a "régimen entreguista." See Cassá, *Historia social y económica de la República Dominicana*, 2:205–8.

11. See, e.g., the opinion of the next Minister of Agriculture after the death of Cáceres: "En la Administración del Presidente Cáceres, fué iniciado la obra de introducir un criterio científico en la agricultura i en la crianza." *Memoria que al*

ciudadano Presidente de la República presenta el Secretario de Estado de Agricultura e Inmigración, 1912 (Santo Domingo: Escobar y Cía., 1913), 3.

12. It is sufficient to see the enthusiastic plans made in 1919 which were never executed. See letter on "Demonstration Plots" from Director of Agriculture to Officer in Charge of the Dept. of Agriculture and Immigration, 30 Sept. 1919, in A/I, box 7. Also see the Memo from J. C. Breckenridge (?) for Brigade Commander, 27 Sept. 1919, on "development of the country," in IP, box 34.

13. This was also the result of the improved financial position of the Dominican state in these years. See Franklin J. Franco, "La crisis del 29 y la génesis del Trujillato," in *América Latina en los años treinta*, ed. Pablo González Casanova (Mexico City: Universidad Nacional Autónoma de Mexico, 1977), 62–64.

14. A famous exception, of course, was Bonó, who in his article "A mis conciudadanos" (1884) rhetorically asked about the sugar plantations: "¿Qué progreso acusa eso?," in Rodríguez Demorizi, *Papeles de Bonó*, 327.

15. This may be compared with the shift from the "Caribbean" model to the "Indian" model which Paul Richards sees in African colonial policy. The former concentrated on the export of cash crops "with little or no thought for indigenous food supply"; the latter gave more attention to peasant cultivation of food crops and farming systems. See Paul Richards, *Indigenous Agricultural Revolution* (London: Hutchinson; and Boulder, Colo.: Westview, 1985), 19.

16. E.g., LeGrand, *Frontier Expansion and Peasant Protest in Colombia.*

17. State attempts to transform the system of land tenure were part of a worldwide process. Joel S. Migdal, in his instructive *Strong Societies and Weak States: State-Society Relations and State Capabilities in the Third World* (Princeton, N.J.: Princeton Univ. Press, 1988), 57–66, writes, "As if in a flash, government after government came to see the hidden potential of changing landholding rights" (57).

18. See, e.g., "Terrenos indivisos o comuneros," RdA 5, no. 3 (June 1909), 50. Here the comunero system is called "una de las causas principales del atraso de la agricultura."

19. See, e.g., the exaggerated description in the government publication *La República Dominicana* (Santo Domingo, 1906), 66: "En una propiedad de mil pesos, por ejemplo, quién compre un peso, aunque sea, tiene derecho a establecerse en cualquiera parte desocupada de ella, explotar los bosques, explotar las minas, y ser copropietario en todo lo que no sea trabajo de otro establecido en la misma propiedad real."

20. In a land conflict in Monte Plata in 1919, it became evident that more than 400 co-owners lived on a property of 93 *caballerías* (some 7,000 hectares): Letter to Colonel Fuller, 23 Oct. 1919, in IP, box 383.

21. Abad, *República Dominicana*, 264.

22. Félix F. Rodríguez, "Por los principios, II," LD 21 (14 Jan. 1910).

23. "Terrenos indivisos o comuneros," RdA 5, no. 3 (Junio 1909), 49.

24. Clausner erroneously dates the earliest attempt to curb collective landholding by means of state legislation to 1895: Marlin D. Clausner, *Rural Santo Domingo:*

Settled, Unsettled and Resettled (Philadelphia: Temple Univ. Press, 1973), 124. It is not clear what is the origin of his mistake.

25. Letter from Governor of Santo Domingo (Pedro Ma. Mejía?), 5 Oct. 1900, in IP, 171.

26. A. Albuquerque, *Títulos de los terrenos comuneros de la República Dominicana* (Ciudad Trujillo: Impresora Dominicana, 1961), 52.

27. This was done in the *Ley sobre inscripción de títulos de terrenos rurales.* See Clausner, *Rural Santo Domingo,* 128.

28. "Senado, 20-4-1911," GO 28, no. 2197 (3 June 1911).

29. Albuquerque, *Títulos de los terrenos comuneros,* 52–57. Also see Bryan, "Transformation of the Dominican Economy," 337.

30. Letter to Secretary of State, 17 June 1911, cited in Bryan, "Transformation of the Dominican Economy," 337.

31. Clearest in this respect is Ruiz Tejada, *Estudio sobre la propiedad inmobiliaria,* 74–75. See also "Terrenos," LIN 2, no. 311 (10 Jan. 1917), which denounced the existence of "fábricas de títulos de propiedad"; and Albuquerque, *Títulos de los terrenos comuneros.*

32. Vicente Tolentino R., Agrimensor, "Terrenos Comuneros," LIN 2, no. 402 (30 Apr. 1917).

33. Manuel de J. Troncoso de la Concha to Col. Rufus H. Lane, 25 May 1918, cited in Clausner, *Rural Santo Domingo,* 130.

34. San Miguel, "Dominican Peasantry," 220. It is worth noting that it was a large-scale tobacco merchant, Ascencio y Cía., who wanted these common lands measured and demarcated.

35. On this sort of collective protest in the nation's plantation-dominated areas, see Michiel Baud, "Transformación capitalista y regionalización en la República Dominicana, 1875–1920," *Investigación y Ciencia* 1, no. 1 (Jan–Apr. 1986): 17–45, esp. 26–27. For the Cibao: San Miguel, "Dominican Peasantry," chap. 5. It would be interesting to investigate whether the geography of present-day peasant mobilization in the Dominican Republic still reflects earlier patterns of comunero landholding. Social cohesion in the countryside as a function of the comunero system seems to have been absent in the region of Villa González.

36. "Ley sobre terrenos comuneros," *El Diario* 8 (1909).

37. See also San Miguel, "Dominican Peasantry," 222. His data make clear that the former sometimes tried to force the latter to measure and demarcate their common lands.

38. E.g., Letter from Ayuntamiento San Carlos, 26 Mar. 1872, says that "los dueños de aquellos se creen hoy con derecho a dichos solares." Also see Letter from Ayuntamiento Monte Plata, 24 Aug. 1872. Both letters in IP, box 16 (1872).

39. "Estado de Agricultura en Azua," EdlO 485 (2 Mar. 1889): "Muchos vecinos y algunos extranjeros ocupan una parte de esos terrenos sin satisfacer al Ayuntamiento el subsidio que repetidas veces se ha impuesto, pero que nunca se ha pagado."

40. "Informe Síndico," BM 36, no. 1186 (31 Dec. 1927).

41. "Ley sobre la concesión gratuita de los terrenos del Estado," GdStD 3, no. 130 (14 July 1876): "Art. 1: Los Dominicanos tienen el derecho de ocupar el terreno del Estado que no esté habitado por otro, para sembrar principalmente en él, caña de azúcar, café, cacao, tabaco, algodon, ú otros frutos mayores. Art. 2: Los inmigrantes extranjeros, cuya ocupación habitual sean los trabajos agrícolas, tienen el mismo derecho."

42. See, e.g., Calder, *Impact of Intervention,* 113. This result of land legislation in the Dominican Republic was far from unique. Migdal, *Strong Societies and Weak States,* 63, recounts "a land-grab of stupendous proportions" in many countries in the world.

43. Government publication *La República Dominicana,* 66. See also note 19, above. The same attitude emerges in E. Deschamps, *La República Dominicana: Directorio y guía general* (Santiago, 1907; rpt. Santo Domingo: Editorial de Santo Domingo, 1974), 131.

44. Calder, *Impact of Intervention,* chap. 4. This is not to say that the U.S. government did not stimulate the penetration of foreign capital in the Dominican Republic; ibid., 240. Also see Baez Evertsz, *Azúcar y Dependencia en la República Dominicana,* 41–44.

45. About this U.S. policy: Equipo de Investigación Socioeconomico, *Desarrollo del capitalismo,* 8.

46. The most complete overview of the 1920 law can be found in Clausner, *Rural Santo Domingo,* 201–10. Also see Albuquerque, *Títulos de los terrenos comuneros.*

47. Calder, *Impact of Intervention,* 73–74, 111. The law was far from clear. Other documents mention a fixed tax of five centavos per tarea. E.g., Director General de Rentas Internas to Secretaria de Estado de Hacienda y Comercio, 23 Aug. 1919, in IP, box 386. The taxation of comunero lands was an unsolved problem and therefore a cause of many complaints: see the letter just cited and one from A. Baez, viuda Guerrero, 4 Nov. 1921, in GM, Hac/Com, box 9. The widow complained that she had to pay the tax, while surveying the land had been impossible: "No puedo venderlos, ni arrendarlos, ni efectuar ninguna operación con ellos."

48. Calder, *Impact of Intervention,* 111.

49. Undated memo from P. F. Silivordes (?), chief assessor, referring to "Propaganda against Payment of Land Taxes," attached to letter from J. Loomis to Secretario de Estado de Hacienda y Comercio, 29 Dec. 1920, in GM, Hac/Com, box 9.

50. Letter from Departamento de Hacienda y Comercio, 17 Sept. 1920, in GM, Hac/Com, box 13.

51. J. Loomis to Secretario de Estado de Hacienda y Comercio, 29 Dec. 1920, in GM, Hac/Com, box 9.

52. Memorandum by D. W. Rose, 15 Nov. 1921, in GM, Hac/Com, box 9 (1921). See also "Santiago y el Impuesto Territorial," LIN 6, no. 2295 (14 Nov. 1921).

53. Calder, *Impact of Intervention,* 113 and 280, n. 72. Calder's emphasis on events in the southern part of the country leads him to underestimate the influence of the movement in the Cibao. He does not understand (p. 112) why the U.S. government diminished the taxes in 1920. It is clear, however, that this move was a direct reaction to the Cibao agitation.

54. This is immediately clear from the archives of the Tribunal de Tierras in Santiago.

55. Abad, *República Dominicana,* 297.

56. "Memoria de la Gobernación de Santo Domingo," 1894, AGN.

57. Compare: *Informe de la Comisión de Investigación de los E.U.A. en Santo Domingo en 1871,* 197: "Estos cerdos son tan salvajes que los cazan con ayuda de perros cuando necesitan carne para alimentarse."

58. Manuel Sención Riches to Alcalde, San Pedro de Macorís, 17 May 1870, in IP, box 12 (1870). The original text is: "Le hago saver que en este lugar tal como yo y otros individuos más tenemos algunos buelles por la razón que tenemos Hacienda de caña y que indispensable debemos moler con Bueyes, y muy pocas bacas de leche por la necesidad de que como aquí no hay crianza de cerdos son de suma necesidad; tanto para socorrer algún enfermo como para sus casas."

59. E.g., Ruiz Tejada, *Estudio sobre la propiedad inmobilaria,* 3: "En Haiti no había terrenos comuneros, pues la existencia de éstos se manifiesta casi siempre en las regiones donde hay crianza libre." Also see Hoetink, *Dominican People,* 11.

60. *Colección de leyes, decretos y resoluciones de los poderes legislativo y ejecutivo de la República, 1893–1894–1895* (Santo Domingo: ONAP, 1983), 13:459–76, Law No. 3522.

61. "Crianza fuera de cercas," RdA 5, no. 9 (Dec. 1909).

62. *Colección de leyes,* 13:463–64. In the original, the size is indicated as ten *caballerías.* One caballería is a little over 75 hectares.

63. Letter to Ministerio de Interior y Policía, 18 Jan. 1900, signed by 151 cattle growers living in Jaguate, San Cristóbal, in IP, box 175.

64. *Colección de Leyes,* 16:20–21: "Num. 3957; Resolución del Congreso Nacional que suspende la ley sobre crianza de animales domésticos" (23-2-1900); and 16:220–21: "Num. 4043; Decreto del Congreso Nacional relativo a la crianza de animales y establecimiento de zonas agrícolas" (3-8-1900). Also "Crianza fuera de cercas," RdA 5, no. 9 (Dec. 1909).

65. Juan B. Alfonseca, "Memoria de Secretario de Estado de Fomento y Obras Públicas," 27 Feb. 1908, in GO 25, no. 1879 (1 Apr. 1908).

66. "Memoria del Gobernador de Santiago," 11 Jan. 1908, in IP, box 240 (italics added).

67. Cited in Patrick A. Bryan, "La producción campesina en la República Dominicana a principios del siglo XX," *Eme Eme Estudios Dominicanos* 7, no. 42 (May–June 1979): 54.

68. Letter from H. Johansen, 7 Sept. 1918, in A/I, box 12 (1918). In an earlier letter (10 Apr. 1918), Johansen had written: "La 'crianza libre' y las 'zonas de crianza' deben ser no solamente desalentadas sino también prohibidas, no importa cuanto los que subscriben las petición defenderlas con su florido lenguaje. . . . Naturalmente, tal especie de agricultura conduce a la desmoralización e indolencia"; in A/I, box 12 (1918).

69. Letter from Junta de Fomento (Juan E. Ariazy?), in F/OP, box 2, folder VII.

70. *Memoria que al ciudadano Presidente de la República presenta el Secretario de Estado de Agricultura e Inmigración (1912),* 13.

71. Director of Agriculture Holger Johansen, to Dept. of Agriculture and Immigration, 31 Aug. 1918, in A/I, box 8.

72. Baron de Candia, "Temas agrícolas," LD 21, no. 6250 (19 Apr. 1910). In the same vein: Grullón, *Sobre nuestro tabaco,* 70–73.

73. "Informe anual del director de agricultura," July 10, 1919—June 30, 1920; in *Memoria que al ciudadano Presidente de la República presenta el Secretario de Estado de Agricultura e Inmigración, 10 July 1919—30 June 1920* (Santo Domingo: El Progreso, 1920), 20; *Memoria que al ciudadano Presidente de la República presenta el Secretario de Estado de Agricultura e Inmigración, July 1918—June 1919* (Santo Domingo: El Progreso, 1919), 19.

74. See Rafael A. Espaillat to Secretario de Estado de Interior y Policía, 22 Apr. 1928, in Sección de Agricultura, 1928.

75. LIN 4, no. 953 (27 Mar. 1919). The problem in the interpretation of such articles is that we do not know exactly who these "campesinos" were.

76. *El Porvenir* 2, no. 18 (4 May 1873).

77. Dr. J. Jover, "El fracaso de muchas empresas, se debe en parte á la poca necesidad del peón Dominicano," *El Anuncio* (San Francisco de Macorís), 26 July 1926.

78. Memo of J. C. Breckenridge (?) for Brigade Commander on "Development of the country," 27 Sept. 1919, in IP, box 34 (1919). Compare also Hans Schmidt, *The United States Occupation of Haiti, 1915–1934* (New Brunswick, N.J.: Rutgers Univ. Press, 1971), 158, citing a U.S. official: "The peasants, living lives which to us seem indolent and shiftless, are enviably carefree; but, if they are to be citizens of an independent self-governing nation, they must acquire, or at least a larger number of them must acquire, a new set of wants."

79. "Agricultura," VdS 1, no. 8 (16 May 1880).

80. See Moya Pons, "The Land Question in Haiti and Santo Domingo," 186. On the "Código Rural": Frank Moya Pons, *La dominación haitiana, 1822–1844* (Santiago: UCMM, 1972), 63–73.

81. *Boletín Oficial* 2, 148 (24 Dec. 1870). In 1855, the "Ley sobre la represión del ocio y la vagancia" already had been issued. See *Memoria correspondiente al año 1927 que al ciudadano Presidente de la República presenta el Sr. Rafael A. Espaillat, Secretario de Estado de Agricultura é Inmigración* (Santo Domingo: García Sucs., 1928), 383–85. According to the governor of Puerto Plata, this "Ley de Vagos" was hardly applied: "Gobernador de Puerto Plata," circular no. 6, *El Porvenir* 4, no. 115 (14 Mar. 1875).

82. To give just two examples: "El Comisionado Especial de Agricultura del distrito de Samaná, Gregorio Rivas, 3-6-1876," GdStD 3, no. 126 (16 June 1876): "Cada habitante está en la obligación de tener el cultivo suficiente para atender con su producto a las necesidades de su familia." Also see "El fiscal intensifica su acción contra la vagancia injustificada," LIN 10, no. 2314 (20 Oct. 1925).

83. See, e.g., Gobernador de La Vega to Ministerio de Interior and Policía, 1 June 1872, in IP, box 15 (1872): "Creo oportuno llenar las vacantes que haga en la Compañía reclutando un número entre los que autoridades rurales presenten como vagos." Also see Pedro T. Garrido, "Memoria del Secretario de Estado de Fomento y Obras Publicas," 24 Feb. 1888, in GO 15, no. 713 (21 Apr. 1888).

84. "Memoria del Gobernador del Seybo [F. Evangelista]," 1896, AGN.

85. "Memoria del Gobernador de Puerto Plata," 1897, AGN.

86. "La Provincia de Santiago," EdP 6, no. 246 (18 Apr. 1889).

87. The Trujillo regime took this repressive policy to its logical conclusion. As early as Sept. 1930, it was reported from Villa González: "Ayer, un pelotón de la PM [Policía Militar] se trasladó a una sección cercana a esta villa y capturó un buen número de hombres que, *aunque no son de todo holgazanos,* se entretenían en violar la ley, estableciendo juegos de azar, donde pierden ya el sustento de su familia o bien el tiempo ¡que es tan precioso!" In "Actividad de la Policía Militar en Villa González," LIN 15, no. 5036 (23 Sept. 1930); italics added.

88. See, e.g., Hoetink, *Dominican People,* 15–16. Also the discourse of Diputado Franco in the National Congress (1895), in Michiel Baud, "The Origins of Capitalist Agriculture in the Dominican Republic," LARR, 22, 2 (1987), 147. In 1880, Bonó expressed a similar judgment concerning the sugar industry: "Todos los pequeños propietarios que hasta hoy han sido ciudadanos vendrán a ser peones o por mejor decir siervos": Rodríguez Demorizi, *Papeles de Bonó,* 252.

89. R. Castillo, "Memoria del Gobernador del Distrito de San Pedro de Macorís, 1891," GO 19, no. 924 (7 May 1892): "En tales condiciones se encuentra Macorís: millares de trabajadores pueblan las seis fincas de caña ubicadas a sus alrededores los cuales en determinados días de la semana entran a la población y la Policía de Gobierno de que dispongo no es suficiente para garantizar el orden según la require la pública moralidad." The governor of Puerto Plata warned in 1894 about large-scale enterprises "creando una situación embarasosa, anomala y preñada de peligros al Estado al convertirse masas numerosas de hombres de propietarios y jefes de familias en hordas de proletarios errantes, viciosos y miserables." Juan Garrido, "Memoria del Gobernador de la Provincia de Puerto Plata," 1894, in IP, box 148, folder 9; also see his letter of 12 July 1895, in IP, box 154, folder 3.

90. López, *El gran pesimismo dominicano,* 57.

91. Hoetink, *Dominican People,* 142–43. Also see Domínguez, *La dictadura de Heureaux,* 43–47. L. Cristóbal Perello made the link between the ideas of Hostos and the improvement of agricultural practice in the Cibao explicit in a speech to the Junta de Fomento of Santiago, 23 Feb. 1908, in F/OP, box A; 1902/07/08: "Lleno de

fe y convencido de la eficacia de su obra [of Hostos], el éxito más completo ha coronado sus esfuerzos y ya se puede asegurar que en poco tiempo la instrucción será útil y provechosa a la juventud dominicana."

92. Compare: José Ramón López, *Censo y catastro de la Común de Santo Domingo* (Santo Domingo: El Progreso, 1919), 35: "Por el nuevo sistema [la instrucción] se difunde entre los campesinos y les enseña, no sólo los fundamentales conocimientos de leer, escribir y contar, sino también la ciencia agrícola, en su parte más práctica, a fin de que las nuevas generaciones reaccionen contra la rutina empírica que les obliga a más cantidad de trabajo y menor volumen de producción."

93. "Correspondencia de Moca, 6-3-1881," VdS 1, no. 51 (13 Mar. 1881).

94. C. Ma. de Rojas, "Memoria del Gobernador de la Provincia Espaillat," 7 Jan. 1891, in GO 18, no. 398 (7 Nov. 1891).

95. For an attempt by José Ramón López to initiate such a discussion, see Baud, "Ideología y campesinado," 77.

96. See, e.g., "Correspondencia de Moca, 27-3-1881," VdS 2, no. 54 (4 Mar. 1881). An attempt to increase taxes on "ventorillos donde se expendiera aguardiente" encountered much resistance from rural merchants and ultimately was abolished. A similar proposal was hotly debated in 1911 and accepted only with many changes: "Cámara de Diputados, 16-5-1911," *Boletín de Congreso* 2, no. 28 (28 July 1911).

97. The quote is from "Policía," *El Orden* 1, no. 13 (11 Nov. 1874). *El Orden* 1, no. 17 (30 Nov. 1874), reported that in Moca "se ha desarrollado la pasión del juego hasta un grado tan alarmante que los padres de familia se ven impedidos de enviar a sus diligencias, a sus hijos y domesticos, pues se juega en los caminos reales, en las veredas, y desde lunes a sabado."

98. "Correspondencia de Moca, 6-3-1881," VdS 1, no. 51 (13 Mar. 1881). Also see "Circular a los Inspectores de Agricultura," BM 3, no. 44 (30 Sept. 1887).

99. "Ley sobre Policía Urbana y Rural," BM 5, no. 118 (24 Aug. 1891).

100. "El fiscal intensifica su acción contra la vagancia injustificada," LIN 10, no. 2314 (20 Oct. 1925). The letter of Procurador Fiscal Germán Martínez Reina, which was reproduced in the newspaper, emphasized that there was work for anyone who wanted to work.

101. "Causas que . . . ," *El Diario* 5, no. 1353 (1 Feb. 1907).

102. Dept. of Justice and Public Instruction to the Dept. of Interior and Police, 26 Nov. 1918, in GM, IP, box 72. To this judgment was added: "The better elements among the Dominicans will not be strong enough to eliminate this corrupting and demoralizing gain." The Military Government, of course, was prepared to help!

103. Letter Brigade Commander to Military Government, 20 Dec. 1917, in GM, IP, box 23: "The Dominican people have for so many years been accustomed to look on cock fighting and its attendant gambling as quite a legitimate sport and pastime, that the restriction of their indulgence in them will have to come gradually."

104. "Juego de Gallos," LIN 3, no. 735 (20 June 1918), recapitulates the discussion.

105. Proclamation of Francisco Antonio Gómez y Moya, General de División del

Ejército Dominicano y Gobernador Civil y Militar de Samaná, 16 Feb. 1900. Considering "que está prohibido por la ley toda clase de juego de envite o azar, y que no obstante ello, existen casas que especulan públicamente con ese vicio que denigra y envilece," he prohibited all gambling. In IP, box 172. Gómez y Moya, born in La Vega, had been a dedicated opponent of Heureaux and, after the death of the latter in 1900, became Ministro de Guerra y Marina. See Martínez, *Diccionario biográfico-histórico dominicano*, 201.

106. See, e.g., the 1922 statement of E. García Santelises, "Inspector de Instrucción Pública" of Puerto Plata: "Muchos son adictos a las velaciones y velorios, y pierden su tiempo frecuentando los establecimientos, en vez de aprovecharlo en el trabajo. Estas tendencias sólo podrán ser modificadas por el Progreso, La Instrucción, y por Leyes sanas bien meditadas"; in Rodríguez Demorizi, *Lengua y folklore de Santo Domingo*, 275.

107. Manuel de J. Tejara, Jefe Superior de la Guardia Republicana, "Orden del Cuerpo," Santo Domingo, 19 Aug. 1908, AGN. Also see Patrick E. Bryan, "La cuestión obrera en la industria azucarera de la República Dominicana a finales del siglo XIX y principios del XX," *Eme Eme Estudios Dominicanos* 7, no. 41 (Mar.–Apr. 1979): 57–77, esp. 73.

108. See, e.g., Rodríguez Demorizi, *Papeles de Bonó*, 161. Also see Hoetink, *Dominican People*, 157–58.

109. Reportero, "De Ingenio Italia," LD 21, no. 6239 (6 Apr. 1910).

110. "Causas que . . . ," *El Diario* 5, no. 1353 (1 Feb. 1907).

111. See Gregorio Rivas to Archbishop, 10 June 1876, in Correspondence of Archbishop, 1876, no. 3253.

112. "La Iglesia y la Agricultura," LIN 3, no. 735 (20 June 1918).

113. The priest Luis F. Henríquez, Altamira, to Luis Martí, Jefe de la Sección VI, Ministerio de Agricultura, 22 Nov. 1927, in SEA, box 64.

114. *Memoria de la Cámara de Comercio, Industria y Agricultura de Santiago, abarcando el período 1922–1923–1924* (Santiago: La Información, 1925), 30.

115. This is not to say that no tension existed between Hostosianism and the Church during the Heureaux regime. See Hoetink, *Dominican People*, 151–53

116. Compare: Migdal, *Strong Societies and Weak States*, 8–9 and passim.

117. Ibid., 136–37 and passim.

9. THE STRUGGLE FOR TECHNOLOGY: IMPROVING THE QUALITY OF DOMINICAN TOBACCO

1. B. Jewsiewicki, "L'innovation technologique et la politique," in B. Jewsiewicki and J. P. Chrétien, eds., *Ambiguïtés de l'innovation: Sociétés rurales et technologies en Afrique centrale et occidentale au XX siècle* (Quebec, Canada: Safi, 1984), 298. See also Alain de Janvry and Luis Crouch, *Technological Change and Peasants in Latin America* (San Francisco: California Agricultural Experiment Station, 1980).

2. No serious research has been done on the social history of tobacco consumption and the influence of changing taste in Europe. A brilliant example of such research for the case of sugar is Sidney W. Mintz, *Sweetness and Power: The Place of Sugar in Modern History* (Harmondsworth, England: Penguin, 1986). For an interesting study, see Peter Taylor, *Smoke Ring: The Politics of Tobacco* (London: Bodley Head, 1984), and Ortiz, *Cuban Counterpoint*.

3. "Cuestión tabaco," *El Orden* 1, no. 11 (18 Oct. 1874).

4. There were some dissident voices, however. "El Tabaco," *La Prensa* 5, no. 1343 (10 May 1897), reported that "personas competentes y observadores" were opposed to seedbeds: "Vale más sembrar el tabaco en surcos en noviembre y no transplantarlo sino arrancar las matitas que sobren."

5. LIN 4, no. 941 (5 Apr. 1919).

6. As early as 1924, José Gabriel Aldebot, in "El tabaco dominicano," *El Diario,* 4 Apr. 1924, wrote that it was necessary "desterrar el mal hábito de regar los semillos al azar, como se acostumbra hacer dentro de los conucos sembrados de maiz y, a veces, con otras plantaciones."

7. Compare: Informe Mensual de la Cámara de Comercio de Santiago, Feb. 1928, in Gobernación de Santiago, 1928, box 7. Tobacco cultivators were warned that "una nueva plaga está invadiendo nuestros tabacos," which was called the "pulga del tabaco."

8. Only in the larger monocultural plantations did they constituted a danger in this period. See Máximo Gómez to J. J. Hungría of the plantation "La Reforma," 12 Feb. 1890, in Rodríguez Demorizi, *Papeles de Máximo Gómez,* 33–34.

9. This criticism became loudest in the 1920s. E.g., J. L. Amargo, "Instrucciones para el cultivo del tabaco" (Santo Domingo, 1919), 9: "El sistema de ranchos abiertos que actualmente se usa es desastroso y debe ser abandonado completamente."

10. P. Pepín, "Memoria del Gobernador de Santiago," 30 Jan. 1892, in GO 19, no. 935 (23 July 1892).

11. It was said in 1928 that "la escasés de ranchos" was the main obstacle to an increase of the tobacco crop: "Nuestros campesinos esperan a última hora para hacer sus ranchos, quizás basados en experiencias amargas de cuando sembraban tarde sus cosechas que la mayoría de las veces se dañaban por la seca o eran destruídas por los gusanos": Anselmo Copello, presidente of the Cámara de Comercio de Santiago, to Gobernador de Santiago, 12 Jan. 1928, in Gobernación de Santiago, 1928, box 3. Also see "Buena preparación del tabaco Dominicano," LIN 10, no. 2185 (19 May 1925).

12. Rodríguez Demorizi, *Papeles de Bonó,* 197–98.

13. Such an interpretation of the Junta system was expressed in 1922 by Américo Jiménez, "Inspector de Instrucción Pública" of Salcedo, who called the Junta "un bonito ejemplo de economía política y de sociabilidad," in Rodríguez Demorizi, *Lengua y folklore de Santo Domingo,* 208.

14. Grullón, *Sobre nuestro tabaco,* 50.

15. Compare, e.g., Grullón, *Sobre nuestro tabaco,* 31: "Al hablar de dichos corredores-comines en los círculos sociales de esta sociedad [Santiago] . . . éstos

claman, sin excepción, contra su existencia, y la condenan como una de las causas que mantienen estancado el movimiento mejorador de la precaria situación tabacalera. . . . Se dice que ellos provocan la mayor confusión de precios y mantienen vivo el sentimiento de inseguridad y desconfianza que reina entre nuestros vegueros respecto a nuestro Comercio especulador."

16. "Tabaco," *Eco del Cibao* (30 May 1905): "Claro está, el interés del cosechero por vender y los reclamos del comerciante que ha avanzado algún dinero porque le traigan la hoja . . . no da tiempo ni a unos, ni a otros para la cojida oportuna, y el *entroje* necesario."

17. "Report on tobacco cultivation . . . ," *Annex to Report of the Director of Agriculture for the Quarter ending Sept. 30 1919,* in Sección de Agricultura, box 7.

18. "Sobre Tabaco, II," *El Diario* 7, no. 2017 (4 May 1909).

19. For such an opinion, see RdA 1, no. 3 (1905), 36.

20. See "La Cosecha de 1886," EdP 4, no. 204 (9 May 1886).

21. For an early reference, see "Sobre tabaco," *Eco del Cibao* 1, no. 101 (11 Mar. 1905): "Nuestros buenos campesinos están ya acostumbrados a que el comerciante *le sirva de criado* teniendo éste que hacer el trabajo de limpieza general de los frutos, acondicionamiento para el embarque, etc."

22. See LIN 2, no. 420 (21 May 1917).

23. "Afán constante," EdP 1, no. 33 (19 Nov. 1882).

24. Compare: J. R. Abad, "El tabaco en el Cibao," RdA 2, no. 15 (June 1906), 211–12. Criollo tobacco, of course, has survived into the present.

25. "Memoria del Gobernador de Santiago," 11 Jan. 1908, in IP, box 240.

26. "Interview con don José J. Díaz," BM 14, no. 382 (10 Apr. 1902).

27. Grullón, *Sobre nuestro tabaco,* 20–21.

28. "Cuestión tabaco," EdP 10, no. 294 (20 June 1891).

29. EdP 1, no. 38 (24 Dec. 1882).

30. "El Departamento de Agricultura—a respecto a la cosecha de tabaco," LIN 13, no. 4125 (31 Aug. 1928)

31. On the González government, see EdP 2, no. 315 (4 June 1892); and Gregorio Rivas, "Comisionado especial de agricultura," GdStD 3, no. 126 (16 June 1876): "Todo el que presentará *cincuenta tareas* de caña recibirá en recompensa un *Trapiche* o ingenio de hierro, sistema 'Victor' . . . ; el que presentará *cien tareas* además de recibir un *trapiche,* será gratificado con dos yuntas de bueyes; o permutará la gratificación por un trapiche de doble precio." Tobacco growers who produced more than 20 quintales would receive 50 centavos per quintal "probando que ha sido cosechado en sus proprias labranzas."

32. For the premium system: "Mención Honorífica," GO 20, no. 1508 (29 Aug. 1903); and nos. 1509 (5 Sept. 1903); 1510 (12 Sept. 1903); 1511 (19 Sept. 1903); 1512 (26 Sept. 1903); 1513 (3 Oct. 1903); 1514 (10 Oct. 1903); and 1515 (17 Oct. 1903).

33. "El tabaco otra vez," EdP 1, no. 17 (30 July 1882).

34. "Observaciones," VdS 1, no. 37 (5 Dec. 1880).

35. For the municipal decree, see "Ayuntamiento, 10-3-1894," BM 7, no. 180 (22 May 1894). A survey of all government measures can be found in Lluberes, "La crisis del tabaco cibaeño," 3–22.

36. "Decreto sobre el tabaco," EdP 6, no. 227 (9 June 1888).

37. "Congreso Nacional, 20-5-1890," GO 17, no. 834 (16 Aug. 1890); and GO 17, no. 824 (7 June 1890).

38. See, e.g., the reaction of one of the most respected commercial houses of Santiago when the government proposed to set a fixed time for the drying and fermentation of the tobacco: "No se puede aceptar ni fijar tiempo determinado para la duración de la troja. Si el tabaco que se entroje queda fermentado en doce días, se podrá autorizar su embarque. Si necesita más tiempo, el empacador tendrá la obligación de esperar a que esté fermentado." Letter from Sres. Bonelly, appended to César Pérez to R. Richards, Inspector Provincial de Frutos, 30 May 1927, in A/I, box 28 (1927). For a similar opinion, see Emilio Almonte, Inspector Especial de Agricultura, to Departamento de Comercio, 22 May 1933: "Cuando el tabaco ha sido fermentado debidamente, se puede embarcar en cualquier época," in A/I, box 28.

39. "La fermentación del tabaco," RdA 1, no. 3 (1905), 36.

40. "Ayuntamiento, 10-3-1894," BM 7, no. 180 (22 May 1894): "El tabaco deberá venderse y comprarse bien fermentado, apartado, con las cabezas cortadas, bien seco, enmanillado y atado con una de sus mismas hojas." In 1917, the "Asociación de Agricultores y Ganaderos" asked the municipal government to enforce this law: BM 29, no. 962 (16 Sept. 1917).

41. "Congreso Nacional, 18-5-1894," GO 21, no. 1041 (4 Aug. 1894), and "Congreso Nacional, 21-5-1894," GO 21, no. 1042 (11 Aug. 1894). For more information about the types of tobacco, see our app. 2.

42. For the varieties of Dominican tobacco, see our app. 2.

43. Decreto del Congreso Nacional, no. 3415, 7 June 1894, in *Colección de Leyes,* 13:281–83.

44. Pedro Ma. Archambault, "La Ley de Frutos," *El Constitucional,* 18 Apr. 1901. He returned to the subject in 1902: Archambault, "Para qué sirve la Ley de Frutos?" BM 14, no. 386 (31 May 1902). His answer to this rhetorical question was: "Para contener la ruina creciente de la depreciación de nuestra riqueza."

45. *El Constitucional,* 27 Apr. 1901.

46. Mario F. Cabral, "Ley de Frutos," *El Constitucional,* 2 May 1901. In the same vein: Ram. Asensio, "Alerta," *El Constitucional,* 29 Apr. 1901.

47. The irony, of course, was that very few of these well-intended articles ever reached the growers. Compare a contemporary opinion, which described the *Revista de Agricultura* as "frequently either of a somewhat remote interest or too strictly technical to be assimilated by the class of people for whom the 'Revista' is primarily meant," in "Yearly Report of the Department of Agriculture, 1917," GM, Agricultura, folder 7. For a similar opinion of José Ramón López, see Muto, "Illusory Promise," 186.

48. See "Memoria de la Secretaría de Estado de Agricultura e Inmigración," 1909, AGN. "La creación de esta Secretaría . . . anunció al país que por primera vez iba a dedicarse seria atención a la agricultura nacional."

49. E.g., "El tabaco y el Cibao," RdA 2, no. 15 (June 1906), 211. Also see chap. 2 of the present volume, "Tobacco and the Cibao."

50. "Memoria Agricultura e Inmigración, 1912," GO 29, no. 2360 (26 Dec. 1912).

51. A. Michels to Secretario de Estado de Agricultura é Inmigración Rafael Díaz, 11 May 1911, in A/I, box 2, folder 3.

52. Albert Michels, Report to E. Montes de Ocoa, Minister of Agriculture and Immigration, 31 Dec. 1912, in *Memoria que al Ciudadano Presidente de la República presenta el Secretario de Estado de Agricultura e Inmigración, 1912,* 47–49.

53. A. Michels to R. Díaz, 12 Jan. 1912, in A/I, box 2, folder 1.

54. Ramón Asensio evaluated Michels' project in 1918: "[El tabaco producido] resultó muy costoso y por consiguiente hubo de abandonarse el cultivo," in Grullón, *Sobre nuestro tabaco,* 57–58.

55. "Muestras de tabaco," *El Diario* 10, no. 3061 (14 Oct. 1912).

56. In Grullón, *Sobre nuestro tabaco,* 58.

57. See, e.g., the report of Dion Williams, District Commander, Northern District, to the Military Governor, 23 Sept. 1919, in GM, box 57 B: "The tobacco industry in Santo Domingo is gradually going backward owing to the ignorance, indolence and avarice of the farmers who raise the tobacco."

58. See Amargo, "Instrucción para cultivo del tabaco."

59. "La forma en que los Inspectores de Frutos. . . . ," LIN 10, no. 2157 (16 Apr. 1925)

60. "Circular del Fiscal Henríquez a los cosecheros de tabaco," Ley que reglamenta la clasificación del tabaco por los productores antes de venderlo, 28 Oct. 1920; Orden Ejecutiva no. 555, included in letter of Daniel C. Henríquez, 20 Mar. 1924, in Sección de Agricultura, box 7.

61. See Andrea Gravina, "Sobre Tabaco, I and II," LIN 6, nos. 2169 (10 June 1921) and 2179 (22 June 1921), and "Los pobres y la cosecha," LIN 8, no. 1928 (18 Dec. 1922).

62. Reporte trimestral, Oct.–Dec. 1920, in Sección de Agricultura, box 7.

63. See "Un semillero de tabaco para toda la provincia," LIN 8, no. 2209 (1 Oct. 1923). Also see "Situación agrícola y comercial en el Cibao," RdA 22, no. 24 (Sept. 1931), 224.

64. César Pérez A. to R. Richards, Inspector Provincial de Frutos, Santiago, 30 May 1927, in A/I, box 28 (1927).

65. Letter from César Pérez, 13 July 1927, in A/I, box 28 (1928).

66. Again, the urban merchants tried to prevent state intervention in their commercial dealings. See "Se protesta contra . . . una ordenanza de frutos," LIN 13, no. 4051 (31 May 1928).

67. "La Cámera de Comercio de Santiago y la próxima cosecha," LIN 12, no. 3070 (23 Aug. 1927); and *Memoria correspondiente al año 1927 que al ciudadano*

Presidente de la República presenta el Sr. Rafael A. Espaillat, Secretario de Estado de Agricultura é Inmigración, 95–97.

68. About the "campaña de arado": LIN 11, no. 2607 (24 June 1926).

69. This information comes from an anonymous speech given at the celebration of the eighteenth anniversary of the Instituto de Tabaco in Santiago in 1984. I am grateful to Iturbides Zaldívar for making a copy available to me.

70. Carballo eventually founded the Instituto del Tabaco in 1962. See Zaldívar, *Producción y comercialización,* 13.

71. See, e.g., Luis F. Mejía, *De Lilís a Trujillo* (Santo Domingo: Editorial de Santo Domingo, 1976), 225.

72. This was the difference from a nineteenth-century man like Pedro F. Bonó, who always remained, before anything, a political moralist.

73. For an early example of this attitude, see "Cuestiones de gran actualidad," LIN 2, no. 355 (3 Mar. 1917).

74. It could be that Mussolini's Italy was the example for Luis Carballo. He called the Italian leader "uno de los hombres más grandes de la época," in "Ponencia dictada por el señor Luis Carballo," 12 Feb. 1928, in Gobernación de Santiago, box 7 (1928).

75. The quotation is from Luis Carballo R., "Informe Mensual de la Cámara de Comercio, etc., de Santiago, Mayo 1928," in Gobernación de Santiago, box 7 (1928). Compare also "Dissertación sobre tabaco leída por el señor Luis Caballo R., 16-8-1934," in SEA, box 194: "El problema del tabaco es para Santiago de vida ó muerte; el tabaco es su principal cosecha, de él vive el 80% de nuestra población; de él vive nuestro comercio y alrededor de él gira la vida económica de la Provincia y por eso, todo Santiagues debe preocuparse de sus diferentes problemas."

76. Luis Carballo, "La Cámara de Comercio de Santiago y la cosecha de tabaco, 1926–27," LIN 12, no. 3038 (5 May 1927). In the following year, the central Cibao had four state-sponsored seedbeds, in Hatillo San Lorenzo, La Herradura, Navarrete, and near the "planta eléctrica": "Informe Mensual de la Cámara de Comercio, etc., de Santiago, Octubre 1928," in Gobernación de Santiago, box 7 (1928).

77. "De la campaña en pro de la siembra de tabaco," LIN 12, no. 3089 (14 Sept. 1927).

78. The German house of Klein even donated a small sum of money to the campaign: LIN 12, no. 3033 (4 Nov. 1927).

79. This was a central issue in the so-called "campañas de tabaco." See, e.g., "Informe Mensual de la Cámara de Comercio, etc., de Santiago, Febrero 1928," in Gobernación de Santiago, box 7 (1928). The quotation is from "Informe de la Cámara de Comercio, Abril 1928," in Gobernación de Santiago, box 7 (1928).

80. An early plea: "Plan para la campaña de tabaco, 1928–29," 14 Sept. 1928, in Gobernación de Santiago, box 7 (1928).

81. "Situación agrícola y comercial en el Cibao," RdA 22, no. 24 (Sept. 1931), 223.

82. "Hay que extender y mejorar el cultivo de los frutos fundamentales de la agricultura nacional; conferencia de Luis Carballo R," LIN 13, no. 2064 (16 Feb. 1928). In the original, the entire paragraph was written in capitals.

83. LIN 13, nos. 3078 (5 Mar. 1928), 3088 (16 Mar. 1928), and 4028 (4 May 1928).

84. "Los bajos precios del tabaco provocan una aguda crisis," LIN 13, no. 4075 (29 June 1928). Also see LIN 13, no. 4079 (4 July 1928).

85. "Informe General sobre créditos para ranchos del tabaco," Santiago, 24 Oct. 1928, in Gobernación de Santiago, box 7 (1928).

86. Luis Carballo R., "Presentación de Informe sobre los préstamos hechos a los cosecheros de tabaco," in Sección de Agricultura, box 11, folder 11 (1931).

87. Letter from Emilio Ceara, 1 Apr. 1931, attached to Emilio Ceara, "Campesinos deudores de esta Cámara por concepto de préstamos según formulario," 27 Mar. 1931, in Sección de Comercio, box 14, no. 280.

88. Luis Caballo to Minister of Agriculture and Commerce Rafael César Tolentino, 6 Mar. 1931, in SEA, box 169.

89. Letter ("particular") of Luis Carballo to Minister of Agriculture and Commerce César Tolentino, 26 Aug. 1931, in SEA, box 117.

90. Ibid.

91. "Hay que extender . . . ," LIN 13, no. 2064 (16 Feb. 1928).

92. E.g., "Informe Mensual de la Cámara de Comercio, etc., de Santiago," Apr.–May 1934, in SEA, box 194: "Es innegable que los cosecheros se están dando cuenta de la necesidad de defender sus productos no ofreciéndolos al mercado con demasiado precipitación." Sometimes he himself advised the cultivators to wait to sell their tobacco: "Informe Mensual de la Cámara de Comercio, etc., de Santiago, Mayo 1933," in Sección de Comercio, box 25, no. 31: "Nuestro consejo al cosechero es que no se precipite a vender hasta que los precios estén reafirmados."

93. See Bidó, *Paginas sencillas*; Ramón E. Jiménez, *Al Amor del Bohío*, 2 vols. (Santo Domingo: Virgilio Montalvo, 1927). The social realism of these authors must be considered the literary complement of the vision described here.

94. Paul Richards, *Coping with Hunger: Hazard and Experiment in an African Rice Farming System* (London: Allen and Unwin, 1986), 144.

95. Compare the dictum in Tzvetan Todorov, *La conquête de l'Amérique: La question de l'autre* (Paris: Seuil, 1982), 133: "Il y a là un enchaînement effrayant, où comprendre conduit à prendre, et prendre à détruire."

96. Dr. Albert Michels, Director Granja Escuela, San Rafael, Mao, Report no. 21, 24 Jan. 1934, in Sección de Agricultura, box 30, no. 362.

97. Grullón, *Sobre nuestro tabaco,* 16: "El corte de la hoja se practica con instrumento cortante. Viene adherido a ella una pequeña parte de tallo, ganchito ó adherencia, que sirve para dar sujeción a las hojas cuando se colocan en los anillos de las sartas, y que debe ser todo lo más reducido que se pueda, para que no se perjudique a la planta."

98. Eric Hobsbawm, "Peasants and Politics," *JPS* 1, no. 1 (1973): 7. This is, of course, also the theme of Scott, *Weapons of the Weak.*

99. "El tabaco y sus problemas.," LIN 11, no. 2602 (8 June 1926).

10. The Cibao Peasantry in Comparative Perspective

1. See, e.g., De Janvry, *The Agrarian Question,* 94–96 and passim. Also see Cooper, "Peasants, Capitalists, and Historians," 286–87.

2. For the Mexican discussion, see A. Lucas, "El debate sobre los campesinos y el capitalismo en México," *Comercio Exterior* 32, no. 4 (1982): 371–83.

3. Ranger, *Peasant Consciousness,* 19–53. See also Geschiere, *Village Communities and the State,* and Cooper et al., *Confronting Historical Paradigms.*

4. Compare: Hill, *Migrant Cocoa-Farmers of Southern Ghana.*

5. See J. Lonsdale and B. Berman, "Coping with the Contradictions: The Development of the Colonial State in Kenya," *Journal of African History* 20 (1979): 487–506. Also see Bates, *Essays on the Political Economy of Rural Africa,* 61–72 and passim. For an interesting discussion on British technological policy in Zambia: S. N. Chipungu, *The State, Technology and Peasant Differentiation in Zambia: A Case Study of the Southern Province, 1930–1986* (Lusaka: Historical Association of Zambia, 1988).

6. For a perceptive analysis of the Colombian case, see Bergquist, *Labor in Latin America,* 274–375. For Costa Rica: L. Gudmundson, "Peasant, Farmer, Proletarian: Class Formation in a Smallholder Coffee Economy, 1850–1950," HAHR 69, no. 2 (1989): 221–57.

7. Ortiz, *Cuban Counterpoint.*

8. Cooper, "Peasants, Capitalists, and Historians," 304.

9. See, e.g., Terry J. Byres, ed., *Sharecropping and Sharecroppers* (London: Frank Cass, 1983).

10. For a similar analysis, compare: Hill, *Migrant Cocoa-Farmers of Southern Ghana,* 116–19.

11. Tabitha Kanogo, *Squatters and the Roots of Mau Mau* (London: James Currey, 1988), 8–34. Colin Bundy, *The Rise and Fall of the South African Peasantry* (London: Heinemann, 1979).

12. Bergad, *Coffee and the Growth of Agrarian Capitalism,* 116 and passim. J. Steward et al., *The People of Puerto Rico,* 194–98 and passim.

13. Compare: Ranger, *Peasant Consciousness,* 32: "Producing white farmers liked having 'squatters' on their lands from whom they could buy grain cheap and levy labour."

14. Lemarchand, "African Peasantries, Reciprocity and the Market," 47.

15. Migdal, *Strong Societies and Weak States.*

16. See also Berry, *Fathers Work for Their Sons,* 12–13: "The best opportunities for accumulation lay not in agriculture but in trade, the professions, and the civil service."

17. Ranger, *Peasant Consciousness*, 46.

18. Bernardo Vega, "El impacto de la depresión económica de 1930 sobre la economía dominicana," *Investigación y Ciencia* 1, no. 1 (Jan.–Apr. 1986): 47–67.

19. Cassá, *Historia social y económica de la República Dominicana*, 2:250–51.

20. These changes in rural society showed strong regional variations. In some regions they were introduced so gradually that they were hardly noticeable. In other places the dictator and his cronies usurped all the land and practically destroyed the viability of peasant production. Neither was it a linear process. Vázquez-Geffroy, "Land Tenure and Resource-Holding Groups," 2–3, shows how the construction of an (unpaved) road caused a regional city to lose its prominent position. Also see Crouch, "The Development of Capitalism."

21. See, e.g., the objectives of the regime in 1935, published in the *Revista de Agricultura* and cited in Roberto Cassá, *Capitalismo y dictadura* (Santo Domingo: UASD, 1982), 124, n. 28.

22. Cassá, *Capitalismo y dictadura*, 113.

23. Cassá, in ibid., 130, suggests that this was the result of a conscious policy of the regime to create a peasantry without viability which would be forced to do wage labor. Also see R. Wendell Werge, "Agricultural Development in Clear Creek: Adaptive Strategies and Economic Roles in a Dominican Settlement" (Ph.D. diss., Univ. of Florida, 1975).

24. Cassá, *Capitalismo y dictadura*, 27–28.

25. E.g., Luis Carballo, "Report of the Cámara de Comercio of Santiago," Aug. 1933, in Sección de Comercio, box 25, no. 31. Carballo reported that prices had improved, adding: "En Bremen las ventas de tabaco dominicano son rápidas y fáciles, habiendo mucha actividad en el mercado para nuestro producto." Cassá too notes the rapid recovery of the tobacco sector: Cassá, *Capitalismo y dictadura*, 28.

26. Equipo de Investigación Socioeconomica, *Desarrollo del capitalismo*, 34.

27. Compare: Byres, *Sharecropping and Sharecroppers*. The research group of the Agrarian Institute of Santiago stresses "la intensidad del uso de mano de obra" in tobacco cultivation in his explanation of sharecropping arrangements. See Equipo de Investigación Socioeconomica, *Desarrollo del capitalismo*, 34–35.

28. Ferrán, *Tabaco y sociedad*, 105.

29. See ibid., 100–103.

30. Carlos Dore y Cabral, *Problemas de la estructura agraria dominicana* (Santo Domingo: Taller, 1982), 44: "En fin, la 'microfinca' menor de 8 tareas no es una unidad económica, sino un malestar social." Also see Rosemary Vargas-Lundius, *Peasants in Distress: Poverty and Unemployment in the Dominican Republic* (Lund, Sweden: Lund Economic Studies, 1988).

31. Ferrán, *Tabaco y sociedad*, 76–77.

32. Ibid., 76, table 18.

33. See, e.g., Del Castillo and Mitchel, *La inmigración dominicana en los Estados Unidos*.

34. For this episode, see Dore y Cabral, *Reforma agraria y luchas sociales.* This law had also a political side. Lozano sees the Balaguer policy as a deliberate "estrategia de la desmovilización popular": Wilfredo Lozano, *El reformismo dependiente* (Santo Domingo: Taller, 1985), 66–71 and passim.

35. For a similar situation in Colombia, see María Cristina Sálazar, *Aparceros en Boyacá: Los condenados del tabaco* (Bogotá: Ediciones Tercer Mundo, 1982), 88–89. She writes, "Este proceso ha dado lugar a que los propietarios establezcan relaciones monetarias con sus propios hijos, 'contratándolos' como aparceros para retener su fuerza de trabajo."

36. I borrowed this qualification from ibid.

37. Grupo Félix, "Ya no tiene ganas," on *Merengue con clase,* Dorado Records, 1984.

38. Mintz, in "From Plantations to Peasantries," 152, even writes: "A successful solution to the problems those (Caribbean) countrysides present may well determine the political future of the entire region."

APPENDIX 1. EXPORT FIGURES AND PRICES OF DOMINICAN TOBACCO, 1870–1930

1. Place, "Memoria sobre el cultivo," 196.

2. "Movimiento de frutos, 1876," EdP 2, no. 56 (29 Apr. 1883).

3. "Tabaco," EdP 3, no. 110 (11 May 1884). Also "La Cosecha," EdP 4, no. 163 (7 June 1885).

4. "Tabaco," EdP 10, no. 317 (3 July 1892).

5. See, for this period, the monthly reports of the Chamber of Commerce of Santiago.

APPENDIX 2. A NOTE ON DOMINICAN TOBACCO, 1870–1930

1. Akehurst, in *Tobacco,* 43, writes: "It is better to regard *N. tabacum* as representing a wide range of continuously variable material with the ability to produce a collection of different products under various environmental conditions."

2. Ibid., 28.

3. Quoted in Gisquet and Hitier, *La Production du Tabac,* 38.

4. Akehurst, *Tobacco,* 43.

5. For the general existence of such a "traditional" type, see ibid., 310.

6. Zaldívar, *Producción y comercialización,* 8, suggests that names are principally commercial devices.

7. Place, "Memoria sobre el cultivo," 186.

8. A. Oquet, "Los Tabacos de Santo Domingo," LIN 11, no. 2610 (16 June 1926). All observations of A. Oquet quoted in this appendix are from this article.

9. See "Informe de la Junta de Fomento de Santiago," RdA 3, no. 24 (Mar. 1907). 385–87.

10. See Sesión del Congreso Nacional, 18 May 1894, in GO 21, no. 1041 (4 Aug. 1894). Also Grullón, *Sobre nuestro tabaco,* 12; and Luis Carballo R., *Cartillo para los agricultores* (Santo Domingo: La Información, 1942), 3.

11. Dr. Albert Michels, Director of the "Campaña tabacalera," "Reporte Anual," 19 Dec. 1934, in Sección de Agricultura, box 29, no. 188.

12. *El Orden* 1, no. 49 (11 July 1875).

13. A. Oquet, "Los Tabacos de Santo Domingo," LIN 11, no. 2610 (16 June 1926).

14. See "Interview con Don José J. Díaz," BM 14, no. 382 (10 Apr. 1902).

15. Grullón, *Sobre nuestro tabaco,* 13–14.

16. See Carballo, *Cartillo para los agricultores,* 3; and Grullón, *Sobre nuestro tabaco,* 12–13.

17. Grullón, *Sobre nuestro tabaco,* 13.

18. See "Informe de la Junta de Fomento de Santiago," RdA 3, no. 24 (Mar. 1907). Deputy Román had a similar opinion in 1894, when he described it as "ancho, elástico y el único que sostenía su precio altísimo." Contrary to other opinions, however, he adds that it "resistía las lluvias": "Congreso Nacional, 18-5-1894," GO 21, no. 1041 (4 Aug. 1894).

19. "Los tabacos de Santo Domingo," LIN 11, no. 2610 (16 June 1926).

20. Grullón, *Sobre nuestro tabaco,* 12.

21. Luis Carballo R., *Cultivo del tabaco* (Santiago: Instituto del Tabaco, 1963), 4.

22. Place, "Memoria sobre el cultivo," 198.

23. Grullón, *Sobre nuestro tabaco,* 33.

24. Luis Carballo R., "Consideraciones sobre el cultivo de tabaco," unpublished speech, Santiago, 2 Aug. 1962, Instituto del Tabaco.

25. Carballo, *Cartillo para los agricultores,* 2–3.

26. J. C. Ariza, "Tabaco Dominicano," Hamburg, 18 Feb. 1909, RdA 5, no. 1 (Apr. 1909), 3–5. The same was true for Emilio Almonte (E. A.) and G. Beliar (G. B.).

27. "Nuestros productos, I," EdlO 424 (17 Dec. 1887).

28. Emilio Almonte, 10 July 1933, to Vicente Tolentino R., Jefe del Departamento de Comercio, Industria y Estadística, in Sección de Comercio, box 28, no. 253.

29. About tampering with the Moca certificate, see R. Pichardo hijo, Inspector de Frutos, to César Pérez A., Jefe de la Sección Segunda, Departamento de Agricultura, 6 Sept. 1927, in A/I, box 28 (1927).

30. "República Dominicana: Inspectoría General de Agricultura de la Provincia de Santiago," RdA 4, no. 8 (Nov. 1908).

31. LIN 10, no. 2229 (10 July 1925); LIN 10, no. 2233 (15 July 1925); and "Las marcas del tabaco," LIN 10, no. 2235 (17 July 1925). R. Pichardo hijo to César Pérez A., Santiago, 6 Sept. 1927, in A/I, box 28.

32. Félix Ma. Nolasco, "Tabaco de la Costa" (8 Aug. 1904), in *El Diario* 3, no. 613 (22 Aug. 1904).

33. A. Michels to E. Gardemann, Jefe de la Secretaria de Agricultura, 6 May 1934, in Sección de Agricultura, box 29, no. 188.

Glossary

Acción	Right to (share of) part of communal land
Alcalde pedáneo	Rural state official
Andullo	Pressed tobacco leaves, smoked in pipes (plug tobacco)
Bandera	Leaves which grow from the armpits of the tobacco plant (also called "sucker"). *Bayoneta*
Baquiní	Wake for a deceased child
Barresuelos	The lowest leaves of a mature tobacco plant
Batata	Sweet potato
Bayoneta	Leaves which grow from the armpits of the tobacco plant (also called "sucker") *Bandera*
Bohío	Rural dwelling
Botado	Land which already has been cultivated, is supposed to be less fertile and is therefore left fallow
Breva	Regional name for cigar
Bulto	Bale made of palm leaves, used to transport tobacco (usually some 60 kilos). *Serón*
Cachimbo	Traditional pipe
Cantero	Seedbed
Capataz	Foreman
Cocolo	British West Indian worker
Colmado	Rural shop. *Pulpería*
Combinación	Secret price agreement of urban tobacco traders
Comín	Intermediary tobacco trader, usually restricted to the local level
Compadrazgo	Ritual coparenthood
Conuco	Food plot
Convite	System of mutual support in rural society and an exchange labor team. *Junta*
Cordel	Oblong piece of property of which only one part, the "mouth," is measured

293

Corredor	Small-scale tobacco trader
Crianza libre	Raising cattle without fences
Criollo	Variety of Dominican tobacco for export (see app. 2)
Décima	Rural song
Ejido	Municipal land (commons)
Fandango	Rural dance party
Hato	Colonial land grant, normally used for extensive cattle raising
Hatero	Large landowner, cattleman
Hortaliza	Small food plot near the house
Indivisos	Communal lands. *Terrenos comuneros*
Ingenio	Sugar mill (originally water-driven)
Junta	An exchange labor team. *Convite*
Marchante	Female peddler in the rural areas
Medianero	Sharecropper who gets half the crop
Montero	Small-scale, traditional agricultural producer
Olor	Variety of Dominican tobacco (see app. 2)
Paca	Packing for export tobacco, made from textile or jute
Peso	Dominican money unit. Also right to part of communal land; *acción*
Platanal	Food plot on which (among other crops) plantains are cultivated
Postura	Small (tobacco) plant
Pulpería	Rural shop. *Colmado*
Quintal	Unit of weight equal to 46 kilos (100 pounds of 0.46 kilo)
Rancho	Drying shed for tobacco
Recua	Herd of pack animals
Resiembra	A second round of planting tobacco plants or seeds
Sancocho	Traditional Dominican soup
Sarta	String of palm leaves used to attach and dry tobacco leaves
Serón	Bag made of palm-leaves used to transport tobacco (usually some 60 kilos). *Bulto*
Solar	Piece of land for house construction
Succesores (Sucs.)	Heirs
Tabaquería	Small-scale cigar factory
Tala y tumba	Local expression for slash-and-burn agriculture
Tarea	Land measure: 0.0625 hectare (16 tarea = 1 hectare)
Terrenos comuneros	Communal lands. *Indivisos*
Troja (troje)	Pile of dry, fermenting tobacco
Velorio	Wake for a deceased person
Ventorilla	Rural store which sells liquor
Yuca	Cassava
Zafra	Harvest

Essay on Sources

1. ABOUT ARCHIVAL SOURCES

This book is based primarily on works housed in the Archivo General de la Nación in Santo Domingo, Dominican Republic. Most secondary literature and published sources were found in the Biblioteca Nacional, Santo Domingo, and the library of the Universidad Autónoma de Santo Domingo. The Biblioteca Nacional allowed me to consult the complete collection of the *Gaceta Oficial*.

In Santiago de los Caballeros, Dominican Republic, I consulted sources more specifically concerned with the Cibao. The Archivo Municipal was difficult to use during the period of my research. Most helpful was the library of the Amantes de la Luz. The library of the Universidad Católica de Madre y Maestra contained some newspapers of the period and useful secondary literature. I consulted the Cibao newspaper *La Información*, which contains very valuable data on the region's twentieth-century history, at the store Franco Hermanos. I consulted the *Boletín Municipal* in the small library of the town hall in Santiago. Complementing my fieldwork in the Villa González region (see below), I consulted material on the Distrito Catastral 4 (Villa González) in the Tribunal de Tierras, Registro de la Propiedad, in Santiago.

In Santo Domingo, Padre Antonio Camilo kindly allowed me to see some of the material concerning the nineteenth-century "Correspondence of the Archbishop," on which he is working.

A few foreign sources were employed in this study. I had the opportunity to work for a few days in the Archivo Histórico Nacional (AHN) in Madrid, Spain, and the Archivo General de las Indias (AGI) in Seville, Spain. Furthermore, I consulted microfilm at the U.S. National Archives of the correspondence of United States consuls in Puerto Plata and Samaná in the 1880s (T 662, 3 films; T 670, 2 films) and the Dutch tobacco journal *De Tabaksplant* for the years 1873–1900.

2. Archivo General de la Nación (AGN)

The Archivo General de la Nación, Santo Domingo, Dominican Republic, suffers from lack of attention and funds. For financial and political reasons, staff turnover is high; therefore, valuable knowledge about the archives is constantly being lost. Some material which I consulted during my first research period could not be found again later. Other collections, notably those of the *Gobierno Militar* and the *Secretaria de Estado de Agricultura*, lack the most basic organization. It was often impossible to consult key collections systematically, and the boxes I have seen represent an arbitrary and haphazard selection from them. Here I shall try to describe the collections I used.

Secretaria de Estado de Interior y Policía (IP)

This collection is well ordered and easily accessible. The material it contains is very heterogeneous, varying from reports of the provincial governors to ministerial circulars and correspondence concerning escaped prisoners. For the period 1870–1900, it is the only source which provides information about social relations and sometimes gives a glimpse of rural society on the local level. For a later period, the material becomes less informative and far too voluminous to be studied completely.
Consulted:
IP, 1870–1900: Boxes 1–181.
IP, 1900–1930: Samples from 1911 and 1919.

Secretaria de Estado de Agricultura e Inmigración (A/I)

This ministry was established in 1909. Its archives are very important for the agricultural history of the country, despite the fact that they give an institutional kind of information and remain very remote from the daily practices of rural society. The archives are most valuable for the information they give about state policy and the vision of rural society within government circles. They are stored without any system.
Consulted:
A/I, 1909–1935: Boxes 3–47 (with gaps). I have assigned some a letter.

Secretaria de Estado de Fomento y Obras Políticas (F/OP)

This collection is very small up to 1900. Still, it contains interesting information about infrastructural plans and projects in the country. After 1900, it became less interesting for the purposes of this book.
Consulted:
F/OP, 1890–1917: Boxes 10–23. I have given some a letter.

Secretaria de Estado de Hacienda y Comercio (Hac/Com)

These archives are very important for understanding relations between the Dominican Republic and the world economy, but for the purposes of this study they were less relevant. They are concerned above all with export figures, financial matters, and import-export taxes.
Consulted:
An arbitrary selection of boxes from the end of the nineteenth century, between numbers 20 and 60.

Gobierno Militar (GM)

This collection of archival material contains very valuable information, but it is completely disorganized. First, it is not clear what the U.S. authorities left behind. Second, the records are stacked in the archive, without any order whatsoever. Typically the records are labeled according to ministries and often contain copies from the archives listed above.
Consulted:
GM, arbitrary selection: Some 30 boxes between numbers 9 and 125.

Sección de Agricultura

This collection concerns the period after the Military Government (although the first four dossiers refer to the years 1914 and 1915). It contains much information about the Vásquez administration and its agricultural policies. The dossiers contain thematic folders, which facilitates consultation.
Consulted:
1924–35: Boxes 1–55 (some boxes missing and some numbered by me)

Sección de Comercio

This collection too deals with the period after the Military Government (although the first four dossiers refer to the years 1914 and 1915). It contains much information about the commercial policies of the Vásquez administration. The dossiers contain thematic folders. In addition to a

wide variety of correspondence on commercial matters, the collection contains much information on export crops and regulation of the tobacco trade.
Consulted:
1924–35: Boxes 1–42 (some boxes missing)

Gobernación de Santiago

This collection contains the correspondence of the provincial governors of Santiago at the end of the Vásquez administration and the beginning of the Trujillo era. It is concerned above all with political matters, but also gives information about economic policy in the region. Here and there it provides unique insights into the organization of political networks and provincial politics. The numbers of the collection begin anew every year.
Consulted:
1926: Boxes 3, 5, 6
1927: Boxes 4, 15, 16, 36–77, 78–88
1928: Boxes 1–15
1930: Boxes 4, 5, 9, 11, 13
1931: Boxes 5, 6.

Secretaria de Estado de Agricultura (SEA)

This ministry was established under the government of Trujillo. Its collection thus refers exclusively to the period after 1930. It is rich but badly organized, and I could consult only an arbitrary selection of the material on the early 1930s.
Consulted:
Boxes 64, 117, 125, 169, 194, 347.

Memorias

All ministries and provincial governors were expected to publish an annual report, called a *memoria*. These could be merely perfunctory, but often they contained very valuable information. The memorias written during the government of Heureaux were not published, and most were lost. Only a few can be consulted in the AGN (in manuscript or typescript). During the government of Ramón Cáceres, the memorias were published in the *Gaceta Oficial*. Some ministerial memorias were published separately. In the 1920s, the provincial memorias were no longer published (or written). The memorias of the ministries as a rule were published separately in that period and can be found in libraries or the AGN.

3. PERIODICALS

This book has benefited greatly from the prolific journalistic activity in the Dominican Republic in the period 1870–1930. Weekly, biweekly, and daily newspapers paid much attention to the social and economic transformation of Dominican society. Established and staffed by the leading intellectuals of the period, they form a valuable source of historical information. Most of these periodicals suffered from financial problems and political suppression, and many were very short-lived. Thus complete collections are difficult to find. In addition, many periodicals can be consulted only in deteriorated condition.

Periodicals Most Important for This Research

El Diario, 1902–30, Santiago
This newspaper is an important source for Cibao history in the first decades of the twentieth century. I consulted the very deteriorated collection of the library of the Amantes de la Luz in Santiago. I found out too late that the Archivo Municipal of Santiago possesses a complete collection in very good condition.

El Eco de la Opinión (EdlO), 1879–93, Santo Domingo
This periodical, based in Santo Domingo, was established to support the sugar industry in the 1870s. It is one of the most important sources on the expanding sugar sector in the southern part of the country. It can be consulted in the AGN.

El Eco del Pueblo (EdP), 1882–92, Santiago
Established in Santiago, this periodical represented the regional interests of the Cibao elite. What EdlO was to sugar, EdP was to tobacco. It is one of the most important sources of information on the late-nineteenth-century tobacco sector in the Cibao. A rapidly deteriorating collection can be consulted in the AGN. Microfilming is planned.
NB: In 1856, a short-lived journal with the same name existed.

Gaceta Oficial (GO), Santo Domingo
This was the official newspaper of the Dominican government. It contained the complete text of laws, transcripts of discussions in the Senate and Congress, and, occasionally, general articles. During short periods, this publication was also called *Gaceta de Santo Domingo* (GdStD) and *Boletín Oficial* (BO). A complete collection of the GO is kept in a locked cabinet in the

Biblioteca Nacional. A deteriorated collection can be consulted in the AGN. It is a very important source of historical information, especially for the period before 1900. After 1914, it becomes an ordinary government publication with little historical value.

La Información (LI), 1915– , Santiago
This was the first daily newspaper of the Cibao. After a hesitant and difficult beginning, twice being suppressed by the U.S. Military Government, *La Información* became the mouthpiece for an active regionalism in the 1920s. Socially engaged intellectuals used its pages to proclaim their opinions, making it the most varied and innovative newspaper of the period. For my research it has been a very important source. The only complete collection that I know of is in private hands, at the business Franco Hermanos, Santiago. Incomplete collections can be found in the Amantes de la Luz library and the Archivo Municipal, both in Santiago.

Revista de Agricultura (RdA), 1905– , Santo Domingo
This magazine was the product of government efforts to improve Dominican agriculture. As such, it is more a source of information about what government officials *wanted* Dominican agriculture to be, than what it *was*. Still, it is a useful source on Dominican agriculture in the first decades of the twentieth century. The best collection is in the Biblioteca Nacional, Santo Domingo.

Other Periodicals

Boletín Municipal (BM) (1887–). Publication of the H. Ayuntamiento de Santiago. Especially in its early years, informative about the regional economy of Santiago.
El Mensajero (1882–1889). Important periodical in the 1880s. Most complete collection is in the Biblioteca Nacional (photocopied).
El Porvenir (1872–94). Published in Puerto Plata. Important periodical for the economic history of the period.
Listín Diario (LD) (1893–). Oldest daily newspaper in the Dominican Republic. Very much centered on events in Santo Domingo.
Boletín del Congreso (1910–11)
Eco del Cibao (1904–5)
El Constitutional (1900–1901)
El Normalismo (1901)

El Noticiero (1908–9)

El Nuevo Régimen (1900)

El Orden (1874–75 and 1887–89)

El Radical (1915–16)

El Santiagués (1889)

El Tiempo (1910)

La Alborada (1883–84)

La Patria (1877)

La Prensa (1896–97)

Producción Nacional (1901)

Voz de Santiago (VdS) (1880–81)

4. About Oral Sources

Part of this book is based on fieldwork and what is usually called "oral history." Most of this research took place during two periods. In the beginning of my research in the Dominican Republic, in 1981, I did a general community study in the region around Villa González. The results of this short investigation were published in the journal *Ciencia y Sociedad* in 1984. When I had made the plan for a broader study, I returned to the region in 1985. This time I tried to obtain more specific information about the processes of differentiation within peasant society. I therefore returned to some of the cultivators I had interviewed before and made some more extensive, open-ended interviews with them and other people.

Simultaneously, I tried to take a representative sample in the region, in order to test some of the conclusions of my previous research. In this endeavor I had the efficient and active support of Juan Peña. Together we did some thirty interviews in the Villa González region, based on a previously prepared list of questions. To obtain an idea of regional differences within the Cibao, we did a small comparative project. With the same list of questions, we went to two regions in other parts of the Cibao, San Victor Abajo (Moca) and Torre Abajo (La Vega). Although these visits could not yield firm conclusions, they offered some interesting comparative insights. Above all, they confirmed my idea that many of the changes in the Villa González region had been happening somewhat earlier in the old center of the Cibao, around the La Vega–Moca axis.

I have used two different systems in referring to the oral history material. First, informants have been given numbers from 1 to 40. The numbers

1 to 28 refer to people living in the Villa González region, numbers 29 to 32 to people in San Victor Abajo, and numbers 33 to 40 to informants in Torre Abajo. Second, I have referred to my key informants using initials.

When information about people in the Villa González region was taken from published sources, real names are used.

Selected Works Consulted

Abad, José Ramón. *La República Dominicana: Reseña general geográfica-estadística.* Santo Domingo: García Hermanos, 1888. Rpt. Santo Domingo: Banco Central, 1973.

Adas, Michael. "From Avoidance to Confrontation: Peasant Protest in Pre-Colonial and Colonial Asia." CSSH 23, no. 2 (1981): 217–47.

Aguirre, Carlos, and Walker, Charles, eds. *Bandoleros, abigeos y montoneros: Criminalidad y violencia en el Perú, siglos XVIII–XX.* Lima: Instituto de Apoyo Agrario, 1990.

Akehurst, B. C. *Tobacco.* London: Longmans, 1968.

Alatas, S. H. *The Myth of the Lazy Native: A Study of the Malays, Filipinos, and Javanese from the Sixteenth to the Twentieth Centuries and Its Function in the Ideology of Colonial Capitalism.* London: Frank Cass, 1977.

Albuquerque, A. *Títulos de los terrenos comuneros de la República Dominicana.* Ciudad Trujillo: Impresora Dominicana, 1961.

Allard, H. A., and Allard, H. F. *Tobacco in the Dominican Republic.* Foreign Agricultural Report, No. 30. Washington, D.C.: U.S. Dept. of Agriculture, 1948.

Amargo, J. L. "Instrucciones para el cultivo del tabaco." Santiago: 1919.

Andrews, Keith R. *The Spanish Caribbean: Trade and Plunder, 1530–1630.* New Haven, Conn.: Yale Univ. Press, 1978.

Ardouin, B. *Etudes sur l'histoire d'Haiti.* 11 vols. Paris, 1853–56. Rpt. Port-au-Prince, Haiti: Dr. François Dalencour, 1958.

Aston, T. H., and Philpin, C. H. E., eds. *The Brenner Debate: Agrarian Class Structure and Economic Development in Pre-Industrial Europe.* Cambridge, England: Cambridge Univ. Press, 1985.

Aubin, E. *En Haiti: Planteurs d'autrefois, nègres d'aujourd'hui.* Paris: Librairie Armand Colin, 1910.

Baez Evertsz, Franc. *Azúcar y Dependencia en la República Dominicana.* Santo Domingo: UASD, 1978.

Bardhan, Pranab K. *Land, Labor, and Rural Poverty: Essays in Development Economics.* London: Oxford Univ. Press, 1984.

Barman, Roderick J. "The Brazilian Peasantry Reexamined: The Implications of the Quebra-Quilo Revolt, 1874–75." HAHR 57, no. 3 (1977): 401–24.

Bass, William C. *Reciprocidad*. Santo Domingo: Imprenta La Cuna de América, 1902.

Bates, Robert H. *Essays on the Political Economy of Rural Africa*. Cambridge, England: Cambridge Univ. Press, 1983.

Batista, Pedro R. *Santiago a principios de siglo*. Santo Domingo: Editorial Panamericana, 1976.

Baud, Michiel. "A Colonial Countereconomy: Tobacco Production on Española, 1500–1870." *Nieuwe West-Indische Gids/New West Indian Guide* 65, nos. 1–2 (1991): 27–49.

———. "La gente del tabaco: Villa González en el siglo veinte." *Ciencia y Sociedad* 9, no. 1 (Jan.–Apr. 1984): 101–37.

———. "German Trade in the Caribbean: The Case of Dominican Tobacco, 1844–1940." *Jahrbuch für Geschichte von Staat, Wirtschaft und Gesellschaft Lateinamerikas* 25 (1988): 83–115.

———. *Historia de un sueño: Los ferrocarriles públicos en la República Dominicana, 1880–1930*. Santo Domingo: Fundación Cultural Dominicana, 1993.

———. "La huelga de los tabaqueros, Santiago, 1919: Un momento de la lucha obrera en la República Dominicana." *Estudios Sociales* 23, no. 81 (July–Sept. 1990): 3–19.

———. "Ideología y campesinado: El pensamiento social de José Ramón López." *Estudios Sociales* 19, no. 64 (Apr.–June 1986): 63–81.

———. "The Origins of Capitalist Agriculture in the Dominican Republic." LARR 22, no. 2 (1987): 135–53.

———. "Para oír a los sin voz: Posibilidades y limitaciones de la historia oral." *Ciencia y Sociedad* 10, no. 4 (Oct.–Dec. 1985): 451–71.

———. "Peasant Society under Siege: Tobacco Cultivators in the Cibao (Dominican Republic), 1870–1930." Ph.D. diss., Univ. of Utrecht, Netherlands, 1991.

———. "The Struggle for Autonomy: Peasant Resistance to Capitalism in the Dominican Republic, 1870–1924." In *Labour in the Caribbean: From Emancipation to Independence*, ed. Malcolm Cross and Gad Heuman, 120–40. London: Macmillan, 1988.

———. "Transformación capitalista y regionalización en la República Dominicana, 1875–1920." *Investigación y Ciencia* 1, no. 1 (Jan.–Apr. 1986): 17–45.

Beckford, G. L. *Persistent Poverty: Underdevelopment in Plantation Economies of the Third World*. Oxford, England: Oxford Univ. Press, 1972.

Bell, Ian. *The Dominican Republic*. Boulder, Colo.: Westview, 1981.

Benítez, José A. *Las Antillas: Colonización, azúcar e imperialismo*. Havana, Cuba: Casa de las Americas, 1977.

Bergad, Laird W. *Coffee and the Growth of Agrarian Capitalism in Nineteenth-Century Puerto Rico*. Princeton, N.J.: Princeton Univ. Press, 1983.

————. *Cuban Rural Society in the Nineteenth Century: The Social and Economic History of Monoculture in Matanzas*. Princeton, N.J.: Princeton Univ. Press, 1990.

Bergquist, Charles. *Labor in Latin America: Comparative Essays on Chile, Argentina, Venezuela, and Colombia*. Stanford, Calif.: Stanford Univ. Press, 1986.

Berry, Sara S. *Cocoa, Custom and Socio-Economic Change in Rural Western Nigeria*. Oxford, England: Clarendon Press, 1975.

————. *Fathers Work for Their Sons: Accumulation, Mobility and Class Formation in an Extended Yoruba Community*. Berkeley: Univ. of California Press, 1985.

Bidó, Amado F. *Páginas sencillas*. Santiago, 1927.

Boesen, J., and Mohele, A. T. *The "Success Story" of Peasant Tobacco Production in Tanzania*. Uppsala, Sweden: Scandinavian Institute of African Studies, 1979.

Boin, Jacqueline, and Serulle Ramia, José. *El proceso de desarrollo del capitalismo en la República Dominicana, 1844–1930*. 2 vols. Santo Domingo: Editorial Gramil, 1979 and 1981.

Bonó, Pedro F. "Apuntes sobre las clases trabajadoras dominicanas." In *Papeles de Pedro F. Bonó*, ed. E. Rodríguez Demorizi. Barcelona: Editorial M. Pareja, 1964. 190–245.

————. *El Montero*. 1856. Rpt. Santo Domingo: Colección Pensamiento Dominicano, 1968.

Boomgaard, Peter. *Children of the Colonial State: Population Growth and Economic Development in Java, 1795–1880*. Amsterdam: Free Univ. Press/Center for Asian Studies, 1989.

Bosch, Juan. *Composición social dominicana: Historia e interpretación*. Santo Domingo: Alfa y Omega, 1979.

————. *La Mañosa*. 1936. Rpt. Santo Domingo: Alfa y Omega, 1984. Novel.

Brading, David A. *Prophecy and Myth in Mexican History*. Cambridge, England: Centre of Latin American Studies, S.A., [1985].

Bray, David B. "Dependency, Class Formation, and the Creation of Caribbean Labor Reserves." Ph.D. diss., Brown Univ., 1983.

Braudel, Fernand. *Civilization and Capitalism*. 3 vols. London: Fontana, 1974–84.

Brea, Ramonina. *Ensayo sobre la formación del estado capitalista en la República Dominicana y Haiti*. Santo Domingo: Editorial Taller, 1983.

Bright, Charles, and Harding, Susan, eds. *Statemaking and Social Movements: Essays in History and Theory*. Ann Arbor: Univ. of Michigan Press, 1984.

Brown, J. *The History and Present Condition of St. Domingo*. 2 vols. 1837. Rpt. London: Frank Cass, 1972.

Bryan, Patrick E. "La cuestión obrera en la industria azucarera de la República Dominicana a finales del siglo XIX y principios del XX." *Eme Eme Estudios Dominicanos* 7, no. 41 (Mar.–Apr. 1979): 57–77.

————. "La producción campesina en la República Dominicana a principios del siglo XX." *Eme Eme Estudios Dominicanos* 7, no. 42 (May–June 1979): 29–62.

————. "The Transformation of the Dominican Economy." Ph.D. diss., Univ. of London, 1978.

Bueno, Arturo. *Santiago: Quién te vió y quién te vé.* Santiago: Impresora Comercial, 1963.

Bundy, Colin. *The Rise and Fall of the South African Peasantry.* London: Heinemann, 1979.

Byres, Terry J., ed. *Sharecropping and Sharecroppers.* London: Frank Cass, 1983.

Calder, Bruce J. *The Impact of Intervention: The Dominican Republic during the U.S. Occupation of 1916–1924.* Austin: Univ. of Texas Press, 1984.

Carballo, Luis. "Cartillo para los agricultores." Santo Domingo: La Información, 1942.

————. *Cultivo del tabaco.* Santiago: Instituto del Tabaco, 1963.

Cardoso, Ciro F. S. *Escravo ou camponês? O protocampesinato negro nas Américas.* São Paulo: Editora Brasiliense, 1987.

Cardoso, Ciro F. S., and Pérez Brignoli, Héctor. *Historia económica de América Latina.* 2 vols. Barcelona, Spain: Editorial Crítica, 1979.

Cassá, Roberto. *Capitalismo y dictadura.* Santo Domingo: UASD, 1982.

————. *Historia social y económica de la República Dominicana.* 2 vols. Santo Domingo: Alfa y Omega, 1977 and 1980.

Censo de población y datos históricos y estadísticos de la ciudad de Santiago de los Caballeros (terminado el 31 de Diciembre de 1916). Santiago: La Información, 1917.

Cestero, Tulio M. *Por el Cibao.* Santo Domingo: Imp. Cuna de America, 1901.

Chayanov, A. V. *The Theory of Peasant Economy,* ed. D. Thorner et al. Homewood, Ill.: Irwin, 1966.

Chevalier, J. M. "There is Nothing Simple about Simple Commodity Production." JPS 10, no. 4 (1983): 153–86.

Chez Checo, J., and Peralta Brito, R. *Azúcar, encomiendas y otros ensayos históricos.* Santo Domingo: Fundación García-Arévalo, 1979.

Chipungu, Samuel N. *The State, Technology and Peasant Differentiation in Zambia: A Case Study of the Southern Province, 1930–1986.* Lusaka: Historical Association of Zambia, 1988.

Christelow, A. "French Interest in the Spanish Empire during the Ministry of the Duc de Choiseuil, 1759–1771." HAHR 21, no. 4 (Nov. 1941): 515–37.

Clausner, Marlin D. *Rural Santo Domingo: Settled, Unsettled and Resettled.* Philadelphia: Temple Univ. Press, 1973.

Collins, Jane L. *Unseasonal Migrations: The Effects of Rural Labor Scarcity in Peru.* Princeton, N.J.: Princeton Univ. Press, 1988.

Concepción, M. "Notas sobre la evolución económica de La Vega en el siglo XIX." *Eme Eme Estudios Dominicanos* 2, no. 9 (Nov.–Dec. 1973): 3–14.

Cooper, Frederick. "Peasants, Capitalists, and Historians: A Review Article." *Journal of South African Studies* 7, no. 2 (1981): 284–314.

Cooper, Frederick, et al. *Confronting Historical Paradigms: Peasants, Labor, and the Capitalist World System in Africa and Latin America.* Madison: Univ. of Wisconsin Press, 1993.

Crassweller, Robert D. *Trujillo: The Life and Times of a Caribbean Dictator.* New York: Macmillan, 1966.

Crouch, Luis A. "The Development of Capitalism in Dominican Agriculture." Ph.D. diss., Univ. of California, 1981.

Deans-Smith, Susan. *Bureaucrats, Planters, and Workers: The Making of the Tobacco Monopoly in Bourbon Mexico.* Austin: Univ. of Texas Press, 1992.

———. "The Money Plant: The Royal Tobacco Monopoly of New Spain, 1765–1821." In *The Economies of Mexico and Peru during the Late Colonial Period, 1760–1810,* ed. N. Jacobsen and H.-J. Puhle, 361–87. Berlin: Colloquium Verlag, 1986.

Deive, Carlos E. *La esclavitud del Negro en Santo Domingo.* 2 vols. Santo Domingo: Museo del Hombre Dominicano, 1980.

———. *Vodu y magia en Santo Domingo.* Santo Domingo: Museo del Hombre Dominicano, 1975.

De Janvry, Alain. *The Agrarian Question and Reformism in Latin America.* Baltimore, Md.: Johns Hopkins Univ. Press, 1981.

De Janvry, Alain, and Crouch, Luis. *Technological Change and Peasants in Latin America.* San Francisco: California Agricultural Experiment Station, 1980.

Del Castillo, José. "Las emigraciones y su aporte a la cultura dominicana (finales del siglo XIX y principios del XX)." *Eme Eme Estudios Dominicanos* 8, no. 45 (Nov.–Dec. 1979): 3–43.

———. "La inmigración de braceros azucareros en la República Dominicana, 1900–1930." *Cuadernos del Cendia* 262, no. 7 (1978). Santo Domingo, Dominican Republic: UASD, 1978.

Del Castillo, José, and Cordero, Walter. *La economía dominicana durante el primer cuarto del siglo XX.* Santo Domingo: Fundación García-Arévalo, 1979.

Del Castillo, José, and Mitchel, C., eds. *La inmigración dominicana en los Estados Unidos.* Santo Domingo: APEC, 1987.

Del Castillo, José, et al. *La Gulf + Western en República Dominicana.* Santo Domingo: Taller/UASD, 1974.

Deschamps, E. *La República Dominicana: Directorio y guía general.* Santiago, 1907. Rpt. Santo Domingo: Editorial de Santo Domingo, 1974.

Domar, E. J. "The Causes of Slavery or Serfdom: A Hypothesis." *Journal of Economic History* 30 (1970): 18–32.

Domínguez, Jaime de J. *La dictadura de Heureaux.* Santo Domingo: UASD, 1986.

———. *Economía y política en la República Dominicana, 1844–1861.* Santo Domingo: UASD, 1977

Dore y Cabral, Carlos. *Problemas de la estructura agraria dominicana.* Santo Domingo: Taller, 1982.

———. *Reforma agraria y luchas sociales en la República Dominicana, 1966–1978.* Santo Domingo: Taller, 1981.

Duarte, Isis. *Capitalismo y superpoblación en Santo Domingo*. Santo Domingo: Codia, 1980.

Dwyer, Daisy, and Bruce, Judith, eds. *A Home Divided: Women and Income in the Third World*. Stanford, Calif.: Stanford Univ. Press, 1988.

Eisner, G. *Jamaica, 1830–1930: A Study in Economic Growth*. Manchester, England: Manchester Univ. Press, 1961.

El libro azul de Santo Domingo/Dominican Blue Book. 1920. Rpt. Santo Domingo: UASD, 1976.

Elwert, G., and Wong, D. "Subsistence Production and Commodity Production in the Third World." *Review* 3, no. 3 (Winter 1980): 501–22.

Enklaar, E. C. *Volledige handleiding voor de teelt en verdere behandeling van den tabak* [*Complete Manual for the Cultivation and Preparation of Tobacco*]. Amsterdam: J. Noorderdorp, 1858.

Erasmus, Charles J. "Culture, Structure, and Process: The Occurrence and Disappearance of Reciprocal Farm Labor." *Southwestern Journal of Anthropology* 12 (1956): 444–69.

Equipo de Investigación Socioeconomica. *Desarrollo del capitalismo en el campo dominicano: Política agraria, pobreza rural y crecimiento agrícola*. Santiago: Instituto Superior de Agricultura, 1979.

Ferrán, Fernando I. *Tabaco y sociedad: La organización del poder en el ecomercado de tabaco dominicano*. Santo Domingo: Fondo para el Avance de las Ciencias Sociales, 1976.

Forman, S. *The Brazilian Peasantry*. New York: Columbia Univ. Press, 1975.

Foweraker, Joel. *The Struggle for Land: A Political Economy of the Pioneer Frontier in Brazil from 1930 to the Present Day*. Cambridge, England : Cambridge Univ. Press, 1981.

Franck, H. A. *Roaming through the West Indies*. New York: Century, 1921.

Franco, Franklin J. "La crisis del 29 y la génesis del Trujillato." In *América Latina en los años treinta*, ed. Pablo González Casanova. Mexico City: Universidad Nacional Autónoma de Mexico, 1977. 52–74.

Franklin, J. *The Present State of Hayti (Saint Domingo), With Remarks on Its Agriculture, Commerce, Laws, Religion, Finances & Population, etc., etc.* 1828. London: Frank Cass, 1971.

Fraser, Peter. "The Fictive Peasantry: Caribbean Rural Groups in the Nineteenth Century." In *Contemporary Caribbean: A Sociological Reader*, ed. Susan Craig, 1:319–47. Maracas (Trinidad and Tobago): College Press, 1981.

Fresco, Louise. *Cassava in Shifting Cultivation: A Systems Approach to Agricultural Technology Development in Africa*. Amsterdam: Royal Tropical Institute, 1986.

García, José Gabriel. *Compendio de la historia de Santo Domingo*. 5 vols. Santo Domingo: García Hermanos, 1894.

García Tamayo, Eduardo. "Cultura campesina en la frontera norte." *Estudios Sociales* 17, no. 55 (Jan.–Mar. 1984): 43–56.

Geschiere, Peter. "La paysannerie africaine est-elle captive?" *Politique africaine* 14 (1984): 13–34.

———. *Village Communities and the State: Changing Relations among the Maka of Southeastern Cameroon since the Colonial Conquest.* London: Kegan Paul International, 1982.

Gisquet, P., and Hitier, H. *La production du tabac.* Paris: Ballière, 1961.

Gomes, P. I., ed. *Rural Development in the Caribbean.* London: Hurst & Co.; New York: St. Martin's Press, 1985.

Gómez, Luis. *Relaciones de producción dominantes en la sociedad dominicana, 1875–1975.* Santo Domingo: Alfa y Omega, 1979.

Gonzales, Michael J. "Capitalist Agriculture and Labour Contracting in Northern Peru, 1880–1905." *Journal of Latin American Studies* 12, no. 2 (1980): 291–314.

———. *Plantation Agriculture and Social Control in Northern Peru, 1875–1933.* Austin: Univ. of Texas Press, 1985.

González, Nancy L. "El cultivo del tabaco en la República Dominicana." *Ciencia* (Dirección de Investigaciones, UASD,) 2, no. 4 (Oct.–Dec. 1975).

González, Raymundo. "Bonó, un intelectual de los pobres." *Estudios Sociales* 18, no. 60 (Apr.–June 1985): 65–77.

Gonzalo Arroyo, S. J., et al. *El campesino dominicano: Un estudio de marginalidad.* Santiago de Chile: Centro para el Desarrolo Económico y Social de América Latina, [1966].

Goody, Jack; Thirsk, Joan; Thompson, E. P., eds. *Family and Inheritance: Rural Society in Western Society, 1200–1800.* Cambridge, England: Cambridge Univ. Press, 1976.

Goslinga, C. C. *The Dutch in the Caribbean and on the Wild Coast, 1580–1680.* Assen, Netherlands: Van Gorcum, 1971.

———. *The Dutch in the Caribbean and the Guianas, 1680–1791.* Assen, Netherlands: Van Gorcum, 1985.

Gould, Jeffrey L. *To Lead as Equals: Rural Protest and Political Consciousness in Chinandega, Nicaragua, 1912–1979.* Chapel Hill: Univ. of North Carolina Press, 1990.

Grasmuck, Sherri, and Pessar, Patricia R. *Between Two Islands: Dominican International Migration.* Berkeley: Univ. of California Press, 1991.

Grieshaber, Erwin P. "Survival of Indian Communities in Nineteenth-Century Bolivia: A Regional Comparison." *Journal of Latin American Studies* 12 (1980): 223–69.

Grindle, Merilee S. *Searching for Rural Development: Labor Migration and Employment in Mexico.* Ithaca, N.Y.: Cornell Univ. Press, 1988.

Grullón, M. C. *Sobre nuestro tabaco.* Santo Domingo: Montalvo Hermano, 1919.

Gudeman, Stephen. "The *Compadrazgo* as a Reflection of the Natural and Spiritual Person." *Proceedings of the Royal Anthropological Institute of Great Britain and Ireland for 1971.* London, 1972. 45–71.

Gudmundson, Lowell. "Peasant, Farmer, Proletarian: Class Formation in a Smallholder Coffee Economy, 1850–1950." HAHR 69, no. 2 (1989): 221–57.

Guerra y Sánchez, R. *Sugar and Society in the Caribbean: An Economic History of Cuban Agriculture*. New Haven, Conn.: Yale Univ. Press, 1964.

Guerrero, Andrés. *La semántica de la dominación: El concertaje de indios*. Quito, Ecuador: Editores Libri Mundi, 1991.

Gutiérrez Escudero, A. *Población y economía en Santo Domingo (1700–1746)*. Seville, Spain: Diputación Provincial, 1985.

Hall, Caroline. *El café y el desarrollo histórico-geográfico de Costa Rica*. San José: Editorial Costa Rica, 1978.

Harrison, D. "The Changing Fortunes of a Trinidad Peasantry." In *Peasants, Plantations and Rural Communities in the Caribbean*, ed. Malcolm Cross and A. Marks. Guildford, England: Univ. of Surrey; Leiden, Netherlands: Dept. of Caribbean Studies, Royal Institute of Linguistics and Anthropology, 1979. 54–85.

Harrison, John Parker. *The Colombian Tobacco Industry from Government Monopoly to Free Trade, 1778–1876*. Bogotá: Universidad de los Andes, Centro de Estudios sobre Desarrollo Económico, 1969.

Hazard, Samuel. *Santo Domingo: Past and Present with a Glance at Hayti*. 1873. Rpt. Santo Domingo: Editorial de Santo Domingo, 1982.

Hewitt de Alcántara, Cynthia. *Boundaries and Paradigms: The Anthropological Study of Rural Life in Post-Revolutionary Mexico*. Leiden: Univ. of Leiden, Leiden Development Studies, 1982.

Hill, Polly. *The Migrant Cocoa Farmers of Southern Ghana*. Cambridge, England: Cambridge Univ. Press, 1963.

Hobsbawm, Eric J. "Peasants and Politics." *Journal of Peasant Studies* 1, no. 1 (1973): 3–22.

———. *Primitive Rebels*. Manchester, England: Manchester Univ. Press, 1959.

Hobsbawm, Eric, and Ranger, Terence, eds. *The Invention of Tradition*. Cambridge, England: Cambridge Univ. Press, 1983.

Hoernel, Robert B. "A Comparison of Sugar and Social Change in Puerto Rico and Oriente, Cuba, 1898–1959." Ph.D. diss., Johns Hopkins Univ., 1977.

Hoetink, H. "El Cibao, 1844–1900: Su aportación a la formación social de la República." *Eme Eme Estudios Dominicanos* 8, no. 48 (May–June 1980): 3–19.

———. *The Dominican People, 1850–1900: Notes for a Historical Sociology*. Spanish original 1972. Trans. Stephen K. Ault. Baltimore, Md.: Johns Hopkins Univ. Press, 1982.

———. "The Dominican Republic, c. 1870–1930." In *Cambridge History of Latin America*, ed. Leslie Bethell, 5:287–305. Cambridge, England: Cambridge Univ. Press, 1986.

———. "'Race' and Color in the Caribbean." In *Caribbean Contours*, ed. Sidney W. Mintz and Sally Price. Baltimore, Md.: Johns Hopkins Univ. Press, 1985.

————. Review of *Papers in Caribbean Anthropology,* ed. I. Rouse and S. W. Mintz. *Caribbean Studies* 1, no. 2 (July 1961): 23–25.

————. *Santo Domingo y el Caribe: Ensayos sobre cultura y sociedad.* Santo Domingo: Fundación Cultural Dominicana, 1994.

Holloway, Thomas. *Immigrants of the Land: Coffee and Society in São Paulo, 1886–1934.* Chapel Hill: Univ. of North Carolina Press, 1980.

Hostos, Eugenio M. de. *Obras.* Havana, Cuba: Casa de las Américas, 1976.

Hyden, Goran. *Beyond Ujamaa in Tanzania: Underdevelopment and an Uncaptured Peasantry.* London: Heinemann, 1980.

————. "The Resilience of the Peasant Mode of Production: The Case of Tanzania." In *Agricultural Development in Africa: Issues of Public Policy,* ed. Robert H. Bates and M. F. Lofchie, 218–43. New York: Praeger, 1980.

Informe de la Comisión de Investigación de los E.U.A. en Santo Domingo en 1871. Preface y notes by E. Rodríguez Demorizi. Ciudad Trujillo: Montalvo, 1960.

Jewsiewicki, B., and Chrétien, J. P., eds. *Ambiguïtés de l'innovation: Sociétés rurales et technologies en Afrique centrale et occidentale au XX siècle.* Quebec, Canada: Safi, 1984.

Jiménez, Michael F. "Class, Gender, and Peasant Resistance in Central Colombia, 1900–1930." In *Everyday Forms of Peasant Resistance,* ed. Forrest D. Colburn, 122–50. Armonk, N.Y.: M. E. Sharp, 1989.

Jiménez, Ramón Emilio. *Al amor del bohío.* 2 vols. Santo Domingo: Virgilio Montalvo, 1927.

————. *Savia Dominicana.* Santiago: El Diario, [1949].

————. *Trujillo y la Paz.* Ciudad Trujillo: Impresora Dominicana, 1952.

Joseph, Gilbert M. "On the Trail of the Latin American Bandits." LARR 25, no. 3 (1990): 7–53.

Kanogo, Tabitha. *Squatters and the Roots of Mau Mau.* London: James Currey, 1988.

Kasfir, N. "Are African Peasants Self-Sufficient?" *Development and Change* 17, no. 2 (Apr. 1986): 335–57.

Kearney, Michael. "From the Invisible Hand to the Visible Feet: Anthropological Studies of Migration and Development." *Annual Review of Anthropology* 15 (1986): 331–61.

Kiszling, R. *Beknopt handboek van de tabakskennis, tabaksteelt en tabaksfabricage* [*Short Handbook of the Knowledge, Cultivation and Manufacture of Tobacco*]. Amsterdam: Kuilenburg, Blom & Oliviers, 1907.

Knight, Melvin M. *The Americans in Santo Domingo.* 1928. Rpt. New York: Arno, 1970.

Kula, Witold. *An Economic Theory of the Feudal System: Toward a Model of the Polish Economy, 1500–1800.* 1962. Trans. Lawrence Garner. Rpt. London: New Left Books, 1976.

Labourt, José. *Sana, sana, culito de rana. . . .* Santo Domingo: Taller, 1982.

311

LeGrand, Catherine. *Frontier Expansion and Peasant Protest in Colombia, 1830–1936*. Albuquerque: Univ. of New Mexico Press, 1986.

Lehmann, David. *Democracy and Development in Latin America: Economics, Politics and Religion in the Postwar Period*. Cambridge, England: Polity Press, 1990.

———. "Two Paths of Agrarian Capitalism, or a Critique of Chayanovian Marxism." CSSH 28 (1986): 601–27.

———, ed. *Ecology and Exchange in the Andes*. Cambridge, England: Cambridge Univ. Press, 1982.

Lemarchand, René. "African Peasantries, Reciprocity and the Market: The Economy of Affection Reconsidered." *Cahiers d'études africaines* 29, no. 113 (1989): 33–67.

Lerner, A. P. "The Myth of the Parasitic Middleman." *Commentary* 8, no. 1 (July 1949): 45–51.

Levine, David. *Reproducing Families: The Political Economy of English Population History*. Cambridge, England: Cambridge Univ. Press, 1987.

Lis, Catharina, and Soly, Hugo. *Poverty and Capitalism in Pre-Industrial Europe*. Brighton, England: Harvester, 1979.

Llanos Company, Manuel. "Evolución de las técnicas para el cultivo del tabaco en las colonias hispano-americanos." *Anuario de Estudios Americanos* 40 (1983): 469–96.

Lluberes, Antonio. "La crisis del tabaco cibaeño, 1879–1930." In Antonio Lluberes, José del Castillo, and Ramón Albuquerque, *Tabaco, azúcar y minería*. 3–22. Santo Domingo: Banco de Desarrollo Interamericana, 1984.

———. "La economía del tabaco en el Cibao en la segunda mitad del siglo XIX." *Eme Eme Estudios Dominicanos* 1, no. 4 (Jan.–Feb. 1973): 35–60.

———. "La Revolución de Julio de 1857." *Eme Eme Estudios Dominicanos* 1, no. 8 (Sept.–Oct. 1973): 18–45.

———. "Las Rutas del Tabaco Dominicano." *Eme Eme Estudios Dominicanos* 4 (Nov.–Dec. 1975): 3–22.

———. "El tabaco dominicano: De la manufactura al monopolio industrial." *Eme Eme Estudios Dominicano* 6, no. 35 (Mar.–Apr. 1978): 3–18.

———. "Tabaco y catalanes en Santo Domingo durante el siglo XVIII." *Eme Eme Estudios Dominicanos* 5, no. 28 (Jan.–Feb. 1977): 13–26.

Lomnitz, Larissa A., and Pérez-Lizaur, Marisol. *A Mexican Elite Family, 1820–1980: Kinship, Class, and Culture*. Princeton, N.J.: Princeton Univ. Press, 1987.

Long, Norman, and Roberts, Bryan. *Miners, Peasants and Entrepreneurs: Regional Development in the Central Highlands of Peru*. Cambridge, England: Cambridge Univ. Press, 1984.

Lonsdale, J., and Berman, B. "Coping with the Contradictions: The Development of the Colonial State in Kenya." *Journal of African History* 20 (1979): 487–506.

López, José Ramón. *Censo y catastro de la Común de Santo Domingo*. Santo Domingo: El Progreso, 1919.

———. *El gran pesimismo dominicano*. Santiago: UCMM, 1975.

Lozano, Wilfredo. *La dominación imperialista en la República Dominicana, 1900–1930.* Santo Domingo: UASD, 1976.

———. *El reformismo dependiente.* Santo Domingo: Taller, 1985.

Lucas, A. "El debate sobre los campesinos y el capitalismo en México." *Comercio Exterior* 32, no. 4 (1982): 371–83.

Ludden, David. *Peasant History in South India.* Princeton, N.J.: Princeton Univ. Press, 1985.

Lugo, Americo. *Historia de Santo Domingo: Desde el 1556 hasta 1608.* 1938. Rpt. Ciudad Trujillo: Editorial Libreria Dominicana, 1952.

Lundahl, Mats, and Bourdet, Y. "Haitian Coffee Marketing Revisited." Paper presented at the 46th International Congress of Americanists, 1988.

Macfarlane, A. *The Origins of English Individualism: The Family, Property and Social Transition.* Oxford, England: Basil Blackwell, 1978.

MacKenzie, C. *Notes on Haiti Made during a Residence in that Republic.* 2 vols. 1830. Rpt. London: Frank Cass, 1971.

Machín, J. "Orígenes del campesinado dominicano durante la ocupación haitiana." *Eme Eme Estudios Dominicano* 1, no. 4 (Jan.–Feb. 1973): 19–34.

Mallon, Florencia E. *The Defense of Community in Peru's Central Highlands: Peasant Struggle and Capitalist Transition, 1860–1940.* Princeton, N.J.: Princeton Univ. Press, 1983.

Manners, R. D., and Steward, J. H. "The Cultural Study of Contemporary Societies: Puerto Rico." *American Journal of Sociology* 59 (July 1953–May 1954): 123–30.

Mariñez, Pablo A. *Resistencia campesina, imperialismo y reforma agraria en República Dominicana.* Santo Domingo: Ediciones Cepae, 1984.

Marte, Roberto. *Estadística y documentos históricos sobre Santo Domingo (1850–1890).* Santo Domingo: Museo Nacional de Historia y Geografía, 1984.

Martínez, Rufino. *Diccionario biográfico-histórico dominicano, 1821–1930.* Santo Domingo: UASD, 1971.

McGreevey, William P. *An Economic History of Colombia.* Cambridge, England: Cambridge Univ. Press, 1971.

Meillassoux, Claude. *Femmes, greniers et capitaux.* Paris: Maspero, 1975.

Mejía, Luis F. *De Lilís a Trujillo.* Santo Domingo: Editorial de Santo Domingo, 1976.

Memoria correspondiente al año 1927 que al ciudadano Presidente de la República presenta el Sr. Rafael A. Espaillat, Secretario de Estado de Agricultura e Inmigración. Santo Domingo: García Sucs., 1928.

Memoria de la Cámara de Comercio, Industria y Agricultura de Santiago, abarcando el período 1922-1923-1924. Santiago: La Información, 1925.

Memoria que al ciudadano Presidente de la República presenta el Secretario de Estado de Agricultura e Inmigración, 1912. Santo Domingo: Escobar y Cía., 1913.

Memoria que al ciudadano Presidente de la República presenta el Secretario de Estado de Agricultura e Inmigración. July 1918–June 1919. Santo Domingo: El Progreso, 1919.

Memoria que al ciudadano Presidente de la República presenta el Secretario de Estado de Agricultura e Inmigración. 10 July 1919–30 June 1920. Santo Domingo: El Progreso, 1920.

Meyer, Jean. *La Cristiada.* 3 vols. Mexico City: Siglo XXI, 1973–74.

Migdal, Joel S. *Peasants, Politics, and Revolution: Pressures toward Political and Social Change in the Third World.* Princeton, N.J.: Princeton Univ. Press, 1974.

———. *Strong Societies and Weak States: State-Society Relations and State Capabilities in the Third World.* Princeton, N.J.: Princeton Univ. Press, 1988.

Mintz, Sidney W. *Caribbean Transformations.* Chicago: Aldine, 1974.

———. "From Plantations to Peasantries in the Caribbean." In *Caribbean Contours,* ed. Sidney W. Mintz and Sally Price, 127–53. Baltimore, Md.: Johns Hopkins Univ. Press, 1985.

———. "Internal Market Systems as Mechanics of Social Articulation." *Proceedings of the 1959 Annual Spring Meeting of the American Ethnological Society.* Seattle: Univ. of Washington Press, 1959.

———. "Peasant Marketplaces and Economic Development in Latin America." Occasional Paper No. 4. Graduate Center for Latin American Studies, Vanderbilt Univ., Nashville, Tenn., 1964.

———. "The Question of Caribbean Peasantries: A Comment." *Caribbean Studies* 1, no. 3 (Oct. 1961): 31–34.

———. "Slavery and the Rise of Peasantries." *Historical Reflections* 6, no 1 (1979): 213–53.

———. "The So-Called World System: Local Initiatives and Local Response." *Dialectical Anthropology* 2 (1977): 253–70.

———. *Sweetness and Power: The Place of Sugar in Modern History.* Harmondsworth, England: Penguin, 1986.

Mintz, Sidney W., and Price, Sally, eds. *Caribbean Contours.* Baltimore, Md.: Johns Hopkins Univ. Press, 1985.

Moore, Barrington. *Injustice: The Social Bases of Obedience and Revolt.* New York: M. E. Sharpe, 1978.

Moore, Henrietta L. *Feminism and Anthropology.* Cambridge, England: Polity Press, 1988.

Moreau de Saint-Méry, M. L. *Descripción de la parte Española de Santo Domingo.* 1797. Rpt. Ciudad Trujillo: Editora Montalvo, 1944.

Moreno Fraginals, Manuel; Moya Pons, Frank; and Engerman, Stanley L., eds. *Between Slavery and Free Labor: The Spanish-Speaking Caribbean in the Nineteenth Century.* Baltimore, Md.: Johns Hopkins Univ. Press, 1985.

Moya Pons, Frank. *La dominación haitiana, 1822–1844.* Santiago: UCMM, 1972.

———. "Haiti and Santo Domingo, 1790–c. 1870." In *The Cambridge History of Latin America,* ed. Leslie Bethell, vol. 3. Cambridge, England: Cambridge Univ. Press, 1985.

————. "The Land Question in Haiti and Santo Domingo: The Sociopolitical Context of the Transition from Slavery to Free Labor, 1801–1843." In *Between Slavery and Free Labor: The Spanish-Speaking Caribbean in the Nineteenth Century,* ed. Manuel Moreno Fraginals, Frank Moya Pons, and Stanley L. Engerman. Baltimore, Md.: Johns Hopkins Univ. Press, 1985. 181–214.

————. "Nuevas consideraciones sobre la historia de la población dominicana: Curvas, tasas y problemas." *Eme Eme Estudios Dominicanos* 3, no. 15 (Nov.–Dec. 1974): 3–28.

Munck, Ronaldo. *Politics and Dependency in the Third World: The Case of Latin America.* London: Zed Press, 1984.

Muto, Jr., Paul. "The Illusory Promise: The Dominican Republic and the Process of Economic Development, 1900–1930." Ph.D. diss., Univ. of Washington, 1976.

Mutto, Paul. "La economía de exportación de la República Dominicana, 1900–1930." *Eme Eme Estudios Dominicanos* 3, no. 15 (Nov.–Dec. 1974): 67–110.

Nazzari, Muriel. *Disappearance of the Dowry: Women, Families, and Social Change in São Paulo, Brazil, 1600–1900.* Stanford, Calif.: Stanford Univ. Press, 1991.

O'Neill, Brian Juan. *Social Inequality in a Portuguese Hamlet: Land, Late Marriage, and Bastardy, 1870–1978.* Cambridge, England: Cambridge Univ. Press, 1987.

Ortiz, Fernando. *Cuban Counterpoint: Tobacco and Sugar.* Spanish original 1940. Trans. Harriet de Onís. New York: Random House, 1970.

Ossio Acuña, J., and Medina García, O. *Familia campesina y economía de mercado.* Lima, Peru: CRESE, 1985.

Paige, Jeffrey M. *Agrarian Revolution: Social Movements and Export Agriculture in the Underdeveloped World.* London: Macmillan, 1975.

————. "Social Theory and Peasant Revolution in Vietnam and Guatemala." *Theory and Society* 12, no. 6 (Nov. 1983): 699–737.

Palacios, Marco. *Coffee in Colombia, 1850–1970: An Economic, Social and Political History.* Cambridge, England: Cambridge Univ. Press, 1980.

Palmer, E. C. "Land Use and Landscape Change along the Dominican-Haitian Borderlands." Ph.D. diss., Univ. of Florida, 1976.

Pelzer, Karl J. *Planter and Peasant: Colonial Policy and the Agrarian Struggle in East Sumatra, 1863–1947.* 's-Gravenhage, Netherlands: Martinus Nijhoff, 1978.

Peña Pérez, Frank. *Antonio Osorio: Monopolio, Contrabando y Despoblación.* Santiago: UCMM, 1980.

————. *Cien Años de Miseria en Santo Domingo, 1600–1700.* Santo Domingo: UNAPEC, [1986].

Pérez, L. A., Jr. *Cuba: Between Reform and Revolution.* Oxford, England: Oxford Univ. Press, 1988.

Pessar, Patricia R. "Kinship Relations of Production in the Migration Process: The Case of Dominican Emigration to the United States." Occasional Papers No. 32. New York Univ., New York, 1982.

Picó, Fernando. *Amargo café (Los pequeños y medianos caficultores de Utuado en la segunda mitad del siglo XIX).* Río Piedras, Puerto Rico: Huracán, 1981.

———. *Historia General de Puerto Rico.* Rio Piedras: Huracán, 1986.

Pitt-Rivers, J. A. *The People of the Sierra.* 1954. Rpt. Chicago: Univ. of Chicago Press, 1971.

Place, Victor. "Memoria sobre el cultivo, la cosecha y la venta de los tabacos." 1849. Rpt. in Jacqueline Boin and José Serulle Ramia, *El proceso de desarrollo del capitalismo en la República Dominicana (1844–1930),* vol. 1: 186–99. Santo Domingo: Editorial Gramil, 1979.

Platt, D. C. M. *Latin America and British Trade, 1806–1914.* New York: Harper and Row, 1973.

Platt, Tristan. "The Role of the Andean *Ayllus* in the Reproduction of the Petty Commodity Regime in Northern Potosí (Bolivia)." In *Ecology and Exchange,* ed. David Lehmann. Cambridge: Cambridge Univ. Press, 1982. 27–69.

Popkin, Samuel L. *The Rational Peasant.* Berkeley: Univ. of California Press, 1976.

Primer Censo Nacional de República Dominicana, 1920. 1923. Rpt. Santo Domingo: UASD, 1975.

Quintero Rivera, Angel G. "The Rural-Urban Dichotomy in the Formation of Puerto Rico's Cultural Identity." *Nieuwe West-Indische Gids/New West Indian Guide* 61, nos. 3–4 (1987): 127–44.

Ranger, Terence. *Peasant Consciousness and Guerrilla War in Zimbabwe.* London: James Currey, 1985.

———. "Recent Discussion of African Peasantries: A Survey." Keynote paper for Conference of African Studies Association of the United Kingdom on "Recent Changes in Development Theory and Africa," Manchester, England, 1980.

Reinhardt, Nola. *Our Daily Bread: The Peasant Question and Family Farming in the Colombian Andes.* Berkeley: Univ. of California Press, 1988.

Repúblic Dominicana. *Colección de leyes, decretos y resoluciones de los poderes legislativo y ejecutivo de la República.* Various years, editions, and publishers.

Richards, Paul. *Coping with Hunger: Hazard and Experiment in an African Rice Farming System.* London: Allen and Unwin, 1986.

———. *Indigenous Agricultural Revolution.* London: Hutchinson, and Boulder, Colo.:Westview, 1985.

Ridings, Eugene W. "Foreign Predominance among Overseas Traders in Nineteenth-Century Latin America." LARR 20, no. 2 (1985): 3–27.

Rippy, J. Fred. "The Initiation of the Customs Receivership in the Dominican Republic." HAHR 17 (1937): 419–57.

Rodney, Walter. *A History of the Guyanese Working People, 1881–1905.* Baltimore, Md.: Johns Hopkins Univ. Press, 1981.

Rodríguez Demorizi, E., ed. *Documentos para la historia de la República Dominicana.* 3 vols. Ciudad Trujillo: Editorial Montalvo, 1944; Santiago: El Diario, 1947; Ciudad Trujillo: Impresora Dominicana, 1959.

————, ed. *La Era de Francia en Santo Domingo: Contribución a su estudio.* Ciudad Trujillo: Editorial del Caribe, 1955.

————, ed. *Hostos en Santo Domingo.* 2 vols. Ciudad Trujillo: García Sucs., 1939.

————, ed. *Lengua y folklore de Santo Domingo* Santiago: UCMM, 1975.

————, ed. *Martí en Santo Domingo.* Barcelona, Spain: M. Pareja, 1978.

————, ed. *Papeles de Monseñor Meriño.* Santo Domingo: Taller, 1983.

————, ed. *Papeles de Pedro F. Bonó.* Barcelona, Spain: M. Pareja, 1980.

————, ed. *Papeles dominicanos de Máximo Gómez.* Ciudad Trujillo: Editorial Montalvo, 1954.

————, ed. *Relaciones Geográficas de Santo Domingo.* Vol. 1. Santo Domingo: Editorial del Caribe, 1970.

Rodríguez J., Julio C., and Velez C., Rosajilda. *El precapitalismo dominicano de la primera mitad del siglo XIX, 1780–1850.* Santo Domingo: UASD, 1980.

Roseberry, William. "Beyond the Agrarian Question in Latin America." In Frederick Cooper et al., *Confronting Historical Paradigms: Peasants, Labor, and the Capitalist World System in Africa and Latin America.* Madison: Univ. of Wisconsin Press, 1993. 318–68.

————. *Coffee and Capitalism in the Venezuelan Andes.* Austin: Univ. of Texas Press, 1983.

————. Review of "Peasants and Peasant Societies." JPS 16, no. 4 (July 1989): 631–34.

Ruiz Tejada, M. R. *Estudio sobre la propiedad inmobiliaria en la República Dominicana.* Santo Domingo: UASD, 1952.

Sabean, David W. *Power in the Blood: Popular Culture and Village Discourse in Early Modern Germany.* Cambridge, England: Cambridge Univ. Press, 1984.

Safford, Frank. *The Ideal of the Practical: Colombia's Struggle to Form a Technical Elite.* Austin: Univ. of Texas Press, 1976.

Samper, Mario. *Generations of Settlers: Rural Households and Markets on the Costa Rican Frontier.* Boulder, Colo.: Westview, 1990.

Sálazar, María Cristina. *Aparceros en Boyacá: Los condenados del tabaco.* Bogotá: Ediciones Tercer Mundo, 1982.

Sánchez Valverde, Antonio. *Idea del valor de la Isla Española.* 1785. Rpt. Santo Domingo: Editorial Nacional, 1971.

Sang, Mukien A. *Ulises Heureaux: Biografía de un dictador.* Santo Domingo: Instituto Tecnológico de Santo Domingo, 1987.

San Miguel, Pedro L. "The Dominican Peasantry and the Market Economy: The Peasants of the Cibao, 1880–1960." Ph.D. diss., Columbia Univ., 1987.

Sauer, C. O. *The Early Spanish Main.* Berkeley: Univ. of California Press, 1966.

Schmidt, Hans. *The United States Occupation of Haiti, 1915–1934.* New Brunswick, N.J.: Rutgers Univ. Press 1971.

Schoenrich, Otto. *Santo Domingo: A Country with a Future.* New York: Macmillan Co., 1918.

Schryer, Frans J. *Ethnicity and Class Conflict in Rural Mexico.* Princeton, N.J.: Princeton Univ. Press, 1990.

Scott, James C. *The Moral Economy of the Peasant: Rebellion and Subsistence in Southeast Asia.* New Haven, Conn.: Yale Univ. Press, 1976.

———. *Weapons of the Weak: Everyday Forms of Peasant Resistance.* New Haven, Conn.: Yale Univ. Press, 1985.

Scott, James C., and Kerkvliet, B. J. "How Traditional Rural Patrons Lose Legitimacy: A Theory with Special Reference to Southeast Asia." *Cultures et développement* (Summer 1973): 501–40.

Seligson, Mitchel A. *Peasants of Costa Rica and the Development of Agrarian Capitalism.* Madison: Univ. of Wisconsin Press, 1980.

Sevilla Soler, M. R. *Santo Domingo: Tierra de Frontera (1750–1800).* Seville, Spain: Escuela de Estudios Hispano-Americanos de Sevilla, 1980.

Shanin, Teodor. *The Awkward Class: Political Sociology of Peasantry in a Developing Country, Russia, 1910–1925.* Oxford, England: Clarendon Press, 1972.

———, ed. *Peasants and Peasant Societies.* Harmondsworth, England: Penguin, 1971. Rev. ed. Oxford, England: Basil Blackwell, 1987.

Sharpe, Kenneth E. *Peasant Politics: Struggle in a Dominican Village.* Baltimore, Md.: Johns Hopkins Univ. Press, 1977.

Shoemaker, R. *The Peasants of El Dorado.* Ithaca, N.Y.: Cornell Univ. Press, 1981.

Silié, Rubén. *Economía, esclavitud y población: Ensayos de interpretación histórica del Santo Domingo español en el siglo XVIII.* Santo Domingo: Taller, 1976.

Singelmann, P. *Structures of Domination and Peasant Movements in Latin America.* Columbia: Univ. of Missouri Press, 1981.

Slicher van Bath, Bernard. *De agrarische geschiedenis van West Europa (500–1850).* Utrecht, Netherlands: Spectrum, 1960.

Sluiter, Engel. "Dutch-Spanish Rivalry in the Caribbean Area, 1594–1609." HAHR 28, no. 2 (May 1948): 165–96.

Smith, Carol A. "Local History in a Global Context: Social and Economic Transition in Western Guatemala." CSSH 26 (1984): 193–228.

Smith, Gavin. *Livelihood and Resistance: Peasants and the Politics of Land in Peru.* Berkeley: Univ. of California Press, 1989.

Smith, Raymond T. "Hierarchy and the Dual Marriage System in West Indian Society." In *Gender and Kinship: Essays Toward a Unified Analysis,* ed. Jane F. Collier and Sylvia J. Yanagisako, 163–96. Stanford, Calif.: Stanford Univ. Press, 1987.

Stern, Steve J. "Feudalism, Capitalism, and the World-System in the Perspective of Latin America and the Caribbean." *American Historical Review* 93, no. 4 (Oct. 1988): 829–72.

Steward, Julien, et al. *The People of Puerto Rico.* Urbana: Univ. of Illinois Press, 1956.

Stubbs, Jean. *Tobacco on the Periphery: A Case Study in Cuban Labour History, 1860–1958.* Cambridge, England: Cambridge Univ. Press, 1985.

Sweezy, Paul, et al. *The Transition from Feudalism to Capitalism.* London: Verso, 1978.

Taussig, Michael. *The Devil and Commodity Fetishism in South America*. Chapel Hill: Univ. of North Carolina Press, 1980.

Taylor, Lewis. *Bandits and Politics in Peru: Landlord and Peasant Violence in Hualgayoc, 1900–1930*. Cambridge: Cambridge Univ., Centre of Latin American Studies, 1988.

Taylor, Peter. *Smoke Ring: The Politics of Tobacco*. London: Bodley Head, 1984.

Tax, Sol. *Penny Capitalism: A Guatemalan Indian Community*. 1953. Rpt. Chicago: Univ. of Chicago Press, 1963.

Thompson, E. P. "The Moral Economy of the English Crowd in the Eighteenth Century." *Past and Present* 50 (Feb. 1971): 76–136.

———. *The Poverty of Theory and Other Essays*. New York: Monthly Review Press, 1978.

Todorov, Tzvetan. *La conquête de l'Amérique: La question de l'autre*. Paris: Seuil, 1982.

Trouillot, Michel-Rolph. *Peasants and Capital: Dominica in the World Economy*. Baltimore, Md.: Johns Hopkins Univ. Press, 1988.

Tutino, John. *From Insurrection to Revolution: Social Bases of Agrarian Violence, 1750–1940*. Princeton, N.J.: Princeton Univ. Press, 1986.

Van Binsbergen, Wim M. J., and Geschiere, Peter, eds. *Old Modes of Production and Capitalist Encroachment: Anthropological Explorations in Africa*. London: Routledge and Kegan, 1985.

Van Schendel, Willem. *Peasant Mobility: The Odds of Life in Rural Bangladesh*. Assen, Netherlands: Van Gorcum, 1981.

Vargas-Lundius, Rosemary. *Peasants in Distress: Poverty and Unemployment in the Dominican Republic*. Lund, Sweden: Lund Economic Studies, 1988.

Vázquez-Geffroy, M. M. "Land Tenure and Resource-Holding Groups in a Dominican Municipio." Ph.D. diss., Univ. of New Mexico, 1977.

Vega, Bernardo. *Imágenes de ayer*. Santo Domingo: Fundación Cultural Dominicana, 1981.

———. "El impacto de la depresión económica de 1930 sobre la economía dominicana." *Investigación y Ciencia* 1, no. 1 (Jan.–Apr. 1986): 47–67.

Vilas, Carlos M. "Notas sobre la formación del estado en el Caribe: La República Dominicana." *Estudios Sociales Centroamericanos* 8, no. 24 (Sept.–Dec. 1979): 117–77.

Walker, D. W. "Business as Usual: The Empresa del Tabaco in Mexico, 1837–44." HAHR 64, no. 4 (Nov. 1984): 675–705.

Warman, Arturo. *Ensayos sobre el campesinado en México*. Mexico City: Editorial Nueva Imagen, 1980.

Wendell Werge, R. "Agricultural Development in Clear Creek: Adaptive Strategies and Economic Roles in a Dominican Settlement." Ph.D. diss., Univ. of Florida, 1975.

Wilbert, Johannes. *Tobacco and Shamanism in South America*. New Haven, Conn.: Yale Univ. Press, 1987.

Wilson, Darrell. *Report on Economic, Financial, and Commercial Conditions in the Dominican Republic.* London: Dept. of Overseas Trade, 1925.

Wolf, Eric R. "Aspects of Group Relations in a Complex Society: Mexico." *American Anthropologist* 58 (1956): 1065–78.

———. *Europe and the People Without History.* Berkeley: Univ. of California Press; and Cambridge, England: Cambridge Univ. Press,1982.

———. *Peasants.* Englewood Cliffs, N.J.: Prentice-Hall, 1966.

———. "Types of Latin American Peasantries: A Preliminary Discussion." *American Anthropologist* 57 (June 1955): 452–70.

———. "The Vicissitudes of the Closed Corporate Peasant Community." *American Ethnologist* 13, no. 2 (May 1986): 325–29.

Womack, John. *Zapata and the Mexican Revolution.* 1968. New York: Vintage, 1970.

Wong, Diana. *Peasants in the Making: Malaysia's Green Revolution.* Singapore: Institute of Southeast Asian Studies, 1987.

Yunén Z., Rafael Emilio. *La isla como es: Hipotesis para su comprobación.* Santiago: UCMM, 1985.

Zaldívar L., Iturbides G. *Producción y comercialización del tabaco negro en la República Dominicana.* Santiago: UCMM, 1979.

Zeller, N. M. "Puerto Plata en el siglo XIX." *Eme Eme Estudios Dominicanos* 5, no. 28 (1977): 27–51.

Index